The American Campaigns of Rochambeau's Army

Jointly Published, 1972, by

PRINCETON UNIVERSITY PRESS · PRINCETON · NEW JERSEY

BROWN UNIVERSITY PRESS · PROVIDENCE · RHODE ISLAND

The American Campaigns of

ROCHAMBEAU'S ARMY

1780, 1781, 1782, 1783

Translated and Edited by Howard C. Rice, Jr., and Anne S. K. Brown

Volume II THE ITINERARIES

MAPS AND VIEWS

The printing of the color reproductions of the
Berthier maps has been made possible by a gift
from Mr. Paul Mellon, who owns a set of the
originals. Mr. Mellon has also provided access
to the rich collection on the Revolution in his
library, from which many illustrations and
references in this book have been taken. The
publishers also gratefully acknowledge gifts
in support of this publication from William D.
Wright and from Herbert S. Bailey, Jr.

This book has been composed in Janson types

Designed by James Wageman
Illustration layout designed by Howard C. Rice, Jr.

Printed in the United States of America by
Princeton University Press, Princeton, New Jersey
Illustrations printed by
the Meriden Gravure Co., Meriden, Connecticut

Volume II

Itineraries

Contents

Maps and Views

Itineraries

Vignette on recto of this page is drawn from a photograph of the 18th-century milestone which once stood in East Hartford, Connecticut, along the route of the French army's march. The stone now belongs to the Connecticut Historical Society and is on display in the Old State House in Hartford.

Editors' Introduction

The six documents published here under the general heading "Itineraries" are translated from hitherto unpublished manuscripts preserved among papers of L.-A. Berthier in the Princeton University Library. As distinguished from the personal journals published in Volume I, these are impersonal documents, characteristic of the meticulous paper work executed by Rochambeau's staff officers in the course of their professional military duties. They provide a detailed description of the overland route taken by the French army when marching from Rhode Island to Virginia in the summer of 1781. Whereas the journals record (from the individual actor's viewpoint) what happened along the route, these itineraries describe the stage of the "theatre of operations." They are thus closely interrelated to the next and final section of this book, the "Maps," and should be studied concurrently with them. Indeed, the cartographers who drew the "figuration" (*figuré* was the technical French term then in use) of roads and campsites were also entrusted with preparing written "itineraries." Dupain de Montesson's manual for topographical engineers, *L'art de lever les Plans* (2nd edn., Paris, 1775), includes a chapter (pp. 179–186) on how to compile itineraries. The engineer marching at the head of a column must, according to this handbook, "note down, as he comes to them, the successive places along the road, the ascents and descents, the woods, the defiles, the rivers, the brooks, the marshes, the bridges, the fords, the nature of the countryside through which the column is proceeding, and finally the different landmarks that he passes on the right- and left-hand sides of the road. . . ." From such field notes maps as well as written descriptions could subsequently be worked up.

As implied in the passage just cited, information for the itineraries was often gathered as the army marched and could serve as a permanent historical record of a campaign. Once recorded, such topographical intelligence could also be used in the planning of future operations, should the fortunes of war bring the army again into the same territory. In the series of documents published below the internal evidence shows that the "Plan for marching the army from Providence to King's Ferry on the east bank of the Hudson River" and most of the "Itinerary" covering the same series of marches were prepared by the quartermaster-general's staff prior to the army's march, but that information for the other itineraries, covering the route from the Hudson to Virginia, was gathered (most probably by Berthier) during the actual march. Our Itineraries describe the route taken during the Campaign of 1781. We have found no comparable documents for the Campaign of 1782—except for a bare schedule of marches—and it seems likely that none were compiled. Since the army then marched northward from Virginia to New England over approximately the same route taken the previous year in the opposite direction, the 1781 itineraries no doubt served as guidance in 1782—and can still do double duty for the historical record.

The Itineraries as printed here follow closely the pattern and layout of the French manuscripts. The material is arranged in two and sometimes three columns, one of which is reserved for running headings or "observations." Our translations, too, are fairly literal approximations of the originals. These are not literary narratives like the journals. The vocabulary is limited. The terse style is repetitive, even monotonous, intended primarily to convey exact topographical information. At times the staccato notations suggest the rapid jottings made by the alert but hurried observer riding along the road. We have tried in our versions to retain the precision of the originals and hope that these itineraries can still, now and then, serve as reliable guides to travelers. The writers when referring to rivers and streams habitually used the terms "right bank" and "left bank." As an added clarification and convenience to readers we have substituted the directional designations, east or west, north or south, as the case may be. The spelling of place names has been standardized according to current norms. Where names of localities have changed over the past two centuries, modern equivalents have been inserted within square brackets. Occasionally the spelling of a proper name as it appears in the manuscript has been retained, when it seems to have some significance. On the whole, the writers maintained a fair average of accuracy in the spelling of names, which can probably be attributed to their training. We find, for example, that an official French army memorandum addressed in 1777 to topographical engineers specifies: "Officers are requested to pay scrupulous attention to the correct spelling of proper names; they should note instances where names have been changed or disfigured on existing maps and record differences between official nomenclature and local usage. . . ." The mistakes found in the manuscripts are generally in names of small places, which could not be verified on such printed maps as were then available, or in names of persons (a tavernkeeper, a local farmer), which the compiler of the itinerary had to transcribe phonetically as his ear caught them. A copying error made when transcribing rough field notes sometimes compounded an initial mistake. If some of the French transcriptions appear amusingly quaint today, they are no more so than the similar examples found in American army documents and correspondence of the same period.

The Editors' annotations provide the indispensable cross-references to the maps in this volume as well as to the journals in Volume 1. We have also included notes on the localities described. Such information has been gathered and verified in the course of our own field trips and with the help of local historians, past and present. We make no claim to exhaustiveness in this respect. There are many puzzles yet to be solved. We like to think that these Itineraries will be an invitation to further explorations and to the nostalgic pastime of "Then and Now." What has become of this old road through the woods? When was that river bridged or dammed? Can this be the same house? Who lives in it now? When did the Baptists oust the Congregationalists from the meetinghouse? Or, when was this hill or that campsite bulldozed off the map? . . . Several centuries ago Captain John Smith wrote in his *Generall Historie of Virginia, New-England and the Summer Isles*: "Before we present you the matters of fact, it is fit to offer to your view the Stage whereon they were acted, for as Geography without History seemeth a carkasse without motion, so History without Geography, wandreth as a Vagrant without a certaine habitation." Thanks to the itineraries and maps prepared by the French officers themselves, the historian of the American Revolution need not treat Rochambeau's army as a "Vagrant without a certaine habitation."

I

PLAN

for Marching the Army from Providence to King's Ferry on the East Bank of the Hudson River in 17 Days, including three Stopovers

Our first document is not strictly speaking an "itinerary" but rather, as the title indicates, a plan for moving the French army from Rhode Island, where it had been quartered for nearly a year, to the Hudson, where it would join the American army under Washington. Although the route is summarily described, this is primarily a schedule or timetable of the projected march. It was prepared in advance under the supervision of General Béville, Rochambeau's quartermaster-general. Béville had himself reconnoitered the roads to the Hudson in April 1781, when he had visited Washington's headquarters at New Windsor and discussed preparations for the expected junction of the allied forces (see Berthier's journal, n. 53). Although our translation is made from a manuscript copy of the "Plan" preserved among L.-A. Berthier's papers, he was not the author, nor is there reason to believe that he had any share in the advance reconnoitering of the routes, as did Mathieu Dumas, another of the quartermaster-general's assistants (cf. Dumas [1], I, 67–68). However, since Berthier was entrusted with guiding one of the divisions on the march, he obviously needed his own copy of the "Plan." Other copies have also survived—for example, in Rochambeau's papers (Library of Congress, Vol. 3, pp. 310 ff.).

The army eventually followed closely the schedule and route indicated here, but only as far as Ridgebury, Connecticut. At that point, because of a quick change in Washington's plans, the French army marched southwestward to join the Americans at Philipsburg near Dobbs Ferry, rather than at Peekskill near King's Ferry (see Clermont-Crèvecœur's journal, n. 31). Partly because of this shift the march from Providence to join with the Americans was accomplished in nineteen days (18 June–6 July 1781) instead of the seventeen called for in the "Plan."

The route can be followed on a map drawn after the fact, the "General Map of the Camps and Marches of the French Army Commanded by General Rochambeau," our No. 162, hereinafter. Another map, not reproduced in the present volume, was, like the "Plan," which it was intended to accompany, prepared in advance of the march; this preliminary map, entitled "Marche de l'armée française de Providence à la rivière du Nord [1781]," is preserved in Rochambeau's papers (Library of Congress, Rochambeau maps, Nos. 42–44); a copy of it is in Cromot Dubourg's journal (1).

The next document, the "Itinerary" proper, covers in more detail the route outlined here in the "Plan." The Editors' topographical notes are in general reserved for the "Itinerary." This "Plan" does, however, supply information, not repeated elsewhere, concerning Lauzun's Legion, which as the "left column" covered the main army's march by a different route farther to the south.

The Princeton manuscript of the "Plan" (Berthier Papers, No. 8), entitled "Projet pour porter l'armée de Providence à King's ferry à la Rive gauche de la rivière du nord en 17 jours de marche y compris trois Séjours," is written on sheets of paper folded and gathered into a "cahier" of 24 pages (22 x 18.5 cm.), of which the last six are blank. It is for the most part in a formal clerical script, with some of the marginal headings added in Berthier's informal hand.

Plan

Order of March

Left Column: Lauzun

Right Column:

Rochambeau

The baggage trains of the Comte de Rochambeau and the Intendant, together with the military chest (*Trésor*), etc., will march at the head of the First Division's baggage train in the right column. The baggage of the general officers will lead the trains of the divisions they command. The Comte de Rochambeau will march at his convenience with those appointed to accompany him. The rest must follow the divisions to which they are attached and must not leave them under any pretext whatever.

Before the army's departure it will be absolutely necessary to determine where the Comte de Rochambeau is to lodge and to halt during his march. He can, for example, go from Providence to Voluntown, from Voluntown to Windham, from Windham to Hartford. By following this course he will find convenient lodgings everywhere without

The army will be split up into five divisions. The first, composed of Lauzun's Corps of Foreign Volunteers, will march independently, forming the left column assigned to cover the left flank of the army, as will be more fully described hereafter.

The other four divisions, forming the right column, will follow one another on successive days, occupying the same camp in succession except in case of a stopover[2] when two divisions, that is, the one stopping over and the one arriving to halt there next day, will camp alongside one another.

The First Division of the right column, under the command of the Comte de Rochambeau, will include the Bourbonnais Regiment, a quarter of the field artillery, part of the baggage train of the headquarters staff, the field hospital of the division, etc.

The Second Division, under the command of the Baron de Vioménil, will be composed of the Royal Deux-Ponts Regiment, a quarter of the field artillery, part of the baggage train of the headquarters staff, the field hospital of the division, etc.

The Third Division, under the command of the Comte de Vioménil, will be composed of the Soissonnais Regiment, a quarter of the field artillery, part of the baggage train of the headquarters staff, and the field hospital of the division.

The Fourth Division, under the command of the Comte de Custine, will be composed of the Saintonge Regiment, a quarter of the field artillery, the rest of the baggage train of the headquarters staff, the field hospital of the division, etc.

---

1. In their writings the French officers used interchangeably the terms *Rivière du Nord* (North River) and Hudson, as was the common practice at the time. We have adopted "Hudson" throughout our translations, since the designation "North River" is now generally limited to the waterfront of Manhattan Island (cf. Pier 57, North River,

etc.). The name dates back to seventeenth-century New Netherlands, when the Dutch maps called the Delaware the "Suydt Rivier" and the Hudson the "Noordt Rivier."

2. The French term is *séjour*, literally "sojourn," which might also be translated as "halt."

interfering with the divisional headquarters.

Sufficient bakeries must be established at Providence to provide the troops with rations for several days.

First day's march of the First Division, led by M. de Béville

Second day's march of the First Division

March of the Second Division, led by M. de Lameth

First Day's March (15 Miles)

The First Division, preceded by 30 pioneers, half of them carrying axes (this applies to the whole march and will not be repeated), will leave the camp at Providence and proceed to camp at Waterman's Tavern. M. de Béville, assistant quartermaster-general,[3] is assigned to take[4] it to the Hudson River.

The camp, though in the middle of a wood, is situated in a rather good position, with a brook in front of it and behind it the tavern and the main road from Providence to Voluntown [Sterling Hill, Connecticut], which is much better than the road via Angell's Tavern.

Lodgings for the divisional headquarters are not very plentiful; however, there are more here than at Angell's Tavern or the Whipple House [on the alternate road].

Second Day's March (15 Miles)

The First Division will leave the Waterman House [Tavern] camp and proceed to camp at Plainfield. This camp is convenient and pleasant: it can be set up in two ways, either in front of the brook [Horse Brook], parallel to the main road from Norwich to Boston, or else beyond the brook on the right-hand side of the road to Windham. There will be a fair number of houses available for the divisional headquarters.

The Second Division, preceded by 15 pioneers, eight of them carrying axes (this applies to the whole march), will leave the Providence camp and proceed to Waterman's Tavern, where it will occupy the camp previously occupied by the First Division.

3. Chevalier Charles de Béville, who was the son of Pierre-François de Béville, quartermaster-general of Rochambeau's army. Contenson, *Cincinnati*, p. 139.
4. The French word is *conduire*, in the sense of "to con- duct, guide or lead." The "conductors" literally led the divisions, whereas their commanders marched at will wherever they pleased.

At Windham the troops will draw bread from the bakeries at Lebanon.

March of the Second Division, and of the Third, led by M. Collot

On approaching Bolton you climb a very steep hill.

March of the Second and Third Divisions, and of the Fourth, led by M. Berthier

The Chevalier [Charles] de Lameth, assistant quartermaster-general, is assigned to take it to the Hudson River.

Third Day's March (15 Miles)

The First Division will leave the Plainfield camp to march to Windham, where it will camp a mile beyond the town. [Either of] two positions may be occupied, the first on the slope above the west bank of the Shetucket, the second in the valley near the bridge, on the right-hand side of the road; the artillery and baggage train will camp on the left. The second camp would be dominated by a wooded slope across the river, but this is not a disadvantage in a region where the enemy is not in evidence. Furthermore, the camp in the valley has a more convenient access to water than the one above.

The divisional headquarters will stay in Windham, which is a rather pretty town.

The Second Division will leave the Waterman's Tavern camp and proceed to camp at Plainfield.

The Third Division, preceded by 15 pioneers, eight of them carrying axes (this applies to each march), will leave the Providence camp and proceed to camp at Waterman's Tavern.

M. [Victor] Collot, assistant quartermaster-general, is assigned to take the Third Division to the Hudson River.

Fourth Day's March (16 Miles)

The First Division will leave the Windham camp and proceed to camp at Bolton. The distance from Windham to Bolton [Center] is 17 miles, but since the camp is to be one mile west of Windham, the march will be only 16 miles long.

At Bolton two sites, which are very near one another and equidistant from a small stream, are available. The wells of the houses will provide additional water.

There are enough houses in Bolton for the divisional headquarters.

The Second Division will arrive at Windham and the Third at Plainfield.

The Fourth Division, preceded by 15 pioneers, eight of them carrying axes (this applies to the

Bakeries must be established at Hartford, from which the troops will draw four days' rations. Each division, furthermore, will be followed by a sufficient number of wagons to carry bread for four more days.[5]

The Hartford ferries: There are 4 boats at the Hartford ferry, two large and two small. These ferry boats are flat-bottomed with low freeboard and are propelled by oars alone. The larger boats can transport 2 wagons and several horses at a time; the smaller can carry from 9 to 10 horses. In order to speed up the crossing, boats must be procured from the neighboring ferries up or downstream. The quartermasters of each state are said to be authorized to make such requisitions when the service of the American army demands it.

whole march), will leave the Providence camp and proceed to camp at Waterman's Tavern.

M. [Louis-Alexandre] Berthier, acting assistant quartermaster-general, is assigned to take this division to the Hudson River.

Fifth Day's March (12½ Miles)

The First Division will leave the Bolton camp and proceed to East Hartford to camp on the east bank of the Connecticut River, where there is a suitable camp ground near the meetinghouse.

The distance from Bolton to the town of Hartford, which is on the west bank of the river, is only 14 miles, but it is preferable to leave the troops at East Hartford on the east bank in order to give the artillery and baggage train, or at least part of it, time to catch up and cross the river the same day. The rest will cross the next day, after the troops.

Another reason for preferring this camp to one on the west bank is that the outskirts of Hartford are full of gardens and orchards, which would require placing the camp too far from the town.

East Hartford is large enough to accommodate the divisional headquarters.

The Second Division will camp this same day at Bolton, the Third at Windham, and the Fourth at Plainfield.

Sixth Day's March and First Stopover

The First Division will halt a day at East Hartford. The Second will leave Bolton and proceed to camp at East Hartford beside the First. The Third will camp at Bolton and the Fourth at Windham.

Seventh Day's March (12½ Miles)

The First Division will leave East Hartford and, after crossing the Connecticut River, proceed to camp

5. In a memorandum to Governor Trumbull, dated Hartford, 22 May 1781 (cited in Crofut, *Guide*, 1, 69, from the Connecticut Archives), Monsieur St. Philippe, "agent for the French Army," states that "he has a number of Labourers employed in building Ovens and makeing the necessary preparations for the accomodation of said Army on their march and he finds no place where to barrack his Labourers, he therefore begs your Excellency to do as may be needfull . . . and give directions that the Barrack Master do furnish Barracks, as the Service can not be effected without." Other preparations for the march, including hospitals, are mentioned in the journal of Claude Blanchard, the commissary general; further documents are to be found in the papers of Jeremiah Wadsworth (Connecticut Historical Society), who served as purchasing agent for the French.

The two roads leading to the Hudson River divide at Farmington; the right-hand road[6] passing through Harwinton, Litchfield, Washington, Morgan's Tavern, the bridge at Bull's Iron Works, Morehouse Tavern, Vanderburg's, Hopewell, Fishkill, and Fishkill Landing [Beacon], where the ferry [across the Hudson] is located; and the left-hand road, which the army will take, passing through Southington, Barnes's Tavern, Waterbury, Break Neck, Southbury, Newtown, Danbury, Ridgebury, Salem, Haight's Tavern, Crompond, Peekskill, and King's Ferry, where you cross the Hudson River. The first route is 74 miles, the second 90.

All the houses along the route, on either side of the road, will be occupied.

at Farmington. The camp may be established a mile beyond the road to Harwinton. This camp has access to water, and Farmington has more than ample accommodations for the divisional headquarters.

The Second Division will halt for a day at East Hartford. The Third will arrive to camp there beside it, and the Fourth Division will camp at Bolton.

Eighth Day's March (13 Miles)

The First Division will leave Farmington and proceed to camp at Barnes's Tavern [in Marion, town of Southington]. It will camp a short way beyond the tavern where there is flat open country. Lodgings for the divisional headquarters will be rather scarce. There are, however, three taverns very close together as well as several small houses.

Ninth Day's March (13 Miles)

The First Division will leave Barnes's Tavern and proceed to camp at Break Neck [in the town of Middlebury]. There is a brook and a camp ground but very few houses for lodging the divisional headquarters. There is, however, a rather good tavern belonging to Isaac Brownson plus several small houses.

The Second Division will camp at Barnes's Tavern, the Third at Farmington, and the Fourth will halt for a day at East Hartford.

Tenth Day's March (15 Miles)

The First Division will leave Break Neck and proceed to camp at Newtown. Camp may be pitched in front of the town, so as to be nearer the water. In this case the headquarters would be located in advance of the camp; this would not, however, be a serious drawback, for it could be guarded by the grenadiers and chasseurs of the division.

If, on the other hand, the town wells were deemed sufficient, the camp could be pitched beyond the town, where it would be a long way from the brook.

6. The so-called upper road to the Hudson. This route is described by Chastellux ([4], I, 78–87), who had taken it during a journey made in November 1780.

Note: If the camp were pushed forward to Salem [Salem Center, in the town of North Salem, Westchester County, New York], it would be more agreeably situated and much nearer water. Here several brooks meet and turn three mills: a grist mill, a sawmill, and a fulling mill. However, this march would be 4½ miles longer for the troops, making a total of 19½ miles, or 6½ *lieues* instead of 5, which would be too far.

This village was partly ruined by the English who burned the meetinghouse and several buildings [in 1779]. The country is quite open and well cultivated.

7. It was at Ridgebury that the army departed from the route prescribed in this "Plan" and proceeded southwesterly via North Castle (Mount Kisco) to the allied camp at Philipsburg. The thirteenth, fourteenth, fifteenth, sixteenth, and seventeenth day's marches did not, therefore,

The Second Division will camp at Break Neck, the Third at Barnes's Tavern, and the Fourth at Farmington.

Eleventh Day's March and Second Stopover

The First Division will halt for a day at Newtown. The Second will set out from Break Neck and proceed to camp beside it at Newtown. The Third Division will camp at Break Neck, and the Fourth at Barnes's Tavern.

Twelfth Day's March (15 Miles)

The First Division will leave Newtown and proceed to camp at Ridgebury, where there is an Anglican church. This is a fairly large settlement made up of houses scattered along an extensive but low plateau. When approaching it from the opposite direction via Crompond, you climb a long hill, which, though steep, wagons can nevertheless negotiate.

Here you must draw water from the wells of the houses, since what little water there is in the vicinity is too far from the suitable campsite. The surrounding country is cleared. Part of it is cultivated, and part is pastureland.

The Second Division will halt for a day at Newtown, where the Third will arrive to camp beside it, and the Fourth will occupy the Break Neck camp.

Thirteenth Day's March (18 Miles)

The First Division will leave Ridgebury and proceed to camp at Crompond.[7] This march is the longest on the route, but the road is good and the divisions can easily accomplish it. There are few houses at Crompond for the divisional headquarters. All those scattered along the road, both on approaching and leaving the camp, will be used. The troops will camp before a little brook, and the headquarters will be situated on the right of the camp.

The Second Division will camp at Ridgebury, the

follow the route outlined here. However, in the autumn of 1782, when marching eastward from the Hudson to New England, the army did take the route from Peekskill via Crompond (Yorktown, Westchester County, New York) to Ridgebury, Connecticut.

As it is not known how long the army will remain at Peekskill, and as it may in fact be there a long time, this camp must be amply provisioned. It has been agreed that bakeries will be established at Fishkill Landing and the bread brought down the Hudson River to the Peekskill camp.[8]

Third will halt for a day at Newtown, and the Fourth will arrive from Break Neck to camp beside it.

Fourteenth Day's March (10 Miles)

The First Division will proceed to camp 2 miles beyond Peekskill in a position that has access to both water and wood. It has previously been occupied in turn by the English and by the Americans.

The headquarters will be established at Peekskill, where there are but few houses; however, it cannot be located elsewhere, or any nearer the camp. It boasts one good house, which is not, incidentally, a tavern. It will be necessary to fall back upon those scattered within a radius of 1 or 2 miles, and even some as far away as Continental Village, just 3 miles behind the camp, where there are a few more houses.

The Second Division will camp at Crompond, the Third at Ridgebury, and the Fourth will halt for a day at Newtown.

Fifteenth Day's March and Third Stopover

The First Division will halt at Peekskill, where the entire army is to assemble, and will remain there until further orders.

The Second Division will march to Peekskill and camp there in line with the First. The Third Division will camp at Crompond, and the Fourth at Ridgebury.

Sixteenth Day's March

The First and Second Divisions will halt at the Peekskill camp, where the Third will arrive to camp in line with them. The Fourth Division will camp at Crompond.

Seventeenth Day's March

The Fourth Division will arrive at the Peekskill camp to join the three others in line.

8. Owing to the last minute shift in plans, by which the allied camp was located in Philipsburg, some 25 miles south of Peekskill, the establishment of bakeries at Fish-

kill Landing (Beacon) eventually proved a handicap. See Clermont-Crèvecœur's journal, n. 39.

On this day the First Division of the right column leaves the Windham camp to march towards Hartford.

March of Lauzun's Corps, led by Sheldon

The crossing of the Connecticut at Middletown is not liable to floods as at Hartford, which would doubtless give it the preference [as a crossing for the army] were the road from Lebanon to Middletown better; however, it is good enough for light troops, who should be able to go anywhere.

To speed up the crossing of the river it will be necessary to supplement the boats ordinarily in service by bringing some up to Middletown from neighboring ferries down river.

First Day's March (15 Miles)

Lauzun's entire Corps of Foreign Volunteers will leave Lebanon[9] and proceed to camp along the Middletown road 7 miles beyond Colchester on the west bank of Salmon Brook [River] opposite the landslide caused by flood waters. This brook can easily be forded. The bed is good but stony. Major Sheldon[10] will be assigned to lead this column.

Second Day's March (11 Miles)

From the camp on the west bank of Salmon Brook the Corps will proceed to camp [at Middletown] on the west bank of the Connecticut River, taking care to ferry its infantry across first. If the entire Corps should not be able to make the crossing in one day, the rest could cross the next day.

Third Day's March and Stopover

As the First Division of the right column is not scheduled to leave East Hartford for its camp at Farmington until the seventh day of its march, Lauzun's Foreign Volunteers will not leave their camp at Middletown until this day, marching through Wallingford, Oxford, North Stratford [Monroe], Ridgefield, Bedford, and Pines Bridge, to cover the left flank of the army.[11]

9. Lauzun's hussars had been quartered in Lebanon during the winter of 1780–1781. Chastellux ([4], I, 229–231) describes a visit there in January 1781.

10. Dominique Sheldon (1757–1801), born in Winchester, England. He began his French service in Dillon's Irish Regiment and eventually rose to the rank of lieutenant general. Sheldon served again under Lauzun in 1792–1793, when the latter, then known as General Biron, commanded successively the Army of the Rhine and the Army of Italy. Contenson, *Cincinnati*, p. 263; Six, *Dict. Biog.*, II, 454; Lauzun (4), 263, 306. Sheldon is mentioned by the Marquise de La Tour du Pin (*née* Henriette Dillon) in her *Journal d'une Femme de Cinquante Ans*, ed. Liederkierke-Beaufort (Paris, 1906 and later reprints), I, 72–73,

and II, 215–217. The Marquise recalls that Sheldon, who was her cousin, was present with the Dillon Regiment at the capture of the British island of Grenada in July 1779 and that he was rewarded for his bravery by being sent to France with the captured standards. However, she adds, court etiquette of the time forbade his appearing before the King in his military uniform when presenting the trophies of victory! This Sheldon is not to be confused with Colonel Elisha Sheldon, commander of dragoons in the American army, who was also present during the allied operations and encampment outside New York in July 1781.

11. As things turned out, Lauzun's Legion did not march beyond Bedford to Pines Bridge (on the Croton River)

Itinerary to be reconnoitered

This road has not yet been reconnoitered.[12] All that is known is that it is passable. It will therefore be indispensable for the Duc de Lauzun to have it reconnoitered in advance as soon as the march of the army is ordered, so as to inform himself of the conditions he may expect along this route, which lies between the Connecticut and Hudson rivers.

Position of the heavy baggage of Lauzun's Corps

If the heavy baggage could not follow this route, or if the Duc de Lauzun wished to avoid being encumbered by it, it could be added to the baggage train of one of the divisions of the right column; however, Lauzun's infantry and hussars must follow this route to protect the march of the army from any threat from Tories or [enemy] troops making a sortie from New York.

---

as planned. At Bedford Lauzun was ordered forward to join an American detachment under General Lincoln for an attempt against the British forts on the northern end of Manhattan Island. See Clermont-Crèvecœur's journal, n. 33.

12. The Legion's route across Connecticut as finally taken is shown, at least approximately, on map, No. 162. No detailed maps of its marches have been found. Local information and traditions concerning the Legion's passage are collected in Crofut, *Guide*, 1, 74–77, "March of the Duke de Lauzun and His Legion in Connecticut." The conflicting evidence concerning the exact route can perhaps be explained by the fact that the Legion (composed of both infantry and hussars) did not necessarily march in a single column. In carrying out the Legion's general assignment detachments of hussars presumably ranged over wide areas and would thus have appeared in scattered localities not on the principal route. In other words, the Legion, which was assigned to protect the main army marching farther north, was itself protected by detachments on its own left flank. The entire Legion eventually joined the rest of the army at the Philipsburg camp near White Plains. Although the British at this time controlled Long Island as well as Manhattan, they made no attempt to disrupt the march of Rochambeau's army across Connecticut; nevertheless, the French correctly envisaged such a possibility in their plans for the march.

ITINERARY

of the Marches of the French Army from Providence to the Camp at Philipsburg

1781

179 Miles

This Itinerary describes in detail the route already outlined in the preceding document. Like the "Plan," the greater part of this road guide appears to have been prepared in advance of the actual march. In the description of the first ten marches (as far as Ridgebury, Connecticut, where the route deviated from the original plan) the future tense is occasionally used, as in the phrase "the camp is to be (*doit être*) on this side of the meetinghouse." However, in describing the subsequent marches (eleventh and twelfth), the past tense is used in such phrases as "a height . . . where the grenadiers and chasseurs camped." It is probable, therefore, that the information included in the latter part of the Itinerary was gathered during the march. When Berthier prepared his copy, he no doubt transcribed an existing document on file at staff headquarters, while adding further information derived from his own field notes. Another copy of this Itinerary in Rochambeau's papers (Library of Congress, with Rochambeau maps, Nos. 42–44) substantiates our supposition. The Rochambeau copy describes only the route as originally planned and lacks the additional information for the tenth and eleventh marches, as well as the "Observations." Otherwise, the two copies are virtually the same, except for occasional variants in spelling. Spellings like "mitten-hause" in the Rochambeau manuscript—corrected in the Berthier copy to "meeting-house"—suggest that the copyist was of Germanic origin, perhaps Rochambeau's aide-de-camp Von Closen. In addition to such small changes, intermediary distances have been added in the Berthier copy.

The following translation has been made from the copy of the Itinerary in the Princeton University Library (Berthier Papers, No. 9). The manuscript, arranged in two columns, is entitled "Itinéraire des Marches qu'a fait l'Armée Française pour se rendre de Providence au camp de Philip'sburg. 179 milles. 1781." It is written throughout in a formal clerical hand on sheets of paper folded and gathered into a "cahier" comprising 32 pages (32 x 20.5 cm.).

The successive marches described in this Itinerary are recorded in the journals of Clermont-Crèvecœur (who marched with an artillery unit attached to the First Division), entries for 18 June–6 July 1781 (pp. 28–32), and of Berthier (who led the Fourth Division), entries for 21 June–6 July 1781 (pp. 247–249). Verger did not march overland from Providence to Philipsburg but remained with a detachment left at Newport under the command of Choisy and eventually went to Virginia with Barras's fleet.

The roads as well as the camps (the terminal points of each day's march) are shown on the maps reproduced in this volume. These maps and the descriptive notes thereto thus complete and illustrate the Itinerary that follows.

Itinerary

OF THE MARCHES OF THE FRENCH ARMY
FROM PROVIDENCE TO THE CAMP AT PHILIPSBURG, 1781

179 Miles

FIRST MARCH

From Providence to Waterman's Tavern[1]

Coming out of Providence, take the Monkey Town[2] road, leaving on the right the road to Hartford via Angell's Tavern.[3] Reaching Monkey Town [Knightsville], which is a cluster of a few houses, first pass on the left a road going to Pawtuxet. Leaving the one you are on, which leads to Greenwich, you turn to the right. *4 Miles*

One mile from Monkey Town you leave the Cranston farm on the left, then continue for about 5 miles over level but stony ground, and go downhill, passing on the right several ponds and a sawmill in a valley where you cross the Pawtuxet River on a wooden bridge. Beyond the bridge the road is still fairly level and still stony. You enter a big wood and proceed through it. You reach a post marking the junction of a road that comes in on the left from Greenwich. It is no more than a mile from this post to Waterman's Tavern,[4] which is situated in the midst of woods behind the camp. *Total: 15 Miles*

SECOND MARCH

From Waterman's Tavern to Plainfield[5]

Shortly after leaving Waterman's Tavern you enter a small wood where you ford several brooks. Beyond this wood, which is only ½ mile wide

1. See maps, Nos. 14, 27, and 28.
2. Written "Monchey Town" in Berthier's manuscript, "Mont Kitown" in the Rochambeau copy, and "Among town" on the road map. The locality, subsequently known as Knightsville, is in the city of Cranston.
3. The tavern kept at this time by Jeremiah Angell (1707–1786) was close to the geographical center of the town of Scituate, Rhode Island, on the banks of the Ponagansett River at a locality later known as Richmond Mills. The site was inundated when the Scituate Reservoir was built in the 1920's; at that time the "road to Hartford via Angell's Tavern" (Plainfield Pike, State Route 14) was partly relocated.
4. Waterman's Tavern, now restored as a private residence, is still standing. A description, with photographs of it as it appeared in the 1920's, is in Forbes and Cadman, I, 164–168.
5. See maps, Nos. 15, 29, and 155.

at most, you reach open country, though surrounded by woods, where the road winds because of the rolling terrain. There are a few houses on the right and left of the road. You reach the Waterman House on the left, opposite which the Providence-Hartford road via Angell's Tavern comes in. At this junction you are 4 miles from Waterman's Tavern, 6 miles from Angell's Tavern, and 7 miles from Voluntown [Sterling Hill, Connecticut].

The road continues straight ahead. You go down a fairly steep slope, leaving on the right Lowe's [?] and Grey's [?] Taverns. Then proceed over fairly level but stony ground, crossing several brooks and several small patches of woodland. You reach the Moosup River, which you cross on a wooden bridge, and then go uphill for a bit. There are several houses on either side of the road. Before entering the forest you cross still another little brook on a wooden bridge. Coming out of the forest you reach Voluntown.[6] Voluntown is a small group of houses, two of which are taverns. Dorrance's Tavern, on the right-hand side of the road as you enter,[7] is the better one; the other, which is on the left on leaving, is called Dexter's.

Coming out of Voluntown, leave a road on the left, continue straight ahead, go through a deep wooded hollow through which flows a small brook. Then go uphill. Soon after you come out of the woods, the road forks. Take the left fork. The right-hand fork, which goes up a rather steep little hill and is difficult for wagons, leads into the center of Plainfield. The left-hand road, less steep, comes in at the far end of town, with Eaton's Tavern[8] on your right. The main road from Norwich to Boston runs through Plainfield. The camp is in the valley on the right-hand side of the road to Windham and beyond the brook, which is spanned by a poor wooden bridge. Wagons cross the brook by the ford.   *15 Miles*

6. Voluntown—written "Valentown" in the manuscript and "Walen Town" on the maps—here and elsewhere in writings of the period refers to the village of Sterling Hill, Windham County, Connecticut. This is not to be confused with the present village of Voluntown, some 9 miles to the south, which is in New London County. In 1781 the township of Voluntown included territory that was subsequently (1794) incorporated separately as the town of Sterling.

7. The tavern kept by Samuel Dorrance—variously written in the manuscript and maps as "Duratsy," "Durancy," and "Dalens" Tavern—is still standing, privately owned, in Sterling Hill, on the northern side of State Road 49, just before the crossroads church when approaching from Oneco. On its eastward march in November 1782, Rochambeau's army camped in the fields to the east of the tavern. Local lore is collected in Forbes and Cadman, I, 165; a description and photograph is in Marian D. Terry, *Old Inns of Connecticut* (Hartford, 1937), 236–237. Details about the Dorrance family, including the story of their unfortunate daughter Susanna, are given at some length by Chastellux ([4], I, 67–69, 252–255), who stopped several times at the tavern.

8. The Eaton Tavern, on the east side of Plainfield's main street, survived into the twentieth century. A commemorative marker now indicates the site.

From Plainfield to Windham[9]

The left of the Plainfield camp adjoins the Windham road, which you take on leaving. The road then becomes more wooded. You reach a fork in the road. The left fork goes to Norwich. You take the right fork, which leads into a rather broad valley through which flows the Quinebaug River. Then follow along the river, which flows a short distance to your left, passing some wooded heights on the right. Then turn left to cross the river on a good but narrow covered wooden bridge.[10] You ascend the opposite slope into Canterbury, a little town on a rather pleasant plateau. Through Canterbury runs a high road that crosses at right angles the one by which you have come. This is the road from Norwich to Boston via Pomfret. The church is on the left, also two taverns, the White Ship and the Black Horse.

5 Miles

One mile beyond Canterbury you go down into a broad valley in the middle of which you cross a brook on a little wooden bridge. After going up the opposite slope you reach several scattered houses where there is a fork in the road. Take the right. Continue uphill, pass a stony road on the right and soon afterwards a meetinghouse and several scattered houses. This place is known as Park House.[11] You soon come to another fork farther on.

3 Miles

You take the left-hand road, leaving some houses on the right, and enter a forest of lofty trees. In the middle of it is a valley through which runs a rather broad stream [Little River] spanned by a wooden bridge. Then you continue up a narrow, steep, and stony road and come out of the forest. You are then only a mile from Scotland, a rather pretty village. Proceed downhill through it. There are two taverns, one on entering,

9. See maps, Nos. 16, 30, 153, and 154.

10. The French manuscript reads "un bon pont de bois couvert de madriers mais étroit." "Madriers" are beams or thick planks. This very early reference should be of interest to covered bridge historians. There is no reference to a covered bridge in this locality in Richard Sanders Allen, *Covered Bridges of the Northeast* (Brattleboro, Vt., 1957), though he mentions a truss bridge over the Shetucket at Norwich built *ca.* 1764 by one John Bliss. A truss bridge (also over the Shetucket near Norwich) built by Elias Bliss, carpenter of New London, is mentioned and illustrated by an engraving in St. John de Crèvecœur, *Lettres d'un Cultivateur Américain* (Paris, 1787), III, 517. It is possible that the covered bridge over the Quinebaug at Canterbury, noted here in the Itinerary, was the handiwork of this same Bliss family.

11. "Parc house" in the Berthier manuscript; "park-hause" in the Rochambeau copy; "cocke's house" [?] on road map, No. 16. This would seem to be the locality of Westminster in the town of Canterbury, where the army was to camp in 1782 (map, No. 154). Cf. Crofut (*Guide*, II, 840), who notes that the "Westminster Society" separated from the traditional Congregational Society in 1769. The Westminster meetinghouse, built in 1770 and rebuilt in 1840, still stands on the north side of Connecticut State Route 14.

another on leaving, and a fine new Anglican church on the right.[12] Leaving Scotland you cross a little brook [Merrick's Brook]. There is a bridge and also a ford. Almost immediately you cross another brook. There are many scattered houses on either side of the road and a pond on the right. You cross several very small brooks in succession, after which you reach Windham.

Windham is a rather substantially built and compact little town. Through it runs a highway that comes in on the left from Norwich and Lebanon and goes off to the right to Boston. You cross a sort of square. The road straight ahead takes you to the banks of the Shetucket 1 mile beyond the town. The camp is to be here in the bottom of the valley, facing the river, with its left adjoining the road leading to the bridge.[13]

15 Miles

FOURTH MARCH

From Windham to Bolton[14]

You start out of the camp on the left and immediately cross the Shetucket River on a good and rather long wooden bridge. At the end of this bridge the road turns. There is a house on the left, beyond which you turn sharp right and go up a fairly steep wooded slope. The road you then pass goes to Lebanon, which is only 6 miles away. At the top of the slope you keep the river on your right without seeing it. You pass the White Ball Tavern on the left and come to another wooden bridge over the same river, 3 miles above Windham. There is another road from Windham to this bridge, but it is a bit longer and not so good as the one just described. You still keep the river, which is now in sight, on your right. It flows over a bed of stones and rocks between fairly low wooded slopes. Halfway up the slope the narrow road is enclosed between steep banks. There are little clumps of trees on either side. You pass through several of these and cross several brooks in succession. On the left you pass Hill's Tavern,[15] which is 6 miles from Windham.

Lauzun's Legion, which had wintered at Lebanon, was assigned to a left-hand column to protect the left flank of the army's march against raiding parties that the enemy or the Tories might disembark along the [Long Island] Sound.

This column set out when the main army reached Windham, first camping on Salmon Brook [River] 13 miles beyond Lebanon; then at Middletown, 13 miles farther; at Wallingford, 15 miles farther; at Oxford, 15 miles beyond; at New Stratford, 11 miles farther; at Ridgefield, 15 miles farther; and then at White Plains, always maintaining communications with the main army at a distance of not more than 9 miles.

12. "Eglise anglicane" in the Berthier manuscript; "église anglaise" in the Rochambeau copy. Although separatism is known to have wracked the church in Scotland, Connecticut, there seems to be no record of an eighteenth-century Anglican church there. It should be borne in mind, however, that the French officers did not generally distinguish between the Protestant sects, often lumping them together as "Presbyterians" or "English."

13. There is a slight discrepancy between this statement situating the camp with its left adjoining the road (i.e., the camp on the right or north side of the road) and the maps, Nos. 16 and 30, both of which show the campsite on the south side of the road, with only the artillery on the north side.

14. See maps, Nos. 17, 31, and 152.

15. Chastellux, in November 1780, had stopped at a tavern kept by a Mrs. Hill

You come to a crossroads. The road on the left comes in from Lebanon. Facing you is Kent [?] Meetinghouse.[16] You take the right fork and go down over a stony road. Enter a wood with a house on the right. Here you are still 10 miles from Bolton. Leave on the left a road coming in from Lebanon Springs House, which is on the left in the angle formed by the two roads. You come to a very wide valley. Two brooks wind through it into the river, which is two musket-shots away. After you cross the bridge over the second brook, the road turns right and ascends the slope. You come into Little Lebanon, a lone house on the right of the road at the top of a bluff. *8 Miles*

Passing Little Lebanon you proceed through a rather pretty little valley, where several brooks flow into the [Hop] river. You are still following the river, which is some distance away on your right. You leave All [Hall's? Hale's?] Tavern on the right. Cross a brook on a wooden bridge. There are several houses on either side of the road. Leave on the right a road through a wood that passes over the river to Coventry. When you are within 4 miles of Bolton, you begin to encounter more houses. The road is then very close to the river. You cross a brook on a wooden bridge. There is a ford beside it and a sawmill on the left. Beyond the bridge you turn left, then go through a small hamlet [Andover?] of scattered houses separated by several little brooks that flow down to the river. You leave on the left Parten's [Parton's?] House, or White's Tavern.[17] You cross a few more brooklets. You go through a little wood where the road climbs sharply. This grade is very steep. At the top you turn sharp right and come to the first houses of Bolton [Bolton Center].

Bolton is a small town comprising many scattered houses, some of which are clustered around the meetinghouse on a spacious but low plateau. Through this part of Bolton runs a high road that goes left to Colchester and right to Boston. The camp is to be located on this [east] side of the meetinghouse. *16 Miles*

----

in what is now Columbia; see Chastellux (4), I, 71–72, 256. Columbia, incorporated as a separate town in 1804, was then in the part of Lebanon known as the North Parish or "The Crank."

16. In the Berthier manuscript the name is written "Kent"; in the Rochambeau copy, "Kant." These are probably misrenderings of "Crank." The Lebanon Crank Meetinghouse was in the present village of Columbia. It was here that the Reverend Eleazar Wheelock presided over Moor's Indian Charity School, before emigrating north to the New Hampshire wilderness to establish Dartmouth College (1770).

17. It is not wholly clear from the manuscript whether "Parten's House" and "Whait Tavern" are the same place or two successive houses. The Rochambeau manuscript of the Itinerary calls the latter "ou hitte Tavern au cheval noir," i.e., White Tavern at the sign of the Black Horse! There was a White's Tavern in Andover; cf. Chastellux (4), II, 639, n. 4. Chastellux and Rochambeau had stopped there when journeying to the Wethersfield Conference in May 1781.

From Bolton to East Hartford[18]

On leaving the camp you proceed to the upper part of the town. You
go past the meetinghouse. Cross the Colchester-Boston highway, with a
wood on the right and some houses on the left. Then enter a small wood.
Coming out of it you go downhill to the stone marking 13 miles to
Hartford. Go through another patch of woods. Coming out of it, turn left.
There are some houses on the right. The road continues downhill. You
pass a few houses on either side of the road. You go through a small wood,
continuing downhill. The road is sandy. To the right you pass by a road
going to Boston.[19] There is a milestone indicating that you are 75 miles
from Boston. Continue downhill on a winding road crossing several small
streams. There are houses here and there on both sides of the road. After
passing Milestone No. 10 you cross a stone bridge. The road continues
as far as Milestone No. 9.[20] There is a cemetery on the left. Ascending
a short grade you turn left, passing a meetinghouse on the right. You
enter a wood. The road is sandy. You come to Milestone No. 8 in a clearing
where there are several houses. Coming out of the wood you turn right
and reach East Hartford.[21]

East Hartford is a small hamlet within the town limits of East Hartford,
which is 7 miles farther along, on the left bank of the Connecticut River.
This hamlet is in a pretty plain with well-cultivated fields, surrounded
by woods within a radius of ½ mile. A small brook can be crossed either
by a ford or a poor bridge. Coming out of the wood you are still on
the plain where you see many houses on the right and a road on the left.
You cross a marshland in the middle of which there is a small bridge.
You cross a highway, going left to Glastonbury and right to East Windsor,
4 miles from Hartford. Entering a wood you come to Milestone No. 4.
The road is narrow. You cross a marsh on a small bridge. The woods
then recede from the roadside. You cross a small stream on a wooden
bridge. There are many houses on either side of the road. Leave a swamp
and a pond on the right. Cross a highway that goes left to Glastonbury.
Turn right and you reach a little valley through which flows a brook
spanned by a wooden bridge. A roadway bordered with trees on either

18. See maps, Nos. 18, 32, and 151.
19. This was the so-called Middle Road from Hartford to Boston, passing
through Coventry, Mansfield, Ashford, Pomfret, etc. Crofut, *Guide*, I, 13–14.
20. Milestone No. 9 was at East Cemetery, East Center Street, Manchester.
Crofut's *Guide* (published in 1937), I, 301, states that five of these milestones
along the road to Hartford were then still standing: Nos. 9, 5, 4, 3, and 2. Milestone No. 2 is now on display as a museum piece in the old Hartford State
House. See vignette, above, on half-title to these Itineraries.
21. Present Manchester. The eastern part of the town of East Hartford was in
1823 separately incorporated as the town of Manchester. The repetitive designations used in the Itinerary, though confusing today, are presumably correct for
the period when they were written. Cf. Crofut, *Guide*, I, 298–302.

side cuts through this valley. You ascend the opposite slope and enter East Hartford. The road forks. The road turning sharp right goes through the town, and the other bearing slightly to the left leads to the ferry. The meetinghouse is in the angle of the fork.   *12½ Miles*

SIXTH MARCH

From East Hartford to Farmington[22]

Upon leaving the camp you cross the meadow between East Hartford and the Connecticut River. You reach the ferry where the boats necessary for crossing the river are to be found.[23] You straightway enter Hartford and, upon reaching the Town Hall,[24] turn sharp left and go through the town, parallel to the river. You cross on a wooden bridge a fairly wide stream with high banks. This cuts the town in two and turns several mills.[25] As you leave the town, the road forks. Take the right fork. The left goes to Wethersfield. A bit farther along, several roads intersect. Take the one on the left. The road leading straight ahead also goes to Farmington, but it is not so good as the left-hand one. The road on the right leads back to town. You then pass by a gallows on the right.[26] You ford a brooklet and about 1 mile farther along cross a small wooden bridge over a brook, which you skirt, now on the right, now on the left-hand side of the road. You go through West Hartford,[27] where you are 4½ miles from Hartford. On leaving the village you turn left. You proceed uphill a bit and leave on the left two taverns, one of which is the Black Horse. You ford a brooklet. From here on the road winds its way to Farmington, passing several scattered houses on either side and crossing several small streams.

Farmington is a small town built along a single street, but a very long one, at the foot of a wooded hill. There is a handsome church[28] on the left of the road. Here you are 10 miles from Hartford. A little before coming out of the town you leave on the right the road to Harwinton, which is closed by a gate, to the right of which is a smithy. This road

22. See maps, Nos. 19, 33, and 149.
23. See above, "Plan," p. 12, "The Hartford Ferries." The Rochambeau copy of the Itinerary includes here a sentence omitted in the Berthier manuscript: "Mr. Dumas est chargé du pouvoir," indicating that Mathieu Dumas, one of the assistant quartermasters, was responsible for getting the army across the river.
24. The State House. The present "old" State House, built in 1796, is on the site of the earlier edifice. Cf. map, No. 19.
25. The Park River, formerly known as the Little River, to distinguish it from the Connecticut or Great River.
26. The French term is "justice." "In Revolutionary times the gallows were on Gallows Hill near the junction of Zachary's Lane (Vernon Street) and Rocky Hill." Crofut, *Guide*, I, 276.
27. On the road map, No. 19, the term "West Division" is used. Crofut, *Guide*, I, 224, 335.
28. The Congregational Church, built in 1771–1772 by Judah Woodruff, is still one of the distinguished landmarks of Farmington.

is the route from Hartford to New Windsor [on the Hudson], called the upper road, passing through Litchfield, Hopewell, and Fishkill.

A mile from Farmington you turn right into a road that leads to the campsite. *12½ Miles*

SEVENTH MARCH

From Farmington to Barnes's Tavern[29]

On leaving the Farmington camp you take the Southington road. A mile farther the road forks. There is a large farm in the angle of the fork. Take the right fork. The left-hand road skirts the foot of a wooded hillside. You come almost at once onto a sandy plain, 5 miles long,[30] covered with a sort of underbrush. Along the road you see several houses surrounded by pastures and plowed fields. You cross on a wooden bridge a little brook that flows to the right into a larger one running parallel to the road. You then come to the territory of Southington with some houses on the right. You pass by Curtiss's Tavern on the left. After recrossing the little brook you enter Southington, skirting several small wooded ridges on the left.

Southington is a little town 9 miles from Farmington and 4 from Barnes's Tavern. Near the middle of the town you pass Adkins's Tavern[31] on the right and a bit farther along, on the left, the road to Middletown. You then turn sharp right, leaving on the left an English church with a steeple, and proceed to cross on a wooden bridge the brook that you skirt on the right before entering into the town.

You then continue over fairly level country. The road makes wide bends, with several little woods on the right and some houses here and there on the left. You cross a brook on a wooden bridge with a pond and a mill on the right. The road is still very winding most of the way to Barnes's Tavern. It finally makes a right-angle turn opposite two taverns, where you turn left. The road that you are leaving and that continues straight ahead goes to Cambridge [?].[32] Barnes's Tavern is a lone house on the right bank of a brook.[33] Shortly before reaching it you pass

29. See maps, Nos. 20 and 34.
30. The "Great Plain," formerly a part of Farmington, named Plainville in 1831 and separately incorporated under this name in 1869. Crofut, *Guide*, I, 311.
31. In the Berthier manuscript the name seems to read "Atquins"; in the Rochambeau copy it is "Hatquins." There was an Adkins family living in this region in the eighteenth century; the wife of Asa Barnes (the next tavernkeeper mentioned) was Phebe Adkins. Cf. Heman R. Timlow, *Ecclesiastical and Other Sketches of Southington, Conn.* (Hartford, 1875), "Southington Genealogies," pp. i–iii (Adkins), xviiff. (Barnes), lxxiii–lxxviii (Curtiss).
32. Thus in the Berthier manuscript; "Campbridge" in the Rochambeau copy. The road "straight ahead" led west (see maps).
33. Concerning Barnes's Tavern, situated in the part of the town of Southington known as Marion, see: Forbes and Cadman, I, 143–144; Crofut, *Guide*, I, 321; Timlow, *op.cit.*, pp. 529–530. Some amusing handed-down local reminiscences

two other taverns on the right. This place is one where there will be the greatest shortage of lodgings for the headquarters. The camp is to lie in front of the brook.   *13 Miles*

EIGHTH MARCH
From Barnes's Tavern to Break Neck[34]

On leaving Barnes's Tavern a wooden bridge takes you across a little brook on which there is a sawmill on the right. You leave on the left a road to Middletown, 18 miles away, and another on the right. You enter an extensive wood in the midst of which are several houses surrounded by tilled fields. Before reaching it you cross several brooks. Parts of the roadbed are made of logs and are generally bad in winter; other parts are filled with stones and are hard to climb. You come to several houses scattered along either side of the road. You are now only 4 miles from Waterbury. You cross in succession several small streams, while passing houses here and there on either side of the road. While still in the wood you come to the bank of a large stream spanned by a wooden bridge. Then you emerge from the wood, skirting on the right a little brook that turns a mill and flows, near the bridge, into the big stream that you have just crossed. You cross several more small brooks that flow into the Naragontad [Mad River, tributary of the Naugatuck], which you follow on your left. You go through a patch of woods and arrive in Waterbury.

Waterbury is a small town whose houses are scattered along the left slope of a wide valley through which flows the Naragontad [Naugatuck] River. You are now 8 miles from Barnes's Tavern. You go through Waterbury, passing the meetinghouse[35] on the right, and make a sharp turn left on leaving, passing a road leading to Litchfield on your right. You cross the river on a good wooden bridge with two rather large arches. You ascend the opposite slope between high banks on a narrow road that is full of stones. At the top, where there are more houses within the town limits of Waterbury, you pass on the right a road to Litchfield, which is only 16 miles away. You then pass through several patches of woodland and cross several little brooks; the last of these is larger than the others and contains several pools. You cross the valley on a raised dike in the middle of which is a wooden bridge. You proceed uphill with a small wood on the left and reach Break Neck.

Break Neck, 5 miles from Waterbury, is a hamlet with but few houses and two taverns belonging to Messrs. Baldwin and Isaac Bronson.[36] The camp is to lie parallel to the road, near the tavern.   *13 Miles*

---

of the passage of the French army were garnered by Timlow, whose book was published in 1875.

34. See maps, Nos. 21 and 35.

35. Situated on the east line of "The Green." Cf. Crofut, *Guide*, ii, 661.

36. Break Neck Hill is in the present town of Middlebury (separately incorporated in 1807 from parts of Waterbury, Woodbury, and Southbury). Bron-

From Break Neck to Newtown[37]

Leaving Break Neck you descend into a small valley where you leave on the left a road with several scattered houses. Turn right, then left up the hill. Next pass a road on the left and a wood on the right and proceed into a wood where you travel up and downhill for a bit. When you come out of it, you are only 1½ miles from Break Neck. Then turn left. The road straight ahead goes to Woodbury.[38] You cross several little brooks and pass close to a very large pond, called Quassapaug Pond [Lake], which is almost entirely surrounded by high hills. You cross several more brooks. There are many houses along the way. The country is wooded and filled with clumps of trees.   *3 Miles*

You cross a wooden bridge over a brook that flows out of the pond nearby. There is a sawmill on the left-hand side of the road. Beyond the bridge there is a long ascent followed by a descent. The road winds a good deal through the woods. You cross several little brooks in succession, then a sparse little wood, and proceed down a rather steep grade. On the right you pass a road going to Waterbury. You go up and downhill a good deal. You pass on the right the belfry of Woodbury,[39] around which many houses are clustered, and soon thereafter a road going to Litchfield. You continue uphill and down. After crossing several brooks you come to the first houses of Southbury, which is a little town strung along the road. A little farther on you skirt on the right a small valley with a flowing brook, crossing several small streams that feed into it. You come to the Stratford [Housatonic] River, which is spanned by a very good wooden

---

son's Tavern, now a private residence, is still standing on present Artillery Road. The road pattern shown on Berthier's maps has substantially survived; the camp itself, however, was situated on a now-abandoned segment of Breakneck Hill Road near the summit of the hill. We are greatly indebted to Dr. Joseph L. Hetzel for a careful study of the locality made in 1968. See also Forbes and Cadman, I, 145–146, 155–156, for observations made in the 1920's.

37. See maps, Nos. 22 and 36.

38. This road junction is clearly shown on Erskine-Dewitt map, No. 102, "Contraction from Hartford, New Haven, Norwalk, Bedford &c." (New-York Historical Society). It should be noted for the interpretation of what follows that the route here described did not continue straight ahead to Woodbury (i.e., the center) but bypassed it when turning left and continuing around the southern end of Quassapaug Pond.

39. The direction of the route is here southwestward. The Woodbury "belfry" was presumably not in the present town of Woodbury, which is farther north. In 1781 the township of Woodbury included the area subsequently incorporated (1787) as the town of Southbury. Thus the localities mentioned here and designated on our 1781 road map as "Woodbury," "Southbury," and "South Britain" are all within the present township of Southbury. Crofut, *Guide*, II, 652. The statement made elsewhere by Crofut (I, 456) that the French army "passed through present-day Woodbury" is open to question.

bridge with three large arches.[40] Turn left, following the river on your left. When you reach a house, you turn right, leaving it on your left, and ascend the opposite slope by a narrow road with steep banks, in which runs a little brook. Cross another brook on a wooden bridge, passing on the left a dam and a mill. Almost immediately you recross the same brook, then proceed uphill and enter Newtown.

Newtown is a fairly compact little town. The camp may be made on either the near or the far side of the town, which is situated on a plateau between two small valleys.[41]   *15 Miles*

TENTH MARCH

From Newtown to Ridgebury[42]

As you leave the town you bear right between two low hills. There are several scattered houses on either side of the road. You go down a stony road, leave a large pond on the left, and then pass through a wood. You cross several little brooks that flow to the right into a larger one. You cross several little woods.

Proceed downhill. The road is very steep. You pass a wood and a pond on the right and then cross a brook on a bad bridge.   *3 Miles*

The road goes up and downhill, crossing several brooks. You pass a small wood on the right. The distance from here to Newtown is 5 miles. You proceed into a small wood and, upon coming out of it, pass on the right a road going to Newbury [?].[43] You enter another small wood and, after passing through it, come into a little valley where you cross a small brook on a bad wooden bridge. Passing a wood on the left you continue uphill on a bad stony road, having a hollow on the left and a wood on the right. Then you wind downhill. Cross a brook on a bridge, next to which there is also a ford. You pass several roads on the right and on the left and several scattered houses. You come to a crossroads. Take the

40. The three arches of the bridge are precisely indicated on the road map, where the name of the bridge has been corrected from Colonel "Groton" to "Carlton." This was presumably the bridge built in 1778, referred to in a memorial addressed to the General Assembly of Connecticut by the inhabitants of Woodbury and Newton (7 October 1780, Connecticut Archives, cited by Crofut, *Guide*, I, 456): "in the latter part of . . . 1778 his Excellency Genl. Washington sent a part of his Army and Built a Bridge across the great River between said Towns at . . . Hinman's Ferry for the benefit of the Army then on their March Eastward and the more convenient transporting of Provisions."

41. According to the map of this encampment (No. 36), the camp was eventually made on the "near side" (i.e., east) of the town, with detachments of grenadiers and chasseurs in a forward position on the "far side" (i.e., west) of the town.

42. See maps, Nos. 23, 37, and 148.

43. So written in both the Berthier and the Rochambeau copies of the Itinerary. It probably refers to a road that went north to join the "upper" route to the Hudson and thus eventually led to Fishkill Landing and Newburgh, New York.

middle road leading to Danbury, which is 10 miles from Newtown and 18 miles from Haight's Tavern [Somers, Westchester County, New York].

Danbury is a fairly large town that has been partly burned by the English.[44] It is situated on a low plateau. A stream called the Still River flows nearby. This is crossed on a wooden bridge, near which there is also a ford. You go out from the center of the town, where you turn left.[45] The road straight ahead goes to Fishkill. You pass through the cemetery,[46] continue uphill, and reach the highway. You cross a brook on a wooden bridge. The road goes up and downhill. After crossing several little brooks you go down a rather steep hill. Leaving a wood on the left you cross a brook on a wooden bridge and then cross several others in succession. There are many houses along the road. Turn right, then left. Cross a brook on a wooden bridge. You pass by several scattered houses, which are still part of Danbury. Continue downhill, crossing over several little brooks where several houses are clustered. There are wooded mountains on the left. You cross a patch of woodland, after which you ascend a fairly steep grade, and then continue downhill. You pass a meetinghouse on the right, many scattered houses, among which is the tavern of S. [Samuel] Keeler, on the right, and you reach Ridgebury.[47] Ridgebury is only a village, where there is an English church,[48] composed of scattered houses on an extensive but not high plateau. The camp will be near Ridgebury. *15 Miles*

44. Tryon's Raid, 26 April 1777. Cf. Crofut, *Guide*, I, 99–100. The fresh evidences of the raid were a reminder that the English, still ensconced in New York in 1781, might again attempt incursions into this region.

45. The French army camped in Danbury when on its eastward march in October 1782. See map, No. 148, and descriptive note.

46. Probably the "Old Town Cemetery" of Danbury on West Wooster Street. General David Wooster, who died in Danbury as a result of wounds received in the 1777 "battles," was first buried here. His remains were transferred in 1852 to a later cemetery, which was named Wooster Cemetery in his honor. Crofut, *Guide*, I, 102–103.

47. It is a bit difficult to reconcile this description (prepared prior to the actual march) with the maps, which show the army's main encampment on the easterly side of Ridgebury's main street, diagonally opposite the meetinghouse (Congregational Church, present edifice dating from 1851 on the same site). Cf. George L. Rockwell, *History of Ridgefield, Conn.* (Ridgefield, 1927), pp. 129–136, Chap. XIII, "The French Troops"; Silvio A. Bedini, *Ridgefield in Review* (Ridgefield, 1958), pp. 130–140, "French Encampments in Ridgefield," and pp. 202–203, "Inns and Taverns of Ridgebury District." Mr. Daniel M. McKeon has made a careful study of the French encampments here. We are indebted to him, as well as to Mr. Richard G. Lucid, for informed and helpful counsel.

48. In addition to the Congregational meetinghouse, there was also at this time an Anglican church in the Ridgebury district of Ridgefield. It is described by Crofut (*Guide*, I, 142, after Rockwell, Teller) and by Bedini (*op.cit.*, p. 315) as standing at the "northerly apex of the triangle at lower end of Ridgebury Street," nearly half a mile south of the Congregational Church.

From Ridgebury to North Castle[49]

On leaving Ridgebury you turn right. At a distance of 2 miles you go down a long and rather steep hill. You pass a road on the right, then cross a brook. You ascend and descend, following along the side of the hill, skirting a brook on the left. There is a road on the right, and another on the left. Several houses on either side of the road. You pass on the right a road going to Peekskill. You cross the brook that you have been skirting. You continue up and downhill and cross a brook, passing a pond [Waccabuc] on the left and a house on the right. You then pass by several houses and a road on the left going [back] to Ridgebury. You continue up and downhill and cross a brook, having several [houses?][50] on either side of the road. You proceed uphill. The road turns right, then left. You continue straight ahead, up and downhill. You come into a road at a right angle. You go over the Cross River on a wooden bridge,[51] then proceed uphill and pass by several houses. Follow along the heights with a hollow on the left. You continue uphill and down. 2 Miles. You go through a little hollow, cross over a plain, and reach the first houses of North Castle [Mount Kisco]. You keep straight ahead, with houses on either side of the road. You pass several roads on the right and left. You turn left, cross a brook, pass a road on the left and then one on the right. There is a pond on the left. The meetinghouse[52] is on the right. The left of the French camp was behind it.   *Total: 17 Miles*

North Castle to Philipsburg[53]

Leaving from the left of the camp, that is, from the meetinghouse, you take the first road to the left. You go up and downhill, cross a brook, continue along the side of the hill, with a pond on the right. You cross a brook, with a little valley on the left, and continuing along the side of the hill you ascend, with a house on the right and another on the left. Cross a brook and leave some mountains on the left. Continue along the

49. See maps, Nos. 24 and 38. At this point the route deviates from the one originally planned. Philipsburg, not King's Ferry, becomes the ultimate destination. This last part of the Itinerary was not prepared in advance but is based on field observations made during the march. There is no counterpart for this text in the Rochambeau copy of the Itinerary. The First and Second Brigades took variant routes from Ridgebury to North Castle. The text here corresponds to the march of the Second Brigade, as does the map, No. 24. Soon after leaving Ridgebury the route crosses the state line, leaving Connecticut and entering Westchester County, New York.

50. There is a word omitted here in the manuscript.

51. The site of the bridge is now covered by the Cross River Reservoir.

52. See descriptive note to map, No. 38.

53. See maps, Nos. 25, 39–41, and 46.

side of the hill, passing several houses. You pass a road on the left, go up and downhill, cross a brook, and come to houses and a road on the left. You come into a hollow; road on the right. You go up, continue along the crest, go down, cross the hollow, and then, proceeding up and down along the hillside, follow a little valley on your right. Road on the left, brook, another road on the left, another brook, then a road on the right. You are now at the foot of a rather steep mountain, which is on the left and on the top of which is the old entrenched camp occupied by the Americans on 1 November 1776. You cross a hollow and a brook, then a plain. You come to a place where the road divides in three directions [*une patte d'oie*]. The right-hand road goes over the Bronx River and also leads to the camp. The left-hand road goes to White Plains. Take the middle road. You go downhill and come to an old camp occupied by the Americans in 1776, where Lauzun's Legion camped [in 1781].[55] Cross a brook, then ford the Bronx River. You go up onto a height, the left of the [French] army's position, where the grenadiers and chasseurs were camped.[56] Continue straight along the road, passing a house on the right. You turn left, come to another house, then to a fork in the road. Take the right fork, go up into the wood, passing a house on the right and another that was General Rochambeau's headquarters.[57] The French camp was in advance of this house, and 1½ miles farther along the same road, after it crosses a brook, was the American camp, with its farthest outposts on the right extending as far as Dobbs Ferry [on the Hudson].

20 Miles

*Continuation of the Route [from Ridgebury]
via Crompond, to Peekskill,
which the army left [at Ridgebury]
From Ridgebury to Crompond (18 Miles)*[58]

Just outside Ridgebury, you ford a brook. You pass a tavern and some houses on the right, go down a very long and steep hill, the road being full of stones and traversed by brooklets. You pass on the left a road going to Ridgefield and another on the right coming in from Danbury. You cross a brook on a wooden bridge. You pass some houses on the right

55. See Clermont-Crèvecœur's journal, n. 38.
56. Chatterton Hill, scene of the Battle of White Plains, 28 October 1776.
57. The Odell House, Ridge Road, Hartsdale (town of Greenburgh, West-chester County). The house is still standing, now maintained as a historic site by the Sons of the American Revolution.
58. Although this route from Ridgebury, Connecticut, to Crompond (York-town, New York) was not taken in 1781, the French army followed it in the opposite direction when proceeding eastward in October 1782. There is no detailed road map for this route, but see the "General Map of Camps and Marches," No. 162.

The American army, having been forced by the English victory over General Putnam to evacuate Long Island and New York, and after having left a strong garrison in Fort Washington [on Manhattan Island], took up positions or small entrenched camps occupying all the heights and strong points from Valentine Hill to White Plains. When the English army, which wanted to force General Washington to engage in battle, had crossed the Sound and landed at Throg's Neck, and then advanced towards White Plains, the Provincials abandoned their various entrenched camps in order to occupy a stronger one on the left [east] bank of the Bronx River at the place where Lauzun's Legion camped [in 1781]. There were several skirmishes between the advance corps. General Washington, who still had the same reasons for avoiding combat, retreated on 1 November and took up a still stronger position along the North Castle road. This position is the one just mentioned, on the left [east] of the route from North Castle to Philipsburg.[54]

54. The "Vieux Camp retranché" shown on map, No. 25.

and on the left-hand side of the road a brick tavern. Going downhill
you then turn right to cross over a big brook on a wooden bridge. Soon
thereafter you cross another stream on a stone bridge. Beyond the bridge
the road turns left. The one you leave goes to Dutchess County, to
Fredericksburg [Patterson, Putnam County, New York], to Hopewell, etc.

You cross in succession two brooklets, one by ford and the other on
a wooden bridge. You turn right and go downhill and cross another
brook on a wooden bridge. There is a mill pond here. You pass on the
right a meetinghouse in bad condition. You cross a brook on a wooden
bridge. You pass by on the right the main road to Fredericksburg.
Continue uphill and pass on the right a fine tavern having for its sign a
ship flying the American flag. You are now in Salem, a little town,
so-called, all the houses of which are scattered over a distance of 5 or 6
miles. On the left you pass by a mill pond that collects several little brooks.
The water from this pond turns the wheels of three mills. You are in a
very pretty little valley. The road is along the side of the slope, lined
on the right by houses belonging to Salem but called Coitton many[?].[59]
Skirting on the left the brook coming out of the mill pond, which forms
another mill race about midway, you pass on the left a road going
over the dam and leading to Bedford, which is 8 to 9 miles away. The
valley narrows a bit, and the road turns right between two wooded
hillocks and continues along over a river on a four-arched wooden bridge
[Croton River, Dean's Bridge] in rather bad condition. You pass some
houses on the right and a road on the left, continue downhill, and enter a
wood. You ford a brooklet. You leave on the right a road going to
Fishkill. You then arrive at Haight's Tavern.[60] This is a lone house on
the right-hand side of the road, 18 miles from Danbury. Opposite it there
is a road going to Bedford, which is only 6 miles away. You are 15 miles
from Peekskill. Leaving the tavern you ford a small brook. There is
also a bad bridge, two houses on the right, and a pond on the left. You
go downhill, turn left, and cross a brook by a ford, with a bad bridge next
to it. You then pass by some houses at some distance from one another.
You come into a little wood, proceed downhill, cross over a big brook on a
plank bridge, continue up and downhill, with houses on both sides of
the road. You leave a little wood on the left. The road winds much less
and continues downhill. You cross several brooks. You pass on the left a
road going to New York, 50 miles away, and another, on the right,
which goes to Fishkill, 25 miles away. You then reach Crompond.[61]

59. Salem Center in the town of North Salem, Westchester County, New York.
See map of the 1782 camp there, No. 147, and descriptive note. The undecipher-
able word appears to read "Coïttsumany" in the Rochambeau copy of this
Itinerary.
60. Also spelled Hait's Tavern. It was situated in the present village of Somers,
in the town of that name.
61. Crompond, taking its name from Crom Pond, is in the present town of
Yorktown, New York. The French army eventually marched through Crompond later in the summer of 1781, after the six weeks' encampment at Philips-

Crompond is only a village, in part ruined by the English, who burned the meetinghouse and several other houses.[62] The troops will camp on this side of a little brook, with the headquarters on the right.

LAST MARCH PLANNED

To Peekskill (10 Miles)[63]

One mile beyond Crompond you go down a long hill. You leave John [?] Tavern on the right. Then turn right and cross a brook on a wooden bridge. Continue downhill and turn left out of the woods. Continuing down you cross several little brooks one after another. You pass scattered houses along the road. You go through a wood, having a hollow on the right. While in the wood you first cross a rather large brook on a wooden bridge and then ford another brook. There is a fork in the road. Take the right branch. The country is fairly open. You cross several little brooks, continuing downhill and passing by several houses on either side of the road. You go through a very thinset wood. Continue down along the hillside, skirting on the right a hollow in which a little brook flows. The hilltops are covered with woods. Continue down. You pass on the right a road that goes by a ford across the brook on the right and immediately thereafter enters Peekskill. As it enters it intersects the road that comes in from Continental Village, which is 3 miles away [to the north] on the Fishkill road. When you are at this point, as far as Peekskill, the road turns left to go to King's Ferry, which is only 5 miles away. You cross a brooklet on a small wooden bridge. Proceed up into a spruce wood, where you cross several more brooklets. The road is not very good. There is a house on the right. You cross a fairly big brook on a wooden bridge. The camp was to have been on this side of the brook.

---

burg, but then approached it from the south and not from the east, as described here and as originally planned. See maps, Nos. 48 and 61. The army was again in Crompond in 1782; see maps, Nos. 145 and 146.

62. The Presbyterian parsonage at Crompond, then used as headquarters by the Committee of Safety, as well as a nearby storehouse for arms of the militia, were both destroyed by Tory raiders under Caleb Morgan on 12 June 1779. During a second raid, on 24 June 1779, under Tarleton and Simcoe the meetinghouse, then used as a barracks, was burned. Otto Hufeland, *Westchester County during the American Revolution* (White Plains, 1926), pp. 292–293.

63. The army, having rejoined this route at Crompond when coming northward in August 1781 from the long Philipsburg encampment, followed the road here described from Crompond to Peekskill—and then continued to King's Ferry for the crossing of the Hudson. See maps, Nos. 48, 61, and 62; Berthier's journal, pp. 254–255, concerning variations in the "prescribed route"; and the next Itinerary.

ITINERARY

of the Marches of the
French Army
from the Camp at Philipsburg
to the Camp before York
in Virginia

1 7 8 1

PART I

From Philipsburg to Whippany
86½ Miles

The French and American armies remained in camp at Philipsburg, in their threatening position north of British-held New York, from early July until the middle of August 1781. The news of the impending arrival of de Grasse's fleet off the Chesapeake Capes, which reached Washington and Rochambeau at Philipsburg on 14 August, determined the next phase of the campaign. The march of the French army to Virginia is described in this Itinerary and the ones following.

The "First March" traces the northward movement of the French army in two columns, by two different but roughly parallel routes, from the Franco-American camp at Philipsburg to Pines Bridge on the Croton River. At this point the route of the two columns converged, and they henceforth followed the same road through Hunt's Tavern, Crompond, and Peekskill, to King's Ferry (Verplanck's Point), where the crossing of the Hudson was made. Meanwhile, the American army, forming the left column of the combined Franco-American army, was marching along a more westerly route close to the Hudson, via Ossining to New Bridge at the mouth of the Croton, and thence to King's Ferry. The schematic map on the following page (if used in conjunction with a modern map) may help to clarify the simultaneous troop movements described below.

After crossing the Hudson at King's Ferry—that is, from Verplanck's Point to Stony Point on the west bank—the French, then marching by brigades, proceeded to "Haverstraw" (Stony Point Village) and to Suffern, New York. Then, entering New Jersey, they continued their march to Pompton Plains and to Whippany, where there was an extra day's halt. The Americans followed a route more to the east, along the foothills of the Jersey mountains. Since the Americans were at this point covering the left flank of the French army, the Lauzun Legion marched with the First Brigade and not as a separate column (as it had done when crossing Connecticut and as it would do again on the march northward through New Jersey in September 1782). The routes of the two armies eventually converged at Trenton for the crossing of the Delaware.

The following translation has been made from the copy of the Itinerary in the Princeton University Library (Berthier Papers, No. 10). No other copy has been found by the Editors. The man-

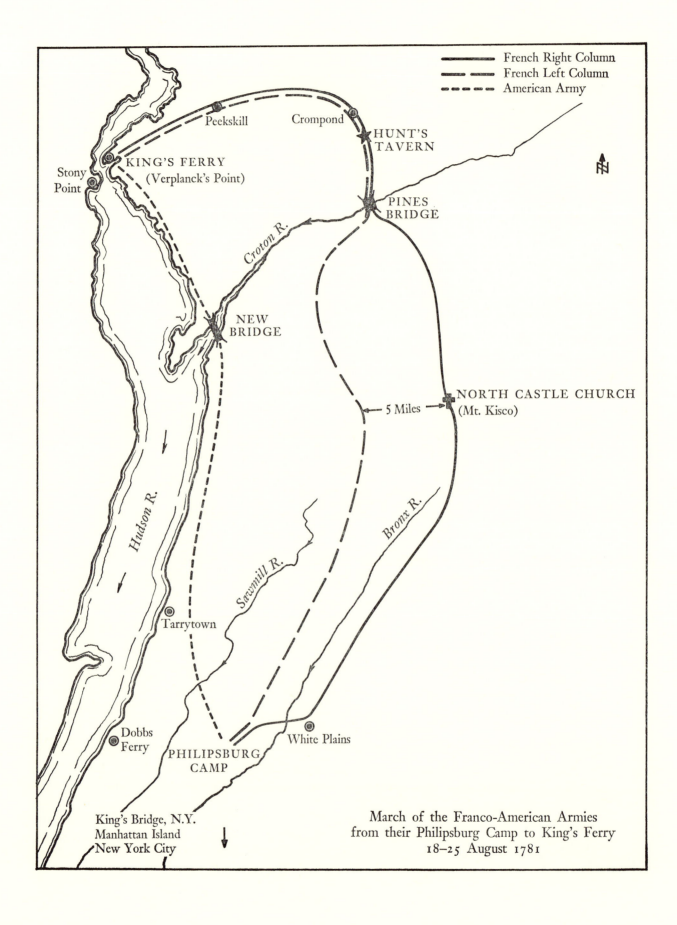

French Right Column
French Left Column
American Army

Peekskill

Crompond

HUNT'S TAVERN

Stony Point

KING'S FERRY
(Verplanck's Point)

PINES BRIDGE

Croton R.

NEW BRIDGE

NORTH CASTLE CHURCH
(Mt. Kisco)

← 5 Miles →

Hudson R.

Bronx R.

Sawmill R.

Tarrytown

Dobbs Ferry

White Plains

PHILIPSBURG CAMP

King's Bridge, N.Y.
Manhattan Island
New York City

March of the Franco-American Armies
from their Philipsburg Camp to King's Ferry
18–25 August 1781

uscript, arranged in two and sometimes three columns, is entitled "Itinéraire des Marches que l'Armée a faits pour se rendre du camp à Philipsburg au camp devant Yorck en Virginie en 1781. Premier Cahier, de Philip'sburg à Wippany, 86 Milles ½." Like the preceding Itinerary, it is written in a formal clerical hand on sheets folded and gathered into a "cahier" of 28 pages (32 x 20.5 cm.).

Since the march to Virginia was determined only at the last moment, with little time for reconnoitering the routes in advance, it seems evident that the present Itinerary is based on observations made for the most part during the actual march. The route is fully covered by the maps of roads and of camps published hereafter. It is also described in Clermont-Crèvecœur's journal. Berthier's personal journal, however, ends with the crossing of the Hudson.

Itinerary

OF THE MARCHES OF THE FRENCH ARMY
FROM THE CAMP AT PHILIPSBURG TO THE CAMP BEFORE YORK
IN VIRGINIA, 1781

Part 1: From Philipsburg to Whippany, 86½ Miles

	FIRST MARCH	
Left Column[1]	*Right Column*[3]	*Observations*
[Artillery and Military Chest[2]] *From Philipsburg to Pines Bridge*	[Infantry] *From Philipsburg to North Castle*	
From the right [west] of the camp you take the communication road between the two general headquarters, turn to the right, go down through the wood, and cross a marshy hollow.[4] *1 Mile*	[same as Left Column] *1 Mile*	In order to preserve the continuity of the itineraries, but at the same time not to miss any interesting details, topographical or military, which may not be directly related to the march, we have placed here in the margin general observations on the country, reconnaissances of specific military positions, lateral branches of the itinerary, and historical accounts of the regions that have already seen military action or occupation earlier in this war, and have thus made the description of the route taken by the army as precise and uninterrupted as possible.
You come out of the wood, go up onto a height, leave the Thomas Tompkins house on the left and, a bit farther on, a road going to Tarrytown. *1 Mile*	[same as Left Column] *1 Mile*	
You go downhill, turning right, cross a brook, cross the meadow that was used as pasturage for the cattle, and reach a triple fork in the road. Take the middle road; the right goes to White Plains,	[same as Left Column]

... Take the right-hand road; the left goes to Tarrytown, and the | In addition to the [two] routes |

1. The left column of the French army left the Philipsburg camp on 18 August 1781, a day ahead of the right column. It was led by L.-A. Berthier, assistant quartermaster-general, who describes the march in his journal (pp. 253 ff.), as does Clermont-Crèvecœur of the artillery (pp. 40 ff.). The greater part of the

route is not specifically shown on any of the maps reproduced hereafter.
2. *Trésor*, i.e., "treasury," is the French term.
3. The northward route of the right column was the same as the one taken in the opposite direction by the whole army when it had marched from North Castle Church (Mount

Kisco) to Philipsburg on 6 July. It is described above in the previous Itinerary under the heading "Twelfth March" and is shown on map, No. 25.
4. The roads leading northward out of the Philipsburg camp are shown in some detail on maps, Nos. 39–41 and 46.

and the left to Tarrytown. You enter a wood.   *1 Mile*

You immediately go up a short but steep hill; the road is stony; you come to a bridge that will eventually need to be repaired. The brook comes out of a meadow on the left, but you can skirt it. On the right you pass by a house belonging to Alexander Larck [?]   *2 Miles*

You then go uphill; the road is bad, but you can pass alongside it through a pasture on the left. You soon come back into the road. You pass a road on the right and on the left a gully washed out by the rains. It would be well to repair the road in this place, though it is of course possible to go around a bad spot. You descend, passing a road on the right. Then you go up on to an open plateau. Enter a thinset wood on the right; coming out of it, you pass a road on the right and another on the left. This is the White Plains road. Continue along the middle road, but skirt it through a pasture in order to avoid a bad stretch. You come back into the road, then pass a house in a hollow. You go downhill, passing on the left a road that also leads to Pines Bridge but is a poor one for wagons.   *1 Mile*

You take the right-hand road, which is a good one, and ford

middle road to Pines Bridge.   *1 Mile*

The road makes a right-angle turn and then, going uphill, resumes its original direction a bit farther along. You come down into the meadow, pass Samuel Horton's house on the left. The road winds as far as Samuel Gilbert Ward's house, which was used as the army's hospital, and you pass on the right a road going to the left [east] wing of the camp.   *1 Mile*

You go up a rather steep slope, enter a wood, then go down to the Bronx River, which is crossed on a bridge.   *1 Mile*

You again go up on to open ground and arrive perpendicularly on the main highway from White Plains to New York. You turn left, leaving on the right the height of White Plains where Lauzun's Legion was camped. At this spot you have on the left, beyond the Bronx River, a high plateau on which the American Army was encamped in 1778 [6?].   *1 Mile*

You go downhill, pass on the left a road that cuts across the Pines Bridge road and continues to the Hudson River. The road turns right, then left, as it goes up, then descends. The road runs halfway up the side of a fairly high mountain on

described in the opposite columns, a communication had been opened from the left [east] wing of the [Philipsburg] camp to a point about 7 miles to the rear, the object of which was to keep control of the right [west] bank of the Bronx River during the army's march, in case any considerable enemy corps were sent to White Plains to oppose our crossing of the Bronx.

Communicating road opened up from the left wing of the camp, at the entrance of the gorges of the Bronx, in the direction of its sources [*alternate route for the Right Column*]:[5]

From the left [east] of the camp you enter the road from King's Bridge, called Tuckahoe Road, which you leave on the right. You turn left after having crossed a little brook below Sicard's house, which you pass on the left. You then cross a brook.   *1 Mile*

After passing by a house on the left, the road bends towards the left. Passing a meadow on the right you reach a fork in the road. Take the right-hand road; the left goes to headquarters. You go uphill a bit, leaving the mountain and the wood on the left, and come to Absalom Gidney's house. Here you leave the White Plains road.   *1 Mile*

---

5. The communicating road, opened up by the French during the encampment at Philipsburg, is shown by a dotted line on map, No. 25.

several brooks. You pass a house on the right and then come to a second, on the left, called James Gea's [?] house.   *1½ Miles*

At this place the road forks. The right-hand road, which you do not take, leads to King Street. You go up a rather steep little pitch to reach the left-hand branch of the fork. Near Joseph Legget's house you pass by a road on the left.   *1 Mile*

You pass by more houses, and come to a ruined shed, where the road makes another fork. Continue on the left-hand road. The right leads to North Castle Church [Mount Kisco], 5 miles distant, and is the best road to travel.   *1 Mile*

The road being followed goes down into a gorge, where it crosses a fairly large brook on a good bridge. Shortly afterwards you cross a brooklet on a rather bad bridge which will soon need some repairs. You then cross the aforementioned brook again, by a good ford in front of a red house.

After crossing the brook you turn sharp left, passing on the left a grist mill, some ponds, then a saw mill and some houses that are outlying parts of North Castle, which is at this point 4 miles

the left [east] bank of the Bronx River. You pass on the left a road that, at a short distance from here, leads into the communicating road opened by the French army.   *1 Mile*

You continue along the side of the mountain and reach a house that you pass on the left.   *1 Mile*

Here you enter the gorges of The Highlands. You ascend a rather steep hill, then go down, cross a little brook, and reach a place where the gorge narrows. You pass by a house on the left. On the height at the head of the gorge can be seen the remains of an American work.[6] The road turns right, then up on the height, down again, and into woods full of rocks.   *3 Miles*

You pass on the left a road that leads into the Pines Bridge route. Crossing a brook you then pass on the right the King Street road. You go down a rather steep hill, cross a brook, proceed through a rather well-cultivated valley, pass by the Adams house on the left, ascend a little hill, and pass on the left the road going to Round Hill.   *2 Miles*

Following along the road, you pass on the right a pond and a grist mill called Wright's Mill.[7]

You pass behind Absalom Gidney's house, cross over a brook, follow along the hillside, passing by the Hughes [?] house on the right. You cut diagonally across the plain to meet the road going to White Plains. You enter the wood, take the first road to the left, cross a marshy hollow, then cross a bridge over a brook.   *1½ Miles*

You go up along the edge of the wood and come into the main highway from Philipsburg to White Plains at Gilbert Ward's house, which was our field hospital.   *½ Mile*

You turn left into the main road, which you follow as far as Samuel Horton's house. Here you bear right across the fields, and after going up the hill, which is rather steep, you head for a house, the only one in sight. From there, proceeding in the same direction, you come into the road from Tarrytown to White Plains.   *2 Miles*

You turn right into this road and then come to a fork. Take the left branch, going down for some time, crossing several brooks on bridges, and when you are at the bottom, skirt on the left a rather swift brook that flows into the Bronx River. Cross this brook, go

---

6. In the previous Itinerary, Twelfth March, this work (*ouvrage*) is described as "an old entrenched camp occupied by the Americans on 1 November 1776."

7. The manuscript reads "Rick Mill," but "Wright" is the spelling given elsewhere (see, e.g., Erskine-Dewitt map, no. 102, New-York Historical

Society). According to our map, No. 25, it would appear that the mill was on the left, rather than on the right, of the road.

away. The country is extremely uneven and the road often very stony and difficult.   *2 Miles*

You go up the road to the left, cross over a little hollow, the view of which is striking, and come to a hamlet with an Indian name. You pass by the meetinghouse on the left.   *1½ Miles*

You continue up the hill, passing between huge rocks split into bizarre and picturesque shapes. You arrive on the height and pass on the right a road going to North Castle, 3 miles away. Then you start down. The road bears left down into the hollow, where you pass White's Tavern on the right.   *2 Miles*

You continue along the road, leaving on the left a road going [back] to Philipsburg over the heights. The road climbs, turning right. You come to a fork. Here you find the house called Stevenson [?], where you turn right. The left-hand road goes to Sing Sing.

The road turns sharp right, along the crest of the hill, with a higher mountain on the right. You proceed down and reach Thomas La——[?]'s Tavern. Continuing along the road, up over another hill, you come to a view of the course of the Croton River, which is on your left.   *1 Mile*

You proceed along the road,

You go up a hill strewn with stones and pass on the left a road going to Sing Sing. Then you cross over a brook, pass Johnson's house on the left, continue gradually uphill, pass through a valley, then down along the foot of a rather high mountain where the grenadiers and chasseurs camped.[8] You come into the road from North Castle to Tarrytown, turn right, cross a brook leaving on the right the pond that is its source, and reach the North Castle Church [Mount Kisco] on the left of the road.   *4½ Miles*
     Total: 17½ Miles

Note: The following part of the Itinerary properly belongs to the Second March [of the Right Column], but we have appended it here to the preceding March in order to be able to describe below the similar route of both columns in a single column of the page, beginning with the crossing of the Croton River.

From North Castle to Pines Bridge

When setting out from the North Castle Church you leave on the right a road going to Bedford, 4 miles away. You follow the road in the bottom of the valley and cross on a wooden bridge a brook that flows left and eventually joins the one [Kisco River] having its source in the pond near the North Castle Church.   *1 Mile*

uphill to a house, which you pass on the left, and follow this road down to the Bronx, which you cross on a rather good bridge. You go uphill again and come in by the left into the main road from White Plains to North Castle.   *2 Miles*
     Total: 8 Miles

---

8. See map of the earlier North Castle camp, No. 38.

continuing upstream along the left [south] bank of the Croton, and reach Pines Bridge. *1 Mile*	You begin the ascent of the sizable mountain that closes the gorge at the bottom of which North Castle is situated. You go down a bit, cross a fairly good-sized brook, or rather some stagnant waters. *1 Mile*
Total: 17 Miles	
	You continue up, wind around the brow of the mountain, cross a brook, and reach the summit. *1 Mile*
	Then you continue downhill, the road bearing left, to Pines Bridge. *1 Mile*
	Total: 4 Miles

From Pines Bridge to Hunt's Tavern

21 [August 1781]

Observations

Pines Bridge is on the Croton River, which flows into the Hudson at a distance of about 15 miles from the bridge. The Croton separates the region called The Highlands from the gorges of White Plains. The river is about 70 yards wide. The bridge is very bad and dangerous for wagons, but the ford downstream from it is very good.[10] After crossing the Croton by this ford you go up on a rather high mountain, the road winding up over several inclines because of the steepness of the escarpment. The road is stony and bad in some places. You go down a bit upon entering the wood and cross over a little brook.   *1 Mile*

You then proceed up to the highest point. From here you have, in one direction, a view of the course of the Croton and the heights of North Castle and, in the other, a view of the small valley of Hunt's Tavern.   *1 Mile*

You continue down into the bottom of this little valley, which is pleasant and well-cultivated. Thus far the road follows the same direction with no forks. From the summit on it is rather good. You pass by some houses on either side of the road, and as you begin to go up the hill that forms the end of the gorge, you reach a fork in the road, in the middle of which is Hunt's Tavern.[11]   *1½ Miles*

The road on the right goes to Haight's Tavern [in Somers, Westchester County, New York] and to Ridgebury [in Connecticut]. The left-hand road, which is the one to be taken, goes to Crompond.

                                                              Total: 3½ Miles

We have already said in other itineraries that The Highlands are a chain, or rather a confused mass, of mountains that extend from the Hudson River to the Stratford [Housatonic] River and cover an area of about 15 to 18 square leagues. The form of each particular mountain is as bizarre as is that of the whole group. One may consider them as bounded on the south by the course of the Croton River, which, flowing from east to west, runs along the foot of the last of them. The mountains beyond this river towards the south rise and fall gradually. This latter mass of mountains served the Americans as a barrier during several campaigns. They held positions there with forces very inferior to those that the English could send out of New York; they had the advantage of being able to send detachments as far as Morrisania Point, with a retreat ensured. We shall have occasion to make a similar remark about the region called The Clove, in the Jerseys, on the other side of the Hudson.

Hunt's Tavern is one of the most important military positions in The Highlands, above the Croton. The camp was to have been made beyond the brook that winds through the little valley and circles a fairly high hillock that overlooks it. On this same hillock might be stationed a detached corps, which would thus occupy the meeting point of the three roads.

For a temporary camp (*camp de passage*) it is preferable to camp in the hollow of the little valley, or halfway up the slope on this side of the brook.

9. See map, No. 48. The localities mentioned in the Itinerary are also shown on the large map of the 1782 encampment near Crompond, No. 146.

10. The site of Pines Bridge and the adjacent ford is now covered by the Croton Reservoir. The name survives in "Pines Bridge Road."

11. See map, No. 61, and descriptive note.

From Hunt's Tavern to King's Ferry

22 [August]

Observations

At Hunt's Tavern you take the left-hand road, and a few paces farther along you leave on the left a road that goes over the mountain to New Bridge on the Croton River [at its mouth], a distance of 16 miles. You go down, cross a brook, and up again. Turning right you pass by the house of ———— [blank in MS] on the right and, a bit farther along, the house of ———— [blank in MS] on the left. The road turns left, then resumes its original direction down into a hollow and crosses a brook.   *1 Mile*

The road turns a bit to the right. You pass by the house of ———— [blank in MS] on the right. The road, turning left a bit, leads down into a marshy bottom, with a wood-covered hillside on the right. You come to a fork. Take the left. The right-hand road is the main highway to Ridgebury.   *1½ Miles*

This road from Ridgebury is the one that the army was to have taken to a camp at Crompond. A description of this branch road is included in the main itinerary of the march from Providence to the Hudson River.[13] The principal points on the road are:

from this fork (at Crompond) to Jonhn [Jonathan?] Hunt's Tavern at —avane [?][14]	*3 Miles*
from Jonhn Hunt's to Haight's Tavern	*7 Miles*
from Haight's Tavern to Salem	*5 Miles*
from Upper Salem to Ridgebury	*4 Miles*
	Total: 19 Miles

Here the left-hand road—the one you are taking—makes a right angle with the one you have been following.[15] You are on an open and rather extensive expanse of ground. You cross in succession two little hollows and as many brooks, which are dry in summer, and reach Crompond. Most of the

Crompond has been destroyed several times by

12. See map, No. 48.

13. See Itinerary 2, pp. 34–35.

14. Jonathan Hunt's Tavern is apparently not the same as

the Hunt's Tavern where the army had camped.

15. The right angle turn to the westward is still clearly identifiable along U.S. Route 202 (State Route 35).

houses are to the right of the route, as is the road or "street" that leads into the center of the village.

1 Mile

You continue along the road, which is very straight and very good. You pass by Cawmen's [?] Tavern on the left. Going uphill you then traverse a rather extensive and very open plain. You cross over a brook and come to a very steep descent.

1 Mile

You go down this mountain, which is very rugged, on a road that is very bad. Going down into the hollow you pass a road on the left and a house on the right and then cross a fairly sizeable brook. Then, as you go up through a little wood, the road bears a bit left, and you cross a brook when coming out of the wood. A bit farther along, when you are proceeding along the mountainside, there is an open and cultivated patch of ground, with several houses on the left. *1 Mile*

Here the road turns right at a right angle. You pass through a little hollow and immediately after, as you climb the rather steep grade, the road resumes its former direction. You pass by some fairly sizeable farms on either side of the road. The road is good, though extremely uneven. It follows the contour of the terrain up to the summit of the mountain. You pass on a height on the left a noteworthy plateau from which you can distinguish perfectly the direction of the valleys. The land continues to appear rather well cultivated. The heights, close at hand, are all covered with woods. You come to Drake Tavern, which you pass on the right. *2 Miles*

You go downhill a bit, pass on the right a road going [north] to Fishkill, then go uphill again as you enter the wood. Soon afterwards you have a view of

bands of refugees [Tories]. You pass by the ruins of the meetinghouse on the right.[16]

From Crompond to Peekskill the ground rises gradually, and from the details given above it can be seen that Crompond is one of the principal *débouchements* from The Highlands and an important military position. The American army has camped there several times.

It was on this eminence that the light troops and the American army were camped when they occupied the position of Peekskill.[17]

16. See Itinerary 2, n. 62. This locality is today known as Yorktown (as distinguished from Yorktown Heights) in the township of that name, which was incorporated only in 1798. The area was originally a part of Cortlandt's Manor.

17. Washington had moved his American forces here in June 1781, at about the time the French were leaving Rhode Island. It was then expected that the two armies would join near King's Ferry, rather than at Philipsburg, near Dobbs Ferry, as was eventually the case.

the North, or Hudson, River. You continue along the stony and rather bad road, the wood opens up, and you descend a bit as far as Peekskill Town, which you pass by on the right.

The part of the Hudson River that you see from here is one of the most extraordinary spots in its course, and this prospect produces a striking effect. It is here that the river comes forth from the narrow channel that it seems to have opened for itself through the very high mountains from West Point to here. It is still contained between very high banks and seems to have difficulty in breaking through the last barrier on its east bank. This mountain, cut horizontally halfway from the top, seems to have been created as a site for a fort. It is called St. [*sic*] Anthony's Nose.

At the foot of the mountain the road turns left and, on this side of the brook, first runs perpendicular to the Hudson River and then turns left along the edge of its bank. You proceed again into the wood, pass a house on the left, cross over a brook, and come to Lent's house on the right-hand side of the road. *1 Mile*

When the Americans were encamped at Peekskill, their camp was beyond the brook on several very flat plateaus situated to the right and left of the main road from West Point.

The road suddenly turns right to cross the creek on a rather good wooden bridge. You leave on the left a road going to ——— [blank in MS]. After crossing the bridge you find a bottom made very marshy by the creek, where the road is frequently impassable for wagons. Then you go uphill and enter the woods. The road winds a great deal because of the heights and the marshy bottoms. Coming out of the wood, you are on the open plateau of King's Ferry. *1 Mile*

This road, continuing in the same direction as the road from Peekskill, runs 2 miles lower and parallel, and very near the eastern bank of the river because of the bend the river takes between Peekskill and King's Ferry. This road goes to New Bridge, Tarrytown, etc.

You follow the very fine road, with the course of the river ½ mile to the right, and on the left a brook that flows into a sizeable creek which, with the one crossed below Lent's house, forms the Verplanck peninsula.
You pass on the right the blockhouse, or Fort La Fayette, formerly called Verplanck, and go down to the wharves of King's Ferry. *1½ Miles*
Total: 14 Miles

While the British occupied Stony Point in 1778, they had a camp of from 2,000 to 3,000 men camped this side of the Verplanck peninsula. They had built several redoubts on the river's edge. This position was a respectable one because there is only a half mile of very uneven and wooded ground between the two creeks that form this peninsula.

From the King's Ferry Crossing to Haverstraw

24 August

Observations

The crossing of the Hudson from the King's Ferry dock to the Stony Point dock is a distance of 1 mile. There are ordinarily 2 large ferry boats serving this ferry, each of which can carry 4 loaded wagons and their horses. There are also flatboats of lesser capacity and some sailboats or "feight [freight?] boats." The docks on either side are spacious and in good condition. The Stony Point dock is a bit upstream[19] from the one at King's Ferry. It is beneath the rock and the fort called Stony Point, which you leave on the left.   *1 Mile*

It is below King's Ferry, and after having gone past the points, that the Hudson resumes its straight and majestic course. Its bed widens considerably and the name of Tappan Sea has been given to the entire stretch of river between King's Ferry and Dobb's Ferry, at which latter place its bed is again narrowed by high cliffs [The Palisades]. See the reconnaissance of the Philipsburg camp.[20]

The fort at Stony Point, which the Americans surprised and took by storm in 1779, is no longer what it was at that time. It has been reduced at its most advanced point, and the works that were on the other peak have been razed.

The blockhouse and the battery are similar to those at Fort La Fayette on the opposite bank.

The Stony Point road, from its base on the river side, is steep and difficult of access from the land side. The creek and marshy bottom that you cross at about a quarter of a mile from the ferry completely surround this first height and detach it from the rest of the mainland.

The English had thought this creek impassable and had reduced their outer defenses to those on the bridge and the causeway. They had thought it impossible for anyone to pass along the riverbank at low tide. The Americans took advantage of their error and, without being discovered, sent columns up over the two peaks that came to the foot of the entrenchments. The more you examine the surrounding terrain and the position of the fort itself, the more brilliant and well-conceived this action appears.

After landing you follow the road at a right angle to the river, passing on the right some poor sheds. You ascend a bit. The road turns left down into a very

---

18. See maps, Nos. 48 and 62.
19. The manuscript clearly reads "au-dessus," i.e., above or upstream, but this is probably a misspelling of "au-dessous," since, according to the maps, the Stony Point dock

is below or downstream from the one at the eastern end of King's Ferry.
20. I.e., map, No. 46.

marshy bottom. You skirt the creek, then cross it on a wooden bridge and a short stretch of causeway, the road turning right and then left. After crossing the bridge you go uphill by stages, following along the side of the brow of the mountain. You cross a little brook on a bridge, pass by a cottage on the left, and on the right reach a spacious and open plateau, extending from the left-hand side of the road to the river. This is very good ground for camping.

This plateau is dominated by the mountain on your right, and you have in front of you a sizeable stream flowing in a very deep ravine (*très encaissé*). The hamlet is called Haverstraw,[21] as is that part of the ground of medium elevation on either side of the brook that extends from the river to the higher mountains on the horizon. *1½ Miles*
Total: 2½ Miles

The Americans occupied this position after the capture of Stony Point. Their camp was on either side of the brook.

FIFTH MARCH[22]

From Haverstraw to Suffern

25 August

You enter the road on the right of the camp and bear left down into the ravine, as if extending forward the front line of the camp. At the bottom of the ravine you bear right, ford a sizeable stream, then cross a branch of the same stream on a bridge. You ascend the opposite bank, which is very steep, and come out on a plateau that is less level but more elevated than the one on the other side. You continue along the road, passing several houses on the left and the two Smith houses on the right. You come to a right-angle fork. Take the right. *1 Mile*

You go uphill for a moment, the road bearing right, then pass some houses on the right, and skirt a rather rapid stream that you ford above a mill. Before fording it you leave on the right a road going

Note: Although the Haverstraw position occupied by the different corps extends towards the mountain beyond Smith's house, we have thought it more convenient to begin the description of the route of the Fifth March with the position at its point nearest to King's Ferry.

Smith's house is famous because of the treason of Arnold, who had assigned this house as his place of rendezvous with Major André.[23]

21. Now called Stony Point Village. See map, No. 63.
22. See map, No. 49.

23. See map of the September 1782 encampment here, No. 142.

to ———— [blank in MS]. You go into the wood and up through it to a house where there is a fork of two roads. Take the right branch. Here you are on fairly level ground, open on the right and very suitable for camping. The road to the left goes to Clarkstown.

1 Mile

Going down a bit as you enter a wood you pass on the right a road that also goes to Suffern through the hollow of the gorge but that is not passable for wagons. You continue along the Kakiat road, going uphill a bit, still in the wood, and over a stony road. The road continues in the same direction as far as Kakiat Meetinghouse [New Hempstead, Rockland County, New York]. Here you meet with a third road. The road continuing straight ahead in the same direction leads to different hamlets. The left-hand road is one of the main roads into the State of New Jersey; it is called the Lower Road. The right-hand road, which is the one to take, leaving Coe's Tavern on the right, is called the Upper Road.

4 Miles

The road turns right at a right angle. You have a fairly sizeable wood on the right. You go downhill, and the road turns left. You pass Holste's [?] Tavern on the left.

1 Mile

You continue down over a very fine road and come to a fork. Take the right. The left-hand road, which continues in the same direction as the one you have been following, goes along into the Lower Road. You go downhill, enter a wood, and cross a smallish brook. When you are in the hollow, the road bears left; then you come to Williams had [head?] Tavern.

3 Miles

24. "Clove" is a regional word of Dutch origin (cf. English "to cleave," "cleft," "cloven hoof," etc.) roughly

This is the position occupied by the American army immediately after the crossing of the Hudson River.

The Lower Road is so called because this route passes along the foot of the last mountains of The Clove[24] and follows the direction of the course of the Hudson River, passing through Hackensack, Newark, and Elizabeth Town.

The Upper Road, on the other hand, passes through the mountains of The Clove, or at least follows their direction, winding through the valleys closest to the highest summits. This is the route to Philadelphia, the shortest and most frequented since the war. It is a good and well-traced road, but extremely uneven.

equivalent to such terms as "gulf," "notch," and "gap."

After leaving this tavern you follow the bottom of
the gorge, which is extremely narrow nearly all the
way. To the right you have a wooded and very
steep mountain. You cross a sizeable stream, which
is henceforth always on your left. You come to
the hamlet of Take Care where the road, still
following the direction of the little river, turns right
and soon afterwards resumes its former direction.

3½ Miles

From this point you go into the wood, pass several
houses on the right, and reach Suffern plain, or
hollow. The tavern is on the right as you come in.
Here at Suffern there is a road that goes to New
Windsor via The Clove and one to the left that
goes to Paramus.

2 Miles
Total: 15½ Miles

The most suitable ground for camping in Suffern
plain is on the right of the road cutting diagonally
across the valley, leaving the course of the brook
forward from the front line of the camp. Beyond
this brook there is a fairly considerable height that
completely closes the gorge and over which the
Pompton and New York roads pass. This height must
be occupied by outposts. This location for the
camp has the further advantage of covering the road
from New Windsor via The Clove. Withdrawal
is easier and better ensured than if the camp were
extended along the left of the road as far as the
brook.[25]

SIXTH MARCH[26]

From Suffern [in New York] to Pompton Meetinghouse [in New Jersey]

26 August

Beyond the crossroads you continue over the plain.
The stream on the left comes nearer the road. Passing
several houses on the right you ford this little river,
which here takes the name Ramapo. The bridge is
in bad condition. You then go uphill, the road turns
right, and you find yourself opposite Samuel Bush's
house. Bear right. The left-hand road goes to
Paramus, Hackensack, etc.

1 Mile

The hamlet or plain of Suffern is also called
New Entrance, because the chain of mountains is
interrupted at this place and leaves a passageway for
penetrating into The Clove. This part of the Upper
Jerseys is no less extraordinary than The Highlands
and seems to be a continuation of them, as if the
Hudson, in determining its course towards the south,
had cut southward through this immense obstacle
and as if the islands at its mouth had been formed
by the debris that it had carried there. The Clove

25. See map, No. 64.

26. See map, No. 50.

The road turns right, you go down a bit, and follow the new direction of the valley, which is approximately southeast. You pass on either side of the road some houses that are an outlying part of the hamlet of Suffern. On the left is the height over which runs the road to New York, and on the right, beyond the river, is the continuation of the same chain of mountains that encloses The Clove. The road curves left and moves away from the river. Reaching a fork, take the right; the left-hand road leads into the New York road. *1 Mile*

The road continues to be fine and becomes less uneven because of the perceptibly lower hills. You pass several houses on the right, the road turns left and, soon afterwards, right. You come to Betorf [Bertolf? Bertholf? Bartholf?] Tavern, which you pass on the right of the road. *1 Mile*

You go uphill a bit, the road bearing left and becoming more uneven. You follow along the hill, pass some houses on the right, go down, crossing a brook, with a pond on the left and Bartoly's [Bertolf? Bartolf?] Mill on the right. You go up again, follow over the hill, leaving Camel's [Campbell?] Tavern on the right and, a bit farther along, a road on the left. *1 Mile*

You go downhill a bit, the road bearing right and coming closer to the river. It then moves away from the river. You go up on to a height, where you pass two houses on the right. You continue over the hill, in the woods, as far as a group of several houses, where the road is almost contiguous with the river. Continuing in the same direction you ford a brook, then another, with steeper banks (*plus encaissé*), on a bridge. *2 Miles*

You proceed through this gorge, which is still very narrow (*très serrée*). You cross a brook near which you pass by several houses on the right. The road runs mostly through the woods, along the side of the hill, up and down, and is sometimes very bad. You reach Fallanel's [Van Allen's?] Mill, where there is

is less extensive than The Highlands, but the mountains are higher and steeper. When coming from the plain [i.e., the New Jersey lowlands], the only passageways into The Clove are the one at Suffern and the one at Pompton, which we shall mention below. The highest elevation is in the neighborhood of West Point and of Butter Hill [Storm King], which closes The Clove towards the north. It is behind this impenetrable curtain that General Washington establishes his winter quarters [e.g., at New Windsor, 1780–1781]. He spreads his troops into The Clove itself, or outside of it but within reach of its principal outlets. The enemy could not attack him, even with very superior forces, except at a great disadvantage, and without great superiority they dare not send large detachments into this part of the Jerseys.

a pond on the left and a mill on the right. You cross the brook on a bridge and come to the marketplace of the hamlet of Herring [Hering? Haring?] plain. This place is triangular. Take the right-hand road and leave on the left the main road going to Paramus.   *2 Miles*

The road now becomes very fine and wide, as you come on to a fairly extensive and well-cultivated plain. The course of the river as well as the mountains recede towards the right. The road is perfectly straight and level as far as Pond Church.
                                                1 Mile

This plain [Pond Flats] is still another interruption in The Clove Mountains, which here open up and gradually become lower. The plain is watered by the Ramapo River, which eventually flows into the Pompton River. In the distance, to the left, you perceive the continuation of the mountain chain that borders the Pompton River. This plain is well-cultivated and seems fertile.

You pass on the left a road going to Hackensack, taking the right-hand road and passing through a little hollow. The road comes closer to the river, and you pass on the left another road that goes into the mountains. Then turn right to reach the bridge over the Ramapo. Before crossing it you pass on the left a road continuing along the left [east] bank of this river.   *1 Mile*

After crossing the bridge you come to a fork. Take the left; the road on the right leads into Schuyler's house. The road then moves away from the river. You cross a little brook with a mill on the left and some houses on both banks. This place is called Bergen County.   *1 Mile*

Here the plain is level and very extensive. The road runs straight as far as a little hollow that you cross and beyond which there is a fork. You take the road to the left; the right-hand road goes to Ringwood and to New Windsor, by the western side of The Clove mountains. The road turns to the left almost at a right angle. You follow the left bank of the first branch of the Pompton River. You pass some houses on the left. You come to a fork in the angle of which there is a tavern on the left-hand side of the road. Take the right-hand road. The main road that you leave on the left goes to Totowa, Acquackanonk [Passaic], and New York. The road turns to the right, you go down into a hollow, cross successively,

This road is the second and principal exit (*débouché*) from The Clove into the lower Jerseys. When considering the course of the waters and the confluence of the Ramapo River and the two branches of the Pompton River, it is easy to see that the southern extremity of The Clove mountains is here at this point. This is one of the most beautiful and most agreeable parts of the Jerseys. The country is well watered, open in all directions, and cultivated with care. If this position is considered in military terms, it is also very important, and what has been said above about the Suffern position applies to it.

over very bad bridges, the two branches of the Pompton River, go up, then reach the village of Pompton, passing a tavern and some houses on the right. *1 Mile*

You come into Pompton plain and continue along the road, which is straight, as far as a fork. There is a cluster of several houses here. You pass Roome's Tavern on the right. Take the left-hand road; the one on the right goes to Charlotteburg Iron Works. *½ Mile*

From here on the road, which is very good and perfectly level, winds over the plain. You pass several houses on both sides of the main road, other roads leading in to the farms, and then reach Pompton Meetinghouse, or Pompton Plains, the course of the river being always ½ mile or sometimes 1 mile to the left. *2½ Miles*
Total: 15 Miles

The Pompton plain is about 6 miles long and 1 mile wide. It is bounded on the east by the bed of the Pompton River and the hillocks on its left bank. On the west it is bounded by wooded but not very high hills, and on the south by woods and terrain that we shall describe in detail in the next march. It is convenient to camp on the right-hand side of the road, behind the church, facing the river.[27] In this way you have in advance of the right wing an outpost at the entrance to the woods and a passage over the river that it is essential to occupy.

SEVENTH MARCH[28]

From Pompton Meetinghouse to Whippany

27 August

After passing the church you leave on the right a road that goes into the fields. On the left you have a wood that extends from the road to the river; you pass on the right some houses and still another road. A bit farther along you pass on the left a road leading to the [Pompton] river. *1½ Miles*

You keep following along the edge of the wood. Very level road. You pass houses on the left and right. The road turns a bit to the right and then back towards the left. In this way you reach a fairly good-sized brook that flows into the Pompton River. You cross over it on a very good bridge. The road then turns to the right. *1½ Miles*

This road leads into the highway to New York. The distance from the road to the river is 1½ miles. The bridge there is in bad condition.

27. See map, No. 65.

28. See map, No. 51.

You pass two houses on the left. The road turns sharp right. You come to a fork. Continue in the same direction, to the right; the left-hand road goes to New York. You pass through more cultivated lands, pass by a fairly good-sized farm on the right, and enter the wood at the foot of the slope.   *1 Mile*

You go up and down a succession of slopes, most of the time in the woods. You come to a fork where Widow Jacobus's house is located. Take the left. The road you leave on the right at a right angle goes [back] to Pompton Meetinghouse, but it is bad for wagons.   *1 Mile*

You follow the road between two slopes; you cross over the brook that is the same as the one previously crossed on a bridge 3 miles from Pompton Meetinghouse. You are still in the woods, you go down into a hollow, and as you come out of it you reach a little hamlet called Picquareek [?].[30] You leave a road on the right.   *1½ Miles*

You go downhill, leaving on the left a road that goes to Riksbutt [?] Town.[32] You continue through the hollow, between two slopes, as far as a brook that you cross on a bridge.   *½ Mile*

You cross another brook a bit farther along. The road keeps turning towards the left. You come out of the wood. You go through the hamlet of Rockaway.[33] The road turns a bit to the left. You come to a fork. Take the right-hand turn. The road to the left goes to Horseneck. The road turns right almost at a right angle. You cross over two brooks (the same as those mentioned above) on bridges, and you come to the bridge over the Rockaway River.[34]   *2 Miles*

After crossing the river you go up on to a fairly

About 3 miles along this road is the place called the Forks,[29] because it is the confluence of the Pompton and the Passaic Rivers. The latter retains its name down to its mouth below Newark, west of Staten Island.

This road goes to Cornelius [?] Doremus's Tavern,[31] and then, turning left, goes on to a bridge over the Rockaway River, but this route is longer and more difficult than the one to the left.

The river is fordable at this spot. The bridge is in bad condition.

29. Now called Two Bridges.
30. So written in the manuscript; "Picquareck hameau" on the road map. This appears to be a faulty transcription of "Pequannock," referring, however, not to the present village of Pequannock but to another locality in the township of that name.
31. Cf. "Doremus Town," near Montville.

32. Perhaps a garbling of Elizabeth Town.
33. See road map, No. 51. This hamlet of Rockaway is obviously not present Rockaway, which is some 10 or 11 miles to the west.
34. This crossing was probably near the present bridge over the Rockaway at Lake Hiawatha.

elevated height. Turning left you leave on the right a road leading to Rockaway Meetinghouse.[35]   ½ *Mile*

You continue uphill, passing several houses on the right. The country is open on the left, and there are woods quite close on the right; you come to a crossroads where you intersect at right angles a highway from Morristown to New York.   ½ *Mile*

You go downhill through a little hollow, passing two houses on the left. Then you go up another slope and go down to Mr. Lott's farm, which is on the left-hand side of the road.[36]   *1 Mile*

Thence you go down to a good-sized brook that is a branch of the Rockaway River. You can cross this brook either by a bridge or by a ford. Then you go uphill, passing on the right a road leading to Mount Hope. You pass through the hamlet called Troy Town [Troy Hills] and come to a fork in the road. Both roads go to Whippany, but the one to the left crosses the plain and the right-hand road crosses a height.[37] The distance is about the same, but the latter is preferable.   *1 Mile*

So you bear right and enter the woods, continuing in the same direction.

This house is the most extensive farm in the Jerseys, and the owner, who is very wealthy, is known as a very good agriculturalist.

35. The "Rockaway Meetinghouse" referred to here has not been positively identified.

36. This was not, strictly speaking, "Mr. Lott's farm." The extensive estate (comparable to Lord Stirling's "plantation" near Basking Ridge) was acquired in 1772 by Lucas Von Beverhoudt of the island of St. Thomas in the Danish West Indies. Von Beverhoudt arrived in New Jersey only in 1778 (and lived at Beverwyck until his death there in 1796). Meanwhile, Abraham Lott of New York served as Von Beverhoudt's agent; at the time of the British occupation of the city Lott moved to Beverwyck, where he resided with his family until the end of the war. See Mrs. Benjamin S. Condit, "The Story of Beverwyck," in New Jersey Historical Society, *Proceedings*, IV (1919), 128–141; Alex D. Fowler, "Notes on the House at 21 South Beverwyck Road, Parsippany, N.J.," in newsletter of Morris County Historical Society, 6 May 1969. See also Clermont-Crèvecœur's journal, n. 63, and Verger's journal, n. 146. The Beverwyck estate (including a nineteenth-century mansion said to include parts of the earlier structure) was

until recently identifiable near the intersection of Beverwyck Road and U.S. Route 46, facing the Parsippany-Troy Hills shopping center. The construction of Interstate Highway 80 has spelled its doom. What was left of the house was consumed by fire in August 1971 (see *Morris County's Daily Record*, 24 August 1971). "Mr. Lott and young Captain Berthier would not know the neighborhood now, all concrete highways and intricate access roads, taverns and junky shops with neon lights, and at all hours, day and night, the roar of traffic. It was a lovely country neighborhood when I was a boy. No farms now, just cheap developments, the wrong word for it, and garden apartments without gardens. Of the old families only a single man lives within a mile of Beverwyck." (Letter to the Editors from Rev. Edwin S. Ford, Fordville, Whippany, New Jersey, 6 October 1971.)

37. The left-hand road corresponds to present South Beverwyck Road, from Troy Hills to Whippany. The right-hand road, the one taken by the French army and shown on the road map, is present Reynolds Avenue.

There are several houses in the clearings. You continue along the high ground and come to a crossroads. The road farthest to the right goes to Parsippany, the one next to it into the fields, and the left-hand road is the one to take.   *2 Miles*

You go down rather abruptly. You cross over the two arms of the little Whippany River; before crossing you leave on the left a road following along the left bank of the river; you go up on the other side and come to a fork, where there is a tavern on the left. The left-hand road goes to Newark, and the right-hand road to Hanover[38] and Morristown. The houses spread around this point form the village of Whippany.   *½ Mile*
                            Total: 14½ Miles

38. Hanover Township, Morris County, includes Whippany (an ancient settlement never incorporated separately) as well as localities designated at various times as Hanover. The village now referred to as "Hanover" is to the east of Whippany, while the locality so designated on our road map, No. 52, corresponds to the locality now known as Monroe.

4

ITINERARY

*of the Marches of the
French Army
from the Camp at Philipsburg
to the Camp before York
in Virginia*

1781

PART 2

From Whippany to Princeton

44 Miles

This continuation of the previous Itinerary is translated from the only known copy, which is in the Princeton University Library (Berthier Papers, No. 11). The manuscript, entitled "Itinéraire des Marches que l'Armée a fait pour se rendre du camp à Philip'sburg au Camp devant Yorck, Deuxième Cahier, de Wipany à Princeton, 44 Milles," comprises 20 pages (last seven blank), similar in format and writing to Itinerary 3.

The march is described in Clermont-Crèvecœur's journal. Berthier's personal journal for this portion of the march has not been found. Verger did not take this route in 1781, but his journal describes the northward march over these same roads in 1782. It was during the march from Whippany to Princeton that the ultimate destination—Virginia—became generally known to the rank and file of the French army. And it was only at this time that the British commander in New York finally realized where the French were headed. "I cannot well ascertain Mr. Washington's real intentions by this move of his army," Sir Henry Clinton reported to Cornwallis on 27 August (the day Rochambeau's First Brigade arrived at Whippany), "but it is possible he means for the present to suspend his offensive operations against this post [New York] and to take a defensive station at the old post of Morristown, from whence he may detach to the southward." On 2 September (when Rochambeau's First Brigade had already left Trenton) Sir Henry surmised: "By intelligence which I have this day received, it would seem that Mr. Washington is moving an army to the southward with an appearance of haste, and gives out that he expects the cooperation of a considerable French armament [fleet]."

EIGHTH MARCH[1]

From Whippany to Bullion's Tavern [Liberty Corner]

Observations

On leaving Whippany you take the Morristown highway, a fine and level road. You turn to the left and, a bit farther along, pass on the left a road leading to Chatham.[2] You enter the wood, proceed uphill a bit and, on going down, come to the first houses of the village of Hanover.[3] In the center of this village you leave on the right the house of ——— [blank in MS] and a road going to Parsippany.

2 Miles

You proceed along the road uphill. On the right you pass still another road, which goes into the fields (*dans les terres*). The road turns a bit to the left and goes up onto a fair-sized hill. Then you go down, passing on the left another road leading to Chatham. You continue through the bottom of a little valley, passing several houses on either side. The road veers towards the right. You cross a little brook that flows into the Whippany River and then proceed up on to the height where Morristown, a good-sized little town, is situated.

On coming into the town you pass on the right a road going to Rockaway. You reach the Morristown marketplace, which is square in shape and spacious. You cross it diagonally, bearing right, passing the church, also on the right. The road that you pass on the left goes to Chatham. There is a fork in the angle on the right. The left-hand road is the one to take. The right-hand road is the route to the mountains.

2 Miles

The most interesting part of the Jerseys being that between the Hudson River and the route we shall be describing, it should be noted here that the mountain range that belongs to the same range as The Clove mountains, and that we left behind us on the east bank of the Pompton River, is prolonged in the same direction as the Hudson River and forms a new barrier protecting the entire interior of the country. This new chain, much less elevated than The Clove range, is formed by the heights called Newark Mountains and those of Springfield. It is bounded on the eastern side by the course of the Passaic River, which has opened a passage for itself at Totowa Falls, and on its southern side by the course of the Raritan River, of which we shall speak in the next march.

Morristown is a rather pretty little town, in an elevated and very agreeable situation. It is almost the center of the State of the Jerseys, and its location on the principal lines of communication favors its trade and growth.

General Washington has made his winter quarters here.[4] In addition to its strategic position, he had the further advantage of being able to sally forth in a single march to the famous position at Springfield.

1. See map, No. 52. The map is reproduced, with identification of key points, in *Historical Booklet of Bernards Township, N.J., published to Commemorate the Bicentennial, 1760–1960* (Basking Ridge, N.J., 1960), p. [15].
2. Washington had his headquarters at Chatham, while the French were encamped farther west at Whippany; see his letter of 28 August 1781 to Rochambeau cited above in Clermont-Crèvecœur's journal, n. 65, and reproduced

as one of our illustrations. It was also at Chatham that the French had set up bakeries as a ruse to make the British believe an attack on New York was imminent.
3. The locality now known as Monroe.
4. In 1777, after the battles of Trenton and Princeton, and again in 1779–1780. (The winter encampment of 1777–1778 had been at Valley Forge, outside British-occupied Philadelphia).

You go down into a rather narrow little valley, having on the right a very high hillside, close to which the road winds while keeping the same general direction. You pass by many farms on either side of the road. You are often in the woods. The country opens up on the left. There is a fairly extensive plain. You cross a brook that is one of the sources of the Passaic River, and you reach Half-Moon Tavern.

4 Miles

The road continues in the same direction; you cross another brook, then a good-sized hamlet, then two more brooks. Here you reach the end of the plain. You go up onto a hill and pass on the left a road leading to Chatham. *2 Miles*

The road turns to the left, still ascending and descending. The hills are not very high. The route is beautiful, and the fields are well-cultivated. You come to a bridge over a fairly swift stream that is one of the principal branches of the Passaic River.[5]

1 Mile

You go uphill again, passing some houses on the right, and come to a fork. You take the left-hand road; the one on the right goes to Veal Town [Bernardsville]. The road veers to the left, and the ground gradually rises. On the left and right you pass roads going into the fields; you then reach the hamlet and meetinghouse[6] of Basking Ridge. *1 Mile*

You follow the road that bears right and passes along the crest of the hills. You come at a right angle to a fork. Take the right-hand turn; the left-hand road goes to Elizabeth Town. On the left you pass near Lord Stirling's house.[7] You go downhill, passing on the right the road to Rockaway. You come to a fork. Take the right; the left-hand road goes to Brunswick. The road bears sharply to the right. You

The brooks that you cross on this route eventually form a sizeable marsh called Great Swamp, on this side of the Long Hill. This may be considered as the source of the Passaic River, which, passing between the Long Hill and the heights of Springfield, flows from south to north, on this side of the mountains, up to the point where it joins the Pompton. It may therefore be concluded that this part of the Jerseys is the highest on this side of the mountains that we mentioned above.

5. See the "Mill" on the road map. U.S. Route 202 now crosses the Passaic at this point, where an "Old Mill Inn," near Bernardsville, is situated.
6. The present Presbyterian Church of Basking Ridge, a mid-nineteenth-century building, is on the site of the

meetinghouse mentioned here. The adjoining churchyard contains many eighteenth-century gravestones dating from the period of the Revolution and earlier.
7. See descriptive note to map, No. 52.

pass houses on either side, then proceed up onto a height that you become aware of as the road winds down from it into the hollow.　　*2 Miles*

You enter the woods, continue up and down, and then down again to reach a brook called Dead River, one of the sources of the Passaic, which flows into the one you crossed before reaching Basking Ridge. After crossing this brook below a red bridge you enter a wood having a fairly high hill on the right and on the left a marshy bottom formed by the course of the stream. You come out of the wood, passing some houses on the right, and reach a stone house belonging to William Annin,[8] which you pass by on the right. Here the road following along the foot of the hill, which has changed direction, turns at a right angle to the left. The brook that is on the left of the road winds through a marshy meadow, eventually coming closer to the road opposite Bullion's Tavern. It can be forded at this point, where you pass on the left a road leading into the main Elizabeth Town road and a road going to Pluckemin on the right.　　*2 Miles*
　　　　　　　　　　　　　　　Total: 16 Miles

This brook, which flows into the Passaic River below the Great Swamp, is no doubt called Dead River because of the slowness of its course.

From this place where you come out of the woods to a quarter of a mile beyond Bullion's Tavern, you have on the right, on this side of the brook, a bare hillside where you can conveniently camp.[9] Beyond the brook are wooded heights that are the beginning of the one known as the Long Hill.

NINTH MARCH[10]

From Bullion's Tavern [Liberty Corner] to Somerset Courthouse [Millstone]

August 30 [1781]

You follow the left [west] bank of the Dead River. Go up the hill, passing some houses and very even and open ground on the right. Go down into the hollow. Cross over the brook on a bridge. Then go uphill into the woods. You follow this road, continuing in the woods, passing by some houses on the right and left. A fairly good road. You reach a fork, where you take the right; the left-hand road goes to Brunswick. Bear right and go down into the hollow, still in the woods. Another fork. Take the left; the right-hand road goes to Pluckemin. Continue

The position of this ground makes it suitable only for a temporary camp.

8. An old photograph of William Annin's stone house, now destroyed, is reproduced in *Historical Booklet of Bernards Township*, p. [18].

9. See map, No. 67, and descriptive note; also map, No. 139.
10. See map, No. 53.

downhill over a stony road. You cross and recross a
brook that winds in and out. Still another fork. Turn
sharp left. You come out of the wood, proceed uphill,
and reach another fork. Take the right; the left-hand
road goes to Quibbletown [New Market]. Bear
right at a right angle and go down into a good-sized
clearing, with cultivated fields. You come to several
houses on either side of the road. The largest one
on the right belongs to Mr. Sebring.   *4 Miles*

Continue downhill, still over a very good road,
into the hollow, where you cross Middle Brook
very near its source.[11] This brook flows into the
Raritan. You go uphill, entering the wood, the road
bearing to the right. You pass houses on both sides of
the road. Continuing up over a series of slopes you
reach the highest point of the mountain [First
Watchung]. The road is stony and rather bad. Then
you begin to descend, bearing to the left.[12] You
discern an immense plain watered by the different
branches of the Raritan. Continue over a series of
ramps to the foot of the mountain. You emerge from
the woods. As you come into the plain you reach a
fork. Take the left; the right-hand road goes to
[Silher's?] Town and to Pluckemin. You turn left
at a right angle and reach Steel's Tavern, which you
pass on the left-hand side of the road.   *2 Miles*

Leave this main highway, which continues
to Brunswick, and take the road that turns
perpendicularly to the right opposite Steel's
Tavern. You go through a little wood and then an
extensive open and sandy terrain where different
roads meet and intersect.[13] Those which you leave
on the left all go to Brunswick, and those on the
right to the northern part of the Jerseys, along the
left bank of what is called the North Branch of
the Raritan. Cross a bridge over a little brook, and

At this point ends the chain of mountains that
we mentioned above. Those that you see along the
road recede in a northwesterly direction. All the
rest of the horizon, as far as the eye can reach, is
below the level of this point here; the view of this
immense plain and the Raritan that waters it forms a
prospect that is as agreeable as it is unexpected. One
is happy to find occasionally such spots as this, from
which can be seen the direction of the principal
mountain chains and of the watercourses. Such
outlooks help you to become acquainted with the
country as a whole and belie or rectify the ideas you
had formed from partial observations.

It may be noticed in the course of this march that
all the roads that turn off to the left, either on the
mountain or in the plain, converge on Brunswick.
The same is true of the rivers and brooks, which all

11. This road corresponds roughly to Newmans Road,
leading southerly out of present Martinsville, which is
behind the rim of First Watchung Mountain. It now
crosses a small causeway over the west branch of Middle
Brook, which has been dammed up to form Washington
Valley Reservoir.
12. This descent from First Watchung Mountain into the

Raritan Valley is still known as Steel's Gap. It is about a
mile and a half west of Chimney Rock Road (State Route
525), the more frequently traveled route from Martinsville
down into the valley.
13. U.S. Route 22, Interstate 287, and several lesser roads
now meet and intersect in this great traffic corridor.

then turn right at a right angle. You pass the Van Veghten House on the right.[14] The road bears left along the north bank of the Raritan, and you reach the bridge over this river.   *2 Miles*

The road turns to the right. After crossing the bridge you go over a very level plain, passing on the right a road that goes to Readingtown. You bear left.   *1 Mile*

On your left you have a cultivated plain and woods at some distance on the right. The road is good and its bed sandy. On the right and left you pass roads leading into the fields. You cross a fairly sizeable brook that eventually flows into the Raritan. Beyond the brook you pass a farmhouse on the right.   *1 Mile*

You come to a fork opposite the house of Abraham Van Nest.[16] Take the right, as the left goes to Brunswick. On this left-hand road, a quarter of a mile from the fork, is the second Millstone Bridge. You go up the slope; in the hollow on the left is the Millstone River, which flows into the Raritan. You pass on the right a road going to Coryel's Ferry on the Delaware [Lambertville]. You follow along this hillside, which is sometimes broken by brooks flowing into the Millstone. You continue in this same direction, following the course of the river. On either

flow into the Raritan. It was therefore a great advantage for General Washington to have held the approaches from Springfield down to the bridge over the Raritan during the winter of 1778. The English, who, after the affairs at Trenton and at Princeton, had withdrawn their headquarters to Brunswick, were unable to send out any detachments or undertake any operation without being discovered by a handful of Americans moving about behind the mountain who could anticipate the English at any point to which they might wish to move.[15]

The Raritan is wide here, where its south and north branches, which have their sources 15 or 20 miles to the north below Brookland [?] forges, have already united. This river is still further swelled by the Millstone, which flows into it 3 miles below the bridge. Thus the Raritan becomes a large river in

14. Substantial parts of the Van Veghten house ("Van Vacter's" on some American maps of the period) still survive on the north bank of the Raritan, a short distance west of the present highway bridge (State Route 533) from Finderne to Manville. General Nathanael Greene made his headquarters in this house during the 1778–1779 winter encampment of the Continental Army on Middle Brook Heights.

15. Cf. C. W. Peale's description of the "sublime prospect" in his diary, 26 June 1777, printed in Charles Coleman Sellers, *Charles Willson Peale* (New York, 1969), pp. 144–145. The advantages of this position are also fully confirmed by British sources. Banastre Tarleton, who was stationed with the Queen's Light Dragoons in the Jersey lowlands in 1777, remarked, when describing operations to a friend in England, that Washington's position "upon the extensive and rugged heights above Bound Brook ren-

dered him formidable to the Jersey Army." The forests and mountains, Tarleton continued, are "strong as human imagination can suggest." "Upon reconnoitering the rebel situation Sir William [Howe] found their mountains inaccessible. . . . Mr. Washington acted the wary part. He kept his strong holds beyond the Rariton and remained quiet in his inaccessible posts. No bait or temptation from Genl. Howe could induce him to leave his mountainous situation." Tarleton, letter of 5 July 1777, printed in Richard M. Ketchum, ed., "New War Letters of Banastre Tarleton," *New-York Historical Society Quarterly*, LI, No. 1 (Jan. 1967), 61–81.

16. Van Nest's (or Vanest's) mill was at the locality now called Weston. See Elizabeth G.C. Menzies, *Millstone Valley* (New Brunswick, 1969), pp. 85–86; also reproduction of Erskine-Dewitt map, No. 74-F, *ibid.*, pp. 230–231.

side of the road you pass outlying houses of Somerset. You go over an open plateau that is very suitable for camping. Then go down a rather steep slope and reach Somerset Courthouse.[17] On entering this small town (*bourg*) you pass on the left a bridge over the Millstone that is in very bad condition. The road over it comes in from Brunswick. You go through the town, which is built on the west bank of the river. The road, following the windings of the riverbed, turns left almost at a right angle as you enter. Before going up the slope to where the church is situated you pass on the right a fine house belonging to Colonel Duryea.[18] The church is on the right-hand side of the road. Here you pass on the right a road that goes to Robinson's Ferry [Stockton] and to Coryel's Ferry [Lambertville.] The ground on the right and on the left of the road as far as the river is suitable for camping.   *2 Miles*
Total: 13 Miles

the vicinity of Brunswick. Its mouth is at Amboy, in Sandy Hook Bay, opposite the southernmost point of Staten Island.

The Millstone River is fordable above the bridge.

It was to Somerset Courthouse that General Washington retired and took his prisoners after the affair at Princeton.

TENTH MARCH[19]

From Somerset Courthouse [Millstone] to Princeton

From the meetinghouse at Somerset Courthouse you follow the road that goes along the river, having on the right a fairly high and entirely open hillside. You pass some houses on the right. At 1½ miles the road turns to the left as it gets closer to the river, and you enter the hamlet of Millstone. You reach Mercer's Mill.[20] Here there is a bridge over the Millstone River. You pass it on the left and continue to follow the road to Princeton. The road over this bridge goes to Brunswick, a distance of 8 miles, to Amboy, a distance of 20 miles, and to Elizabeth Town, a distance of 26 miles.

17. See map, No. 68, and descriptive note.
18. The name is written "Dorrié" in the manuscript. "The property on each side of Peace Brook had passed into the hands of Abram Duryea, of New York. In 1790 he sold it to Gen. Frederick Frelinghuysen for £1500. It contained 29 acres, extending about a mile and a quarter west from the church lot. . . ." James P. Snell, comp., *History*

of Hunterdon and Somerset Counties, New Jersey (Philadelphia, 1881), p. 777.
19. See map, No. 54.
20. Written "Messer" in the manuscript. "Archibald Mercer was the proprietor of the mill subsequently known as Blackwell's Mills." Snell, *op.cit.*, p. 785.

The road continues to follow the windings of the course of the Millstone River, running most of the way along the crest of the slopes on its west bank. A half mile beyond Mercer's Mill you pass by a road on the right that goes to Sourland, being separated from the river only by fields and having at the right now houses, now woods, but usually open lands. *2 Miles*

Here the road approaches closer to the river. You go down the slope, marching into the bottom land where it flows. Following this direction you reach the bridge and the hamlet called Griggstown. You leave on the right another road going to Sourland. *2 Miles*

You cross over the bridge. You pass on the left the houses that make up the hamlet, and you reach a crossroads, where you take the right; the left-hand road goes to Brunswick. The road turns to the right at a right angle to follow the east bank of the Millstone along the foot of the hillside. You reach Mr. Greg's [Grigg's] mill, which you pass on the right. *1 Mile*

You can still see the remains of the camp made here by General Washington after the affair at Princeton.[21]

You keep following the east bank of the Millstone River, staying in the bottom land and sometimes very close to the stream, until you reach a fork in the road: both roads go to Princeton, the left-hand road via Kingston and the right-hand road via Rocky Hill.[22]

Left-hand Road	*Right-hand Road*

From the fork just mentioned, the road is stony and rather bad. You have on your right the heights called Mount Lucas and some houses on both sides. *2 Miles*

The ground rises on reaching Kingston. The country is open. The Millstone River flows at the

From the above-mentioned fork you cross the Rocky Hill bridge. You go uphill, leaving some houses on the left. You come to a second fork. The right-hand road goes to Blawenburg.[23] You follow the left-hand road for a mile. Here you come into some woods. You reach another fork. The right-hand road goes to Hopewell. You keep to the left, the

21. Along the present road, which borders the Delaware and Raritan Canal, is a marker recalling that "by this route Washington and his army retired after his victory at Princeton, January, 1777."

22. The army marched from here to Princeton over the right-hand road, i.e., via Rocky Hill and Mount Lucas.
23. "Blue humbert" in the manuscript.

right. You go through Kingston.[24] You pass on your left a road going to Brunswick, a distance of 12 miles. You cross the Millstone and pass on your left a road that goes to Monmouth. Continuing over the plain you reach Princeton. The road runs in the same direction as the main street of Princeton.

3 Miles
Total: 15 Miles

road being uphill as far as a house on the left side of the road. This place is called Mount Lucas.[25]

2 Miles

From there you gradually go downhill until you are a mile from the town. You come out of the woods, pass on the right a road that goes to Pennington, and then go uphill to reach the height on which Princeton is situated. This road runs in a direction perpendicular to the street.[26]   *2 Miles*

Total: 14 Miles

24. When the French marched northward over the same route in September 1782, Lauzun's Legion (then commanded by Colonel Dillon) took a more easterly route through New Jersey, to cover the main corps on its right. The Legion then camped at or near Kingston (perhaps near the junction of present Routes 27 and 518) to protect the New Brunswick road against a possible enemy sortie from New York. See map, No. 162, and descriptive note to No. 138. See also George Grieve's note on the perils of traveling along the New Brunswick road, in Chastellux (4), I, 334–335.

25. According to the will of Richard Stockton, dated 20 May 1780, he left to his daughter, Julia Rush, a "plantation" known as Mount Lucas, consisting of 500 acres with a "mansion house." Certified copy of Stockton's will in Princeton University Library, Manuscripts Department (Pyne-Henry 924). The Editors are indebted to Mrs. Constance Greiff for calling their attention to this document.

26. Junction of present Witherspoon and Nassau Streets, opposite Nassau Hall. See map, No. 69.

5

ITINERARY

*of the Marches of the
French Army
from the Camp at Philipsburg
to the Camp before York
in Virginia*

1781

PART 3

From Princeton to Head of Elk

89½ Miles

This is the third installment of the description of the route from the Hudson to Virginia, translated from the Princeton manuscript (Berthier Papers, No. 12) entitled "Itinéraire des Marches que L'armée a fait pour se rendre du Camp à Philip'sburg au Camp devant Yorck, Troisième Cahier, de Princeton à Head of Elk, 89 Milles ½." The manuscript of 20 pages (last 4 blank) is similar to the previous "cahier" in size and is written in the same copyist's formal hand.

Up to this point the Itineraries have described the inland route the army was obliged to take in order to circumvent New York City and the surrounding areas then occupied by the enemy. From Princeton southward the army followed the main colonial post road—roughly equivalent to present U.S. Route 1. At this point also the routes of the American and French armies converged, the Americans preceding the French by a day or so. The portion of the route covered in this Itinerary is described in Clermont-Crèvecœur's journal (also in Verger's journal, for the northward 1782 march) and is fully illustrated by the road maps and camp plans. The route took the marchers through the largest city in the United States, Philadelphia, where they passed in review before the Continental Congress.

ELEVENTH MARCH

From Princeton to Trenton[1]

Observations

Coming out of Princeton you find open ground suitable for camping on the left and the house of Mr. Stockton on the right. Following the main road you gradually descend a rather gentle slope, with open cultivated country on either side. You pass a tavern on the left and reach the foot of the hill, with a wood on the right. You cross a small brook that winds into the road, then reach the hamlet of Stony Brook and the bridge over the river of the same name.

1½ Miles

After crossing Stony Brook you go up into the wood. The road continues along the crest of the hill. Parallel to the road on the right is a hollow, beyond which are wood-covered heights. On the left you have level wooded ground. After leaving behind the last houses of Stony Brook, and after passing some houses on either side of the road, you come to a fork. Take the left; the right-hand road goes to Pennington.

2½ Miles

The road continues along the height of land, bearing left. You go down into the hollow where you cross a brook and pass on the left the road going to Burlington. Then going uphill again, you come to

After the Battle of Trenton [December 1776] the American army, having been reinforced by some Pennsylvania militia, crossed the Delaware again to attack the English forces that Lord Cornwallis had just reassembled.[2] The Americans took a position that was covered by Trenton [Assunpink] Creek and occupied the bridge over which you pass. The English general, believing that General Washington had decided to await battle, hastened to take measures for offering it to him. Cornwallis took a position on the other side of the creek and gave orders to the troops quartered in Princeton and nearby to make forced marches to rejoin him [in Trenton]. The American general, too wise to risk a general action, and having left his campfires burning, silently decamped at nightfall, marched to the right, crossed the creek, and headed in two columns towards Princeton. He arrived there at dawn just as two English regiments were leaving for Trenton. The [American] left column took the main road out of Trenton, with the right column marching at some distance to the right in order to be able to turn the enemy's left. The American left column opened an attack on one of the English regiments that was already on the march. This regiment gave way with

1. See map, No. 55. The road south from Princeton via Trenton, Philadelphia, and Wilmington to Head of Elk can also be traced in the earliest American road book, Christopher Colles's *A Survey of the Roads of the United States of America* (New York, 1789), Plates 44ff. A facsimile edition, with introduction and notes by Walter W. Ristow, was published in 1961, in "the John Harvard Library," by Harvard University Press. According to Ristow (p. 45): "The road book was very probably conceived during the Revolution and some of the surveys were undoubtedly made by Colles . . . before the close of the war. The compilation of the first series of maps and the engraving of the plates and title page were accomplished quite likely between 1784 and 1789." For some of his maps Colles made use of the surveys prepared during

the war by Robert Erskine and Simeon DeWitt, military geographers and successive surveyors-general in the Continental Army. The French staff officers when marching southward in 1781 must also have been acquainted with the Erskine-DeWitt maps. There is, however, no evidence to show that Colles ever saw the road maps prepared by the French, which have remained unpublished until now. Colles's *Survey of the Roads* and Berthier's *Figuré de la route de l'armée*, though roughly contemporary, may be considered independent enterprises.

2. The officer engaged in compiling an itinerary also observed, as a matter of course and of training, the earlier battlefields along the route. Cf. the somewhat similar account of the Battle of Princeton included in Clermont-Crèvecœur's journal, p. 44.

outlying houses of the village of Maidenhead on either side of the road. Here you have a sizeable plain on the left and, at some distance to the right, some wooded heights. You pass on the right a road called the little Pennington road. At the top of the hill you arrive at Maidenhead [Lawrenceville], which is a fair-sized village, but with widely separated houses.

1 Mile

Coming out of Maidenhead the road turns left. You pass on the right a road going to Pennington and to Coryel's Ferry [Lambertville] on the Delaware. Continue in the same direction along the high ground, with woods on the left. Then you go down, pass a road going to Allentown [in New Jersey] on the left, cross a brook, and go up onto a height and through a thickset wood, where you pass several roads on the right, all leading to Pennington. Pass several houses on the right-hand side of the road and go down again into a fairly deep ravine, where you cross Shabakunk Brook on a bridge.

3 Miles

You go up into the woods and pass on the left roads going to Burlington and a road going to the ferry over the Delaware on the right. At this point you are in a sizeable clearing. You cross another little hollow, go up onto the high ground again and into another wood. Coming out of the wood you can see the town of Trenton. Going down again, the road bearing right, and then up, you reach the first houses of Trenton. On the left you have very open ground, and wooded heights on the right. *4 Miles*

Total: 12 Miles

the exception of the grenadiers, who broke through with bayonets. All the rest withdrew towards Princeton where the second regiment was just beginning to march. The American left column continued to march and press the enemy, while the right column arrived near the College. Thereupon there was extreme disorder among the English troops. They thought they were surrounded, put up a poor defense, and surrendered.

General Washington crossed the Millstone River and then proceeded to occupy a protected position beyond the Raritan, which we have mentioned above. [See previous Itinerary.] Cornwallis, who feared for the large quantities of supplies assembled at New Brunswick, withdrew there in haste.

Note: The order and direction of the march to which these observations are necessarily subordinated oblige us to treat historical events in reverse chronological order.

Trenton is a fairly large and well-built town.[3] Its situation is as pleasant as it is advantageous, thanks to the navigation of the Delaware. It will be forever famous in the history of America as the scene of General Washington's victories.

TWELFTH MARCH

From Trenton to Red Lion[4]

2 September [*1781*]

You go through the town of Trenton, crossing a stone bridge over the little river [Assunpink] that

3. See map, No. 70.

The campaign of 1776 had been very unlucky for the Americans. The loss of the battles of Long Island,

4. See map, No. 56.

divides it in two and flows into the Delaware. Proceeding uphill and out of town you have the Delaware about a half-mile away on your right and some woods on the left. On the right is the road going to the ford and another going directly to the ferry. You enter the woods and pass the Burlington road on the left. Crossing an open plain, which is most suitable for camping, the road makes a sharp turn so that it is perpendicular to the river. You reach the ferry, where there are several houses.[5] At this spot the river is 800 yards wide. There are generally 2 ferryboats and some sailboats available for crossing. This is the highest point for small vessels coming up river, as navigation is interrupted by the falls that are above the ferry. You can ford the Delaware above the falls, opposite Colonel Cox's house.[6] The ford is good, but care must be taken to face upstream against the current as far as a point above the little island, after which you can head straight for the opposite bank.   *1½ Miles*

From the right bank of the Delaware you follow the main highway. As the road bears left you enter some woods interspersed with clearings, in which you pass by roads on the right and on the left. The

of New York, of Fort Lee, of the different posts on the Hudson, and of all the country between the Hudson and the Delaware had followed in rapid succession. General Washington's army, defeated, discouraged, and reduced by sickness, could no longer sustain the campaign, and the General, crossing over to the west bank of the Delaware, placed this barrier between his victorious enemies and his downhearted troops. He thereupon burned all the boats. The English, who had pushed their quarters forward as far as the east bank of the river, only awaited the moment when it should freeze over in order to cross it and enter Philadelphia in triumph.

It took no less than the eloquence of Mr. Mifflin and the extreme confidence that people had in General Washington to succeed in raising in haste a corps of 5,000 men, with which General Washington resolved to surprise the enemy in their winter quarters along the Delaware. He marched during the night of 27 [25–26] December in bitter cold weather.[7] He had divided his little army into three corps. The first, commanded by General [James] Ewing, was to cross the Delaware at Trenton Ferry, 1 mile below the town. The second, commanded by General Cadwalader, was to cross still lower down, towards

---

5. There were two ferries across the Delaware: the so-called Trenton Ferry (referred to here) and the Continental Ferry farther downstream at Lamberton. See the section on "Ferries" in Trenton Historical Society, comp., *A History of Trenton*, 2 vols. (Princeton, 1929), I, 263–272. Both ferries are shown on the road maps, Nos. 55 and 56, but only the Trenton Ferry on the camp map, No. 70. The first bridge across the Delaware at Trenton was completed only in 1806.

6. Colonel John Cox, assistant quartermaster-general of the Continental Army, was the owner of the Trent House (still in existence) from 1778 to 1792. This house is the "Chateau" shown on the separate map of the ford, No. 71. A watercolor view of Trenton, including the falls and the Trent House, drawn *ca.* 1798 by a French veteran of the American war, is in the Edwin A. Ely Collection, New Jersey Historical Society (which published a color reproduction of it in 1962). The artist, Colbert de Maulevrier (see "Checklist of Journals") was then residing in the United States as an émigré.

7. Clermont-Crèvecœur's journal (p. 45) also includes

an account of the Battle of Trenton. Several maps of the Battles of Trenton and Princeton drawn by French officers *ca.* 1780–1781 have survived. Among those noted by the Editors are: two maps on the same sheet entitled "Plans de la surprise de Trenton, et de la marche sur Princeton et Somerset, par le Général Washington," Bibliothèque du Ministère des Armées "Terre," Paris, L.I.D. 166; two insets on sheet of four maps by Colbert de Maulevrier, entitled respectively "Plan de la surprise de Trenton . . ." and "Marche sur Princeton et Sommerset . . . ," William L. Clements Library, Brun, *Guide*, No. 469; "Marche sur Princeton et Sommerset par le Gal. Vashington le 2 janvier 1777," Library of Paul Mellon, Crublier d'Opterre MS No. 13. Such maps, following a similar pattern and obviously derived from secondary sources, bear evidence of errors in copying. For example, in the Colbert de Maulevrier versions the title of the Trenton map has been given to the Princeton map and vice versa. Despite its title, the Crublier d'Opterre map is actually the Trenton "surprise" and not the march to Princeton and Somerset Courthouse! Cf. Berthier's journal, n. 72.

country is very flat, the terrain sandy, the road very good and very smooth. You meet with dwellings here and there and come to a fairly good-sized stream, which you cross on a bridge.　　*4 Miles*

You gradually come out of the woods. The road turns left and comes closer to the river, as it rises gradually onto the heights that overlook this bank. The ground is open and well cultivated. You come to the edge of the Delaware. Here the road turns right and follows the windings of the river. You can see Burlington Island and, farther in the distance on the east bank, the little town of Burlington. You continue to skirt the river, cross on a bridge a little brook flowing into it, and come to Bristol, which is a charmingly situated little town. Midway along the street of Bristol the road turns right and away from the Delaware. Coming out of town you pass on the right a road going to Newtown [in Bucks County, Pennsylvania].　　*5 Miles*

The road turns left; you are on a plain that extends to the river. Cross a brook on a bridge and continue along the road, which is wide, straight, and very smooth. You come to a symmetrical fork. Both roads lead to the north bank of the Neshaminy River. The one to the right goes to the ford, and the one to the left, which is the one to take, to the ferry.　　*1 Mile*

Passing a house on the right at the fork you follow the left-hand road, which runs very straight in this new direction. On the left you pass a road going to the Delaware River, then cross a little brook on a bridge. You meet with good-sized clearings, first on the left, then on the right. The road turns right and descends to the Neshaminy ferry. This river, or creek, is about 100 yards wide. It is crossed by means of a rope ferry (*bac à traite*), which has a maximum capacity of 15 horses. The ford over this

8. "King's Ferry" in the manuscript—evidently a copyist's error, probably from analogy with King's Ferry on the Hudson. On the maps mentioned in the previous note

Burlington, to attack Colonel Donop's brigade. Finally, the principal column, commanded by General Washington in person, was to cross at McKonkey's Ferry,[8] 9 miles above Trenton. The great masses of floating ice caused the failure of the expeditions led by Generals Ewing and Cadwalader. This obstacle did not stop General Washington. He had expected to surprise the enemy under cover of darkness, but continuous sleet rendered the crossing of his artillery so difficult and so long that he arrived in Trenton only at eight o'clock the next morning. He nevertheless surprised the Hessians, who had kept a poor watch. After the crossing of the Delaware General Washington had separated his corps into two divisions, one of which had turned to the right and taken the lower Trenton road, while the other, with which the General marched, had taken the upper route, called the Pennington Road.

The American columns were not long in surprising the Hessian posts, which were very near the town, into which the fugitives carried the alarm. Colonel Rall, who was in command there, scarcely had time to form his troops. He was mortally wounded. The defeat of the Hessians was total. They surrendered almost without fighting.

After this action General Washington, informed of the lack of success of Generals Ewing and Cadwalader, crossed back over the Delaware and returned to Philadelphia, followed by 1,200 prisoners and 6 pieces of cannon.

Before the affairs of Trenton and Princeton General Washington occupied the west bank of the Delaware from Bristol to a point above Trenton. It can be seen from the direction of the road and the windings of the river that the part of the country where he had chosen his position was the more

"McKonkey's Ferry" is written "Bac de Kenty." This is the spot now known as Washington Crossing.

creek is about ¾ mile upstream from the ferry.

2 Miles

After crossing Neshaminy Creek you proceed
uphill, passing the ferry house on the right. You
enter the woods, pass on the right the road coming
out of the wood, march through a clearing, closely
bordered by woods on either side, go down over a
brook, then up again, passing on either side roads
going into the fields. The ground becomes uneven,
and the horizon is still closed in by woods. The
road bears left, rising up onto a height and continuing
along it. You pass on the right several houses
belonging to the hamlet of Red Lion. The road
turns right and down into a hollow where the
Poquessing Creek flows. You pass Red Lion Tavern
on the right and immediately afterwards a road that
turns right up onto the height. You cross the creek
on a stone bridge, then go up through the woods
onto the opposite height, where the road resumes its
former direction. On either side of the road you have
open ground suitable for camping, surrounded by
the course of the creek.

4 Miles

Total: 17½ Miles

advantageous inasmuch as the enemy, who were
quartered on the opposite bank, were obliged by the
very course of the river to occupy widely separated
cantonments. This gave the Americans a great
advantage for the defense of the crossing and
facilities for concealing their attacks—circumstances
that General Washington made the most of.

Beyond this creek, on the open knoll, is a fine
position for a camp. It is convenient, well suited
for defense, and midway between Trenton and
Philadelphia. The creek has steep wooded banks,
and the hollow in which it flows is extremely marshy.[9]

THIRTEENTH MARCH

From Red Lion to Philadelphia[10]

You continue along the road, still on the crest of
the height. Pass on the right some outlying farms
of the hamlet of Red Lion. You come to a fork where
you pass a church on the left. Take the right-hand
road; the one to the left goes to the Delaware River.
This church is called Pennypack Church. You enter
the woods, then go down by stages to a brook that
is crossed on a stone bridge.

2 Miles

After crossing the brook you ascend. The road
bears left, and you pass on the right a road going
into the fields. Continue up onto a height where you
find several houses clustered together. This place
is called Ho——— [?].[11]

1 Mile

9. See map, No. 72.
10. See map, No. 57.
11. The name, which looks like "Hohurtovn" in the man-

uscript, has been garbled by the copyist. It should probably read "Holmes's Tavern," as shown in Colles, *Survey*,
Plate 47.

You go into the wood, down into a hollow, and up out of it. Coming out of the wood you are in flat and open country. A very fine road. On the right you pass a road going to Newtown. There are many houses along the road. You cross at right angles several roads going to the river and reach Frankford, a fair-sized village. *4 Miles*

Here you cross a creek [Frankford Creek] that flows into the Delaware; one of its branches comes from Germantown. The road, which bends a bit to cross the creek, resumes its former direction across this beautiful plain. You pass on the right a road going to Germantown and come to the Black Horse Tavern on the right-hand side of the road. *2 Miles*

You continue in the same direction over the plain, having open and cultivated ground on the left as far as the river and on the right, dwelling houses interspersed with woods. You reach the Taverne du Mouton [Sheep Tavern?]. *1 Mile*

The road bears right a bit but nevertheless comes closer to the river. On either side of the road you find woods, country houses, and ruins that are monuments to the wrath of the English. Half a mile from the city you see remains of General Howe's lines. Soon you cross one of the works that the English had built for the defense of the town. The road turns left, you cross a brook called Cohocksink Creek, pass through the suburb of Kensington, and reach Philadelphia. *2 Miles*

You traverse part of this city, the streets of which are perpendicular to the west bank of the Delaware, before turning sharp right into the Congress road.[12] You leave town by the Chester road, crossing the ground lying between the Delaware and the Schuylkill, an area of about 1½ miles, on which

Philadelphia's fine situation at the confluence of the Delaware and the Schuylkill is most advantageous for trade. This city has thus grown rapidly. The plan on which it is built is simple and spacious. It includes an area of nearly 3 miles between the two rivers. The tracing of the streets is perpendicular to the Delaware and cut at right angles by streets parallel to this same river. Only a third of this space has been built up, without in any way changing the original plan. The wharves and docks have not been entirely completed, but the largest vessels can load at those available.

Situated between the northern and southern provinces, Philadelphia receives via the Chesapeake Bay the tobacco of Virginia and via the Delaware the grain and cattle of the Jerseys, which are prosperous branches of trade with the islands of America [West Indies]. There are very few public buildings in Philadelphia, and none of any special beauty. The terrain on which the city is built and laid out is perfectly level.

General Howe, after having defeated the Americans at Brandywine on 4 October 1777, took possession of Philadelphia, but because of the very position of this city this conquest did not have the consequences the English government had expected. General Washington occupied an impregnable position at Whitemarsh. In the state of crisis through which the different provinces of America were then passing, Philadelphia was not regarded by all as their capital and seat of government.[13] Congress continued to function and withdrew to Baltimore. And this campaign, which appeared so brilliant when viewed from England, served only to make the Americans aware of the strength of their geographical position and of their own resources.

12. "Le chemin du Congrès" in the manuscript, meaning the road leading to and past the seat of the Continental Congress (Pennsylvania State House, present Independence Hall), i.e., Chestnut Street.
13. "Dans l'état de crise où étaient les différentes Provinces de l'Amérique Philadelphie n'était pas regardé

comme la première patrie et le siège du gouvernement." The meaning seems to be that the particularist states did not instinctively think of Philadelphia, despite the presence of Congress there, as a national capital worth defending at all costs. Its loss was not, therefore, the coup de grâce that the British thought it would be.

the plan for the rest of the city is already traced,
and reach the banks of the Schuylkill.[14]   *2 Miles*
                                    Total: 14 Miles

FOURTEENTH MARCH
From Philadelphia to Chester[15]

From the camp on the east bank of the Schuylkill
you cross this river on a pontoon bridge (*pont
flottant*). At this place the river is about 200 yards
wide.

After crossing this bridge you come to a fork.
Take the left; the right is the Lancaster road. The
road turns left. You go down in a hollow where
you cross a brook flowing into the Schuylkill.

1 Mile

Coming up from the hollow you enter the wood.
Still in the wood, you go down into a hollow,
continuing through it, as the road comes closer to
the bed of the Schuylkill. You can still see on the
east bank of this river the redoubts that the Americans
had built there to defend the crossings. You come
to a fork. Take the right; the left goes back to
Philadelphia. On this latter road, about a mile from
the fork, is the Lower Ferry,[16] so called because you
cross the Schuylkill there below Philadelphia. This
road is the regular route from Philadelphia to Chester,
whereas the one you have been following from
the bridge is only a cross road from the Lancaster
highway to the Chester highway.   *2 Miles*

The road turns right a bit and moves away from
the river. You cross a little brook, then reach a

During this entire march you skirt the Delaware,
and although the route is separated from it by the
marshes at the confluence of the two rivers, we
shall nevertheless note here the works defending
both banks of the Delaware,[17] which formerly had
such importance.

After the Battle of Brandywine, when the English
army had taken possession of Philadelphia, the
only hope remaining to the Americans was to starve
the English army, which would soon have to have
had recourse to its ships to procure provisions. The
navigation of the Delaware was interrupted by
enormous chevaux-de-frise invented by Dr. Franklin,
who had formerly persuaded the English government
to make this expenditure in order to protect
Philadelphia from a raid. These chevaux-de-frise,
armed with sharp iron points, are an insurmountable
obstacle to vessels. The channel was imperceptibly
reduced to a slight width. The forts on Mud Island,
so called because this island is low and marshy, and
the Red Bank fort, which is opposite it, on the
east bank of the Delaware, prevent the approach
of vessels that might attempt to pass up the river.
Red Bank was attacked on 22 October 1777 by the
Hessians commanded by Colonel Donop, who was
killed there, lost 800 men, and failed to capture it.
Credit for this fine defense of Red Bank was due

14. See map, No. 73. The campsite near the banks of the
Schuylkill was then well outside the populated part of
town.
15. See map, No. 58.
16. Present Gray's Ferry Avenue indicates the site of the
Lower Ferry, which was also known as Gray's (or Grey's)
Ferry.

17. The "works defending both banks of the Delaware"—
the so-called River Forts—are shown on the road map for
the previous march, No. 57. For a convenient recapitulation of the role of these river defenses in 1777, based on a
reexamination of original sources, see Samuel Stelle Smith,
Fight for the Delaware, 1777 (Monmouth Beach, N.J.,
1970).

crossroads where you have on the left a fairly good-sized residence (*habitation*). The road you cross joins up with the Lancaster road. You go into the wood, the road continuing in the same direction. It is a fine road, though uneven because of the hills over which it passes. Pass on the right and left several taverns, the best known of which is Wattemen's [?]. You then reach the bridge over Cobb's River [Creek]. Before crossing it you pass on the left a road leading to farms that are in the marshes at the mouth of the Schuylkill. Crossing the bridge you pass on the right a tobacco mill. The road bears right, and you reach Derby, which is a fair-sized little town (*bourg*).

3 Miles

Coming out of Derby the road bears left. You pass on the right a road going to Lancaster. You cross Derby Creek, which joins with Cobb's Creek a mile below the village. The road turns right, and you enter the woods. You cross in succession several hollows and several brooks. The country is inhabited and cultivated at intervals.

You gradually come nearer the Delaware, as you can notice from the greater depth of the ravines and the volume of water in the different creeks [Little Crum, Crum, and Ridley creeks] that you cross one after another at about 1½ miles from Chester. The country is so much the same and the direction of the road so unvarying that the same description would have to be repeated. You reach Chester, a rather pretty and regularly built little town on the west bank of the Delaware.[20]

8 Miles

Total: 14 Miles

M. de Mauduit.[18] The fort at Mud Island held out for three weeks against the fire of the English squadron. M. de Fleury was serving as engineer there.[19] The English, finally surmising, correctly, that the obstacle created by the chevaux-de-frise must have hollowed out another channel between Mud Island and the west bank of the Delaware, risked sending in a vessel, which moored within pistol-shot of the fort. They flooded the works and forced the Americans to evacuate.

After the Battle of Brandywine the left column of the American army withdrew to Chester. During the entire next march you follow the march of this

18. Mauduit du Plessis was one of the French officers serving in the American army in 1777, before his country's official participation in the war. After returning to France in 1779, he came back to America with Rochambeau's army, in which he was serving during the 1781 march to Yorktown. At this time Rochambeau took the river route from Philadelphia to Chester in order to observe the forts. Mauduit himself, a veteran of the 1777 campaign, was in the General's party and could thus serve as an informed guide (mindful of his own earlier exploits). See Von Closen, pp. 121–123; "Checklist of Journals," *s.v.* Mauduit; references to Mauduit in Berthier's journal (con-

sult general Index). During his visit to Philadelphia in December 1780, Chastellux had inspected the river forts, also in Mauduit's company; see Chastellux (4), I, 154–160, 315–318. An unsigned manuscript map of Fort Mercer showing the attack of October 1777 ("Esquisse du Fort Mercer"), probably drawn by Mauduit, is reproduced in Smith, *op.cit.*, p. 17, from the original in the Historical Society of Pennsylvania.

19. See "Checklist of Journals," *s.v.* Fleury. Like Mauduit, Fleury served in the Continental Army, returned to France, and then came back with Rochambeau's forces.

20. See map, No. 74.

same column and notice the points where the Americans sometimes resisted in order to protect their retreat.

When you reach Milltown on the Brandywine Creek, 1 mile from Wilmington, you are 7 miles south of the battlefield.[21] The American successes at Trenton and Princeton having forced General Howe to give up his plan of making himself master of Philadelphia, he again attempted at the beginning of the 1777 campaign to penetrate by land [from New York] as far as the Delaware, but failing to force General Washington to leave his position on the Middle Brook [in New Jersey], he embarked his army and left Sandy Hook on 23 July. These forces consisted of 32 English or Hessian battalions, a corps of Queen's Rangers, a regiment of light horse, and a formidable artillery.

It was not until 25 August that General Howe made his landing at the head of Chesapeake Bay, at the points we shall mention in the course of subsequent marches.

The American army had taken a position on Red Clay Creek, which it left to retire behind the Brandywine.

General Washington occupied the heights that are on the east bank of this river, threw up defenses at the ford, and appeared determined to dispute the crossing.

The English army marched forth on 11 September to attack the American army. The right, commanded by General Knyphausen, marched to Chadds Ford, which was about at the American center and where they expected the main attack to take place, because it was the most feasible here. At ten o'clock the cannonade began. The English general made preparations to attack Chadds Ford. During this

21. Another similar account of the Battle of Brandywine is inserted in Clermont-Crèvecœur's journal, p. 51. See also Chastellux (4), 1, 148–152, 313–314, for his account of a visit to the Brandywine battlefield in December 1780, when he had the benefit of Lafayette's recollections of the battle. Derivative maps of the Battle of Brandywine by French draftsmen (comparable to those of Princeton and Trenton mentioned above, n. 7) are extant: e.g., "Figuré de la Bataille de Brandywine donnée le 11 7bre 1777 entre les Américains commandés pas le général Waginston et les Anglois commandés par le général Howe," Library of Paul Mellon, Crublier d'Opterre mss Nos. 1 and 2. Such maps were evidently based to a great extent on the engraved map published in London in 1778 by William Faden, "Battle of Brandywine in which the Rebels were defeated, September the 11th 1777, by the Army under the Command of General Sir William Howe."

From Chester to Wilmington[22]

Observations

To leave Chester you turn right, cross a bridge over a good-sized creek, and continue along the road that turns right and moves away from the river. You have open ground on either side of the road. That on the right, this side of the brook and woods, is very suitable for camping.   *1 Mile*

The road continues along the west bank of the Delaware, moving away from it a bit. On the right you still have woods interspersed with clearings. You pass houses on either side and a road on the right. You come to a wooden bridge over Naaman Creek and pass by Robertson's Mill a bit to the left.
   4 Miles

From Naaman Creek the fine road continues over flat ground for about half a mile. Then the terrain becomes uneven and stony, continuing so as far as Shellpot's Creek, over which there is no bridge.
   4½ Miles

From Shellpot's Creek to Allet's [Ellett's?] Tavern the terrain is still stony and mountainous.   *1½ Miles*

From Allet's Tavern you cross a bridge over Brandywine Creek. The hamlet, which is on either side of the different branches of this creek, is called

22. See map, No. 59.

time General Cornwallis, with the second column, marched on the left and made a wide detour to reach the forks of the Brandywine. He crossed the river unopposed at Ramble [?] Ford and Jefferies Ford and then took the road for Dilworth in order to turn the American right. General Washington, informed of this movement, detached General Sullivan, with all the troops he could draw from the center of his army, to oppose Lord Cornwallis.

General Sullivan took an advantageous position on the heights above Birmingham [Friends] Meeting House, his left extending as far as the Brandywine River and his columns resting on some very thick woods. Lord Cornwallis, having formed his troops on the other side of the church, attacked the Americans, broke their line, and pursued them in disorder into the woods in their rear. A part of the American right, which had not broken, took a second position in the woods, where it was soon dislodged by detachments from the enemy line.

General Knyphausen, after having successfully deceived the Americans with the idea of an attack he had no wish to make, did in fact cross the river at Chadds Ford as soon as he knew that the affair was well engaged on the right, and captured a battery of 9 cannon, creating such disorder among the Americans that they fled in all directions. A part of General Conway's brigade withdrew in good order by the Chester road.

The Americans lost in this action 300 killed, 600 wounded, 400 prisoners, and 10 pieces of cannon.

General Howe has been criticized for failing to take advantage of his victory and not having marched at once on Chester.

Milltown [now absorbed by Wilmington], because of the large number of mills above and below the bridge. The road turns right, and you go up onto the height where Wilmington is situated.[23]

Total: 11 Miles

Wilmington is a fairly sizeable town, well built and advantageously situated at the mouth of Christina Creek, which flows into the Delaware. William Penn had good reason to be charmed with its pretty position and made his first settlement there. This town, in spite of the rivalry of Philadelphia, carried on very extensive trade before the war. Ships coming down the Delaware can stop here to load tobacco that has been transported overland from Head of Elk [on the Chesapeake Bay] and bring flour and cattle from the Jerseys, which are a precious object of exchange for the West Indies.

After leaving Wilmington and moving away from the Delaware River you notice that the terrain gradually rises as far as Iron Hill, which is the highest elevation between the Chesapeake Bay and the Delaware. On Iron Hill you see the old camps made there by the English army after its debarkation at Head of Elk [in August 1777].

SIXTEENTH MARCH

From Wilmington to Head of Elk[24]

From the camp at Wilmington you go up Roberson [Robinson?] Mountain, keeping the Delaware and Mill Creek on the left. You then go downhill and reach the village of Newport.   *3½ Miles*

From Newport you continue along the road, enter a thinset wood, pass over another little height, and come to a wooden bridge over Red Clay Creek.

2 Miles

From Red Clay Creek to White Clay Creek.

1 Mile

After White Clay Creek the road becomes uneven. You reach the little village of Christiana.   *3 Miles*

23. See map, No. 75.   24. See map, No. 60.

At Christiana you pass on the left a bridge and a
road going to Dover. There are then no side roads
and only a few dwellings, on the right and left, as
far as the bridge called Cooch's Bridge.   *5 Miles*

Here there are three different roads. All three
go to Head of Elk. The one you pass on the right
before crossing the bridge goes around to the right
of Iron Hill. The one straight ahead from the bridge
goes over the crest of this same mountain. The road
to the left beyond the bridge goes around to the left
of Iron Hill. The shortest of the three roads is the
one straight ahead, but it is also the hardest for
wagons; they should take the left-hand road after
crossing the bridge. After having come around or over
Iron Hill you go up over Gray's Hill. Then the three
routes merge, first the right-hand road, then
the left-hand road, a mile before reaching the
bridge called Elk Bridge.   *5 or 6 Miles*

From Elk Bridge to Head of Elk.[25]   *½ Mile*
                    Total: 20 or 21 Miles

25. See map, No. 76.

6

ITINERARY

of the Wagon Train of the Army from the Camp at Annapolis to Williamsburg

1781

219 Miles

The previous Itineraries have brought the description of the army's route as far as Head of Elk at the uppermost northeastern tip of Chesapeake Bay. It had been expected that the entire Franco-American army would embark here and be transported down the Bay to Williamsburg, where the allied forces were assembling to besiege Cornwallis in Yorktown. However, contrary to expectations, insufficient boats were available at Head of Elk. Only an advanced corps of French grenadiers and chasseurs could be embarked here. (Their tribulations are mentioned in the entry for 8 September 1781 in the journal of Clermont-Crèvecœur, who congratulated himself on not having been in this convoy). Thereupon the rest of the French army continued its march to Baltimore (via Lower Ferry over the Susquehanna, Bush, and White Marsh, 9–12 September) under the command of the Baron de Vioménil. Rochambeau had temporarily left his troops to ride ahead overland to Williamsburg with Washington and Chastellux. Again, at Baltimore, the hoped-for transports were inadequate. The few ships available were ceded to the Americans and preparations made for an overland march of the French army to the rendezvous at Williamsburg. Heading for Georgetown and Alexandria, they proceeded to their first camp (16 September) at Spurrier's Tavern, 15 miles from Baltimore. At this point came the news that, thanks to the arrival of Barras's squadron from Rhode Island, transports were being sent under escort up the Bay to Annapolis. Vioménil therefore changed direction and, instead of proceeding ahead towards the Potomac, marched his army down to Annapolis, where the troops and field artillery were embarked on 21 September. (Barras's ships had brought the siege artillery from Rhode Island.) They arrived off Archer's Hope, at the mouth of College Creek near Williamsburg, on 24 September. Nevertheless, the transports available at Annapolis proved inadequate for the wagons and horses. These had to be sent overland under the escort of Victor Collot and Louis-Alexandre Berthier, assistant quartermasters-general. According to Berthier ("Extrait des Opérations de la Campagne de l'Armée combinée," Berthier Papers No. 26):

"Lauzun's Legion [the hussars], the artillery horses, and the army wagon train formed a column numbering 1,500 horses, 800 oxen, and 220 wagons and marched overland to Williamsburg, crossing the Patuxent, Potomac, and Rappahannock rivers, traveling 230 miles. This column, led and commanded by the assistant quartermasters-general Collot and Berthier, executed their march, despite its manifold difficulties, with great dispatch. After marching 17 days they arrived on 6 October, before the first trench was opened, thereby furnishing transport for the artillery and ammunition."

This march from Annapolis to Williamsburg is described in the following Itinerary. In view of the pressure of events and the rapidly changing plans, all within a span of ten days, it is not surprising that there are no itineraries or road maps for the prior marches from Head of Elk to Baltimore and Annapolis. This gap in the series is in some measure bridged by the "General Map of the Camps and Marches," No. 162, and by the plans of the camps at Lower Ferry, Bush, White Marsh, and Baltimore, Nos. 77–81. Clermont-Crèvecœur's journal also supplies details about the army's movements during this period.

This last Itinerary in our series is entitled "Itinéraire des marches faittes par les Equipages de L'armée pour se rendre du Camp d'Anapolis à Williamsburg, 219 Milles, 1781." The only copy known to the Editors is this one, preserved in the Princeton University Library (Berthier Papers, No. 13). The manuscript comprises a "cahier" of 32 pages (last twelve blank), similar in format and handwriting to Itineraries 2–5. Inasmuch as Berthier was one of the "conductors" of the wagon train's march, there is every reason to believe that he himself was the compiler of this Itinerary. The increasingly staccato style of the writing seems to reflect the urgency of the march. Bare notations replace the more detailed observations of the earlier itineraries. In spite of his multiple responsibilities and the rapidity of the march, Berthier found time to reconnoiter possible campsites for the main army "in case it should take this route." This information is included in marginal "observations," which suggest that the successful embarkation of the army was still in some doubt when the wagon train set out from Annapolis. As things turned out, the army as a whole did not have to take this route in September 1781. However, Berthier's observations were not wasted. The following year, when the French army moved northward from Virginia, it did in fact camp at a number of the sites pointed out in the wagon-train itinerary. These are recorded in our series of 1782 camp plans, Nos. 108ff., which can in turn serve to illustrate this Itinerary of the wagon train's march in 1781.

Itinerary

OF THE WAGON TRAIN OF THE ARMY
FROM THE CAMP AT ANNAPOLIS TO WILLIAMSBURG, 1781

219 Miles

Observations	Description of Marches	Observations, in case the army were to take this route

FIRST MARCH

21 September [1781] · From Annapolis to the Plantation of the John Easton brothers[1]

	On leaving Annapolis, take the Baltimore road and follow it for ½ mile, where you come to a fork. Both roads lead to Georgetown, but the one on the right, which is 5 miles longer, is the only one suitable for wagons. You come to Scotland Tavern. *4 Miles*	
	Next you reach Scott House[2] and a fork whose right branch runs straight to Frederic Town [Frederick, Maryland]. Take the left. The road is good; however, there are a few short, steep grades. You go down a steep hill into a hollow. Halfway down you pass a house on the left. *10 Miles*	
This would make a good position for a camp, since there is water and forage available.	You climb the opposite slope and come to a small wood in a marshland, which you pass through. *2 Miles*	
	You cross several fields, with houses on either side of the road. You descend into another wood as marshy as the last, and reach the	

---

1. See map, No. 162.
2. The Scott House was along the road leading back to Baltimore from Annapolis. When marching from Baltimore to Annapolis the army had

made its 36th camp here, as shown on map, No. 162. Cf. Deux-Ponts ([1], pp. 46, 131), who notes that on 17 September "we took the route for Annapolis [from Spurrier's Tavern]

and encamped at Scott's Plantation." Thus the wagon train retraced its steps back to this point before striking out westward towards Bladensburg and Georgetown.

Observations	Description of Marches	Observations, in case the army were to take this route
Both the entrance and exit of the ford, which is very poor, need repair.	bank of the Patuxent, which you cross. It is not more than 60 yards wide. The riverbed is firm and smooth. *2 Miles*	
	You continue through the woods for ½ mile, and on the left, ½ mile from the road, you come to the house of John Easton.[3] *Total: 18 Miles*	*At John Easton's — 1st Camp (17 Miles)* The army can camp here, since there is abundant forage and water within reach. Lodgings for the headquarters would be scarce.

SECOND MARCH

22 September

From the John Easton brothers' Plantation to the Age[?] House[4]

You leave John Easton's house by a road that reenters the Georgetown highway 200 paces farther on. You pass quite a fine house on the left.   *2 Miles*

The road continues to be very good, with woods on the right and some clearings on the left. You come to a tavern.   *3 Miles*

You cross two small brooks on bridges, the second of which is in bad condition. There are woods and clearings on either side of the road. You come to another brook. The wagons camped to the right of the road, ahead of the brook.   *4 Miles*

The wagon train, which had loaded a day's forage at John Easton's house, parked at this place to rest the oxen. These had suffered considerably the day before, since, having left Annapolis at noon, they did not arrive until the middle of the night.

After crossing the brook you go uphill and reach the Age[?] House.[5]   *Total: 9 Miles*

3. The Easton brothers' plantation—not further identified—was not far from the west bank of the Patuxent River, which here forms the boundary between Anne Arundel and

Prince Georges Counties. The general direction of the march is very roughly that of present State Route 450.

4. See map, No. 162.

5. This name has not been confirmed. It is clearly written "Age" in the manuscript, as on the map. In the heading above, "Age" appears to be followed by another syllable, "bet,"

THIRD MARCH

23 September

From the Age [?] House to Georgetown[6]

Take the road in front of the Age[?] House and go through the woods, in which there are several clearings. When you emerge on high and open ground, you will catch sight of Bladensburg.[7] You go down into the town, which you enter at right angles to a wide street. Turn right after crossing the town, leaving the road to Baltimore on your right, then ford a little river called East Branch, which is only 40 yards wide and is the east branch of the Potomac [Anacostia].   *5 Miles*

At Bladensburg — 2nd Camp (15 Miles)
The army could camp at Bladensburg, where the headquarters would be well lodged on either side of the river. There are fine campsites here, as well as pastures and forage.

Beyond the river the ground rises on the left-hand side of the road. There is a very fine site here for a camp of 10,000 men.[8]

Leaving the river the road turns left. You go through a hollow. On the left the ground rises. You continue along the road, which is excellent. You pass some woods, with occasional clearings on either side. You go up and down some gentle slopes, then descend a steep hill to the edge of Rock Creek, only 20 yards wide, which you ford.[9]   *7½ Miles*

You climb a short, steep hill, then go to the top of another hill where Georgetown is situated, overlooking the Potomac. Several

At Georgetown — 3rd Camp (8 Miles)
The army could camp at Georgetown, and the headquarters

Although this little town on the east bank of the Potomac contains very few houses, it has two fairly

---

which has been crossed out. Other possibilities: Ayer? Eager? Hager? This house was evidently not far from Bladensburg.
6. See map, No. 162.

7. See map, No. 126, which shows the camp made at Bladensburg in July 1782, when the army was on its northbound march.

8. The future site of Washington, D.C.
9. See map, No. 125, showing the army's camp near Rock Creek in July 1782.

large taverns. Here you cross the Potomac, which is at this point about 1,000 yards wide. At the ferry there are: 2 large boats, each of which can carry 2 wagons or 4 two-wheeled ox carts; 3 that can carry 1 wagon or 2 two-wheeled ox carts; and 2 small boats able to carry 3 horses each.

Note: The latter are very dangerous, since they are very small and liable to capsize. During the crossing of the wagon train 1 horse and 1 man were drowned. In good weather the crossing takes 22 minutes.

streets descend to the river's edge, where there are some houses.

½ Mile
Total: 13 Miles

Note: The oxen proceed 3 miles up the Potomac above Georgetown to a ferry where the river is only 150 to 200 yards wide. Here they can swim across without difficulty, with the aid of a small boat kept there for this purpose.

would cross the Potomac there and go on to Alexandria, 8 miles beyond, where it would be well lodged for the two-day halt indispensable for the crossing of the wagons, which, as soon as they crossed, would proceed to Alexandria.

FOURTH MARCH

From the West Bank of the Potomac, opposite Georgetown, to Alexandria[10]

You go uphill and turn left along the Potomac. As you begin to leave the river you enter the woods. After 1½ miles you cross a brook. You turn, leaving on your right a road and the house of one Cameron, an Irishman.

6 Miles

You pass on the right another road, which leads to Scot Tavern, 2 miles beyond.   *½ Mile*

This town, which is very pretty and substantially built, lies on the west bank of the Potomac, which

The road is superb and is straight as far as Alexandria.[11]

1½ Miles
Total: 8 Miles

At Alexandria — 4th Camp
(8 Miles)
This camp would be the third

10. See map, No. 162.

11. Map, No. 124, shows the army's camp at Alexandria in July 1782.

here is 1 mile wide and is crossed by a ferry. Frigates can come up the river to Alexandria; its trade thereby prospers and flourishes.

for the headquarters and the fourth for the army, the two-day halt being divided between Georgetown and Alexandria.

FIFTH MARCH

26 September
From Alexandria to Colchester[12]

Leaving Alexandria, take the main road, off which you turned to enter town. At a fork, whose right branch goes to Frederic Town [Frederick, Maryland], 60 miles away, you take the left. The road is very good. You pass a road on the right,   *1 Mile*

then Colonel West's [?] house on the left.   *1 Mile*

You come to a fork, where there is a cluster of several houses called Cameron.[13] The right branch leads to Loudon County, 22 miles away. You take the left and cross Hunting Creek.   *1 Mile*

You enter a wood and come to a fork. The left-hand road leads to General Washington's house, 8 miles beyond.[14] You take the right fork and cross a large clearing.   *1 Mile*

You cross a brook and pass a house known as Creek Mills House.
                    ½ Mile

You enter the woods. Passing

12. See map, No. 162.

13. Cf. "McAllister," Colles, *Survey*, Plate 66.

14. Mount Vernon.

	a house on your left, you cross a clearing and pass another house on your right. You cross a brook and pass a road on the left at Swepplett [Triplett] House.	
	2½ Miles	
As it stopped by the house, the wagon train loaded 30 _milles_ of hay. Since the house has both water and fine pastures, 10,000 men could camp here.	You climb a fairly steep hill, passing a house on the left. _1½ Miles_	

You cross a clearing, leaving a
house on the left, then a road on
the right. You remain in the
woods. You go up and downhill.
You come to a clearing with a
house on the left. Cross a brook.
2½ Miles

You follow a little river[15] for
½ mile, go through some clearings,
and ford the river, passing a road
on the right. _1 Mile_

You go uphill, past a house
on the left and a road on the right.
There is a church on the right.[16]
You are still in the woods. _½ Mile_

You pass a road on your right,
then one on the left that leads
to Posey's Ferry, 7 miles beyond.[17]
There is a house on the left. You
cross two little brooks. You pass a
road on the right and another on
the left. _1 Mile_

You remain in the woods,
passing through several clearings,

15. Accotink Creek. "Accohick Creek," Colles, _Survey_, Plate 66.
16. Pohick Church, a brick building completed in 1774, recently restored. This was the home church of Mount Vernon; Washington, one of the vestrymen, was a member of the building committee.
17. This was a ferry across the Potomac. See _Papers of TJ_, II, 454–463,

"A Bill for Establishing Public Ferries," in which it is listed as going "From Posey's, in Fairfax [County, Virginia], to Brooks's, in Maryland."

with negro cabins[18] on either side. You go uphill, then down over a brook.　　　　　　*2 Miles*

Colchester is a small town, which is almost deserted. It is on the left bank of Occoquan Creek, 120 yards wide, which is crossed by a single ferry able to carry but one four-wheeled wagon. Four hundred yards below the town the river widens considerably into a bay that encroaches upon the surrounding fields. It is still quite broad where it flows into the Potomac several miles beyond.

You go up another hill, come out into a clearing, and arrive at Colchester.[19]　　　　　*1 Mile*
　　　　　　　Total: 16 Miles

At Colchester — 5th Camp
(15 Miles)
The headquarters would be fairly well quartered here, and the camp could be pitched on the heights above the entrance to the town. The army would have to be ferried across the Occoquan, and the wagons, horses, etc., would go upstream to the ford, 7 miles from Colchester.

SIXTH MARCH

27 September
From Colchester to Marumsco Creek[20]

If you take the Occoquan ferry at Colchester, Marumsco Creek is only 1½ miles beyond the town, but the limited capacity of the ferry boat makes it necessary to send the wagon train upstream to the ford, which is narrow and very good.

Before entering the town of Colchester you take a road to the right that follows the north bank of the Occoquan. A good road leads to the ford, which is narrow and very good.　　　*7 Miles*

After fording the Occoquan you go down the creek again by the road leading to the forges.
　　　　　　　1 Mile

You proceed from the forges to the furnaces,　　*½ Mile*

and from the furnaces to Marumsco Creek.　*2½ Miles*
　　　　　Total: 11 Miles

The army's baggage train would take this same route in order to cross at the ford and would continue as far as Dumfries, where the army's 5th [6th] camp could be made. This day's march would be only 19 miles.

18. *Baraques* is the French word used here and subsequently in the manu-

script. It might also be translated as "wooden huts" or "shanties."
19. Map No. 123 shows the army's

camp at Colchester in July 1782.
20. See map, No. 162.

28 September
From Marumsco Creek to Aquia Run near Peyton's Tavern[21]

Observations	Description of Marches	Observations, in case the army were to take this route
	From the Marumsco camp you go through some woods with occasional clearings. You cross a brook. *2 Miles*	
There is plenty of hay in this neighborhood.	You pass some fine meadows on the left. You go uphill and down. You proceed through the woods, passing Blackburn House on the left.[22] *2 Miles*	
Pasturage is abundant in this neighborhood.	For about 1 mile you cross a beautiful valley, which extends towards the Potomac.[23] *1 Mile*	
	You pass a house on the right. When you come to a fork, take the left, cross a brook, go uphill, passing a house on the left, and cross another brook. *1 Mile*	
	At the top of the hill you pass a house on the right. You go through some woods with occasional clearings and some negro cabins and arrive at Dumfries.[24] *2 Miles*	
Dumfries is a small town containing 15 houses, situated in a hollow at the head of a meadow that extends to the marshes along the Potomac a mile or so beyond.		*At Dumfries* *6th Camp* { *for the baggage train (19 Miles) for the army (9 Miles)* } This day is not too long, since the road is excellent. The headquarters and the camp would be well situated.

21. See map, No. 162. Peyton's Tavern was also known as Peyton's Ordinary.
22. Rippon Lodge, built *ca.* 1725 by Richard Blackburn, an architect who later designed the original Mount Vernon. Colonel Thomas Blackburn was the occupant in 1781.
23. The valley formed by Neabasco Creek.
24. See map, No. 122, which shows the camp made here by the French when on their northward march in July 1782.

	After passing through Dumfries you keep on your left Quantico Creek, which you ford ½ mile from town. You pass a road on your left. You proceed through the woods and pass a road on the right. *4 Miles*	
In general this country is covered with woods, with here and there some clearings and negro cabins.	You go down into a hollow, which you follow as it becomes a small valley. This valley leads to the bay of the Potomac. You pass a road on the left, then ford Chopawamsic Creek. Keep on through the meadow, where there are houses on either side. The road turns right. You pass woods on the left and a collection of houses on the right called Chopawamsic. *1 Mile*	93 *Itinerary* · 6 ·

This position would be too confined for the camp of a whole regiment.	Keep on through the woods and come to Aquia Run near PayTown Tavern [Peyton's Ordinary].[25]
	    4 Miles
	    Total: 17 Miles	

EIGHTH MARCH

29 September
From Aquia Run to Fredericksburg[26]

Leaving the camp you cross a
brook and go up a steep rise. You
pass a poor tavern and enter a
wood. Cross several clearings with
negroes' cabins. You go uphill
and down and cross a brook.
    2 Miles

25. Part of the army camped at Peyton's Ordinary in July 1782, as shown on map, No. 121. 26. See map, No. 162.

Observations	Description of Marches	Observations, in case the army were to take this route
	You continue through the woods. You go uphill and down and arrive at Colonel Garrot's [?] Tavern, where there are several houses. *2 Miles*	*At Garrott's [Garrett's?] Tavern — 7th Camp (13 Miles)* This position is better than the one at Aquia Run (near Peyton's Ordinary). The headquarters would be less inconvenient and the camp better.[27]

Observations	Description of Marches	
	You enter the woods ¼ mile farther on and come to a fork. Take the right. You are still in the woods. You go uphill and down and cross the ford over Aquia Creek. *2½ Miles*	
	You are still in the woods. You go uphill and down, then cross Potomac Creek. *3 Miles*	
This site is one of the pleasantest in Virginia. You can see Falmouth and the course of the Rappahannock, which on the right roars over the rocks and on the left flows peacefully through steep banks past Fredericksburg, one of the prettiest towns in Virginia, and off through a vast plain covered with plantations.	You continue in the woods. You reach a wooded plateau. On the left you pass Fitzhugh House.[28] You can now see Falmouth. You descend into the town, which is very small and contains but few houses.[29] It lies on the north bank of the Rappahannock, which can be forded. *6 Miles*	
	The Rappahannock is forded at a point where there are two islands, forming three branches of the river, each 60 yards wide and full of rocks, which are more alarming than dangerous, since the water is only 2 feet deep.[30] On leaving the ford you go up a very rough and steep little grade. For ¼ mile you follow the south	

27. The First Division of the French army camped at Garrott's Tavern in July 1782. However, as the water supply was inadequate, the other divisions continued their march to Peyton's Ordinary.

28. Chatham, the estate of William Fitzhugh. See Thomas Waterman, *The Mansions of Virginia, 1706–1776* (Chapel Hill, N.C., 1946), pp. 360–363, 415.

29. See map, No. 119, which shows the French encampment at Falmouth in July 1782.
30. Map No. 120 is a detailed chart of the ford.

	bank of the river. Then the road turns left, and you go straight on into Fredericksburg. *1½ Miles* *Total: 17 Miles*	[At] *Fredericksburg — 8th Camp* *(12 Miles)* The camp and headquarters would be very comfortably situated.[31]
Fredericksburg is a pretty town with a single fine street running parallel to the right bank of the Rappahannock, which you cross at a ferry between 80 and 100 yards wide. There is only one ferry boat. In time of peace trade prospers here because of the ease with which 500-ton ships can be brought upstream to this point. There are many fine houses in the vicinity. Hay is beginning to be scarce, and the horses must be fed corn shucks.		

NINTH MARCH

1 October
From Fredericksburg to Colonel Dangerfield's House[32]

	Leaving Fredericksburg, follow the road straight ahead. You pass some houses and some woods on either side of the road. You proceed uphill and reach a fork. The right-hand road goes to Bowling Green. *7½ Miles*	
This short day's march was required to find forage.	*Note*: The wagon train took the left-hand road and camped at Colonel Dangerfield's, 1 mile from the fork.[33] *1 Mile* *Total: 8½ Miles*	*At Colonel Dangerfield's* *— 9th Camp (8½ Miles)* The headquarters would remain in Fredericksburg.

31. Although the army marched north through Fredericksburg in 1782, it did not camp there.
32. See map, No. 162.
33. The detour via Colonel Danger-field's is described more fully by Berthier in a memorandum preserved in

the Princeton University Library (Berthier Papers, No. 31). This stray scrap, hastily written on both sides of a small sheet in Berthier's unmistakable scrawly handwriting, is the only sample found of his on-the-spot field notes, which he later wrote up

for his journal (missing for this period) or the itineraries. This nearly illegible fragment reads:

2 October 1781

Left Fredericksburg 1 October. Leaving town you go downhill, turn left across a ravine, climb out

2 October
From Colonel Dangerfield's House to Bowling Green[34]

Observations	Description of Marches	Observations, in case the army were to take this route

You leave Colonel Dangerfield's plantation on the same road by which you arrived, returning to the main road, which you enter at a right angle. Turn left. *½ Mile*

The road is excellent. There are woods on the left and a road that crosses it from right to left.
2 Miles

You pass through a grove of trees, then a road on your left.
1 Mile

Four hundred yards to the right of the road there are woods, and also some houses on the left. You enter the woods, passing a clearing on the right. You arrive at Todd's Tavern.[35] *2 Miles*

of it and turn right, then left. You pass a house on the right. You follow a very good straight road across a very beautiful plain, following the Rappahannock at a distance of 1 or 2 miles on your left. You pass a road on the right and come to a brook 5½ miles from Fredericksburg. You go up a hill, with a grove of trees on the left. A half mile farther on you come to a fork. The right-hand road goes to Williamsburg via New Castle, the left follows the Rappahannock. There is a house to the right of the fork. You are 6 miles from Fredericksburg. Taking the left-hand road you proceed ¾ mile to Colonel Dangerfield's house, where he gave us lodgings for the night. This short day's march of 7 miles was made necessary in order to procure

forage at Colonel Dangerfield's on the banks of the Rappahannock. The Colonel has a very large and beautiful plantation. He raises wheat, cotton and corn, and very good horses. He gave us an excellent dinner, which was amply repaid by the high price [we paid] for his beverages at 18 pence the bottle. The forage cost 5 pounds a ton.

This country is full of little partridge and small hares for which the local name is "rabbits." Nevertheless, they are more like hares than rabbits. They have the same shape, same fur, do not rear up, and thus differ only in their size, which is the same as a rabbit's. There are many birds: the cardinal, a superb red; the blue bird, the blue jay; and a great number of varied

species. Up in the hills there are many deer.

Left for Bowling Green.

2 October 1781

A letter from Arthur Lee (then residing at Chatham, near Fredericksburg) written to Colonel Theodorick Bland, 27 September 1781, reported: "Col. Dangerfield and his family are well; and he has touched some hard money from the French, for his hay, which being unusual [the hard money!] is very delightful." Charles Campbell, ed., *The Bland Papers*, 2 vols. (Petersburg, 1840–1843), II, 77.
34. See map, No. 162.
35. Todd's Ordinary, as it was also called, was located in present Villboro, along the road from Fredericksburg to Hanover—roughly present State Route 2.

Half a mile from the tavern you enter a wood. You pass a road on the left, go through some clearings, and pass a road on the right.   *1 Mile*

The road continues through the woods. You cross a brook.
                              1½ Miles

You pass a road on the right, then one on the left. You come to a large clearing where there is a fine house belonging to Charles Thornton.[36]   *1 Mile*

You pass a road on the left. There are woods on the right and woods receding from the road on the left. You come to the bank of a brook at right angles to the road. The bridge across it is called Downer's [?] Bridge. You follow the brook, keeping it on your right.   *1½ Miles*

The army could camp on this site.

Turn left. There is a wood on the right and a clearing on the left. A fine house belonging to Widow Thornton.[37] You cross the brook that you were following on your right over two wooden bridges. You are now in the woods. You come to another brook, which you ford. Go uphill, through a clearing, and reach Peck [?] House.   *3½ Miles*

You go through a wood, then

36. In July 1782, when marching northward, the army camped near Charles Thornton's house. See map, No. 118.

37. Written "Towten" in the manuscript. The house is shown in Colles, *Survey*, Plate 71.

a clearing, passing a wood on
your left.   *1½ Miles*

You pass several cabins on the
right and on the left a clearing.
You go through a little grove of
trees and arrive at Bowling Green
Tavern.[38]   *2½ Miles*
            Total: 18 Miles

*At Bowling Green — 10th Camp
(18 Miles)*
Neither camp nor headquarters
would be very well situated
here. It is nevertheless better than
any other campsite in this
neighborhood.

A quarter of a mile from the
tavern there is a fine house.

ELEVENTH MARCH

3 October
From Bowling Green to Lynch's Tavern[39]

The wagons (*équipages*) went
to this plantation, ½ mile from
the road, to load hay. This

On leaving the camp you enter
the woods. You pass through
several clearings and come to a
fork. Take the left. The right-hand
road goes to Mr. Baylor's
plantation.[40]   *3½ Miles*

38. The French camped at Bowling
Green when on their northward
march in July 1782. See map, No. 117,
and descriptive note. In 1781 the
routes of the army's wagon train and
of Lauzun's cavalry, which had been
following the same route since
Georgetown, diverged here at Bowling Green. A letter from General
Rochambeau, dated Williamsburg, 16
September 1781, containing instructions for Colonel d'Arrot, commanding Lauzun's cavalry, and also for the
army's wagon train, was brought by
messenger to Bowling Green (Manuscript Collections of Colonial Williamsburg). Colonel d'Arrot was instructed to take his cavalry (with its
own wagon train as well as the train
of Lauzun's infantry) to join Briga-
dier General Weedon's forces at

Gloucester Courthouse, where he
would be joined by the Duc de Lauzun and the Legion's infantry which
was being transported down Chesapeake Bay. D'Arrot was to proceed
to his destination via Todd's Bridge
and King and Queen Courthouse. On
the other hand, the army's wagon
train was to march from Bowling
Green to Williamsburg, as originally
planned. Rochambeau noted, however, that since the New Castle bridge
was broken, the preferred route
would be via Todd's Bridge and Ruffin's Ferry. Assuming that the present
Itinerary describes the route actually
taken by the wagon train, it appears
that the alternate route proposed by
Rochambeau was not the one taken.
Rochambeau's letter also specifies that
the agent for procurement of provi-

sions (Wadsworth & Co.) then attached to Colonel d'Arrot's unit
would continue to Williamsburg
with the army's train, since the latter would be moving into a badly
devastated region, while d'Arrot
would be going through less devastated country.
39. See map, No. 162.
40. The Baylor mansion, known as
"Newmarket," is no longer standing.
The owner of the plantation in 1781
was Colonel George Baylor (1752–
1784). See Writers Program (WPA),
*Virginia, A Guide to the Old Do-
minion* (New York, 1940, and later
printings), p. 364. Baylor was aide-de-
camp to Washington and commander
of the Third Continental Dragoons,
whose uniform is illustrated in the
Leipziger Jahrbuch of 1784.

plantation is a pretty one. The whole family speaks French.	On the right you pass by a road coming from Mr. Baylor's. You are still in the woods. Go through some clearings and come to the red house.[41] *3½ Miles*	
	You pass roads on the right and left. Then, farther on, another road on the left and a house. *1 Mile*	
This river flows into the York River at West Point, 40 miles away. A camp could be located in front of Burk's Bridge.	There are clearings to the right of the road. You turn right. You go down across the Mattaponi River, which is 40 yards wide, on a good wooden bridge called Burk's Bridge.[42] *1 Mile*	
	You are in the woods, with occasional clearings. In a hollow you cross some marshes on logs. You pass a meetinghouse on the left. *½ Mile*	
	You come to a pond formed by a brook. The road forks. Bayork's[43] [?] Tavern is on the left. The right-hand road leads to Orange County in the mountains. Take the left. *½ Mile*	
	You cross the brook by a ford and by a wooden bridge. You pass a road on the left and come to a fork. Take the right. Cross a brook. You are still in the woods. You go uphill to Lynch's Tavern.[44] *3 Miles* *Total: 14 Miles*	*At Lynch's Tavern — 11th Camp (14 Miles)* A good position may be found by crossing the brook at the foot of the mountain. The headquarters would be quite a distance away from it.

41. The army camped in this vicinity in July 1782. See map, No. 116, where the house is called "Kenner's Tavern."

42. See map, No. 116.

43. The manuscript clearly reads "Bayork's," which is probably a garbling or copyist's error, perhaps for "Burk."

44. Lynch's Tavern was also called "Head Lynch's Ordinary." See map, No. 107, and descriptive note. Al-

4 October
From Lynch's Tavern to Hanovertown[45]

Observations	Description of Marches	Observations, in case the army were to take this route

Leaving Lynch's Tavern you go downhill, cross a brook, go through some woods and clearings, and pass a road on the right.
1½ Miles

You pass another road on the right and continue through woods and clearings, with plantations on either side. You arrive at [————?] House.[46] *1½ Miles*

The road forks. Take the right and go through a clearing, with a house on the right. You come to Crean [?] House, a fine plantation.[47] *4 Miles*

Twelve hundred men could camp here, before crossing the river. The Pamunkey flows into the York River at West Point, 40 to 50 miles beyond.

You go downhill and follow a brook on your right. You enter a very large clearing where there are several houses. You continue through it for a mile, then go down to the bank of the Pamunkey, a river 40 yards wide, running between steep banks, which you cross on a wooden bridge. You pass a crossroads, then another road on the left. You come to a triple fork (*patte d'oie*). Take the left. The first road on the right leads to a plantation, and the second to the mountains. You pass

---

though the army marched over this route in July 1782, it did not camp at Lynch's Tavern, as suggested in the marginal observations.

45. See map, No. 162.
46. The name, as written in the manuscript, looks like "Mest somme house" or "New sound house."

47. "Crean" should perhaps read "Graham." Cf. map, No. 115, showing the army's 1782 camp at Littlepage's Bridge or Graham's house.

Observations	Description of Marches	Observations, in case the army were to take this route
There is a very fine and large inn here.	a house on the left and arrive at Hanover Courthouse.[48] *3 Miles*	
	You go downhill, cross a brook on two wooden bridges, then climb again. You pass a house on the left and enter the woods. You pass a house on the right and another on the left. *2 Miles*	
	You pass a fine house on the left. You come to a fork. Take the left, through woods and clearings, past negro cabins.[49] You pass a road on the left and arrive at Hensen [Anderson?] House.[50] *1 Mile*	
	The country is more open. You cross a brook on two bridges. *1 Mile*	
	You pass a plantation on the left and a road on the right. *1 Mile*	
One of these houses is a very large and handsome brick warehouse.	You pass several houses ½ mile to the left of the road. Go downhill to a brook, which you cross on a bridge, and enter woods. *2 Miles*	
Hanovertown, a small town on the south bank of the Pamunkey,	House on the left. You pass a crossroad. House on the right. The road forks. The right fork goes to New Castle, and the left also, but via Hanovertown. *½ Mile*	

48. Hanover Courthouse (present Hanover) is not to be confused with Hanovertown, the terminal point of

this march. See Chastellux (4), II, 380–381, 569–570.

49. Colles, *Survey*, Plate 74, uses the term "Negro pens."
50. Cf. Colles, *Survey*, Plate 74.

Observations	Description of Marches	Observations, in case the army were to take this route
has suffered war damage. Cornwallis had the fine warehouses burned, as well as several private houses whose owners were suspected of devotion to the cause of independence. There was once a bridge, which is now broken.	You are now out of the woods. You cross a small plain and arrive at Hanovertown on the bank of the Pamunkey River.[51] ½ *Mile* *Total: 18 Miles*	*At Hanovertown — 12th Camp* *(18 Miles)* A camp would be well situated here, as would the headquarters.

102

Itinerary

· 6 ·

THIRTEENTH MARCH

5 October
From Hanovertown to Hartfield[52]

Follow the New Castle road to a crossroads (*patte d'oie*). Take the left. The right-hand road is the one you passed ½ mile from Hanovertown. The middle road leads to a plantation.   ½ *Mile*

The road turns left and is excellent. You cross a marshy bottom on two bridges.   *1 Mile*

New Castle is a small town with very few houses, situated on high ground. It is almost deserted. There are many plantations in the neighborhood.

You go uphill, through thinned-out woods, to New Castle.[53]
    2½ Miles

Coming out of New Castle you pass a crossroads. You proceed downhill, cross a brook, go uphill, then down into some woods. Clearings and cabins. A fork. Take the right. A mile beyond you cross a brook.   *3 Miles*

51. See map, No. 114, which shows the army's camp at Hanovertown in July 1782.
52. See map, No. 162. In addition to Colles's *Survey* (published 1789), Erskine-Dewitt maps, Nos. 124–125

(New-York Historical Society), show this region as it was in the 1780's. The main thoroughfares have now been moved inland from the Pamunkey River.

53. See map, No. 113, and descriptive note. The army camped at New Castle in July 1782, its 5th camp after setting out from Williamsburg. This small town is now extinct.

As you come out of the woods, the ground is higher and more open. Plantations on the right and left. You cross a brook over two bridges. Mill pond and mill on the left.   *2 Miles*

You proceed uphill. At a fork you take the left. Clearings.
                                      1 Mile

Houses on the right. You pass a road on the right. Fork. Take the left.   *½ Mile*

Another fork. Take the right. Several houses on the left. The country is open. Crossroads.
                                      1 Mile

Twelve miles from Hanover-town. A camp could be pitched on this site. There are some houses for the headquarters.

You pass a road on the left and cross a brook. You pass another road on the left and cross a brook. The road forks. Take the left. Half a mile beyond you go down over a brook, which is crossed by two bridges and a ford.
                                      2 Miles

Since this brook runs through a marshy bottom, the bridge needs repairs.

You cross another brook. Fork. Take the left. You cross a ravine on a bridge. House on the left. You enter the woods.   *1 Mile*

You cross a brook.   *2 Miles*

The road forks. Take the right.
                                      ½ Mile

You are still in the woods. You cross a brook.   *1 Mile*

You come to a clearing where

Observations	Description of Marches	Observations, in case the army were to take this route

This is a poor location for a camp.

the wagon train camped. There is a house on the right and another ahead on the left on the height called Hartfield.[54] *1 Mile*
Total: 19 Miles

At Hartfield House — 13th Camp (19 Miles)

This site is very poor for the headquarters, and also for a camp. I think it preferable to camp at the site indicated above, 12 miles from Hanovertown, and from there to march 10 miles to New Kent Courthouse for the next camp.

FOURTEENTH MARCH

6 October
From Hartfield to Byrd's Tavern[55]

Half a mile from the camp you pass a very small tavern on the left and a road on the right. You enter the woods and go through several clearings. Houses on the right and left. You pass a road on the left, another farther on, also on the left, and a fine house. You arrive at New Kent Courthouse.[56] *3 Miles*

There is a fine tavern here.

[At New Kent Courthouse]
[Alternative 13th Camp]
Ten miles from the preferred campsite indicated above [12 miles beyond Hanovertown], camp could be pitched at New Kent Courthouse. There would be some houses available for the headquarters. It would be only 14 miles to Byrd's Tavern.

You leave on the left a road leading into the fields. You are still in the woods. Go through some clearings. Pass on the left a road going to West Point, 10 miles away.[57] *3 Miles*

54. In spite of the reservations expressed here in the marginal observation, the French army made its 4th camp at Hartfield House in July 1782, when marching northward through Virginia. See map, No. 112, and descriptive note.
55. See map, No. 162, also Colles, *Survey*, Plates 75-77.
56. After the conclusion of the Siege

of Yorktown, while the French army was in its 1781-1782 winter quarters, hussars were stationed at James Warren's tavern in New Kent Courthouse, as part of the "chain of expresses," set up to maintain communications with the north. See map, No. 107, and descriptive note. Chastellux ([4], II, 377-380, 566) describes his stop at New Kent Courthouse in

April 1782. The New Kent Ordinary, now a private residence, is still standing and has recently been restored (letters to H. C. Rice from Hunter W. Martin, Richmond, 1963-1964).
57. West Point—"West Point du Sud," as the French sometimes designated it—at the confluence of the Mattaponi and Pamunkey rivers (i.e., head of York River). Artillery units

House on the right. You pass
a road, also on the right, which
leads back into the one you are
on, but it is very bad. You come
to a clearing. Cabins on the left.
1 Mile

You cross a brook in a hollow.
2 Miles

You pass a house on the left.
1 Mile

You proceed downhill and
through a marshy bottom. Then
uphill. Plantations on the right.
You come to [——— ?][58] Tavern
to the left of the road.   *1 Mile*

A road forking left goes to
Ruffin's Ferry, 8 miles beyond.[59]
Take the right.   *1 Mile*

You pass Valentine's house on
the right.[60] Go down to a brook in
a hollow. You are still in the
woods.   *1 Mile*

Go uphill. Leave a house and a
road on the left. You come to
a fork. The left goes to Ruffin's
Ferry, 10 miles away, and to West
Point, 8 miles away. Take the
right.   *2 Miles*

Plantation on the right. You
pass a road on the left and some

---

of Rochambeau's army were quartered at West Point during the winter of 1781–1782. See maps, Nos. 104
and 105, also Clermont-Crèvecœur's
journal.

58. The name, as written in the manuscript, appears to be "Tonyreer's"
or "Congrere."
59. Ruffin's Ferry crossed the Pamunkey River, on the road leading north-

ward from Williamsburg to Port
Royal on the Rappahannock. Cf.
Virginia *Guide*, p. 602.
60. Colles, *Survey*, Plate 76.

Observations	Description of Marches	Observations, in case the army were to take this route
	houses on the right, then some cabins and a road on the left leading toward the York River. You pass a road on the right and arrive at Byrd's Tavern.[61] *2 Miles* *Total: 17 Miles*	[At] Byrd's Tavern — *14th Camp* (*17 Miles*) The camp would be well situated. The tavern is large. There are several houses in the neighborhood for lodging the headquarters staff.

FIFTEENTH MARCH

7 October
From Byrd's Tavern to Williamsburg[62]

Leaving Byrd's Tavern the road is very good. You pass through large clearings, then enter the woods. You pass a meetinghouse on the left.[63] *3 Miles*

You come out of the woods and pass [Ruperthes?] House on the left. You come to a fork where there are two old chimneys.[64] The right-hand road goes to Petersburg via Cole's Ferry [over the Chickahominy]. Take the left-hand road. *1 Mile*

You pass on the right a road leading to Jamestown. *1 Mile*

You are in the woods. You pass through several clearings and leave a road on the left. *1 Mile*

You pass another road on the left; *1 Mile*

61. Byrd's Tavern, also known as Doncastle's Ordinary, was at present Barhamsville. Chastellux ([4], II, 378, 566) describes his stop there in April 1782 and records Mr. Byrd's stories

of Loyalist plundering. The French army camped 2 miles from Byrd's Tavern in July 1782; see map, No. 110.
62. See map, No. 162.

63. Hickory Nut Church, according to Colles, *Survey*, Plate 77.
64. Burnt Ordinary, or "Burnt brick Ordinary," according to Colles, *Survey*, Plate 77.

then still another road on the left and one on the right, also several houses. The country is wooded, with clearings. You come to Allen's Tavern.   *2½ Miles*

   You pass through a large clearing with houses to the right and left. You come out in open country with a house on the left and cabins on the right. You catch sight of Williamsburg and presently arrive in the town.   *6 Miles*
                    Total: 15½ Miles

Total mileage covered by the wagon train of the army from Annapolis to Williamsburg:
                    219 Miles[65]

65. There are slight discrepancies between this summary and Berthier's statement cited above in the introduction to this Itinerary. In the latter he says that the wagon train traveled 230 miles, in 17 days, arriving on 6 October. It will be noted that in this Itinerary the dates run from 21 September to 7 October, but as 30 September has been skipped, this does make a total of 17 days. No doubt the arrival at Williamsburg was spread out over a day or two. Cf. Verger's journal, p. 138 and n. 68, where he mentions the shortage of horses and wagons as of 28 September and says that the train was expected only on 5 October.

Maps and Views

The maps reproduced in this volume form a substantially complete cartographical record of the American campaigns of Rochambeau's army from its arrival in Rhode Island in July 1780 until its return to Brest in June 1783. The original manuscripts from which the reproductions have been made are now scattered in various repositories in France and the United States. They have, however, a common origin, since all of them were drawn by French officers who took part in the war of the American Revolution. A number of them (as well as many others not reproduced here) have been preserved in France with the official records of the French army and navy. Others, which are now in America, once formed part of General Rochambeau's personal archives at the Château de Rochambeau. Still others were preserved at the Château de Grosbois among the personal papers of Louis-Alexandre Berthier until they were dispersed by his descendants in the twentieth-century and likewise found their way to America. The dispersal of family collections also accounts for the presence in the United States of further examples, such as the maps by the engineer Crublier d'Opterre or those illustrating the personal journals of Sublieutenant Jean-Baptiste-Antoine de Verger and of Sublieutenant Joachim du Perron.

The maps are here placed in historical sequence, following the chronology of the campaigns and of the successive "positions" represented. It is thus possible to determine precisely where Rochambeau's army was at a given date. Most of these finished maps were not completed at the moment shown thereon, but all of them presuppose observations or rough sketches made on the spot. The fair copies were carefully drawn and colored, as circumstances permitted, to serve as a record of the campaigns—a record which could eventually be of use in planning future campaigns. With the possible exception of Nos. 43–45 (the New York reconnaissance of July 1781), none of them can be considered "operational" maps. Berthier's maps of the army's marches and campsites, for example, were not prepared in advance as guidance for those directing the marches (although the routes had been reconnoitered and less precise maps were available) but were drawn after the event on the basis of information noted during the actual march. A rough on-the-spot pencil sketch of the 1782 camp at Farmington, Connecticut, and the corresponding finished version of the same (Nos. 149–150) provide evidence of this procedure. In the same way the maps of the Siege of Yorktown (Nos. 87–89) are not the maps actually used in conducting the siege but were drawn shortly thereafter as a record of the event.

Taken as a whole, the maps provide the essential chronological and topographical framework for the narrative journals published in Volume 1 and for the Itineraries in this volume. We hope, too, that they may henceforth serve as a starting point for any serious study of the French participation in the American Revolution by bringing events closer to the realities of time and place. Although our first consideration has been to restore to each map its full historical and military significance, we are aware that they will also be of interest to many people as maps of given localities, since not a few of them are early, if not the earliest, surviving maps of various small areas in the eastern United States. The local antiquarians, the searchers after old roads and old houses, must nevertheless be reminded that, although this is an "atlas" of Rochambeau's campaigns, it is not a geographical atlas providing systematic coverage of states or regions. By definition the maps represent only the areas where the French army sojourned or through which it passed. Nothing but the immediate vicinity of the camps and marches is depicted. In those places where the army remained for longer periods—Rhode Island, Westchester County, and Virginia—larger areas are shown. Finally, since the maps will interest others as examples of cartography, and of eighteenth-century French military cartography in particular, some further comment on the background and training of the cartographers and on the organization of map making in the French army seems appropriate.

An acquaintance with map reading and at least some elementary skill in map making were as a matter of course part of every officer's background. More specialized knowledge and professional training in cartography were cultivated in two branches of the French service in particular: the Corps Royal du Génie (Royal Corps of Engineers) and the Ingénieurs Géographes (Topographical Engineers). The history of these military cartographers—a somewhat intricate one, owing to frequent administrative reorganizations and bureaucratic changes—has been traced in detail in Colonel Berthaut's *Les Ingénieurs géographes militaires*, a work based on the official archives of the French Ministry of War.[1]

In the course of the seventeenth and eighteenth centuries there gradually developed certain distinctions between the "engineers" and the "topographical engineers," the latter being often referred to as the Ingénieurs-Géographes des Camps et Armées du Roi. The engineers, strictly speaking, traditionally concerned themselves primarily with fortifications and related military works, designed according to the principles laid down by Marshal Vauban, whereas the topographical engineers gradually came to have wider responsibilities: "They were expected to reconnoiter and survey the terrain in

1. Colonel Henri M.-A. Berthaut, *Les Ingénieurs géographes militaires, 1624–1831, Etude historique*, 2 vols. (Paris, Imprimerie du Service Géographique, 1902). The subject is also treated more briefly in Berthaut's companion work, *La Carte de France, 1750–1898, Etude historique*, 2 vols. (Paris, Imprimerie du Service Géographique, 1898). The following paragraphs are based on Berthaut's works. See also *Mémorial topographique et militaire rédigé au Dépôt Général de la Guerre*, 5 vols. (Paris, Imprimerie de la République, 1802–1803); Vol. 2, pp. 1–41, includes a "Notice historique sur le Dépôt Général de la Guerre."

advance of the army and especially the routes to be followed; then to draw up plans of the itineraries of the columns on march, of the camps and their exits (*débouchés*); to reconnoiter the enemy's positions, to survey battlefields, fortifications, and localities suitable for defense or for cantonments. In general they executed any topographical work that the commanding officers might need for the conduct of operations, and any that might eventually be useful for drawing up narrative reports on the campaigns."

By the middle of the eighteenth century the topographical service had progressively assumed greater importance. Topographical engineers at work during the War of the Austrian Succession, wearing their own distinctive uniform, are depicted in the colored frontispiece (attributed to Pierre L'Enfant) of an album of manuscript plans of the Battle of Laaffelt (1747).[2] The plans themselves, showing successive phases of the battle, which were meticulously executed by Jean-Baptiste Berthier (1721–1804) and presented to the King in 1748, evidently attracted favorable attention to the work of the topographical engineers.[3] In the course of the next war—the Seven Years' War—Berthier was promoted chief engineer, with ten or more persons under his command. A decree of 1759 defined in detail the functions of the topographical engineers in time of war and of peace. With the completion in 1760 of the Hôtel de la Guerre, a new building in Versailles designed to centralize the hitherto scattered branches of the Ministry of War, the topographical engineers were attached to the Dépôt des Cartes et Plans, maintained by the chief engineer. Berthier père, who had himself designed the building, held the post of "governor" (resident administrative director) of the Hôtel, as well as of the soon-to-be-completed adjacent building housing the Ministries of Marine and Foreign Affairs, which he also designed.[4] During the peaceful interlude following the Seven Years' War the activities of the map makers were thus centered in Versailles. Some of them were completing maps of the recent campaigns. Others were sent overseas to the colonies. Still others were assigned to the mapping of the coasts of France or the frontiers of the kingdom. Under the leadership of J.-B. Berthier the topographical engineers extended their efforts to less strictly military work, such as the so-called "Carte des Chasses du Roi," a detailed map of the King's hunting preserves, which was actually a comprehensive and careful mapping of the environs of Paris.[5] Meanwhile, cartographical techniques were being developed and perfected in line with general scientific progress in this field.[6] Dupain de Montesson,

113

Maps and Views

2. The uniform of the Ingénieurs Géographes, as prescribed by an ordinance of 2 September 1775, is described in detail in the *Etat militaire* for 1776, p. 443. It is depicted in the series of watercolor drawings of uniforms in the Anne S.K. Brown Collection; cf. Vol. I, frontispiece to Clermont-Crèvecœur journal, showing artillerymen taken from this same album.

3. This album is now in the Bibliothèque du Ministère des Armées "Terre" in Paris.

4. See L.-A. Berthier's journal, Vol. I, n. 2 and illustration.

5. See map, No. 10.

6. Instruments and geodetic methods are fully discussed and illustrated by Berthaut (see n. 1). His *Carte de France* (I, 1–70) treats of the famous Cassini map of France, an undertaking that ran parallel to the work of the military engineers during the latter part of the eighteenth century. This "Carte topographique de la France" (sometimes referred to as the "Carte de l'Académie," or the "Carte de l'Observatoire"), begun under the direction of Cassini de Thury in 1750, was eventually completed in 1815, totaling some 180 sheets. Soon after its inception under government auspices it passed into the hands of a privately incorporated com-

one of the topographical engineers, published in 1763 his *L'Art de lever les plans*, an authoritative manual that served as a textbook for new recruits.[7] Among the young men who learned the art of map making at Versailles, under the tutelage of such experts as Dupain de Montesson, were J.-B. Berthier's own sons, Louis-Alexandre and Charles-Louis, who were subsequently to map the camps and marches of Rochambeau's army in America.

In spite of the apparently flourishing state of the topographical engineers (numbering in 1768 twelve captains and sixteen lieutenants, grouped in four brigades of seven), various administrative changes soon troubled the surface calm. In 1772 J.-B. Berthier, though retaining his other functions, was replaced as chief of the topographical engineers by M. de Villaret. In 1776 a royal ordinance assigned the topographers to the Direction du Génie, that is, to the Royal Corps of Engineers, on the grounds that the responsibilities of these two branches of the service had become for all practical purposes inseparable. This amalgamation, which amounted to the suppression of the topographical engineers as a distinct corps, inevitably provoked a lively reaction. In protesting against the reorganization the topographical engineers again redefined what they considered their special functions: "Plans of the camps and their exits (*débouchés*), plans of the marches, surveys of the terrain in advance of the marches, reconnaissances of enemy positions and of any other unforeseen situations—such tasks, executed for the General Staff, for the commanding general as well as for the quartermaster-general, and even for His Majesty himself and his ministers, have always continued to be the basic functions of the topographical engineers. . . ."

The protests had some effect. Two months later an ordinance dated 26 February 1777 redefined the functions of the Royal Corps of Engineers and the Topographical Engineers, entrusting them con-

---

pany (1756), where it remained until it was eventually taken over again by the government in 1793. As Berthaut points out (1, 57), the parallel work of the Cassini engineers and of the military engineers led to considerable duplication of effort and a lack of mutually advantageous interchange. A readable account of the Cassini enterprise and of the development of French cartography in the eighteenth century will be found in Lloyd A. Brown, *The Story of Maps* (Boston, 1949), pp. 241ff.

7. *L'Art de lever les plans, De tout ce qui a rapport à la Guerre, à l'Architecture civile et champêtre . . .* Par M. Dupain de Montesson, Capitaine d'Infanterie, Ingénieur-Géographe des Camps et Armées du Roi (Paris, Chez Ch. Ant. Jombert, Libraire du Roi pour le Génie et l'Artillerie, rue Dauphine, 1763). A second revised edition was published in 1775, a third in 1792; all of them have an engraved frontispiece (Chevalier after Delafue) showing cartographers at work. Among Dupain de Montesson's other publications is his *La Science des Ombres* (Paris, Jombert, 1750), which in-

cludes a section entitled "Le Dessinateur au cabinet et à l'armée." An earlier manual, Jacques Ozanam's *Méthode de lever les plans et les cartes de terre et de mer avec toutes sortes d'instrumens et sans instrumens . . .*, first published in 1693, was reissued several times during the eighteenth century; an edition completely revised by Audierne appeared as late as 1781. The *Mémorial topographique et militaire* (cited above, n. 1) has much material on methods of surveying and executing maps, including (v, 1–64) a report of 1802 on the standardization of conventional symbols used on maps. This report, approved and countersigned by Alexandre Berthier, then minister of war, is illustrated by plates showing "Signes conventionnels pour l'Armée de terre," "Signes conventionnels pour l'Armée de mer," etc. A valuable recent reference work is François de Dainville's *Le Langage des Géographes: Termes, Signes, Couleurs des Cartes anciennes, 1500–1800* (Paris, 1964). An example of a "map in process," showing how the color was applied, etc., is reproduced below, No. 91.

jointly with topographical surveys, on the frontiers in time of peace and with the armies in time of war. It is evident, however, that there was considerable rivalry, even antagonism, between these two hitherto separate branches of the army professionally concerned with cartography. Nevertheless, General de Vault, who was then in charge, continued to issue circulars prescribing high standards for the practitioners, noting among other things that well-executed maps required appropriate harmony "between typography and topography."[8] Thus, as France entered another war, map making was being fostered in the French army both as an art and as a practical necessity.

When planning the expedition to America in 1780 General Rochambeau and his staff not only foresaw the need for competent cartographers but also took pains to gather such cartographical information as was already available. Presumably they found in the Dépôt de la Guerre, or in the corresponding navy map depository, information dating back to the previous war when the French had fought in Canada and the West Indies. Nor were they the first to land on American shores even in the present war. The naval expedition under Admiral d'Estaing, which joined the Americans in Rhode Island in the summer of 1778, had subsequently remained for several months at Boston and had participated the following year in the Siege of Savannah. After the unsuccessful siege several of d'Estaing's ships had visited the Chesapeake Bay; the *Fendant* remained for some weeks during the winter of 1779–1780 in Virginian waters, at which time some of the officers had consulted with Governor Jefferson concerning the defenses of the Yorktown peninsula.[9] Nor should it be forgotten that French engineers had been serving in the American army even before France's official intervention in the war. A map of the "Theatre of War in North America," engraved after a drawing by one of these volunteers (Lafayette's aide, Michel Capitaine du Chesnoy), had already been published in Paris in 1779.[10] Numerous other engraved maps, chiefly of English origin, were available in France and must have been assiduously studied by the officers assigned to Rochambeau's staff. These included both prewar maps of the British colonies and more recent "war maps," drawn by British engineers and subsequently issued as engraved maps by William Faden and other London publishers. They related, for example, to the 1775–1776 campaign in New England, the New York and Long Island campaign of 1776, the campaigns of 1777 and 1778 in New Jersey and Pennsylvania, and to Burgoyne's expedition down the Champlain Valley. Furthermore, geographical publishers in Paris, such as Le Rouge and Beaurain, were keeping abreast of the times by adapting or copying English maps.[11] Characteristic

8. Berthaut, *Ingénieurs géographes*, I, 78.

9. See Clermont-Crèvecœur's journal, Vol. I, n. 140.

10. "Carte du Théâtre de la Guerre dans l'Amérique Septentrionale, pendant les Années 1775, 76, 77, et 78, où se trouvent les principaux Camps avec les différentes Places et Epoques des Batailles qui se sont données pendant ces Campagnes. Gravée d'après le Dessein Original qui a été présenté au Roi, fait par le Sr. Capitaine du Chesnoy Officier Français, Aide de Camp de M. le Marquis de La Fayette, servant alors dans l'Armée Américaine" (Chez Perrier Graveur . . . Et

Chez Fortin, Ingénieur Méchanicien du Roi pour les Globes et Spheres). Reproduced in Doniol, III, between pp. 856 and 857.

11. For example: "Baye de Chesapeake, en 4 feuilles, avec les Bas fonds, Passes, Entrées, Sondes et Routes, où l'on donne les parties Navigables des Rivières Patowmack, Patapsco, et Nord-Est, d'après les Dessins de Navigateurs Expérimentés, principalement d'après A: Smith Pilote de St. Marys; comparée avec les Nouvelles Levées de Virginie et Maryland. Publié à Londres en juillet 1776. Traduit de l'Anglais, A Paris, Chez

examples of engraved maps that Rochambeau used in America are still preserved, as are others once belonging to Crublier d'Opterre, an engineer serving under his command.[12] Thus the officers of Rochambeau's army were not illiterate, cartographically speaking, when they embarked for the United States. The engraved maps that accompanied them as part of their equipment supplied them with the general outlines of the country where they were to campaign. They had the preliminary base maps. The cartographers of Rochambeau's army would supplement and expand these, filling in the details in the course of their own original surveys in the field.

Engineers from the Royal Corps of Engineers were of course assigned to Rochambeau's army. Eight of them, under the command of Colonel Desandroüins, who had already served in America during the Seven Years' War, landed in Newport in July 1780 and immediately set to work surveying the defenses there.[13] The General had also provided for other map makers to be attached to his staff. Writing to Montbarey, the minister of war, as he was setting sail from Brest, Rochambeau mentioned that he had filled in the blank commissions that the minister had given him to complete the General Staff. But, he said, instead of offering the monthly pay of 1,000 francs allowed by the King, he had reduced this to 800 francs, "reserving the balance to pay cadets or officers skilled in drawing who are to be attached to the staff (*élèves ou officiers dessinateurs à la suite de l'état-major*)." The latter would thus cost the King nothing, and everybody would be satisfied. "I have already," he continued, "selected two for this employment: M. Dumas, one of my aides-de-camp, and the Baron von Closen, of the Royal Deux-Ponts Regiment, a relative of the late general of that name, both of whom are good draftsmen."[14] Neither of these "promising young men" was, strictly speaking, a professional

Le Rouge, rue des Grands Augustins, 1778"; collection of William P. Davisson, Marlboro, Vermont. Concerning the English prototype for this map—Anthony Smith's "A New and Accurate Chart of the Bay of Chesapeake"—see note in Baltimore Museum of Art exhibition catalogue *The World Encompassed* (1952), No. 247.

12. Rochambeau's personal collection of engraved maps (as distinguished from the manuscript maps of the American campaigns, which were acquired by the Library of Congress with other Rochambeau papers in 1883) is now in the Library of Paul Mellon, Upperville, Virginia. The Crublier d'Opterre material, also in the Paul Mellon Collection, includes: John Montresor's "A Plan of the City of New York and its Environs . . . Surveyed in the Winter, 1775" (London, A. Drury, 1776); and "The Province of New Jersey, Divided into East and West, commonly called The Jerseys" (London, William Faden, 1 December 1777). This latter map has manuscript additions showing the French army's march from Connecticut to Maryland, the New York reconnaissance, and the battlefields of

Trenton, Monmouth, Germantown, Brandywine, etc. Also in the Crublier d'Opterre papers is a reduced manuscript copy of the Joshua Fry and Peter Jefferson "Map of the most Inhabited Part of Virginia . . ." (London, 1755), on which d'Opterre has added the marches of Rochambeau's army through Virginia.

13. The Engineers who arrived at Newport with Rochambeau's army were: colonel, Desandroüins; lieutenant colonels, Querenet de La Combe, Palys de Montrepos; captains, Crublier d'Opterre, Garavaque, d'Oyré, Turpin; lieutenant, Plancher. Lieutenant Bouan joined them in May 1781. They were reinforced at Yorktown by other Engineers who had come from the West Indies with Saint-Simon's army; see note to map, No. 87. This roster is based on letters of Desandroüins and other Engineers (Archives du Génie, 15-1-7, 34), Library of Congress, Rochambeau Papers, Vol. 3, and *Etat militaire*, 1781, 1782.

14. Rochambeau to Montbarey, on board the *Duc de Bourgogne*, 5 May 1780, printed in Doniol, v, 339, from original in the Archives de la Guerre, A¹3733, fol. 49.

cartographer, though Mathieu Dumas had had considerable previous experience in drafting maps.[15] At the beginning of October there arrived in Newport by a circuitous route two other "good draftsmen," who were soon to find employment as staff map makers. These were the Berthier brothers—Louis-Alexandre and Charles-Louis—both of whom had begun their military careers with professional training as topographical engineers. Indeed, as Louis-Alexandre later wrote, "I grew up in the Dépôt de la Guerre and with the Ingénieurs Géographes."[16] Although they were no longer officially members of this corps (both came to America as captains of dragoons attached to the Soissonnais Regiment), Rochambeau soon recognized their special talents and they straightway set to work surveying the island where the army was encamped. Their large signed "Plan of Rhode Island" (Nos. 7–9) was transmitted, with appropriate commendation from the General, to the ministry in Versailles early in 1781.[17] At the same time Rochambeau noted that he had appointed Louis-Alexandre a supernumerary assistant quartermaster-general (*aide maréchal-général-des-logis surnuméraire*), thus placing him under the direct command of General Béville, the quartermaster-general, in which role he could perform, among other duties, the tasks of a cartographer. Berthier was subsequently to prepare maps of the "camps and marches" of the army, one of the traditional functions of the topographical engineers.

The maps reproduced hereafter give typical samples of the work of these different categories of cartographers. The amateurs or semi-professionals are represented by Dumas (No. 4), Du Perron (Nos. 3, 84, 90, 166), and Verger (in Volume 1). The Royal Corps of Engineers has contributed maps by Crublier d'Opterre and others (Nos. 5, 6, 43, 44, 45, 102, 103, 160, 161). Most of the

15. As a youth Dumas had hoped to enter the engineering school at Mézières but, failing to be admitted there, began his military career in 1773 as a sublieutenant in the Médoc Regiment of infantry. While the regiment was stationed at Briançon in the Alps, Dumas spent much time surveying and drawing maps of the region, under the guidance of M. Doumet, commander of this fortress. See Dumas (1), I, 7–9. Much later, after the Napoleonic Wars (in which he had played a considerable role), Dumas devoted himself to writing on military history and the art of war. In his *Précis des Evénemens militaires, ou Essais historiques sur les Campagnes de 1799 à 1814*, 19 vols. (Paris and Hamburg, 1817–1826) he included short essays "Sur la Topographie" (I, 420–424) and "Sur le service des Etats-Majors" (II, 430–446), in which he reviewed the development of map making and the role of the Topographical Engineers in the planning and conduct of operations.

16. This statement occurs in a memorandum addressed in 1791 by Berthier to Duportail, the same who had served in the American army as Washington's chief of engineers. Duportail was then the French minister of war, a post he held from October 1790 to December 1791 during the final period of the monarchy. Berthier's memorandum is entitled "Mémoire à Monsieur Duportail, Ministre de la Guerre, à l'époque de la nomination de M. Dumas comme Directeur du Dépôt des Cartes et Plans de la Guerre, et dont copie a été remise à M. Dumas" (Archives de la Guerre, Berthier dossier, pièces 59–60). After the death of General de Vault in 1790 the post of Director of the Dépôt de la Guerre went to Mathieu Dumas, Berthier's comrade-in-arms in America and friend of long standing. While admitting Dumas's obvious qualifications, Berthier was evidently chagrined to find that what he considered the even more compelling claims of his father and himself had been overlooked. Seeking security for his family at a moment when events were taking an unpredictable turn, Berthier asked to be made a deputy (*adjoint*) to Dumas, "in special charge of topographical matters"—without pay, and desiring only "to be useful."

17. Rochambeau to Montbarey, Newport, 1 February 1781, printed in Doniol, v, 406–407, from original in the Archives de la Guerre, A¹3733, fol. 193.

other maps come from the papers of Louis-Alexandre Berthier and can thus represent the tradition of the Topographical Engineers. Only a few of the maps are signed. "The Plan of Rhode Island" (No. 7), for example, specifies that it was both surveyed and drawn (*levé et dessiné*) by the Berthier brothers. A bare signature, however, does not necessarily mean that the observations or surveys for the map were made by the signatory, who may merely have drawn it after another's original surveys. Although it is possible in some instances, by reference to signed examples and through similarities or peculiarities of draftsmanship, to deduce the authorship of the unsigned maps, the whole problem of attribution is full of pitfalls. Draftsmen with a common training naturally used the same symbols and the formal impersonal penmanship or lettering they had been taught. Furthermore, once the basic prototype map had been executed, manuscript copies by various hands could be multiplied. The maps on file at headquarters constituted a cartographic pool. Any officer who had access to them could copy them and in turn pass his copy along to be traced by another—perhaps to illustrate a personal journal. Even after the American campaign was over and maps had found their way back into the Dépôt de la Guerre in France, copies could still be made. As indicated in the descriptive notes below (e.g., No. 43), we have in the course of our own investigations found numerous examples of these multiple copies or variant versions of the same map. Authorship, however, is essentially less important for our present purpose than the subject of the map and the information it is intended to convey. These military cartographers could well take pride in their work and were often artists in their craft, but they were in general less concerned with personal glory than their confreres in the "fine arts," such as painters and sculptors. Their maps were a means to an end, designed to serve a practical purpose in the conduct and recording of the war. By the same token the content of the map rather than the author has determined our selection for this volume.

Eschewing the delicate question of the authorship of individual maps and viewing them as a whole, we can nevertheless safely attribute them collectively to the French army. In this respect they invite comparison with the maps produced during the American Revolution by map makers of the American and of the British armies. As one would expect, they are more competently drawn and show greater professional skill than the average American map of the period.[18] The Continental Army was on the whole a nonprofessional army, forged under the pressure of circumstance. The lack of technical engineering skills was one of Washington's early preoccupations and accounts for his continuing dependence on foreign volunteers. Washington's "chief geographer and surveyor-general," Robert Erskine, was born in Scotland and had had training as a civil engineer before coming to America in 1771 to manage iron works in New Jersey for a London syndicate. The surveys made

18. An excellent recapitulation of American maps will be found in Peter J. Guthorn's *American Maps and Map Makers of the Revolution* (Monmouth Beach, N.J., Philip Freneau Press, 1966). See also Albert H. Heusser, *The Forgotten General, Robert Erskine, F.R.S. (1735–1780)* (Paterson, N.J., 1928); new edition by Hubert G. Schmidt, under the title *George Washington's Map Maker, A Biography of Robert Erskine* (New Brunswick, N.J., Rutgers University Press, 1966). Engraved maps pertaining to the Revolution are listed in James Clements Wheat and Christian F. Brun, *Maps and Charts Published in America before 1800, A Bibliography* (New Haven and London, Yale University Press, 1969); manuscript maps do not fall within the purview of this bibliography.

under the direction of Erskine (who was succeeded, after his death in 1780, by Simeon Dewitt) were a notable contribution to American military operations and are still a valuable cartographic source for the study of the war. But, aside from the Erskine maps, most of the surviving American maps, despite their undeniable usefulness at the time, are the work of amateurs. Some of the most finished "American" war maps were done by such French volunteers as Capitaine du Chesnoy, Duportail, Villefranche, and Rochefontaine.

On the other hand, the large corpus of maps emanating from the British army (and navy) and their German auxiliaries can properly be compared to those produced by the French.[19] British engineers and surveyors had been mapping the North American colonies even before the rebellion, so that their war maps were part of a continuing enterprise. The British war maps—many of them published soon after the event—depicted chiefly the localities where hostilities took place. Since the British were involved in the war for a longer period than were the French, the historian will find wider geographical coverage in their maps. Although many of the localities shown in the present volume are also depicted in maps of British origin, there is not complete duplication. In one respect at least the French maps make a unique contribution to the cartography of the American Revolution. To the best of our knowledge the British produced no series of maps like those of the "camps and marches" of Rochambeau's army—possibly because such a concept was peculiar to the French. In recording their campaigns in this manner the French military cartographers labored to better purpose than they knew, by providing Americans of a later generation with a unique and invaluable record of the lay of the land as it was in "megalopolis" some two hundred years ago.

In addition to maps, this volume also includes several views and related pictorial documents. It might be supposed that a number of the French officers would have illustrated their journals with drawings or left sketchbooks of landscapes and other American scenes. This does not, however, appear to be the case. Among the many surviving journals Verger's drawings of American military types and of Indians (reproduced in Volume I) are exceptional.[20] The view of Newport (No. 11) and the small vignette of Yorktown (No. 98) reproduced below are the only such on-the-spot views we have

19. Many examples of these British maps are now in American collections, notably those forming part of Sir Henry Clinton's papers in the Clements Library. See Christian Brun, comp., *Guide to the Manuscript Maps in the William L. Clements Library* (Ann Arbor, University of Michigan, 1959). Maps from the papers of John Graves Simcoe (formerly in the Church collection) are in the Henry E. Huntington Library, San Marino, California, and in the Manuscript Collections of Colonial Williamsburg. Manuscript maps from the papers of Major André are reproduced in Henry Cabot Lodge, ed., *Major André's Journal, 1777–1778 . . . with facsimile reproductions of original maps and plans*, 2 vols. (Boston, 1903). The André maps are now in the Huntington Library. Peter Guthorn has in preparation a companion volume to his *American Maps and Map Makers*, on British maps and map makers of the Revolution. Several of the map makers in the German regiments employed by the British had earlier had training in the French army: for example, Montluisant and Gironcourt de Vomécourt. See also Walter W. Ristow, "Maps of the American Revolution, A Preliminary Survey," *Quarterly Journal of the Library of Congress*, XXVIII, No. 3 (July 1971), 196–215.

20. The sketches reproduced in Evelyn Acomb's edition of Von Closen's journal (cf. "Checklist of Journals," Vol. I) were apparently copied from Verger's journal, as explained below in the descriptive note to No. 47. In addition to these sketches, Von Closen also had in his collection some silhouettes of American ladies, which he brought back from America.

found, though we suspect that others may be hidden away in French family archives. The inclusion of Van Blarenberghe's pictures of the Siege and the Surrender of Yorktown (Nos. 92–97) needs no justification. These were not actually executed in America but are nevertheless based upon documents supplied by officers who were there. They are executed with the meticulous care for authentic detail characteristic of the "battle painters," who were closely associated with the Topographical Engineers at the Hôtel de la Guerre in Versailles. To supplement these French views we have added glimpses of Rochambeau and his army in America as depicted by the American artists James Peale and John Trumbull (Nos. 101 and 144). Since we have not found examples of the maps drawn by officers of Rochambeau's army during their 1783 campaign in the Caribbean, we have reconstructed the record from other French sources with engraved maps and views by their near contemporaries.

The descriptive notes hereinafter constitute both a *catalogue raisonné* of the maps and views and a table of contents. The military significance of the maps and their relation to the events of the war have been primary considerations in their selection. The short titles are a translation or close paraphrase of the French titles appearing on the maps. Essential verbal information on the maps themselves or in the legends has also been translated as an aid to readers unfamiliar with French. In our notes place names have been normalized in accordance with standard present-day usage. Modern equivalents of those place names that have changed since the eighteenth century have been explained or inserted in square brackets. Natural features and other points of reference not named on the maps have been identified in order to facilitate correlation with twentieth-century maps. Some of the changes brought about by the subsequent growth of roads, cities, dams, and other public works have been noted as a further aid to identification of the localities shown. The present ownership of the original maps is indicated. Similar maps, not reproduced, are also located. Although practical considerations have made it impossible to reproduce all the maps in actual size, the dimensions of the original are consistently recorded in our descriptive notes. Many of the maps include their own scale. In a few instances the distances are expressed in miles (e.g., Nos. 4, 40, 102, 162). The Berthier brothers' large map of Rhode Island (No. 7) has a double scale using both the *lieue commune de France* (common league of France, about 2.5 miles) and the *lieue commune d'Angleterre* (English league, about 3 miles). On the maps showing more limited areas the cartographers generally used the old French measures of their time, the *pouce* (inch), *pied* (foot), and the *toise*, which was equivalent to 1.949 meters, that is, approximately 2 English yards. (The metric system was not adopted in France until 1795.) In some instances (notably in the series of road maps and campsites) the maps have been rearranged on our pages, thus eliminating the blank spaces and margins of the original sheets; the content of the map itself, however, has been retained complete. We deem ourselves fortunate in being able to reproduce a large proportion of the maps in color, for color is part of the cartographer's language and much is lost when they are restricted to black and white.

The maps and views (as well as the illustrations in Volume 1) have been reproduced in offset lithography by The Meriden Gravure Company, which has shown great patience and much ingenuity in devising means to preserve the spirit and the artistry of the originals. Roughly two-thirds of the maps have not hitherto been reproduced in any form.

Synopsis

MAPS AND VIEWS RECORDING ROCHAMBEAU'S AMERICAN CAMPAIGNS

121
*Maps
and
Views*

122
*Maps
and
Views*

Maps and Views

DESCRIPTIVE NOTES

Departure from Brest
May 1780

*1 Brest, Entrance to the
Port, by Louis-Nicolas
Van Blarenberghe, 1776*

Rochambeau's army departed for America from Brest in the ships of Ternay's fleet on 2 May 1780. Vaudreuil's fleet brought the army back to Brest on 17 June 1783. Brest was France's principal Atlantic naval base (with Toulon as its Mediterranean counterpart) and the main port of embarkation for troops going overseas.

The first of Van Blarenberghe's views shows the entrance to the port, looking from the battery on the western side of the Penfeld across to the fortified Château on the opposite bank (see "A" on map, next page). At the far right is the bay and roadstead of Brest. In the background to the left of the Château part of the city can be discerned; far left of the picture is the part of the town known as Recouvrance. The two ships (not further identified) entering the port have presumably been damaged in a storm.

These views of Brest are the work of the same artist who did the "Siege" and "Surrender" of Yorktown, reproduced below, Nos. 92–97.

Watercolor and gouache, 37 x 59.5 cm. Signed, lower right, "Van Bla . . . ," no date (perhaps cut off), but presumably same as its companion piece. Musée du Louvre, Cabinet des Dessins, RF 3475.

*2 Brest, the Inner Port,
by Louis-Nicolas Van
Blarenberghe, 1776*

The second view of Brest shows part of the inner port, with the arsenal and other installations of the French Royal Navy.

Returning to Brest after his three years of campaigning overseas, Verger noted in his journal (p. 180): "At Brest you see a sample of the power of the King of France in the multiple storehouses filled with all necessary provisions to equip several fleets, the large number of workmen employed in the port, the special machines to keep the harbor from silting, the yard where the masts of vessels are stepped, the superb drydocks where vessels are repaired, the mechanical pumps to expel water, and many other devices revealing to what heights man's industry has carried him in this field."

Watercolor and gouache, 38.2 x 60 cm. Signed and dated, lower right, "Van Blarenberghe 1776." Musée du Louvre, Cabinet des Dessins, RF 3476.

3 Brest and Environs, Map by Du Perron, 1780

This map was drawn by Joachim du Perron in the summer of 1780, not long after the departure of Rochambeau's army. The road from Paris, via Landerneau, leads in from the right to the fortified city of Brest, divided into two sections by the Penfeld River, which constitued the "port" or harbor proper. The ancient "Château" (right of the letter "A") defended the entrance to the port and protected the anchorage for warships ("mouillage des vaisseaux de guerre"). To the left (west) of "G" is "Le Goulet," the narrow channel leading out from the bay and roadstead of Brest to the open sea. "H" indicates the fort at Bertheaume; "K," Pointe de Saint-Mathieu.

At this time the defenses of the city were being strengthened by the construction of an outer ring of forts at "B," "C," "D," "E," "F," and "G." Du Perron notes that men from his detachment were put to work on the forts while awaiting embarkation and remarks that many people thought them useless. Sublieutenant du Perron was with a detachment from the "Régiment d'Infanterie de Monsieur" quartered at Le Conquet ("L," upper left of map). Towards the end of July their enforced residence in this small fishing village was enlivened by an incident described in du Perron's journal (printed version, pp. 10–11, "Une petite alerte") and represented here on his map: "R" designates the French cutter *Levrette*, commanded by the Chevalier de La Bourdonnaye, which had been chased from near Ushant by the 70-gun English warship *Nonsuch* ("S"). The *Levrette* reached the protection of the coastal battery at Kermorvan ("M") just in time to head off a French convoy ("q") coming down the channel from Saint-Malo under escort of the corvette *Prince Henri* ("P"). The English ship, which had hoisted the Spanish flag as a ruse, headed towards Brest but eventually veered about and sailed out to sea again.

"Les Pierres Noires," the dangerous reef mentioned in Verger's journal (p. 180), is shown here to the left (west) of "S." In the upper left corner of the map are the Molène Islands, situated some 6 miles southeast of the island of Ouessant (Ushant), which is not included here.

MS, 37 x 47 cm. (sheet measurement). Princeton University Library, in MS journal of Joachim du Perron, comte de Revel, folding plate between pp. 4 and 5. Hitherto unpublished; not reproduced in printed version of journal.

4 *Plan of Newport and Vicinity showing the Camp occupied by the Troops commanded by the Comte de Rochambeau, with the Anchorage of the Warships and Transports commanded by the Chevalier de Ternay, by Mathieu Dumas, July 1780*

The map is signed by Rochambeau's aide-de-camp Mathieu Dumas and dated 12 July 1780. It was thus drawn at the time of the landing and may rank as the first of the numerous extant maps of Newport and vicinity subsequently made by officers of Rochambeau's army. Rochambeau and his aides went ashore on 11 July; the landing of the troops began on the 12th. In a dispatch to the minister of war, Montbarey, dated Newport, 19 July 1780, Rochambeau wrote: "I have the honor of sending you herewith the plan of our position and that of the fleet; it is most correct and was drawn by my aide-de-camp, M. Dumas" (Doniol, v, 346). Upon leaving France Rochambeau had informed the Minister that he intended to use two of his promising young staff officers for map work: "M. Dumas, one of my aides-de-camp, and the Baron de Closen, a relative of the late general of that name, both of whom are good draftsmen" (Rochambeau to Montbarey, 5 May 1780, in Doniol, v, 339). An example of Von Closen's draftsmanship, an untitled manuscript plan of the island of Rhode Island signed "Closen fecit," is in the John Carter Brown Library in Providence.

Dumas's map, as indicated, was drawn "at sight" (*levé à vue*), that is, free hand, without benefit of surveying instruments. No. 1 indicates the position of the army's camp; 2, the vanguard (on The Neck); 3, different outposts of the army and vanguard; 4, former English lines and new redoubts built by the French; 5, artillery and munitions (*réserve*); 6, park; and 7, new batteries.

Comparison with the following maps shows that the ships are not yet at the anchorage they subsequently took after the alert of 21 July. See Clermont-Crèvecœur's journal, p. 18, and Verger's journal, p. 120.

MS, 42.5 x 52.5 cm. Bibliothèque du Ministère des Armées "Terre," Paris, L.I.D. 113 ("C" of five items classified under this number).

5 *Camp of the French Army, near Newport, Rhode Island, Map by Crublier d'Opterre*

This is a detail from "Plan de la Ville, Rade, et Environs de Newport, avec le Campement de l'Armée Françoise près de cette Place en 1780, La Disposition des Ouvrages qu'elle a exécuté et le Mouillage de l'Escadre," by Henri Crublier d'Opterre, captain in the Royal Corps of Engineers.

The colors used here to designate the different units correspond to the colors of their uniforms. All French infantry regiments (in contradistinction to foreign regiments in French service and to staff officers, artillery, engineers, etc.) wore white uniforms with various colored facings to identify the regiment. No. 47 on the map is the Saintonge Regiment, whose white uniforms had green cuffs and piping; 46 is the Soissonnais, white with crimson lapels and cuffs; 45 is the Royal Deux-Ponts, who wore light blue uniforms with yellow lapels and cuffs; 44 is the Bourbonnais, white with black cuffs and piping. No. 43 designates the Auxonne artillery, whose uniforms (like those of other artillery regiments) were dark blue with red collars, cuffs, and tail facings. (See frontispiece to Clermont-Crèvecœur's journal.) Lauzun's Legion of Foreign Volunteers, stationed near Castle Hill on The Neck, 48, is tinted light blue and yellow, denoting the uniform color of its hussars.

Crublier d'Opterre's map in its complete form is similar (both in area covered and in legend) to maps done at this same time by other officers of the Royal Corps of Engineers; cf. the next item. In a letter written from Newport, 13 August 1780 (Archives du Génie, 15–1–7, pièce 34–1), Crublier d'Opterre reported that he and the other engineers had been continuously occupied since their arrival, first in repairing the old English fortifications and then in constructing new ones: "We are establishing around this town a line of defense formed by strong redoubts that will be linked by communications." He apologized for the illegibility of his letter by saying that he was writing it outdoors while supervising work on the defenses, which he had been doing from morning to night ever since his arrival. Querenet de La Combe, lieutenant colonel in the Corps of Engineers, in a letter to his superiors in France, reported on 8 September: "M. Desandroüins is now able, or will be shortly, to send you very detailed plans and reports" (Archives du Génie, 15–1–7, pièce 34–3).

Thus these engineers' maps of Newport and vicinity (or their prototypes) must have been completed by 1 October 1780. The Berthier brothers, who did not reach Newport until 30 September, would have been able to consult them when preparing their own large map of Rhode Island, reproduced here as No. 7.

MS, 48.2 x 59.2 cm. (dimensions of complete map). Library of Paul Mellon, Upperville, Virginia, Crublier d'Opterre MS No. 5.

6 Position of the French Army around Newport, 1780

This is a detail from a very large map compiled in the autumn of 1780 by the Royal Corps of Engineers under the direction of Colonel Desandroüins. The map as a whole was intended primarily to indicate field fortifications: new works constructed by the French, old works built by the English during their occupation of the town and now repaired by the French, and abandoned or nearly ruined English works. Among the new French works shown on the portion of the map reproduced here are:

6. Saintonge redoubt
7. Tail-of-the-Pond redoubt
8. Head-of-the-Pond redoubt
9. Left lunette of the camp
10. Right lunette of the camp

Among the English works repaired by the French are:

22. Dyer's Point battery
28. *Flèche* ruined by Sullivan
29. Redoubt on left of Flood Road
30. Easton redoubt
31. Artillery Park battery

Ruined English works include: Nos. 36–37, communication lines. No. 40

indicates flood dikes; 41, battery above Easton's beach. Nos. 43–47 designate the regimental camps, as on the preceding map.

There are several smaller versions of this same map: e.g., in Archives du Génie, 15–1–7, pièce 27, signed by Desandroüins; and a copy by Colbert de Maulevrier in the William L. Clements Library (Brun, No. 281, reproduced opposite p. 68).

MS, 150 x 117 cm. (dimensions of complete map, which is entitled "Plan de la Position de l'Armée Françoise autour de Newport et du Mouillage de l'Escadre dans la Rade de cette Ville, 1780"). The detail reproduced here is about one-half actual size. Library of Congress, Map Division, Rochambeau Map No. 41.

7 *Plan of Rhode Island occupied by the French Army under the Orders of the Comte de Rochambeau, and of the French Fleet commanded by M. Destouches, with the Islands and Channels between it and the Mainland, by L.-A. and C.-L. Berthier*

This is the large map of the whole island surveyed by L.-A. Berthier and his brother Charles during the late autumn and early winter of 1780, mentioned in the elder Berthier's journal (n. 40). It was transmitted by Rochambeau to Montbarey, minister of war, in a dispatch dated 1 February 1781. The map reflects the techniques and skills acquired by the Berthier brothers in the course of their recent work on the "Carte des Chasses du Roi" under the direction of their father, director of the Ministry of War's Dépôt des Cartes in Versailles.

MS, 120.7 x 114.6 cm. Signed, lower left, "Levé et dessiné par Berthier et Berthier de Berlui Capitaines de Dragons servant à la suite du Régiment d'Infanterie de Soissonnais." Bibliothèque du Ministère des Armées "Terre," Paris, L.I.D. 140. A similar map, unsigned, is preserved at the Château de Grosbois (until recently the estate of Berthier's descendants, and now owned by the Société d'Encouragement à l'Elevage du Cheval Français).

8 *Newport and Harbor, Detail from the Berthier Brothers' Plan of Rhode Island*

The position of the French navy's ships are shown, with the range of their guns, as well as the coastal batteries protecting the entrance to the Harbor.

9 *Neighborhood of Newport, Detail from the Berthier Brothers' Plan of Rhode Island*

This portion of the map includes parts of the towns of Middletown and of Portsmouth. The road running diagonally across the sheet is the East Main Road (State Route 138), here called "Chemin du Passage [du Bac]."

Comparing this map with the next facing it, one is tempted to retitle it "Carte des Chasses du Rhode Island."

10 *"Carte des Chasses du Roi," Detail showing Château de Grosbois*

See Berthier's journal, n. 2, for a discussion of this famous map, in which the Berthier family had a large share. From surveys begun as early as 1764 finished maps were gradually accumulated but were not published in engraved form until 1807. The detail reproduced here shows Grosbois, the estate southeast of Paris acquired by Berthier in the early 1800's. Among the titles bestowed upon him by Napoleon was that of "Grand Veneur" (Grand Master of the Hunt). On Grosbois, see Editors' Introduction to Berthier's journal, n. 42.

Detail, actual size, from sheet 9 of *Carte Topographique des Environs de Versailles, dite des Chasses Impériales* (as the "Carte des Chasses du Roi" was called when published in 12 sheets, Paris, 1807). Engraving by Dondan, Tardieu l'aîné, and Boudet. Modern restrike from original plates, Princeton University Library.

11 View of the City, Harbor, and Roadstead of Newport [March–April 1781]

This view was presumably drawn in March or April 1781, since it shows among the ships (K) the *Romulus*, which was captured from the English off the Chesapeake Capes on 19 February 1781 and brought into Newport on the 24th; the full title refers to the commander of the French squadron as Destouches, who relinquished his temporary command to Admiral Barras on 10 May. Cf. Clermont-Crèvecœur's journal, nn. 15 and 21. The view is taken from the south side of the harbor looking north; Brenton's Point (where Fort Adams is now situated) is in the foreground, far left (G). The tallest of the spires is Trinity Church. To the right of it is the spire of the First Congregational Church (Mill Street); to the left, the spire of the Second Congregational Church (Clarke Street) and then the Colony House. This drawing, quite possibly the work of L.-A. Berthier, was included as an extra-illustration to the manuscript journal of Cromot Dubourg, who did not himself reach Newport until May 1781.

Pen and watercolor drawing, 19 x 48 cm. Historical Society of Pennsylvania, Philadelphia. Formerly with Cromot Dubourg's manuscript journal (AM 6360), but now classified with Prints and Drawings, Bc 68 R 346.

12 Engagement of 16 March 1781, between the French Squadron commanded by Destouches and the English Squadron commanded by Arbuthnot, at the Entrance to the Chesapeake Bay

Successive phases of the encounter of the two squadrons are shown here in a series of ten diagrams. Destouches's squadron, with troops from Rochambeau's army aboard, left Newport on 8 March 1781 and returned there on the 26th, after an indecisive engagement with the English on 16 March. The expedition—a preview of the later, successful Yorktown operation—was expected to effect a junction of French and American forces for a joint operation against the English in Virginia. An official *Relation* of the Destouches expedition is included in Verger's journal, pp. 126–128 and nn. 30–33. The journal of Berthier (who was on the *Neptune*) also describes the engagement depicted here (pp. 242–244).

MS, approx. 45 x 72 cm. Bibliothèque du Ministère des Armées "Terre," Paris, L.I.D. 43.

March from Rhode Island to the Hudson June - July 1781

Road Maps

13 Figuration of the Route and of the different Camps occupied by the French Army from Providence to the Junction of the Two Armies at the Philipsburg Camp

This heading appears on the cover of the first of a series of "cahiers" containing the road maps of the army's march. Each sheet includes the route for one day's march, usually covered on four successive days by the four divisions. The point of departure is at the left, the destination at the right. The campsites are shown in more detail in another series of maps, below, Nos. 26ff. The large "General Map of Camps and Marches" (No. 162) covering the entire Atlantic seaboard from New England to Virginia provides a recapitulation and summary of the route. The "Itineraries," above, give a detailed description of the route and should be read as a commentary on the road maps; further identification of localities is given in the notes to the "Itineraries." See also the pertinent portions of Clermont-Crèvecœur's journal (pp. 28ff.) and of Berthier's journal (pp. 246ff.).

MS, 22.5 x 15.5 cm. (dimensions of cahier when closed; the fold-out sheets are of varying width). Princeton University Library, Berthier Papers, No. 14 (1–12). No other set of these road maps has been found. The wash in this cahier (our Nos. 14–25) is brownish yellow, but green in those following (our Nos. 48ff.).

14 First Day's March: from Providence to Waterman's Tavern

This map shows the route taken by the four divisions, successively, on 18–21 June 1781. The composition of the divisions is explained in the "Plan for taking the Army from Providence to King's Ferry on the east bank of the Hudson River . . . ," above, Itinerary 1. "Among Town" is Monkey Town (Knightsville). The "Patasket" is the Pawtuxet River. Waterman's Tavern was in the town of Coventry, Rhode Island (near present Pottersville).

MS, 22.5 x 27.5 cm. Princeton University Library, Berthier Papers, No. 14-1. The dimensions given here for the road maps are those of the sheet on which the original was drawn; as reproduced, the blank margins have been eliminated and the maps themselves repositioned on the pages.

15 Second Day's March: from Waterman's Tavern to Plainfield [in Connecticut]

19–22 June 1781. The "Musclover" is the Moosup River. "Walen Town" is Voluntown (now Sterling Hill, Connecticut); "Dalens Taverne" is Dorrance's Tavern. The army camped here on its return march the following year, 8–9 November 1782; see No. 155, below.

MS, 22.5 x 40 cm. Princeton University Library, Berthier Papers, No. 14-2.

16 Third Day's March: from Plainfield to Windham

20–23 June 1781. The curious reversed lettering of "chemin de Boston," left of Windham on the map, is presumably a copyist's error, perhaps arising from some tracing device used when making a fair copy of the map.

MS, 22.5 x 36 cm. Princeton University Library, Berthier Papers, No. 14-3.

17 Fourth Day's March: from Windham to Bolton

21–24 June 1781. The "Rivière de Windham" is now called the Shetucket. The 4th camp was located in the town of Bolton, at the spot now known as Bolton Center.

MS, 22.5 x 38 cm. Princeton University Library, Berthier Papers, No. 14-4.

18 Fifth Day's March: from Bolton to East Hartford

The four divisions arrived in succession on 22, 23, 24, and 25 June 1781. Each division halted here for two extra days, the Fourth leaving only on 28 June. The artillery park (indicated here and elsewhere in pink) was ferried across the river and camped beyond Hartford while the infantry regiments were encamped in East Hartford; cf. Berthier's journal, p. 247.

MS, 22.5 x 32 cm. Princeton University Library, Berthier Papers, No. 14-5.

19 Sixth Day's March: from East Hartford to Farmington

25–28 June 1781. The white square to the left of the word "Hartford" corresponds to the present site of the Old State House (built in 1796). The symbol resembling two posts (I I) on the crest of the hill, above the letter

"D" of Hartford, designated the gallows on Gallows Hill. See Itinerary 2, n. 26, where this "justice" is mentioned; cf. François de Dainville, *Le Langage des Géographes* (Paris, 1964), pp. 301–302, Fig. 44. "West Division" is the older term for West Hartford, which was set up as a separate town only in 1854.

MS, 22.5 x 32.5 cm. Princeton University Library, Berthier Papers, No. 14–6.

20 Seventh Day's March: from Farmington to Barnes's Tavern

26–29 June 1781. The cluster of houses designated here as "Formington. Village" is within the boundaries of the present town of Plainville (incorporated in 1869). "Soudington" is Southington. "Baron's Taverne," where the army camped, was Barnes's Tavern, in present Marion in the town of Southington, Connecticut, on what was later named French Hill. The "Chn. de meridon," beyond Barnes's Tavern, is the Meriden Road.

MS, 22.5 x 27 cm. Princeton University Library, Berthier Papers, No. 14–7.

21 Eighth Day's March: from Barnes's Tavern to Break Neck

27–30 June 1781. The "Nacketack" is the Naugatuck River at Waterbury. Break Neck Hill, where the army camped, is in the town of Middlebury, a high point between the watershed of the Naugatuck to the east and the Housatonic to the west. The French all seemed to agree (cf. Clermont-Crèvecœur's journal, p. 30) that Break Neck was indeed a *casse-cou*.

MS, 22.5 x 32 cm. Princeton University Library, Berthier Papers, No. 14–8.

22 Ninth Day's March: from Break Neck to Newtown

The four divisions arrived successively at the Newtown camp on 28, 29, 30 June, and 1 July 1781. The first three each halted here an extra day, but the fourth (including the Saintonge Regiment) made no extra day's halt. From here on the army marched by brigades of two divisions each. The First Brigade (including the Bourbonnais and Deux-Ponts regiments) left Newtown during the night of 30 June–1 July; the Second Brigade (including the Soissonnais and Saintonge regiments) left on 2 July. "Woodbury" here designates, not the present town of Woodbury, which is farther north, but a part of Southbury, which was separately incorporated from Woodbury only in 1787. The "Rivière de Stratford" is now called the Housatonic; the crossing shown here is near the site of the present Shepaug Dam.

MS, 22.5 x 37.5 cm. Princeton University Library, Berthier Papers, No. 14–9.

23 Tenth Day's March: from Newtown to Ridgebury

1–2 July 1781. The army was now marching by brigades. The camp was at Ridgebury, a locality or parish in the northern part of the town of Ridgefield, Connecticut. Ridgebury is some 5 miles north of the village of Ridgefield proper. The map shows the camp by brigades, with a detachment of grenadiers and chasseurs in an advanced position. "Miry Broug" is Miry Brook.

MS, 22.5 x 31.5 cm. Princeton University Library, Berthier Papers, No. 14–10.

24 Eleventh Day's March: from Ridgebury [in Connecticut] to North Castle [in New York]

While the French were camped at Ridgebury, orders were received for a change of itinerary. Instead of proceeding westward from Ridgebury to join the Americans at Peekskill on the Hudson, as originally planned, the French army now veered to the southwest to join their allies at Philipsburg.

See Clermont-Crèvecœur's journal, nn. 31–32, and Berthier's journal, p. 248. The First Brigade, leaving Ridgebury on 2 July, bivouacked at Bedford (present Bedford Village) and proceeded next day to the camp at North Castle (present Mount Kisco, Westchester County, New York). The Second Brigade covered the whole distance from Ridgebury to North Castle, by a slightly different route, in a single day's march on 3 July 1781. This road map shows only the route of the Second Brigade. The "Pond" indicated midway along the route is Lake Waccabuc. The bridge over the Cross River is now inundated by the Cross River Reservoir. The "justice," noted along the route between the Cross River and North Castle, indicates a gallows, commemorated in the present name of Hangman's Hill.

MS, 22.5 x 48 cm. (including hinged square, upper right). Princeton University Library, Berthier Papers, No. 14–11.

25 Twelfth Day's March: from North Castle to Philipsburg

On 6 July 1781 the French army marched in a single column from its camp at North Castle (Mount Kisco) south to Philipsburg, where it joined the American army. The Philipsburg camp, where the allied armies remained until 18–19 August, was on the heights between the Bronx and Sawmill rivers within the limits of the present town of Greenburgh, Westchester County, New York.

The right column of the French army followed this route again, in the opposite direction, when marching northward to King's Ferry, 19 August 1781. See Itinerary 3.

MS, 22.5 x 51 cm. Princeton University Library, Berthier Papers, No. 14–12.

March from Rhode Island to the Hudson June - July 1781

Camp Plans

26 Plans of the Different Camps occupied by the Army under the Orders of the Comte de Rochambeau: Campaign of 1781

This is the cover of a "cahier" containing maps of the army's camps from Rhode Island to Virginia. The key indicates that artillery units are tinted in pink, French troops yellow, and American troops green. Light-green tinted areas marked "b" show "bois," i.e., woods; blue designates water. Note also that the yellow-tinted symbols for French regiments, when enclosed in a dotted line, indicate positions occupied in 1782 (on the northward return march from Virginia to New England) by the Royal Deux-Ponts and Saintonge regiments, then marching together as a brigade. Since some of these maps thus combine information concerning the 1781 and 1782 campaigns, it is evident that the finished copies reproduced here were not completed until after 1782, perhaps after Berthier's return to France. For a single surviving example of the rough field sketches made on the spot, see No. 150. The maps of the 1781 camps illustrated here are reproduced from a set in the Berthier Papers, Princeton University Library, formerly in the Château de Grosbois. A second set, now in the Library of Paul Mellon, was once among Rochambeau's papers in the Château de Rochambeau. A few minor variations, such as the omission of certain names, seem to signify that the General's set was copied from Berthier's own set. Still another series of these camp plans, somewhat similar to the Berthier set but much smaller in size, are included in a manuscript entitled "Précis des Opérations et des Marches de l'Armée combinée française et américaine pendant la Campagne de 1781," in the Henry E. Huntington Library, San Marino, California (MS HM 621); see "Checklist of Journals," *s.v.* Soissonnais Regiment.

For further commentary on the localities represented, see Itineraries 1 and 2, and the pertinent parts of the journals of Clermont-Crèvecœur and of Berthier.

MS, 32 x 21 cm. Princeton University Library, Berthier Papers, No. 21. The dimensions noted for the camp plans are the outside measurements of the sheet on which the original was drawn. In the reproductions two plans have in many cases been regrouped on a single page, thus eliminating blank portions of the original sheets.

27 *First Camp at Providence*

10–11 June 1781. As stated in the heading, the troops had come from Newport to Providence by water. The road junction above the letter "P" in the word Providence represents the corner of present Westminster and Weybosset Streets. The "chemin de Waterman's Tavern" (leading to the next campsite) is present Cranston Street.

The army camped again on this site in November 1782, where the units shown within dotted lines are positioned on the present map; see note to No. 156.

MS, 32 x 21 cm. Princeton University Library, Berthier Papers, No. 21–1. Rochambeau's copy is in the Library of Paul Mellon, Upperville, Virginia.

28 *Second Camp at Waterman's Tavern*

18–21 June 1781. Fifteen miles from the preceding camp at Providence. The dates on the maps of the camps, here and subsequently, are those of the arrival of the First Division. Since the army was marching in four divisions, each camp was occupied on at least four successive days. The maps are so oriented that the direction of the march is at the top of the sheet. The incoming and outgoing roads are generally designated by the point of departure of the day's march and by the next day's destination: in this instance, the Providence road and the Plainfield road. Waterman's Tavern is in the town of Coventry, Rhode Island. The "chemin de Providence" is now Matteson Road. The tavern itself is on Maple Valley Road. The "meeting-house" is no longer standing; State of Rhode Island Historic Cemetery, Coventry 37, is near the site. The stream on the left is Turkey Meadow Brook.

The army camped again on this site, by brigades, in November 1782, as indicated here by the units enclosed in dotted lines.

MS, 32 x 21 cm. Princeton University Library, Berthier Papers, No. 21–2. Rochambeau's copy is in the Library of Paul Mellon, Upperville, Virginia.

29 Third Camp at Plainfield [in Connecticut]

19–22 June 1781. Fifteen miles from the preceding camp at Waterman's Tavern. Plainfield's main street, running from south to north (left to right on the map), is present State Route 12. The stream, to the west of which the camp was located, is Horse Brook.

MS, 32 x 21 cm. Princeton University Library, Berthier Papers, No. 21–3. Rochambeau's copy is in the Library of Paul Mellon, Upperville, Virginia.

30 Fourth Camp at Windham

20–23 June 1781. Fifteen miles from the preceding camp at Plainfield. The pattern of the town, as shown here, is readily recognizable today. The "Windham River," on the east bank of which the army camped, is now called the Shetucket. "Chemin de Marshfield" is presumably an error for Mansfield.

On its return march in November 1782 the army camped again at Windham, but on a different site, east of the town; see No. 153.

MS, 32 x 21 cm. Princeton University Library, Berthier Papers, No. 21–4. Rochambeau's copy is in the Library of Paul Mellon, Upperville, Virginia.

31 Fifth Camp at Bolton

21–24 June 1781. Sixteen miles from the preceding camp at Windham. Bolton, with its "meeting house," is now known as Bolton Center. The present main highway (U.S. Route 6) passes northeast of Bolton Center, along the Hop River valley and over Bolton Notch.

The army marched through Bolton Center again in November 1782 but camped "2 miles beyond Bolton Meetinghouse," as shown on map, No. 152.

MS, 32 x 21 cm. Princeton University Library, Berthier Papers, No. 21–5. Rochambeau's copy is in the Library of Paul Mellon, Upperville, Virginia.

32 Sixth Camp at East Hartford

22–28 June 1781. Twelve and a half miles from the preceding camp at Bolton Center. Each of the four infantry regiments halted here for two extra days. The positions shown nearest to the Connecticut River indicate the camp of the Bourbonnais on the right (22–23–24 June, replaced by the Saintonge, 25–26–27 June) and the Royal Deux-Ponts on the left (23–24–25 June). The position along the road from Bolton, in the lower part of the map, is that of the Soissonnais (24–25–26 June). Since the Saintonge departed only on 28 June, the East Hartford camp was occupied continuously from the 22nd to the 28th. The stream at the lower part of the map is the Hockanum River.

The 1782 encampment at East Hartford is shown on map, No. 151.

MS, 32 x 21 cm. Princeton University Library, Berthier Papers, No. 21–6. Rochambeau's copy is in the Library of Paul Mellon, Upperville, Virginia.

33 Seventh Camp at Farmington

25–28 June 1781. Twelve and a half miles from the preceding camp at East Hartford. This map shows only the southern part of Farmington's Main Street (cf. map of the 1782 camp, No. 149, which includes the northern part of the street). The brook at the bottom of the map, flowing under the road and into the larger stream at the right (Pequabuck), is Diamond Glen Brook. The camp ("a mile from Farmington," according to Itinerary 2, above) was on the west side of the main road (present Route 10) just beyond its junction with Scott Swamp Road (present Route 6).

34 Eighth Camp at Barnes's Tavern

26–29 June 1781. Thirteen miles from the preceding camp at Farmington. The tavern kept by Asa Barnes was in the locality now known as Marion in the southwestern part of the town of Southington. A local historian, the Reverend Herman R. Timlow, in his *Sketches of Southington, Conn.* (Hartford, 1875) notes that in June 1781 "the French army, under the command of Count de Rochambeau passed through the town," and adds: "Marshall[!] Berthier was aid to the Count."

The position shown within dotted lines denotes the second of two regiments that camped here together on 26–27 October 1782, when the army was marching by brigades.

ms, 32 x 21 cm. Princeton University Library, Berthier Papers, No. 21–8. Rochambeau's copy is in the Library of Paul Mellon, Upperville, Virginia.

35 Ninth Camp at Break Neck

27–30 June 1781. Thirteen miles from the preceding camp at Barnes's Tavern. Break Neck Hill is in the town of Middlebury. The stream is Hop Brook; its enlargement is now called Abbott's Pond. Bronson's Tavern (here shown left of letter "B") is on present Artillery Road. The portion of the road passing through the encampment (artillery on left side) is now abandoned; only the right-hand swing of the loop remains. As denoted by the regimental symbol enclosed in a dotted line, the French camped here again in October 1782 when marching in the opposite direction on their way to Hartford and Providence.

ms, 32 x 21 cm. Princeton University Library, Berthier Papers, No. 21–9. Rochambeau's copy is in the Library of Paul Mellon, Upperville, Virginia.

36 Tenth Camp at Newtown

28 June–2 July 1781. Fifteen miles from the preceding camp at Break Neck. The four divisions are shown, with a detachment of grenadiers and chasseurs in a forward position west of Newtown's Main Street (which runs roughly north and south). The army camped again at Newtown on 24–26 October 1782.

ms, 32 x 21 cm. Princeton University Library, Berthier Papers, No. 21–10. Rochambeau's copy is in the Library of Paul Mellon, Upperville, Virginia.

37 Eleventh Camp at Ridgebury [in Connecticut]

1–3 July 1781. Fifteen miles from the preceding camp at Newtown. Ridgebury, not far from the New York State line, is a hamlet in the northern part of the town of Ridgefield. The present Congregational Church (built in 1851) is on the site of the "meeting-house" shown on the map.

The army marched over this route again in October 1782 but did not then stop to camp at Ridgebury.

ms, 32 x 21 cm. Princeton University Library, Berthier Papers, No. 21–11. Rochambeau's copy is in the Library of Paul Mellon, Upperville, Virginia.

38 Thirteenth Camp at North Castle [Mount Kisco, New York]

3–6 July 1781. The First Brigade, which left the Ridgebury camp on 2 July and bivouacked that night at Bedford, and the Second Brigade, which marched the whole distance from Ridgebury on 3 July, both reached

North Castle on 3 July. As mentioned in the heading of the map, no plan of the Bedford (Village) bivouac of the First Brigade was drawn. North Castle is present Mount Kisco, Westchester County, New York. The "Etang" or pond, formerly known as Kirby Pond, no longer exists; the area is part of present Leonard Recreation Park. The stream flowing out of the pond is the Kisco River. The North Castle "meeting house," shown here, was St. George's Church (built in 1761); it no longer stands, but an old cemetery still marks the site. See Richard G. Lucid and Arthur I. Bernhard, "Northcastle Camp," *The Westchester Historian* (Westchester County Historical Society), xxxv, No. 1 (Jan.–March 1959), 3–8.

A French hospital was maintained at North Castle during the period of the long encampment farther south at Philipsburg. See Blanchard's journal (1), p. 82; Dawson, *Français Morts aux Etats Unis*, pp. 30, 56, 71. There was a bivouac here at North Castle, 20 August 1781, when the army was proceeding north from Philipsburg to King's Ferry; see notes to Nos. 48 and 61.

MS, 32 x 21 cm. Princeton University Library, Berthier Papers, No. 21–12/13. Rochambeau's copy is in the Library of Paul Mellon, Upperville, Virginia.

The Allied Encampment at Philipsburg, New York

July - August 1781

39 *Fourteenth Camp at Philipsburg*

Seventeen and a half miles from the preceding camp at North Castle. Rochambeau's army camped here with Washington's army from 5 July 1781 until 19 August. Both French and American campsites are shown: French in yellow, American dark green. South is at the top of the map. The Bronx River is at the left, the Sawmill River at the right. The Dobbs Ferry road, upper right, leads to the banks of the Hudson.

MS, 32 x 21 cm. Princeton University Library, Berthier Papers, No. 21–14. Rochambeau's copy is in the Library of Paul Mellon, Upperville, Virginia.

40 *Position of the American and French Army at Philipsburg . . . from 6 July 1781*

This places the preceding map in a broader setting. South is on the left, facing the enemy, who occupied Manhattan Island. As stated in the full title, the position was 12 miles from King's Bridge (i.e., the northern tip of the Island) and 25 miles from New York (i.e., the city proper, then confined to the southern end of the Island). The unnamed stream shown here below the Sawmill River is Sprain Brook. Areas tinted yellowish are wooded.

MS, 33.7 x 40.2 cm. New-York Historical Society. The map was reproduced in the *Magazine of American History*, iv, No. 1 (Jan. 1880), between pp. 10 and 11; it was then in the possession of James F. Dwight of New York City. A similar

41 Lodgings of Staff Headquarters [Philipsburg Camp]

This map designates more precisely than do the other extant maps of the Philipsburg area the location of houses occupied by the General Staff officers during the six weeks' encampment there. Washington's HQ (1) was near the site of present Ardsley High School. Rochambeau's HQ (2) was the Odell farm, still standing on present Ridge Road (in Hartsdale, town of Greenburgh) and now owned by the Sons of the American Revolution. The rustic retreat described by Berthier in his journal (pp. 250–251) was near Béville's HQ (3). Chastellux's HQ (4) was a farmhouse then owned by a Tory absentee, Frederick Philipse, on present Healey Avenue South, Scarsdale, along the eastern border of Sunningdale Country Club. Lodgings of the two Vioménils (5,6), the *intendant* Tarlé (7), the commissary-general Blanchard (11), and others are also located.

MS, 29.5 x 36 cm. Historical Society of Pennsylvania, Philadelphia. The map was formerly with Cromot Dubourg's MS journal (though probably not drawn by him) but is now in a separate portfolio (AM 63601). It was reproduced in the *Magazine of American History*, IV, No. 4 (April 1880), between 296 and 297.

42 Plan of Huntington Bay, Long Island [July 1781]

This map provides a record of the unsuccessful attack on the fort at Lloyd Neck by a force of some 200 French under Colonel d'Angély. The raiding party was transported from Newport in ships commanded by La Villebrune; the *Romulus*, *Gentille*, and *Ariel* are shown here. The expedition, undertaken for the purpose of destroying British stores at Huntington while the main allied army was poised at Philipsburg, left Newport on 11 July and returned there on the 14th, without having accomplished its purpose. For details, see Verger's journal, pp. 130–132, nn. 42–47 and the map drawn by Verger, who participated in the expedition. Note here the inscription at right: "Bay into which the American pilots should have taken the ships." The larger bay where the ships actually went is farther to the left. The somewhat imprecise outlines of the map, which was probably drawn by one of the naval officers soon after the event, confirm Choisy's statement that "we were badly informed about the location of the stores." Despite the compass arrow, north would seem to be at the bottom of the map. Another rough map, labeled "Description of Huntington Bay according to the report made to me," which probably served as preliminary intelligence, is in the Destouches Papers, No. 34 (Henry E. Huntington Library, San Marino, California).

MS, 35.4 x 50 cm. Service Hydrographique de la Marine, 137-7-7, now on deposit in the Bibliothèque Nationale, Section des Cartes et Plans.

43 Reconnaissance of the Works on the Northern Part of the Island of New York, the Principal

This map incorporates the results of the King's Bridge reconnaissance, the first of the surveys made on 22 July by Generals Washington and Rochambeau with their engineers, as described in Berthier's journal (p. 253, n. 77). See also Clermont-Crèvecœur's journal, pp. 36–37. Several of the engineers returned here the next day to complete their observations without interruption from skirmishers.

"A" is Fort Washington (or Knyphausen), situated on present Fort Washington Avenue at 183rd Street. "B" is Fort Laurel Hill (or George), located on the crest of Laurel Hill, on present Audubon Avenue at Fort George Avenue. "C" is Fort Tryon, situated on present Fort Washington Avenue on a line with 190th Street. The Cock Hill fort, "I," on the northwestern tip of the island was on the summit of Inwood Hill, near present Bolton Road. "K" designates Fort Charles (or Prince Charles), which overlooked King's Bridge, the bridge connecting the island with the mainland. Marble Hill, on which the fort was located, was severed from the island by the completion in 1895 of the Harlem River Ship Canal and has been joined to the mainland by the gradual filling-in of the northern loop of Spuyten Duyvil Creek; it is nevertheless still a part of the Borough of Manhattan. Present Fort Charles Place preserves the name of the former British work. "M" designates Fort Independence, a former American fort that had been razed before 1781. Its site was at the upper end of present Giles Place near the Jerome Park Reservoir in the Bronx. A nearby strip of land along the reservoir has been designated Fort Independence Park. In the lower right corner of the map is "Col. Cortland," now known as the Van Cortlandt Mansion in Van Cortlandt Park. Following down the east bank of Harlem Creek the map shows "Deighton Bridge," i.e., Dyckman's Bridge, and "Howlands," i.e., Hollands Ferry. On the heights above this ferry, designated by the letter "L," is Redoubt No. 8, situated on the present University Heights campus of New York University in the Bronx.

The fortifications and other localities shown on this and the following map are precisely identified, on the basis of archeological investigations made in the early years of the twentieth century, by Reginald Pelham Bolton in his *Relics of the Revolution, The Story of the Discovery of the Buried Remains of Military Life in Forts and Camps on Manhattan Island* (New York, 1916), and *Washington Heights, Manhattan, Its Eventful Past* (New York, 1924). *Relics of the Revolution* was also printed (but with fewer illustrations) as Appendix A of the *Annual Report*, 1915, of the American Scenic and Historic Preservation Society, pp. 347–501.

The numerous extant versions of this map emphasize its significance as a preparatory reconnaissance of the proposed allied attack on New York. These include: the map reproduced here (Library of Congress, Rochambeau Map No. 32); another (perhaps a preliminary version) also in Library of Congress, Rochambeau Map No. 28; map signed by Desandroüins, chief French engineer, Archives du Génie, 14–1–5; map signed by Crublier d'Opterre, captain in the Royal Corps of Engineers, Library of Paul Mellon, Upperville, Virginia. There is a similar map, signed by Rochefontaine of the American engineers, among the Service Hydrographique de la Marine maps, 135–14–6–P, now deposited in the Bibliothèque Nationale, Section des Cartes et Plans; and still another version, accompanying an "Analyse d'un mémoire sur l'attaque de l'Isle de New York . . . ," in the

Archives du Génie, 14–§–1 (Places Etrangères: New York). Another such map, attributed to Colbert de Maulevrier, is in the William L. Clements Library (Brun, No. 359), Ann Arbor, Michigan. A copy of the map is also in Cromot Dubourg's journal, Historical Society of Pennsylvania (reproduced in the *Magazine of American History*, IV, No. 4 [April 1880], facing 306); another version is in the Service Historique de la Marine, Fonds du Service Hydrographique, MS No. 2847, Cromot Dubourg's "Atlas," No. 4–b.

MS, 45.5 x 53.5 cm. Library of Congress, Rochambeau Map No. 32.

44 Reconnaissance of the Part of the Island of New York that faces the Entrance of the Sound [22–23 July 1781]

After making the reconnaissance shown in the preceding map, the generals and their engineers moved forward down the east bank of the Harlem River to Morrisania, where this second survey was made. The map reproduced here was drawn by Crublier d'Opterre, then a captain in the Royal Corps of Engineers. A similar map, signed by the chief engineer, Desandroüins, has the more explicit title: "Plan of the eastern part of the Island of New York opposite the mouth of the Sound in the left branch of the Hudson called Harlem Creek, reconnoitered 22 and 23 July 1781." Buchanan Island is present Ward's Island; Montresor Island, Randall's Island. "A" is Horn's Hook, at present 89th Street, Carl Schurz Park, and site of Gracie Mansion, residence of the mayor of New York City. The British redoubt marked "B" and the blockhouse "C" were on the heights in the vicinity of present 130th(?) Street; the batteries on the river shore, "D," were near present 125th Street.

Similar maps are: the one signed by Desandroüins, Archives du Génie, 14–1–4 (Places Etrangères: New York); Library of Congress, Rochambeau Map No. 29; Historical Society of Pennsylvania, Cromot Dubourg journal (reproduced in the *Magazine of American History*, IV, No. 4 [April 1880], 294); Service Historique de la Marine, Fonds du Service Hydrographique, MS No. 2847, Cromot Dubourg's "Atlas," No. 4–a.

MS, 22.5 x 36.7 cm. Library of Paul Mellon, Upperville, Virginia, Crublier d'Opterre MS No. 8.

45 Throgs Neck Reconnaissance, 23 July 1781

On 23 July the generals and their engineers moved eastward to Throgs Neck to observe the British defenses across the Sound on the northern shore of Long Island. See Clermont-Crèvecœur's journal, n. 51. This part of the Long Island shore at the narrowest passage between the island and the mainland was a possible allied landing point in the projected attack against the British. Another version of this map, signed by Desandroüins (Archives du Génie, 15–1–17, pièce 28), supplies the title: "Plan of the peninsula of Frogs Neck and of the part of the Sound that separates it from Long Island, with the battery built by the English to defend the passage which is one of the most suitable for crossing from the mainland to the Island. Reconnoitered 23 July 1781." The portion of the island shown here is the Whitestone and Little Bay section of the present Borough of Queens. The Throgs Neck Bridge now crosses the Sound at this point. Throck's or Throg's Neck, as it was originally named and is now known, was often called Frog's Neck in the eighteenth century. The designation on this map follows American usage of the time and is not a French misrendering of the name. The map shows the base line used in making observations and thus provides an illustration of the cartographic methods used by the engineers. Similar maps are in the Historical Society of Pennsylvania, Cromot Dubourg journal (1), reproduced in the *Magazine of American History*, IV, No. 4 (April 1880), 294; and in the Service Historique de la Marine, Fonds du Service Hydrographique, MS No. 2847, Cromot Dubourg's "Atlas," No. 4-a.

MS, 38 x 46.5 cm. Library of Congress, Rochambeau Map No. 30.

46 *Position of the Camp of the Combined Army at Philipsburg from 6 July to 19 August 1781*

This map shows the Philipsburg camp in relation to the Hudson River, Long Island Sound, and British-held Manhattan Island and thus explains and clarifies allied strategy. An attack on New York was still envisaged until 14 August when news was received of the impending arrival of de Grasse's fleet, not at New York, but off the Chesapeake Capes. Thereupon the decision to march to Virginia was made. This map may be attributed to L.-A. Berthier, who mentions in his journal (p. 249) that the frequent foraging expeditions enabled him to reconnoiter the country between the Philipsburg camp and Long Island Sound. The map also incorporates information concerning the Manhattan forts obtained during the reconnaissance of 21–22 July (see Nos. 43 and 44). Information on the lower parts of Manhattan and New York Harbor was presumably obtained from available American or British maps (including, probably, such engraved maps as William Faden's "A Plan of New York Island, with part of Long Island, Staten Island & East Jersey . . . ," London, 1776, and Claude Joseph Sauthier's "A Topographical Map of the North Part of New York Island . . . ," published by Faden, London, 1777). Two other versions of this same map now at the Château de Grosbois, which once belonged to Berthier, are further evidence of his authorship. One of them, of the same dimensions as the Rochambeau map and with a similar legend, has a few place names that have not been completed on the Rochambeau version; the road from the western end of Dobbs Ferry to Fort Lee is indicated. The second of the Grosbois maps, drawn on a larger scale, is incomplete. Although the outlines have been sketched in pencil, only the area of the Philipsburg camp and the northern end of Manhattan have been added. A key, intended to indicate the lodgings of the staff headquarters, is included in a blank space, upper right. Both Grosbois maps are in sections, mounted on linen and folded.

MS, approx. 48 x 104 cm. Library of Congress, Rochambeau Map No. 21.

47 *Skirmish at Morrisania, 22 July 1781, Painting by Albrecht Adam, depicting Von*

This canvas, by the Bavarian battle-painter Albrecht Adam, was commissioned by Baron Von Closen's son Karl to commemorate his father's participation in the War of American Independence. It is based on the elder Von Closen's description of the skirmish (see Evelyn Acomb's edition of his journal, pp. 99–100), which is also described in Berthier's journal (pp. 252–253) and mentioned in Clermont-Crèvecœur's journal (p. 37). Adam's painting was exhibited at the Kunstverein in Munich in 1826, at which time the local news sheet *Flora* (No. 45, 19 March 1826, a copy of which may be found in the Clarence Winthrop Bowen Papers, American Antiquarian Society) published an article about it entitled "Eine Kriegscene von Hrn. A. Adam mit dem Porträt des Hrn. Generals Frhrn. v. Closen." The article states that the artist painted the retired septuagenarian general from life, though he portrayed him as a younger man, as he might have appeared when serving as Rochambeau's aide. Von Closen's own journal (quoted in the article) supplied the theme for the central incident, showing the young captain recovering his hat amidst enemy fire. A dead British dragoon and his fallen steed also appear in the foreground. Two of Rochambeau's aides ride toward the horsemen on the ridge. In the forefront of the group is General Washington, copied by the artist from a portrait in Von Closen's possession, given to him by Governor John Hancock (cf. reproduction in *Century Magazine*, February 1907, p. 533). Next to Washington is General Rochambeau, observing the enemy's position through a field glass. At the far right an American dragoon leads in a prisoner. Others in the group, representing "various uniforms and arms," are, according to the *Flora* article (footnote signed "C," i.e., Von Closen or perhaps his son), "for the most part after drawings in a Journal kept by a still living general in the Royal Bavarian service, who also fought in the American war and who has most willingly lent it for the painting." Although this general is not named, it could only have been J.-B.-A. von Verger, then living in Munich as commander of the Bavarian Gendarmerie Korps, who, like Von Closen, had served in the Royal Deux-Ponts Regiment in America. The drawings used by Adam are those reproduced above in Verger's journal. The black light infantryman of the First Rhode Island Regiment (far right in the Adam painting) and the musketeer in felt tricorn hat next to him are easily recognized. At the far left, middleground of the painting, an Indian firing from a thicket can be dimly discerned. A note to the *Flora* article explains that the Indians were divided in their allegiance, some of them allied to the British and others to the Americans and French; in this connection the article includes a quotation from the Indians' address to Rochambeau at Newport as transcribed in Verger's journal (p. 122). Finally, for good measure, *Flora* informs us that the exotic plant introduced by the artist in the left foreground is *Rhododendron maximum*. Thus, although Adam's painting is a conventionalized rendering of the scene, done long after the event, the details have been carefully documented from the journals of two veterans of the American war.

Albrecht Adam began his career as a battle painter during the Napoleonic Wars. In 1809 at Schönbrunn, following the Battle of Wagram, the young artist's work attracted the attention of French officers, including the Viceroy of Italy, Prince Eugène de Beauharnais, who employed him for several years thereafter. Adam accompanied Eugène during the Russian

Campaign of 1812. After 1815 he worked chiefly in Munich. A series of lithographs from Adam's drawings was published under the title *Voyage pittoresque et militaire de Willenberg en Prusse jusqu'à Moscou, fait en 1812, pris sur le terrein même* (Munich, 1827–1833). In the 1840's Eugène's son, Duke Maximilian von Leuchtenberg (who married a daughter of Czar Nicholas I), commissioned for his palace in St. Petersburg a series of paintings commemorating his father's campaigns of 1809–1812. Adam's autobiography, edited by Hyazinth Holland, was published at Stuttgart in 1886 under the title *Albrecht Adam (1786–1862), Aus dem Leben eines Schlachtenmalers, Selbstbiographie.* Following the artist's death many of his drawings were dispersed at auction; an example in the Anne S.K. Brown Military Collection, Brown University (cf. *The Anatomy of Glory*, Plate 93) is a design for a painting now in the Winter Palace, Leningrad.

Through the efforts of Clarence Winthrop Bowen, Adam's painting of the Morrisania skirmish was lent by Von Closen's descendants for display at the St. Louis Exposition in 1904 and was in the custody of the Smithsonian Institution before its return to Germany in 1905. At that time a photograph was made; a small half-tone reproduction of it was published by Bowen in his article "A French Officer with Washington and Rochambeau," *Century Magazine*, LXXIII, No. 4 (Feb. 1907), 533. The original painting was destroyed, with other Von Closen souvenirs, in a fire at the castle of Gern, Bavaria, in 1921. The Editors are indebted to Mrs. Evelyn Acomb-Walker, Mrs. Louise Scheide-Marshall, Mr. David Jeremy, Mr. Maurice Callahan, Jr., and others at the American Antiquarian Society and the Smithsonian Institution, for their assistance in locating a print of the 1905 photograph.

Oil painting by Albrecht Adam (1786–1862), *ca.* 1825, dimensions unknown. Reproduced from photograph made in 1905, archives of Smithsonian Institution, Washington, D.C.

March from the Hudson to Virginia August-September 1781

Road Maps, from Philipsburg to Head of Elk

48 March from Newcastle, via Pines Bridge and Crompond, to King's Ferry and Stony Point,

This is the first of another series of road maps (no other copies of which have been found) showing the army's route from the Hudson to the head of Chesapeake Bay. Leaving the Philipsburg camp on 18–19 August 1781, the French army proceeded northward in two columns to Pines Bridge on the Croton River and thence in a single column to King's Ferry, while the

including a Plan of West Point

American army marched via New Bridge at the mouth of the Croton over a route closer to the Hudson. The marches from Philipsburg to King's Ferry are described in detail in the journals of both Clermont-Crèvecœur and Berthier (pp. 40–42 and 253–55, respectively) as well as in Itinerary 3. There is no new map for the first march from Philipsburg to North Castle (Mount Kisco), but No. 25, showing the southward march on 6 July, indicates the route over which the right column of the French army retraced its steps in the opposite direction some six weeks later.

The map reproduced here represents the second, third, and fourth marches extending over the period 20–25 August. The portion at far left traces the road over Crow Hill from North Castle (not shown) to Pines Bridge on the Croton River. "New-castl," used in the inscription, designated the general area and is now the name of the township of Newcastle, established in 1791. Between the Croton River and "Crompon" (present town of Yorktown) is the Hunt's Tavern camp (shown on the map, but not so designated); cf. No. 61. The next encampment at Verplanck's Point near the eastern end of King's Ferry, also shown here, is depicted in greater detail in the series of camp maps, No. 62. Finally, across the Hudson, beyond the Stony Point peninsula, is the so-called Haverstraw camp (present village of Stony Point), also depicted in the campsite maps, No. 63.

This map is extended to include The Highlands and a plan of West Point, though the army's route did not pass through the area north of Peekskill. General Rochambeau and several of his officers, accompanied by Washington, visited the key American stronghold on 23 August. See Clermont-Crèvecœur's journal, p. 41 and n. 57. Other maps showing West Point at approximately this same time are: Crublier d'Opterre MS No. 15, Library of Paul Mellon; Historical Society of Pennsylvania, Cromot Dubourg journal (reproduced in the *Magazine of American History*, IV, No. 4 [April 1880], between 304 and 305); Service Historique de la Marine, Fonds du Service Hydrographique, MS No. 2847, Cromot Dubourg's "Atlas," No. 5; Library of Congress, Map Division, "Plan de West-Pointe du Nord" (reproduced in *Quarterly Journal of the Library of Congress*, XXVIII, No. 3 [July 1971], 213).

MS, 22 (26.5 with fold-out extension, upper right) x 52.5 cm. Princeton University Library, Berthier Papers, No. 15–1. The component parts of the map have been rearranged in the reproduction.

49 *March from Haverstraw to Suffern*

25–26 August 1781. This was the first march after the crossing of the Hudson at King's Ferry, made on successive days by the First Brigade (including the Bourbonnais and Deux-Ponts regiments) and Second Brigade (including the Soissonnais and Saintonge). The route led from the Haverstraw camp (i.e., Stony Point village) via Kakiat (present New Hempstead, Rockland County, New York) to Suffern, New York. Kakiat ("meeting house," "Coff taverne," "Keycit place" on map) was a pivotal point on the eighteenth-century routes leading from the Hudson into northern New Jersey: the "lower road," indicated here, went south along the Saddle River to Paramus and the Jersey lowlands, while the upper road taken by the French army went via Suffern into the Ramapo Valley, which was protected by mountains on the east. Suffern was likewise an important road junction: the road from New Windsor, north of West Point and The Highlands, via The Clove, came in here.

Earlier road surveys of this region (now in the New-York Historical Society) prepared under the direction of Robert Erskine, geographer to Washington's army, which were probably available to the French, provide a useful complement to the Berthier road maps; cf. Peter J. Guthorn, *American Maps and Map Makers of the Revolution* (Monmouth Beach, N.J., 1966), pp. 17ff. See also Washington's letter of 29 August 1781 to Simeon DeWitt (Erskine's successor), *Writings of GW*, XXIII, 68–69: "Immediately upon receipt of this you will begin to Survey the road . . . to Princeton, thence (through Maidenhead) to Trenton, thence to Philadelphia, thence to the head of Elk through Darby, Chester, Wilmington, Christiana Bridge. At the head of Elk, you will receive further orders. . . ."

In preparation for the march through New Jersey, Jeremiah Wadsworth and John Carter (Church), purchasing agents for the French army, instructed their agent, David Reynolds, to assemble supplies (15 tons of hay, 20 tons of straw, 230 bushels of corn, 5 cords of wood) at each of the following "staging posts": Suffern, Pompton, Whippany, Bullion's Tavern, Somerset Courthouse, and Princeton. Wadsworth and Carter to Reynolds, Philipsburg, 18 August 1781, in Wadsworth Papers (Connecticut Historical Society), Box 153, Letterbook B, p. 108.

MS, 22 x 30.5 cm. Princeton University Library, Berthier Papers, No. 15–2.

50 March from Suffern [in New York] to Pompton [in New Jersey]

26–27 August 1781. The route along the Ramapo Valley corresponds closely to present U.S. Route 202. "Pompton," the terminus of this march, is the locality now known as Pompton Plains. The curious words "her scaller house," designating a property between Pond's Church and the Pompton River, is a draftsman's miscopying of "Mr. [Casparus] Schuyler's House." "Bartoli moulin" is probably Bartolf's (or Bertolf's) Mill; "Fanallen's Mills," Van Allen's. The march through New Jersey is described in Clermont-Crèvecœur's journal (pp. 42ff.) and in Itineraries 3 and 4.

MS, 22 x 26 cm. Princeton University Library, Berthier Papers, No. 15–3.

51 March from Pompton to Whippany

27–29 August 1781. The First Brigade halted here an extra day, not leaving until the 29th; the whole army was thus camped at Whippany on the 28th. The upper branches of the Passaic River are sketched here in pencil; "fork," under the word "Wippany" in the heading, indicates present Two Bridges, at the confluence of the Pompton and Passaic rivers. "Ferme de Mr. Lot," to the left of Troy Town on the map, is Beverwyck, the estate of Lucas von Beverhoudt, then also the residence of Abraham Lott, a patriot refugee from New York City. See Itinerary 3, p. 57 and n. 36.

MS, 22 x 28.5 cm. Princeton University Library, Berthier Papers, No. 15–4.

52 *March from Whippany to Bullion's Tavern*

29–30 August 1781. "Hanovre's V.ᵘ [Village]" at the left of the map is the locality to the west of Whippany now known as Monroe; Whippany, an ancient settlement never incorporated separately, is still a part of Hanover Township. The "Mill" shown here was Lewis's (later Van Dorn's) Mill, on the Passaic River, which here forms the present boundary between Morris and Somerset counties. The "Maison du lord Sterling" was the estate of William Alexander ("Lord Stirling"), southeast of Basking Ridge, near the site of the present Somerset Hills Airport. Bullion's (or Boylan's) Tavern was at present Liberty Corner. It was at this point in the march that the troops began to realize that they would not be attacking the British in New York via Staten Island but that Virginia was their destination.

MS, 22 x 28 cm. Princeton University Library, Berthier Papers, No. 15–5.

53 *March from Bullion's Tavern to Somerset Courthouse*

30–31 August 1781. The "Black-men road," left of map, is the road to Pluckemin. The "montagne très roide et très longue à monter" is the Second Watchung Mountain, north of present Martinsville. The descent over First Watchung Mountain down into the Raritan Valley was via Steele's Gap, as described above in Itinerary 4. "Vinvington house" is the Van Veghten house, near Van Veghten's Bridge (the present bridge at Manville, State Route 533). Somerset Courthouse is present Millstone on the river of that name; the county seat was later moved to Somerville.

MS, 22 x 28 cm. Princeton University Library, Berthier Papers, No. 15–6.

54 *March from Somerset Courthouse to Princeton*

31 August–1 September 1781. The "Mill" at left of map, then belonging to Archibald Mercer, is the locality subsequently known as Blackwell's Mills. The route crossed to the east bank of the Millstone River at Griggstown (not named here) where several taverns are shown. The Delaware and Raritan Canal now runs parallel to this part of the Millstone. The army's route recrossed to the west side of the river at Rocky Hill (not named on map) and thence to Princeton via Mount Lucas Road, the last stretch of which is now called Witherspoon Street. The property shown across the road (present Stockton Street) from the army's campsite is "Morven," then the residence of Annis Boudinot, widow of Richard Stockton, "The Signer," who had died earlier that year.

Describing the army's march from Princeton to Somerset Courthouse a year later (8 September 1782), Von Closen notes (p. 235): "We did not take the same road as the previous year, but a new passage was opened up along the Millstone River which was on our *right* [i.e., when going north] all the way."

MS, 22 x 27 cm. Princeton University Library, Berthier Papers, No. 16–1.

55 *March from Princeton to Trenton*

1–2 September 1781. The route follows closely present U.S. Route 206. "Stony brug hameau," at left of map, indicates the "hamlet" at Stony Brook (Worth's Mill), one of the earliest settlements (*ca.* 1700) in what later became the town of Princeton. "Maidenhead" is present Lawrenceville, so renamed in honor of Captain James Lawrence, naval hero of the War of 1812. At Trenton two ferries are shown below the falls: Trenton Ferry, which crossed the Delaware from the foot of Ferry Street near the present

Pennsylvania Railroad bridge, and Continental Ferry, lower down, which crossed from a point below the present site of Riverview Cemetery (Lamberton Road).

MS, 22 x 26 cm. Princeton University Library, Berthier Papers, No. 16–2.

56 *March from Trenton to Red Lion Tavern*

2–3 September 1781. The army had now reached Pennsylvania. The river to the right of Bristol on the map is the Neshaminy. As indicated in Clermont-Crèvecœur's journal (p. 45), the artillery crossed it at a ford, several miles upstream, while the infantry used the ferry. Dr. James Thacher, who was marching with the American army at the same time, notes in his *Military Journal* (Boston, 1823), p. 325, that on 1 September "we crossed a small river at Shammany's rope ferry. Our boats were pulled across with facility by a rope made fast at each shore." Red Lion Tavern, the terminus of this march, was on present U.S. Route 13, at Poquessing Creek, which now forms the northern boundary of the City (and County) of Philadelphia.

MS, 22 x 28 cm. Princeton University Library, Berthier Papers, No. 16–3.

57 *March from Red Lion Tavern to Philadelphia*

3–4 September 1781. There was an extra day's halt in Philadelphia, the First Brigade departing on the 5th, the Second on the 6th. See Clermont-Crèvecœur's journal, p. 46, for an account of the march-past of the French army before the Continental Congress. The "ancienne ligne Angloise," shown on the map beyond Kensington and to the north of the then-populated part of Philadelphia, extended from the mouth of Conoquonoque Creek on the Delaware (a bit to the north of the present Benjamin Franklin Bridge) westward to the height of land above the Schuylkill now occupied by the Philadelphia Museum of Art; this line of fortifications, built by the British during their occupancy of the city in 1777–1778, ran approximately between present Callowhill and Spring Garden Streets. The map shows, upper right, the river forts: Billingsport and Red Bank (Fort Mercer) on the New Jersey shore of the Delaware, and Fort Mifflin (or Mud Island) on the Pennsylvania side. General Rochambeau sailed down the river to Chester in order to inspect these forts; cf. Clermont-Crèvecœur's journal, n. 83. The "Maison à Mr. le Ch[evali]er de la Luzern," shown on the map below the Falls of Schuylkill, lower right, was "Laurel Hill" (also known as the Randolph Mansion), a country house rented by the Chevalier de La Luzerne, the French minister; it still stands on the bluff overlooking the Schuylkill in East Fairmount Park, between "Ormiston" and "Strawberry Mansion."

MS, 22 x 33 cm. Princeton University Library, Berthier Papers, No. 16–4.

58 *March from Philadelphia to Chester*

5–6 September 1781. The river, far left of map, is the Schuylkill, with the pontoon bridge shown on the previous map. The route from Philadelphia, via Darby, to Chester is described in Itinerary 5. It was at Chester that Washington greeted Rochambeau (who had come down the Delaware from Philadelphia by boat) with the joyful news that de Grasse's fleet had arrived in the Chesapeake Bay; cf. Clermont-Crèvecœur's journal, n. 85.

MS, 22 x 31 cm. Princeton University Library, Berthier Papers, No. 16–5.

59 *March from Chester
[in Pennsylvania] to
Wilmington and to
Newport [in Delaware]*

6–7 September 1781. After Marcus Hook the route crossed Naaman Creek, several smaller streams, then the Brandywine, before entering Wilmington. As clearly shown here, Wilmington was originally built facing Christina Creek, according to a pattern similar to that of Philadelphia, with its Front Street along the Christina corresponding to Philadelphia's Front Street along the Delaware. The map indicates that one brigade (the Second) camped beyond Wilmington at Newport. The following year, when bound north, the army camped only at Newport (the four divisions in succession, 29 August–1 September 1782), and marched through Wilmington without halting there to camp; see No. 135.

MS, 22 x 27 cm. Princeton University Library, Berthier Papers, No. 16–6.

60 *March from Newport
[in Delaware] to Head
of Elk [in Maryland]*

7–8 September 1781. The route follows closely the "Old Baltimore Pike" (which has now been eclipsed in importance by U.S. Route 40 to the south of it and Interstate 95 to the north). Proceeding from the left of the map, "Whytly Crick" is White Clay Creek, "Christine Bridge" is now called Christiana, and "Couche's Bridge" is Cooch's Bridge, near which there stands today an eighteenth-century house still owned by the Cooch family. A monument by the bridge commemorates the "Battle of Cooch's Bridge," i.e., the skirmish of 3 September 1777 between Washington's troops and the British, led by Cornwallis, who had landed at Head of Elk and were proceeding towards the Brandywine and Philadelphia. Beyond Cooch's Bridge the route goes over Iron Hill, the height of land between the Delaware and the upper reaches of Chesapeake Bay. It was expected that the army would embark at Head of Elk.

This is the last in the series of detailed road maps depicting the army's marches. Two blank leaves that follow it and that precede the last map in the "cahier" (the plan of Baltimore, No. 81) suggest that Berthier intended to continue and complete the series.

MS, 22 x 34.5 cm. Princeton University Library, Berthier Papers, No. 16–7.

March from the Hudson to Virginia August - September 1781

Camp Plans, from Philipsburg to Head of Elk, Baltimore, and Annapolis

61 *Sixteenth Camp at
Hunt's Tavern*

21 August 1781. This was the second camp after Philipsburg. There is no map of the previous day's bivouac at North Castle (Mount Kisco). Hunt's Tavern was situated in present Yorktown, Westchester County, New York,

on what is now designated as State Route 35 (U.S. 202) near the corner of Hallock's Mill Road, opposite Baldwin Road. The two ponds (*étangs*) shown on the map are Mohansic Lake and Crom Pond. The roads at the left of the sheet lead westward to New Bridge at the mouth of the Croton River. The four divisions with field artillery units are shown, as well as detachments of grenadiers and chasseurs, and Lauzun's Legion, the latter serving here as a rear guard facing the enemy to the southward.

The French army camped here again in the autumn of 1782 when returning from Virginia to New England. See Nos. 145 and 146, the map of its so-called Crompond encampment, where it remained from 17 September to 20 October 1782.

MS, 32 x 21 cm. Princeton University Library, Berthier Papers, No. 21-15/16. Like the others in the series of the southbound camps of 1781, this map is duplicated in the Rochambeau manuscripts now in the Library of Paul Mellon, Upperville, Virginia.

62 Seventeenth Camp at King's Ferry or Verplanck

22–24 August 1781. Fourteen miles from the preceding camp at Hunt's Tavern. The crossing of the Hudson at King's Ferry is described in Clermont-Crèvecœur's journal (p. 40) and in Berthier's journal (p. 255). Berthier, who supervised the crossing of the wagons, notes that the last vehicle had crossed the river by midnight on 25 August. The road to New Bridge, at the left of the map, is the route by which the Americans reached King's Ferry. The fort shown here above the letters "nk" of "Verplank" is Fort La Fayette, on the east bank of the Hudson.

MS, 32 x 21 cm. Princeton University Library, Berthier Papers, No. 21-17. Rochambeau's copy is in the Library of Paul Mellon, Upperville, Virginia.

63 Eighteenth Camp at Haverstraw

24–25 August 1781. Two miles from King's Ferry. The army was now marching by brigades of two divisions each. The date on the map is that of the arrival of the First Brigade. The "Haverstraw" camp, the first after the crossing of the Hudson (and the eighteenth since the departure from Providence, Rhode Island) was in the locality now known as Stony Point Village (as distinguished from the Point proper). The designation "Haverstraw" is correct, since the name applied in 1781 to a larger area than the present town of Haverstraw, which is farther south. The larger of the two streams shown here is Cedar Pond Brook, flowing eastward into the Hudson.

In September 1782 one brigade camped again on this site; see No. 142.

MS, 32 x 21 cm. Princeton University Library, Berthier Papers, No. 21-18. Rochambeau's copy is in the Library of Paul Mellon, Upperville, Virginia.

64 Nineteenth Camp at Suffern [in New York]

25–26 August 1781. Fifteen and a half miles from the preceding camp at Haverstraw (Stony Point Village). The stream at the left of the map is the Ramapo River, here flowing roughly south.

The army camped here again in 1782, as shown on map, No. 141.

MS, 32 x 21 cm. Princeton University Library, Berthier Papers, No. 21-19. Rochambeau's copy is in the Library of Paul Mellon, Upperville, Virginia.

**65 *Twentieth Camp at
Pompton Meetinghouse
[in New Jersey]***

26–27 August 1781. Fifteen miles from the preceding camp at Suffern. The "meeting-house" shown on the map is the Dutch Reformed Church; the present church building and adjacent cemetery are on the same site, along the Newark-Pompton Turnpike, the main street of Pompton Plains, Morris County, New Jersey.

The army camped again at Pompton Plains on its return march in September 1782, as shown on map, No. 140.

MS, 32 x 21 cm. Princeton University Library, Berthier Papers, No. 21–20. Rochambeau's copy is in the Library of Paul Mellon, Upperville, Virginia.

**66 *Twenty-first Camp at
Whippany***

27–29 August 1781. Fifteen miles from the preceding camp at Pompton Plains. The First Brigade halted here a second day, so that the entire army was in camp here on the 28th. Both brigades are shown. The map also indicates, by means of dotted lines, positions occupied when the army camped here again, northward bound, on 10–11 September 1782. The camp was located on grounds now occupied by the Bell Telephone Laboratories, the Seeing Eye, and some adjacent houses on the high ground between Whippany Road (the main east-west road on the map, i.e., the road from Whippany to Morristown) and the northwest edge of the Black (or Columbia) Meadows. The top of the map is approximately south. Roads leading off the left edge of the map went eastward to Chatham, the sightly position where Rochambeau had decoy bake ovens built to make the British believe an attack on New York was imminent. Washington, who led the American army through New Jersey by a route paralleling the French to the east, had his headquarters temporarily at Chatham. The road leading off the right of the map went to Morristown (and eventually to Bullion's Tavern, the destination of the next march). "Hanover" was, and is, the name of the township of which Whippany is a part.

MS, 32 x 21 cm. Princeton University Library, Berthier Papers, No. 21–21. Rochambeau's copy is in the Library of Paul Mellon, Upperville, Virginia.

**67 *Twenty-second Camp at
Bullion's Tavern
[Liberty Corner]***

29–30 August 1781. Sixteen miles from the preceding camp at Whippany. Bullion's Tavern was at the locality later called Liberty Corner, in Bernards Township, Somerset County, New Jersey. The spelling "Bullion" (probably a corruption of Boylan) also appears on American maps of the period. The stream shown on the map is Harrison's Brook, a tributary of Dead River, which in turn joins the Passaic. The sharp right-angle turn in the road still provides an unmistakable point of reference for identification of the site of the French camp. The road at top of map, left, was the route leading eventually to Quibbletown (New Market), Scotch Plains, or Chatham.

The army's 1782 encampment at Bullion's Tavern is shown on map, No. 139.

MS, 32 x 21 cm. Princeton University Library, Berthier Papers, No. 21–22. Rochambeau's copy is in the Library of Paul Mellon, Upperville, Virginia.

68 Twenty-third Camp at Somerset Courthouse [Millstone]

30–31 August 1781. Thirteen miles from the preceding camp at Bullion's Tavern. Somerset Courthouse is now called Millstone. The stream, which flows north into the Raritan, is the Millstone River. The courthouse, near the second of the three bridges shown here, had been burned in October 1779 by British raiders under Lieutenant Colonel Simcoe. The road through the village taken by the army is essentially present State Route 533, which has been straightened to eliminate the bow leading down to the bridge. The two infantry regiments and artillery camped near the Dutch Reformed Church (present edifice [1827] and adjacent cemetery on same site) at the junction of present State Routes 533 and 514. Beyond the encampment, at a bend in the road, is the Van Doren house, still standing on this site. Photographs of the Van Doren house and of the site of the courthouse are in Elizabeth G.C. Menzies, *Millstone Valley* (New Brunswick, 1969), pp. 146, 236, 244, 262.

The separate unit, on right of the map, represents Lauzun's Legion. Rumors of a British sortie from New York reached the army here at Somerset Courthouse. Fearing an attack, the Baron de Vioménil (who was then in command, Rochambeau having ridden ahead) ordered patrols to the eastward. Lauzun ([2], p. 293) relates that he himself with 50 of his hussars rode 10 miles out along the New Brunswick road: "I met two or three sizeable patrols of light troops, who retired after exchanging a few shots with my hussars. I satisfied myself that the English army was not on the march, and then returned to reassure the Baron."

The army camped again at Millstone on its return march in 1782; see No. 138.

MS, 32 x 21 cm. Princeton University Library, Berthier Papers, No. 21–33. Rochambeau's copy is in the Library of Paul Mellon, Upperville, Virginia.

69 Twenty-fourth Camp at Princeton

31 August–1 September 1781. Fourteen miles from the preceding camp at Somerset Courthouse. The "Collège" is Nassau Hall. The road leading in from the right of the map—here called the road from Somerset Courthouse, since that was the starting point of the day's march—is present Witherspoon Street. The army camped across the main road (Stockton Street, present U.S. Route 206) from the Richard Stockton residence (Morven), indicated here with its private entrance road (dotted lines). The camp extended across Mercer Street (which did not exist in 1781) on to grounds now occupied by the Princeton Theological Seminary. The crossroads at the lower part of the map is the present intersection of Nassau and Harrison Streets (Queenston, Jugtown). The stream at the left of the map is Stony Brook, now enlarged at this point to form a part of Carnegie Lake.

The army camped again in Princeton, 7–8 September 1782, presumably on this same site, since no new map was drawn for the series representing the 1782 camps.

MS, 32 x 21 cm. Princeton University Library, Berthier Papers, No. 21–24. The word "Collège" does not appear on the Rochambeau copy of this map, Library of Paul Mellon, Upperville, Virginia.

70 *Twenty-fifth Camp at Trenton*

1–2 September 1781. Twelve and a half miles from the preceding camp at Princeton. The stream flowing into the Delaware, shown on the map between the letters "n" and "t" of "Trenton," is the Assunpink. The infantry regiments camped beside the "Burlington Road" to the east of the Assunpink. The artillery unit was opposite the Trent House (then the resident of Colonel John Cox), shown here with its formally laid-out grounds.

Dotted lines indicate the position occupied by one brigade a year later, when the army camped again in Trenton, 3–7 September 1782, on its northbound march.

MS, 32 x 21 cm. Princeton University Library, Berthier Papers, No. 21–25. Rochambeau's copy is in the Library of Paul Mellon, Upperville, Virginia.

71 *Ford across the Delaware at Trenton*

As stated on the map, "this ford at its greatest depth is about two and a half feet." The "Chateau," shown here as a directional point of reference, is Bloomsbury Court, the William Trent House, built *ca.* 1719, restored and still standing on South Warren Street. Cf. description of the ford in Itinerary 5. Clermont-Crèvecœur in his journal (p. 45) mentions that the crossing of the Delaware was made by both ford and ferry.

MS, 14 x 14.5 cm. Princeton University Library, Berthier Papers, No. 17.

72 *Twenty-sixth Camp at Red Lion Tavern*

2–3 September 1781. Seventeen miles from the preceding camp at Trenton. This was the last place the army camped before entering Philadelphia. The stream is Poquessing Creek, which flows into the Delaware. The tavern itself was in the depression formed by the creek, the camp on the higher ground beyond it. The road corresponds to U.S. Route 13, now paralleled by Interstate 95, which runs still closer to the Delaware.

MS, 32 x 21 cm. Princeton University Library, Berthier Papers, No. 21–26. Rochambeau's copy is in the Library of Paul Mellon, Upperville, Virginia.

73 *Twenty-seventh Camp at Philadelphia*

3–6 September 1781. Fourteen miles from the preceding camp at Red Lion Tavern. The entire army was assembled here before resuming its march. The Lauzun Legion (both the infantry and the cavalry, or hussars), which had marched with the First Brigade after the Hudson crossing at King's Ferry, is shown on the right-hand side of the road. The widest of the streets shown (on a line with the second "i" in "Philadelphie" and the second "a" in "Delawar") is Market Street. The pontoon bridge across the Schuylkill was near the site of the present Market Street bridge.

When the army stopped in Philadelphia a year later, the camp was on the northern outskirts of the city; see No. 137.

MS, 32 x 21 cm. Princeton University Library, Berthier Papers, No. 21–27. Rochambeau's copy is in the Library of Paul Mellon, Upperville, Virginia.

74 *Twenty-eighth Camp at Chester [in Pennsylvania]*

5–6 September 1781. Sixteen miles from Philadelphia. The street pattern shown here is still readily discernible in the heart of the modern city of Chester. The army's route from Philadelphia came in via present Market (formerly High) Street. The first intersection shown corresponds to present Sixth Street, after which come Fifth, Fourth, then Market Square. The old market in the center of the intersection is represented on the map. Here the route turned sharp right along present Third Street and over the bridge across Chester Creek. The camp was southwest of the town on higher ground along the road to Wilmington; the site is well inside the present city.

A year later, when marching in the opposite direction, the army camped again at Chester, by divisions, on 30 August–2 September 1782. The camp was then northeast of the town, on the road to Philadelphia, between Ridley and Crum creeks; see No. 136.

MS, 32 x 21 cm. Princeton University Library, Berthier Papers, No. 21–28. Rochambeau's copy is in the Library of Paul Mellon, Upperville, Virginia.

75 *Twenty-ninth Camp at Wilmington* [*in Delaware*]

6 September 1781. Eleven and a half miles from the preceding camp at Chester. As shown on the road map above, No. 59, the Second Brigade did not camp in Wilmington but marched through and beyond the city to Newport, where it camped on 7 September. The route of the march through Wilmington and the campsite of the First Brigade there can be precisely determined by reference to the church and surrounding burial ground (small crosses) shown on the map. This is the Friends' Meeting House situated in the block bounded by West, Fifth, Fourth, and Pasture (present Washington) Streets; the original building was replaced by the present structure in the early nineteenth century. Thus the street at the top of the grid is Front Street, the one at right angles to it, far left, is Orange Street. The "Corderie," lower right, is a rope walk then on the property of Mordecai Woodward. A small dotted line shows the army's route: coming into town via a road passing from the Brandywine Creek up over the height now crowned by the Du Pont and Nemours buildings, the army veered into West Street, marching as far as Fifth, thence right into Pasture Street, down which it marched towards Front. The camp of the First Brigade was on a line with Second Street, in an area, then open fields, now included between Justison and Adams Streets. The camp faced Front Street (and its extension, the Lancaster Pike) and was close to the road leading to Newport and Head of Elk (present Maryland Avenue), over which the troops would resume their march the next day.

MS, 32 x 21 cm. Princeton University Library, Berthier Papers, No. 21–29. Rochambeau's copy is in the Library of Paul Mellon, Upperville, Virginia.

76 *Thirtieth Camp at Head of Elk* [*in Maryland*]

7–8 September 1781. Twenty miles from the preceding camp at Wilmington. The First Brigade halted an extra day, so that both brigades were camped here together on the 8th, to the north of the main road leading through the village of Head of Elk, or Elkton. Elk Landing, a mile or so south of the village, was on the "Head of Elk River" (formed by the confluence of Big Elk and Little Elk creeks) at one of the northernmost tips of the Chesapeake Bay. The once busy waterfront, shown here with its wharves at the left of the map, is today an overgrown backwater; its former importance as the western gateway of the portage route from the Chesapeake Bay to the Delaware River was largely eliminated by the completion in 1829 of the Chesapeake and Delaware Canal a few miles to the south.

It was hoped that the armies, both French and American, could embark at Head of Elk and be ferried down the Bay to Virginia. In spite of Washington's efforts to have sufficient transport vessels assembled here (see, e.g., his letter to Governor Thomas Sim Lee of Maryland, 27 August 1781, in *Writings of GW*, XXIII, 57–58), only a limited number of troops could be accommodated. These included a French detachment commanded by Colonel Custine; cf. Clermont-Crèvecœur's journal, nn. 89–90. These units are shown on the map close to the landing (within and below the letter "H" of "Head of Elk").

The main part of the army thus continued its route towards Baltimore (and eventually Annapolis). The series of detailed road maps depicting the daily marches does not continue beyond Head of Elk, but the routes are schematically indicated on the comprehensive map of camps and marches, No. 162.

The French army camped again at Elkton, by divisions, on 28–31 August 1782; see No. 134.

MS, 32 x 21 cm. Princeton University Library, Berthier Papers, No. 21–30. Rochambeau's copy is in the Library of Paul Mellon, Upperville, Virginia.

77 *Bivouac at Lower Ferry*

9 September 1781. Fifteen miles from the preceding camp at Head of Elk. After being ferried across the Susquehanna the four infantry regiments, as shown here, bivouacked together along the northern edge of the Baltimore road. "Lower Ferry" corresponds to the present Perryville–Havre de Grace crossing. ("Upper Ferry" was near Port Deposit.) The town of Havre de Grace did not exist in 1781, though when the French army passed over this route again in 1782 (No. 133) several officers noted in their journals that such a town was then being planned; see Verger's journal, n. 134. The "Tavern" shown on the map is presumably the "Ferry House" (later the Lafayette Hotel).

No artillery units are shown on this map. The wagons and artillery, escorted by Lauzun's hussars under Colonel d'Arrot (the Duc de Lauzun himself and his Legion's infantry had embarked at Head of Elk), took a more circuitous route via Bald Friar Ford, which was some 7 miles upstream (above present Conowingo Dam). Their route is shown on the general map of camps and marches, No. 162. They camped at Cummings Tavern (Battle Swamp) east of the Susquehanna and, after the crossing by Bald Friar Ford, at "Dear Church" (Deer Creek Friends Meeting, Darlington) to the west of the river. Their route, via Churchville, then merged into that of the infantry at Bush. Clermont-Crèvecœur made this detour with the artillery, as described in his journal (p. 53 and nn. 92–93).

MS, 32 x 21 cm. Princeton University Library, Berthier Papers, No. 21–31. Rochambeau's copy is in the Library of Paul Mellon, Upperville, Virginia.

78 *Bivouac at Bush Town, or Harford*

10 September 1781. Twelve miles from Lower Ferry. Bush, originally called Harford Town, was the county seat of Harford County until 1783, when

the seat was moved to Bel Air. Bush is still a small hamlet very similar in its general pattern to the one shown on this map. It is on the "old Philadelphia road," present State Route 7, which has now been superseded as the main traffic artery by parallel highways to the east (U.S. 40) and west (Interstate 95) of it. The stream flowing eastward (left of map), beyond which the infantry regiments bivouacked, is Bynum Run, a tributary of Bush River, which in turn flows into the Chesapeake Bay. The road coming into the main road from the right of the map (below letter "B" of "Bush Town") is the route (present Calvary Road) over which the artillery and wagons arrived from Bald Friar Ford. As recorded in Clermont-Crèvecœur's journal (p. 53), they reached Bush on 10 September, joining up the next day with the infantry regiments at a point beyond White Marsh.

The following year the army camped again at Bush, by divisions, on 25–28 August 1782, in a slightly different position. Cf. No. 132.

MS, 32 x 21 cm. Princeton University Library, Berthier Papers, No. 21–32. Rochambeau's copy is in the Library of Paul Mellon, Upperville, Virginia.

79 *Thirty-third Camp at White Marsh*

11 September 1781. Two brigades, including the artillery, are shown. The distances noted in the headings of this and the following map indicate that this so-called White Marsh camp was 15 miles from Bush and 10 miles from the next camp in Baltimore. This would place the camp some 3 miles southwest of White Marsh Forges (where the army camped on its northbound march in 1782, as shown on map, No. 131). The site was probably along the old Philadelphia road (State Route 7) near the corner of present Mohrs Lane. The stream shown on the map is a branch of White Marsh Run. The building across the road from the camp may be the mansion house of White Marsh Plantation, headquarters of the Nottingham Company, which managed the iron works at White Marsh Forges—or perhaps a tavern. Clermont-Crèvecœur (p. 54) places the camp at a "Tavern," which he does not identify by name.

MS, 32 x 21 cm. Princeton University Library, Berthier Papers, No. 21–33. Rochambeau's copy is in the Library of Paul Mellon, Upperville, Virginia.

80 *Thirty-fourth Camp at Baltimore*

12–15 September 1781. The street pattern shown on the map still underlies the section of modern Baltimore adjacent to the Basin, or "Port," as it is designated here. North is at the right of the map, west at the top. Charles Street runs along the west side of the "Port"; above it (running diagonally) is Liberty Street. The street running west to east through the middle of the grid is Market (now Baltimore) Street. The stream flowing from the north into the Basin is Jones's Falls; below it is Old Town, next is a depression known as the Harford Run, then a street (Point Lane, now Broadway) leading out to Fell's Point (not named on the map).

One brigade (the Soissonnais and Saintonge, with artillery) is shown to the left (south) of the "chemin de Spurier's Tavern," i.e., the road (approximately U.S. Route 1) leading to Georgetown; on a height to the right (north) of this road are more artillery and wagons, as well as two other units (including Lauzun's hussars, indicated by the cartographer's customary symbol for cavalry). Another brigade (the Bourbonnais and Deux-Ponts, with artillery) was camped in Old Town, east of Jones's Falls, in readiness for embarkation.

The expected embarkation did not take place at Baltimore. Again, as at Head of Elk, transports proved inadequate; cf. Clermont-Crèvecœur's journal, n. 98, and also Matthew Ridley's letter to Governor Lee, 9 September 1781, conveying Washington's urgent request "for collecting Vessels from all parts" at Baltimore, in *Archives of Maryland*, Vol. XLVII: *Journal and Correspondence of the State Council of Maryland (Letters to the Governor and Council)*, 7, 1781, ed. J. Hall Pleasants (Baltimore, 1930), pp. 482–483. Thereupon the army, now under the command of the Baron de Vioménil (Rochambeau having proceeded ahead with Washington overland to Williamsburg), resumed its march on 16 September, bound for Georgetown and Alexandria on the Potomac. Upon reaching the next camp at Spurrier's Tavern, news of the arrival of La Villebrune's squadron at Annapolis determined a countermarch back to the shores of the Chesapeake Bay. This route is schematically shown on the general map of camps and marches, No. 162.

MS, 32 x 21 cm. Princeton University Library, Berthier Papers, No. 21–34. Rochambeau's copy is in the Library of Paul Mellon, Upperville, Virginia.

81 Roadstead and Harbor of Baltimore

This map, included in the series of road maps for the 1781 marches (see note to No. 60), shows a larger area than the preceding map. It is extended eastward to include Whetstone Point and its fortifications (now Fort McHenry National Monument) and Gorsuch's Point opposite. In addition to the army units shown on the preceding map, this one indicates four other regiments, lower right. Although the identifying colors have not been completed, these probably represent American regiments under General Lincoln.

Other maps of Baltimore drawn the following year when the French army halted here from 24 July to 24 August 1782, are reproduced below, Nos. 129 to 130. The rapid growth of Baltimore during the decades following the Revolution may be traced by comparing Berthier's maps with the engraved map by A. P. Folie ("French Geographer"), "Plan of the Town of Baltimore and Its Environs" (1792), and with Warner and Hanna's engraved "Plan of the City and Environs of Baltimore" (1801).

MS, 22 x 19.5 cm. Princeton University Library, Berthier Papers, No. 16–8.

82 Ford across the Elkridge River

After leaving Baltimore and proceeding towards Spurrier's Tavern the army crossed the "Elkridge," i.e., the main branch of the Patapsco River, forming the boundary between Baltimore and Howard Counties. The ford, above the town then known as Elk Ridge Landing, is described in the note included on the map: "The detour that must be taken to cross by the ford is not great and I estimate the difference as about three-fourths of a mile, or a mile. The road leading to the ford is bad and filled with stones and foot-high stumps. As it approaches the ford the road is dangerous along the bank of the river, which is very deep in those places where the waters are dammed up to operate the forges. This ford is very good if you pass between the big stones as marked here; if you stray from this line, you find large rocks and holes." The inscription, upper left, indicates that the little road up over the bluff ("la montagne") is "passable only for troops on foot."

There is no map for the 35th camp at Spurrier's Tavern (16 September 1781), but see below, No. 128, which shows the camp made there on 23–26 August 1782 when the army was returning northward from Virginia. MS, 11 x 20 cm. Princeton University Library, Berthier Papers, No. 18.

83 *Plan of the Harbour and City of Annapolis . . . [March–April 1781]*

As indicated in the heading to No. 85, maps are lacking in this series (presumably not drawn) for the army's 35th camp at Spurrier's Tavern (16 September 1781), 36th camp at Scott's House (17 September 1781), and 37th camp at Annapolis (18–21 September 1781). There are, however, small plans of the camps at Spurrier's Tavern and at Annapolis in Huntington Library MS No. 621, described above in the "Checklist of Journals," *s.v.* Soissonnais Regiment.

The plan of Annapolis reproduced here, though not showing the camp of Rochambeau's army in September 1781, depicts the city as it was only five months earlier. This map was drawn by Michel Capitaine du Chesnoy (signed, lower right) to show the position of the American units under the command of Lafayette when they camped at Annapolis, *ca.* 13 March–6 April 1781, "previous to the opening of the Campaign in Virginia." Cf. Lafayette's letters to Jefferson, 27 March, 4 April 1781, *Papers of TJ*, v, 261–262, 342–344; Verger's journal, n. 33; and Berthier's journal, n. 48. The map shows the encampment of the American light infantry, several Annapolis landmarks, as well as two blockading British vessels (the sloops *Hope* and *General Monk*). Michel Capitaine du Chesnoy (1746–1804), an aide to Lafayette with the rank of major in the American army, had, like Berthier, been trained as a topographical engineer; for other examples of his maps, see list in Peter J. Guthorn, *American Maps and Map Makers of the Revolution* (Monmouth Beach, N.J., 1966), pp. 9–12.

The main part of the army (the Americans as well as the French), including the field artillery, set sail from Annapolis on 21 September and arrived in the James River on the 24th. On the next day they made their 38th camp at Archer's Hope at the mouth of College Creek, near Jamestown and Williamsburg. The wagon train (*équipages*), however, did not embark at Annapolis but proceeded overland to Williamsburg via the route summarily shown on the general map of camps and marches, No. 162, and described in detail in Berthier's Itinerary 6.

MS, 70 x 48 cm. Bibliothèque du Ministère des Armées "Terre," Paris, L.I.D. 11.

84 Chesapeake Expedition

This map by Joachim du Perron, comte de Revel, who arrived in Virginia from the West Indies with de Grasse's fleet, provides a comprehensive view of the entrance to the Chesapeake Bay and Yorktown peninsula and of the events that had preceded the arrival of Rochambeau's army from the north. Du Perron, a sublieutenant in the Régiment d'Infanterie de Monsieur, was serving in the ship's garrison of the *Languedoc*. The map was drawn to illustrate his personal journal and is not the work of a professional engineer.

"C" indicates the first anchorage of de Grasse's fleet off Cape Henry and Lynnhaven Roads, where it arrived on 31 August 1781. "F" (top of map) is Jamestown Island, where the regiments under Saint-Simon (Agenois, Gâtinais, Touraine) landed on 2 September. "D" (bottom of map) shows the position of the British fleet commanded by Admiral Graves when it was sighted by the French on 5 September. De Grasse's victory of that day (the first phase of the Battle of the Chesapeake) and the failure of the British on succeeding days to outmaneuver their enemy's fleet gave control of the entrance to the Chesapeake Bay to the French navy. "N" indicates the second anchorage of de Grasse's fleet between Horseshoe shoal ("A") and Middle Ground ("B"), to which it moved on 25 September. Other points shown on the map are: "M," French ships (*Réfléchi, Ardent, Triton, Romulus*) blocking the mouth of the James; up river at "H," the landing place for the siege artillery, Trebell's Landing; inland, "G," Williamsburg; on the York River side of the peninsula, "E," Cornwallis's positions at Yorktown and at Gloucester Point across the river, with the British ships under command of Thomas Symonds; "L," three French ships (*Vaillant, Expériment, Railleuse*) blockading the mouth of York River; "O," two French corvettes reinforcing the blockade; "I" (Deacon's Neck, Ware River), the landing point of the detachment of 800 men from the ships' garrisons (including du Perron himself) under the command of Choisy, who proceeded overland via "K" (Gloucester Courthouse) to besiege Gloucester Point. See Du Perron's map of the Environs of Gloucester, No. 90.

This map thus represents summarily the situation into which Rochambeau's army moved when it came down the Bay from Annapolis.

MS, 33 x 46 cm. Princeton University Library, in manuscript journal of Joachim du Perron, comte de Revel, between pp. 64 and 65. A redrawn version of the map is reproduced in the printed version of the journal (pp. 120–121).

85 Thirty-Eighth Camp at Archer's Hope

25 September 1781. The transports that had brought the combined French and American forces from Annapolis are shown off the landing point at

Archer's Hope, which was about 7 miles southeast of Williamsburg to the west of the mouth of College Creek. Washington (*Diaries*, II, 261) refers to the spot as "the upper point of College Creek." The present Colonial Parkway passes along this shore. Archer's Hope is east of Jamestown Island, where Saint-Simon's forces from the West Indies had landed on 2 September. About 3½ miles downstream and east of Archer's Hope was Trebell's Landing, the landing point for the siege artillery, at the mouth of Grove Creek near Carter's Grove. The Archer's Hope encampment, depicted here near the shore along the road leading to Williamsburg, shows both French regiments (yellow) and the American units (green).

MS, 32 x 21 cm. Princeton University Library, Berthier Papers, No. 21–35/38. Rochambeau's copy is in the Library of Paul Mellon, Upperville, Virginia.

86 *Thirty-ninth Camp at Williamsburg*

26–27 September 1781. The road from Archer's Hope over which the army marched to its positions "at the gates of Williamsburg" is at the lower center of the map (below the word "Rich-mill's"). Clermont-Crèvecœur's journal (p. 56) notes that the field artillery was brought up College Creek in boats and unloaded at College Landing (lower right of map). The new arrivals found Saint-Simon's regiments already encamped to the northwest of the town (lower left, tinted yellow) and Lafayette's Americans (tinted green) west and south of the College of William and Mary. The French detachment that had been brought from Newport in Barras's squadron was also in camp (cf. Verger's journal, p. 137), as was the vanguard under Custine that had embarked at Head of Elk. Rochambeau's regiments (tinted yellow) made their camp to the east of town behind the Capitol, while Washington's Americans (tinted green) took a position farther to the south. The encampment at Williamsburg marked the 39th camp of Rochambeau's army since its departure from its 1st camp at Providence, Rhode Island, on 18 June. This map is the last in the "cahier" of the 1781 camps. The 40th and final camp of this "campaign," referred to at the bottom of the sheet, is included in the next plate.

MS, 32 x 21 cm. Princeton University Library, Berthier Papers, No. 21–39. Rochambeau's copy is in the Library of Paul Mellon, Upperville, Virginia.

87 *Plan of the Siege of York, by L.-A. and C.-L. Berthier*

The map is signed, below the border, lower right: "figuré à vue par Berthier frères à la hâte" ("drawn freehand by the Berthier brothers in haste"). The term *figuré à vue*, also used in the title of the map, indicates freehand drawing without the guidance of instruments, as distinguished from such surveyors' terms as *levé* or *déterminé géométriquement* (cf. Nos. 7 and 43). Administrative memoranda filed with a copy of a letter addressed to Rochambeau by the Marquis de Ségur, minister of war, dated Versailles, 5 December 1781, in reply to the General's recommendations in favor of the Berthier brothers, mention that "the elder has sent several maps and in particular the plan of York after the capture" (Archives de la Guerre, dossier of L.-A. Berthier, pièces 31–35). This presumably refers to the plan reproduced here, which must therefore have reached France in late November with the first batch of official dispatches sent by Rochambeau; on the couriers, cf. Clermont-Crèvecœur's journal, n. 127. Another similar map (without the hinged overlay), though unsigned, may be attributed to the Berthier brothers on the basis of style and handwriting; this is preserved with an anonymous 17-page manuscript text entitled "Siège d'Yorck deffendu par le Lord Corno Wallis . . ." in the Archives du Génie, 15 ("Sièges: Yorck aux Etats-Unis"), pièce 2.

Of the numerous extant French maps of Yorktown this is the only one found by the Editors that uses the hinged "flap" to depict the successive stages of the siege. A similar device is used, however, on several of the British maps of this period: e.g., "A Plan of the Posts of York and Gloucester . . . Established by His Majesty's Army under the Command of . . . Cornwallis . . . with the Attacks and Operations of the American & French Forces Commanded by General Washington and the Count of Rochambeau, Which Terminated in the Surrender of the said Posts and Army . . . ," surveyed by Capt. Fage of the Royal Artillery, published 4 June 1782; included in *The Atlantic Neptune*, J.F.W. Des Barres, comp. (facsimile reproduction, Barre Publishers, Barre, Mass., Series III, No. 41).

The left and lower parts of the Berthier brothers' map show in a broad semicircle the French (yellow) and American (green) camps, from which the troops moved in rotation and with clocklike regularity into the trenches of the siege lines. The French regiments are numbered: (1) Bourbonnais and (2) Royal Deux-Ponts, forming the Bourbonnais Brigade; (3) Soissonnais and (4) Saintonge, forming the Soissonnais Brigade; (5) Agenois and (6) Gâtinais, forming the Agenois Brigade; (7) Touraine; (8) Saint-Simon's volunteers. Moore's House, where the capitulation was signed, is shown at the lower right. A note in the "Legende" states that the English position at Gloucester Point "was drawn from York with a field-glass (*lunette d'approche*)."

Numerous other French maps of the Siege of Yorktown (many of them deriving from the basic engineers' maps) are extant. A partial list is in Coolie Verner, *Maps of the Yorktown Campaign . . . A Preliminary Checklist of Printed and Manuscript Maps Prior to 1800* (London, The Map Collectors' Circle, Map Collectors' Series, No. 18, 1965), pp. 45–52. A fine map by Crublier d'Opterre (not listed by Verner) is in the Library of Paul Mellon: "Carte des Environs d'York avec les attaques et la position des Armées Française et Américaine devant cette place." Notable among the maps still preserved, appropriately, in the archives of the Royal Corps of Engineers are several by the acting chief French engineer, Querenet de La Combe, sent by him to France immediately after the capitulation (Archives du Génie, 14, 15, "Sièges: Yorck aux Etats-Unis"). The Engineers had an essential role in the planning and conduct of the Siege of Yorktown and could there apply their specialized training that was based upon the precepts formulated a century earlier by Vauban in such works as his *Traité de l'attaque des places*. All the engineers at Yorktown, whether in the American or French service, were Frenchmen. Duportail commanded the Americans; Querenet de La Combe (replacing Desandroüins, who was sick), the French. Under them three divisions were formed, composed as follows: (1) Gouvion (American), d'Oyré, Turpin, Plancher; (2) Palys, Crublier d'Opterre, Rochefontaine (American), Courregeolles; (3) Ancteville, Garavaque, Bouan, Géante.

MS, 53 x 51.5 cm. Bibliothèque du Ministère des Armées "Terre," Paris, L.I.D. 174.

<table>
<tr><td>88 First Parallel, Detail from the Berthier Brothers' Plan</td><td>The hinged overlay shows the "first parallel," or siege line, established on 6 October 1781. The besieged British regiments are shown in red.

Detail from previous map. Reproduced actual size.</td></tr>
</table>

88 *First Parallel, Detail from the Berthier Brothers' Plan*

The hinged overlay shows the "first parallel," or siege line, established on 6 October 1781. The besieged British regiments are shown in red.

Detail from previous map. Reproduced actual size.

89 *Second Parallel, Detail from the Berthier Brothers' Plan*

The hinged overlay is here raised, showing the "second parallel" established on 15 October. Far right, near the riverbank, is the "redoute enlevée par les Américains," generally identified today as "Redoubt No. 10" (the British number for it), which was stormed by the Americans (led by Alexander Hamilton) during the night of 14–15 October. To the left of it is the "redoute enlevée par les Français" (British No. 9), which was taken by the French that same night (led by Guillaume de Deux-Ponts). See Clermont-Crèvecœur's journal, pp. 59–60, and Verger's journal, pp. 141–142. The British requested a truce on 17 October; the capitulation was signed on 19 October 1781.

Detail from No. 87. Reproduced actual size.

90 *Environs of Gloucester*

"Glocester" here refers to Gloucester Point, not to Gloucester Courthouse, now known as Gloucester, which is some 13 miles north of the Point and not shown on this map. Although Gloucester Point is summarily shown on most of the extant French maps of the Siege of Yorktown, this is the only one found by the Editors that depicts the surrounding area in detail. It was drawn by Sublieutenant Du Perron, whose journal contains a lively account of the Gloucester operations, in which he himself took part. A small schematic map of the Gloucester area, indicating roads from the Courthouse to the Point, is preserved with other papers of the Vicomte d'Arrot, colonel in Lauzun's Legion, in the Manuscript Collections of Colonial Williamsburg.

The road running from top (north) to bottom of the sheet closely follows the course of present U.S. Route 17. The "crique" at the left is Timberneck Creek; on the right are the northwest and northeast branches of Sarah Creek. The Marquis de Choisy (who had remained with the detachments at Newport, Rhode Island, when Rochambeau's army marched southward and subsequently arrived in Virginia in Barras's squadron) was assigned to the overall command of the operations at Gloucester Point. His forces included General Weedon's American militia, Lauzun's Legion, and the 800 troops lent by de Grasse from the ships' garrisons. The latter landed on 1 October at the head of Ware River (Deacon's Neck) and proceeded to the vicinity of Gloucester Courthouse, where Lauzun's

Legion and the American militia were already in camp (cf. No. 84, "I" and "K"). On 3 October Choisy's forces moved forward to positions shown here as "A," the French to the west of the road, the Americans to the east; the camp of Lauzun's Legion is at "B." These positions are south of Abingdon Church, "D," which was to serve as a hospital and was also fortified as a defensive position in case Cornwallis succeeded in crossing the river from Yorktown, and "C," which Du Perron calls "Saul's Tavern" (the locality now known as Ordinary). General Weedon had his headquarters in this tavern, General Choisy at the house marked "E." However, before these positions were fully occupied, a skirmish took place on 3 October between Lauzun's hussars and Tarleton's dragoons: "F" shows Tarleton's position, "H" the British infantry when attempting to outflank the French, who were drawn up at "G" (dotted lines). Concerning this engagement, see Clermont-Crèvecœur's journal, n. 113.

Farther down the road, at "K," is a redoubt constructed by the French, near the locality known as The Hook, now Hayes' Store. Various outposts are designated by letters, "o," "r," "L," etc. "M" is a detachment of enemy cavalry. The skirmish of 3 October—"Tarleton's last fight"—was the only significant engagement in the Gloucester sector of the siege, though Choisy's forces played an essential role by containing the British garrison within the Point. Cornwallis failed to make his escape across the river. The British forces at Gloucester formally surrendered on 19 October as a part of the general capitulation. The next day, when Du Perron made a personal (and unauthorized) inspection of the British fortifications, he discovered to his surprise that "Gloucester was only four houses situated on a point of land projecting into the river opposite York."

MS, 42 x 31 cm. Princeton University Library, in manuscript journal of Joachim du Perron, comte de Revel, between pp. 90 and 91. A redrawn version of the original map is included in the printed edition of the journal (pp. 146–147).

91 *Yorktown Peninsula Detail from unfinished Map*

This is a detail from an unfinished map preserved in the library of the Château de Grosbois, formerly Berthier's estate. It was apparently overlooked when other papers of his were dispersed in the 1930's. Had the map been completed, it would have included the entire peninsula between the James and York rivers, as well as the area as far north as the Ware River, and would have been a show piece comparable to the Berthier brothers' "Plan of Rhode Island," No. 7. The map provides an unusual example of the map maker's techniques. The entire map has been faintly sketched in pencil; certain portions have been traced over in black. A reddish brown ground color has been added to show relief, but the green and blue tints (for woods and water) have not been completed. As distinguished from No. 87, which was drawn freehand "in haste," Berthier probably worked on the present map during the winter quarters at Williamsburg when there was time to examine and survey the ground at leisure.

Another unfinished map—an outline ground plan of the siege lines at

Yorktown and Gloucester Point, in black and white—has also remained, hitherto unidentified, in the library at Grosbois.

MS, 68 x 83 cm. (entire map). Cut in sections and mounted on linen. Château de Grosbois (now owned by the Société d'Encouragement à l'Elevage du Cheval Français). The map has been misidentified by some nineteenth-century family archivist as "Environs de Baltimore."

92 The Siege of Yorktown, by Louis-Nicolas Van Blarenberghe, 1784

Van Blarenberghe's painting of the "Siege" and its companion piece depicting the "Surrender" (No. 95), dated respectively 1784 and 1785, were executed for the King's collection and are still in the former royal palace at Versailles. Replicas made for General Rochambeau, dated 1786, have remained at the Château de Rochambeau.

In a letter dated 30 May 1785 (preserved among the Berthier Papers, Princeton University Library) Rochambeau wrote to the Marquis de Ségur, minister of war: "When you presented to the King the first painting of the Siege of York, you were good enough to promise me a copy of it for my cabinet. Will you, Sir, accord me the favor of ordering M. Blarenberg to make me copies of the two paintings to place on the right and left of the portrait of Washington in my cabinet, and allow this letter to serve as a reminder to give the order to M. Berthier. . . ." Rochambeau's letter is endorsed by Ségur "M. Berthier, speak to me about this," indicating that he transmitted it for appropriate action to Jean-Baptiste Berthier, then governor of the Hôtel de la Guerre in Versailles under whose aegis the battle painters like Van Blarenberghe worked. Shortly afterwards, on 2 June 1785, Rochambeau wrote (in English) to Washington: "It has been presented yesterday to the King, my Dear Général, two pictures to put in his closet which have been done by an excellent painter, one representing the Siege of York and th'other the defile of the British army between the american and french armies. Mr. le marshal de Ségur promised me copies of them which I will place in my closet on the right and left sides of your picture [by Charles Willson Peale]—besides that they are excellent paintings, they have been drawn, both by the truth and by an excellent design done by the young Berthier whom was deputed quarter-master general at the said siege . . ." (Library of Congress, Washington Papers). Rochambeau's English term "design" is presumably his (or his secretary's) translation of the French *dessin*, a drawing. It can thus be plausibly inferred that "the excellent design done by the young Berthier [i.e., Louis-Alexandre]" was a pictorial sketch, since young Berthier was trained to draw views as well as maps. Such views of Yorktown, if they have survived, have not been located by the Editors. In any case, it is clear from Rochambeau's statement to Washington that Van Blarenberghe's paintings of Yorktown were based upon first-hand topographical information supplied by L.-A. Berthier, whether in the form of views or maps.

Louis-Nicolas Van Blarenberghe (1716–1794), a native of Lille, was one of the several battle painters (*peintres de batailles*) then attached to the Dépôt de la Guerre. Pierre L'Enfant (1704–1787), father of the designer of the city of Washington, was another. Although these documentary painters were not strictly speaking "combat artists," they nevertheless based their work on authentic battle plans and maps. Between 1779 and 1790 Van Blarenberghe executed a series recording the battles of the reign of Louis XV (Menin, Ypres, Fribourg, Fontenoy, Tournai, etc.), which may be seen today in the Château de Versailles. His "Battle of Fontenoy" (11 May 1745) is dated 1779; his "Battle of Melle" (9 July 1745), 1784. The artist thus interrupted this retrospective series to paint the recent victory in America. The Yorktown paintings are the same size as those of the earlier battles and are strikingly similar in lighting, color, and general composition. The meticulous detail characteristic of these battle scenes is also evident in the miniature landscapes and portraits with which Van Blarenberghe decorated snuff-boxes (examples in the Louvre, Cabinet des Dessins). Still other examples of his work are the city views (Warsaw, Berlin, etc.) framed in ornamental panels above the doorways in the archive rooms of the former Hôtel des Affaires Etrangères (now the Bibliothèque Municipale de Versailles). See also Van Blarenberghe's views of Brest, Nos. 1–2.

Van Blarenberghe's battle paintings are pictorial projections of diagrammatic ground plans or maps. There is, for example, a close correlation between his "Siege of Yorktown" and such plans as our No. 87. In the distance, center, is the besieged town of York and Gloucester Point on the far side of the river. Below this the second parallel can be traced, with puffs of smoke rising from the redoubts; and below this are the outlines of the inactive first parallel. The group of general officers and their staff is placed to the rear of the first parallel. From the left French troops are marching into the trenches; at the far right the Americans are advancing into their sector, which was closer to the river. Various appurtenances of the siege, such as fascines and gabions, can be distinguished in the foreground.

Gouache, 59 x 94 cm. Signed, lower center, "van Blarenberghe—1784." Musée de Versailles (2264). A replica (with some variant details) made for the Comte de Rochambeau signed, lower right, "Van Blarenberghe 1786," is in the Château de Rochambeau.

93 Rochambeau and his Officers, Detail from Van Blarenberghe's "Siege," 1784

The central group as depicted in the original version (Versailles) of Van Blarenberghe's "Siege of Yorktown." These are of course symbolic figures representing the participants in the siege rather than portraits from the life. It is nevertheless possible to identify many of them, thanks to the artist's accurate depiction of the uniforms. Rochambeau (wearing his Cross of Saint-Louis) stands towards the left, with raised arm. The figure in blue and red uniform behind Rochambeau's outstretched arm is presumably the Intendant (Tarlé), the chief administrative officer, who was responsible for the logistics of the campaign. The bare-headed figure in white uniform at the far left, with his sword down at the salute, is the colonel of the Soissonnais Regiment (Saint-Maîme), while the other with the tip of his sword in his left hand represents the colonel of the Bourbonnais Regiment (Laval). A group in the center evokes the Engineers: the man in an American uniform wearing the black American cockade, looking at the map, must be Duportail; the two holding either end of the map are French engineers (perhaps Desandroüins and Querenet de La Combe), as the black facings on their uniforms clearly show. Other generals and regimental officers complete this "conversation piece." The man mounting a horse, at the far right of the group, can be identified, from the musicians' lace sewn on the seams of his yellow coat, as a drummer of the Royal Deux-Ponts—who is probably being sent to beat an order for the troops.

Detail from Van Blarenberghe's gouache and watercolor painting, described under previous number. Musée de Versailles. The reproduction is approximately two-thirds the size of the original.

94 Rochambeau and his Officers, Detail from Van Blarenberghe's "Siege," 1786

The central group as depicted in the replica of the "Siege" executed by Van Blarenberghe for Rochambeau. Various changes have been made here, no doubt following Rochambeau's suggestions. The General himself, for example, is shown more formally, in his red full dress waistcoat and breeches, whereas in the earlier version he is wearing a white waistcoat and breeches (permitted in extreme hot weather). The Intendant, who was partially concealed by Rochambeau's arm in the first painting, has here been given a more prominent position, with his decoration (the Cross of Saint-Louis, which he received only in December 1781) proudly displayed. The colonel of the Soissonnais now has his hat on. In the foreground, to the right of Rochambeau, his four *maréchaux de camp* (Baron de Vioménil, Comte de Vioménil, Chevalier de Chastellux, Marquis de Saint-Simon) have been more carefully distinguished. Of these, Chastellux can be identified in the center of the group of three talking together, since he has the double cuff lace of the *major-général* (chief of staff) as well as the Cross of Saint-Louis. The next group of three represents, from the left: an officer of the Royal Deux-Ponts in a blue coat with yellow facings, an officer of the Gâtinais (standing) with blue lapels and the Cross of Saint-Louis, and an officer of the Agenois (seated) with light blue cuffs. The group of Engineers (Duportail pointing to the map) appears again here. To the right of the Engineers are several figures in American uniforms (white shoulder belts) who have no counterpart in the earlier version. The soldiers in the foreground (not included in the King's painting) represent the workmen who dug the trenches and emplaced the guns. Those depicted here in their *tenue de corvée* are wearing caps or *bonnets de police* in the colors of the Royal Deux-Ponts Regiment. The wounded man and stretcher-bearers (the one discernible here in this detail, lower right, is black) have likewise been given a more prominent place in the foreground.

Detail from Van Blarenberghe's gouache and watercolor painting. Replica for General Rochambeau. Château de Rochambeau, Thoré (Loir-et-Cher). Courtesy of Comte Michel de Rochambeau.

95 The Surrender of Yorktown, by Louis-Nicolas Van Blarenberghe, 1785

Van Blarenberghe's companion piece to his "Siege" represents (as Rochambeau phrased it) "the defile of the British army between the american and french armies," on 19 October 1781. The defeated army is shown, colors cased, marching out from Yorktown (far right) to the field (lower left) where they grounded their arms, as specified in the Articles of Capitulation (Article 3). The same afternoon a similar ceremony took place on the "Gloucester Side" of the York River. The French are drawn up along the left of the road (from the viewer's standpoint), the Americans on the right. The local observers in the foreground, including the fair Virginian Amazon, were undoubtedly inspired by descriptions given the artist by officers who had been on the spot.

Gouache, 59 x 94 cm. Signed, lower center, "van Blarenberghe. 1785." Musée de Versailles (2265). A replica (with some variant details) made for the Comte de Rochambeau signed, lower center, "Van Blarenberghe 1786," is in the Château de Rochambeau.

Van Blarenberghe's depiction of the surrender field provides visual confirmation of the many verbal descriptions of the dramatic conclusion of the siege.

Detail from Van Blarenberghe's "Surrender," 1785. Described above under the previous number. Musée de Versailles. The reproduction is approximately two-thirds the size of the original.

The French regiments drawn up along the right of the road leading out from Yorktown (the senior regiments nearest the town) are identified by their flags. The regimental color of the Royal Deux-Ponts (the "youngest" of the regiments present at Yorktown) can be distinguished at the far left of this detail. Preceding it (not included in this detail, but see the complete picture, opposite) is the colonel's color of the Royal Deux-Ponts. The colonel's color, i.e., his personal standard as distinguished from the regimental color, was paraded whenever the colonel was present with the regiment. To the right of the Royal Deux-Ponts (who wear blue coats) come the colonel's color, then the regimental color of the Saintonge (white coats), followed by the regimental color of Royal-Artillerie (blue coats again). Beyond the artillery come the colonel's color and the regimental color of the Soissonnais (white coats), and then the colonel's color and the regimental color of the Touraine. Still other regiments (Gâtinais, Agenois, and Bourbonnais), not visible in this detail, line the road as far back as the town.

Of the flags shown on the American side, the blue flag with white stars, far left in this detail, can be positively identified as Washington's Headquarters flag (illustrated in E. Schermerhorn, *American and French Flags of the Revolution, 1775–1783* [Philadelphia, 1948], Plate III).

The rejoicing Virginians, center foreground, were probably suggested to the artist by Berthier or other officers familiar with the locality. Berthier had himself sketched similar scenes when he visited the Comte de Ségur's plantation in Saint-Domingue during his journey back to France. See Berthier's journal, n. 134.

Detail from Van Blarenberghe's gouache and watercolor painting, 1786. Replica for General Rochambeau. Château de Rochambeau, Thoré (Loir-et-Cher). Courtesy of Comte Michel de Rochambeau.

98 View of York

This sketch of the Yorktown skyline, seen from the York River side, appears as a vignette in the lower right corner of a comprehensive map entitled "Plan of the Landing and March of the Division commanded by the Marquis de Saint-Simon, its junction with the Corps commanded by the Marquis de la Fayette, and with the combined army of Washington and Rochambeau, and the Siege of York, 1781." Although the map is not signed, it can be assumed from the title that it was drawn by a French officer who came to Virginia from the West Indies. Since Saint-Simon's forces were reembarked on de Grasse's ships that set sail on 4 November 1781, the sketch (or its prototype) was in all likelihood drawn towards the end of October only a few days after the surrender of the town.

The large house at the left appears to be the shell of Secretary Nelson's house. The building with a cupola to the left of the flag (no doubt the stars and stripes) near the edge of the bluff is Grace Church. Directly below the letter "Y" of "Yorck" is the Thomas Nelson, Jr., house.

MS, detail from "Plan du debarquement et de la Marche de la division Commandée par le Mis. de St. Simon . . . ," 22.6 x 36 cm. Bibliothèque du Ministère des Armées "Terre," Paris, L.I.D. 174 (one of several items under this classification number).

99 Plan of Yorktown to be used for establishing the Winter Quarters of the Soissonnais Regiment, and of the Grenadiers and Chasseurs of the Saintonge Regiment, 12 November 1781

This map provides a record of Yorktown buildings as they existed immediately after the siege. At the upper left (colored darker than the others) is "Secretary Nelson's" house, where Cornwallis had his headquarters at the opening of the siege and which later suffered heavily from allied artillery bombardment. The building set back slightly from the south side of the main street (below the word "hyver" in the heading) was another Nelson house belonging to Secretary Nelson's nephew, Thomas Nelson, Jr., governor of Virginia and commander of the American militia during the siege. Both Nelson houses figure in the annals of the siege; see, e.g., Clermont-Crèvecœur's journal, n. 137. The Thomas Nelson, Jr., house ("York Hall"), still standing, can be distinguished in the distant view of Yorktown included in Van Blarenberghe's paintings (Nos. 92 and 95). See also the "View of York," which was drawn at about the same time as this ground plan and which is similarly oriented, with the York River in the foreground. Other buildings surviving today (the Customs House, Grace Church, etc.) may be identified by reference to the map of "Old Houses and Other Places of Interest in the 'Town of York,'" in Charles E. Hatch, Jr., *Yorktown and the Siege of 1781*, National Park Service, Historical Handbook No. 14 (Washington, 1954, and subsequent editions).

MS, 28.5 x 45.5 cm. Princeton University Library, Berthier Papers, No. 29.

100 Profile of Yorktown Fortifications

These sketches, which appear as an inset in the lower right corner of a "Plan du Siège d'York . . . ," represent the two main types of works constructed by the British to form the rampart defending the town of York.

MS, detail from "Plan du Siège d'York, en Virginie par l'armée alliée d'Amérique et de France sous les Ordres des G[énér]aux Washington et Cte. de

Rochambeau; contre l'Armée Anglaise Commandée par Lord Cornwallis en Octobre 1781," 47.2 x 30.8 cm. Service Hydrographique de la Marine, 136–7–3, now on deposit in the Bibliothèque Nationale, Section des Cartes et Plans. A similar map, including the vignette, is in the Bibliothèque du Génie, MS A 224, "Atlas de la Guerre d'Amérique," fol. 79.

101 *Generals of the French and American Armies at Yorktown after the Surrender, by James Peale*

This is a studio composition, painted not earlier than 1782 and probably even later. Nevertheless, the view of Yorktown is based on authentic documents, as are the portraits of the officers. "After the surrender of Cornwallis at Yorktown, James Peale [brother of Charles Willson Peale] appears to have visited the scene . . . to get a timely and appropriate background for Washington portraits" (Sellers, *Portraits by CWP*, p. 232). Portions of this same view appear in the background of portraits of Washington executed in the Peale atelier, *ca.* 1782, for Rochambeau and for Chastellux. Rochambeau's Washington portrait is at the Château de Rochambeau (Sellers, No. 919); Chastellux's (not recorded in Sellers) is still owned by collateral descendants. The appropriateness of the Yorktown background in these instances is evident, recalling as it does the allied victory in which Rochambeau and Chastellux were Washington's partners.

James Peale's view can, furthermore, be correlated with the contemporary maps of Yorktown. The generals are standing by the riverbank, west of the town and west of Yorktown Creek (visible here, with a small footbridge), near the "Fusiliers' Redoubt" (shown under fire of the "Volontaires de S. Simon" on the Berthier brothers' "Plan of the Siege," No. 87). The towerlike building, left center of the painting, is the windmill, which can also be discerned in Van Blarenberghe's paintings (Nos. 92 and 95). At the far left is Gloucester Point. Masts of sunken enemy ships project from the surface of the river. Dead horses have been washed ashore along the beach. French ships, flying white pennants, ride at anchor in the distance.

It can be assumed that the officers' heads are copied from authentic life portraits that were available to James Peale in the family studio in Philadelphia. A comparison of the faces depicted here with the portraits painted by Charles Willson Peale leads to the following identifications, which differ in some cases from those previously suggested by others. Washington is unmistakable. On his right (from the viewer's standpoint) is General Rochambeau, wearing a dark blue and red uniform with the insignia of the Order of Saint-Louis (cf. Sellers, No. 750). Lafayette, in his American general's uniform, stands in the foreground at Washington's left (cf. Sellers, Nos. 445 and 935). At the far right, holding the Articles of Capitulation, is Colonel Tench Tilghman, Washington's aide (and friend of the Peale family), who was chosen to carry news of the surrender to Congress in Philadelphia (cf. Sellers, No. 935). The figure in the second row, between Washington and Lafayette, is General Benjamin Lincoln (cf. Sellers, No. 483), who, like Lafayette, has the American feather in his hat (as prescribed by Washington in June 1780). The other figure in the second row, between Rochambeau and Tilghman, wearing a French uniform and decoration, is Rochambeau's chief of staff, General Chastellux (cf. Sellers, No. 140; Chastellux [4], II, frontispiece). All the officers wear the black-and-white cockade of the Franco-American alliance.

James Peale's painting of the generals at Yorktown was originally owned by Robert Gilmor (1748–1822) of Baltimore, whose son, another Robert Gilmor, presented it in 1845 to the Maryland Historical Society. At least two replicas were made in the Peale studio: one for Francis Bailey of Philadelphia, another for Lafayette. Concerning the painting done for Bailey, which was acquired in 1958 by Colonial Williamsburg, see Charles Coleman Sellers, "Francis Bailey and the Peales," *Antiques*, December 1954, pp. 492–493. The Bailey-Williamsburg version differs in some of its details from the Maryland Historical Society canvas, notably in the faces, which are less carefully individualized. The painting done for Lafayette (present location unknown to the Editors) was exhibited in the "Exposition Historique des Souvenirs Franco-Américains de la Guerre de l'Indépendance" in the French Pavilion at the Chicago World's Fair, 1893. In the catalogue of that exhibition (p. 48, item No. 43), it is described as being signed "York Painted by James Peale in 1786 (?)" and as having been lent by "Madame la Barrone de Perron," a granddaughter of Lafayette. Baroness Perrone di San Martino (née Jenny de La Tour-Maubourg, 1812–1897) was the daughter of Lafayette's daughter Anastasie. According to information in the J. Hall Pleasants Collection (Maryland Historical Society), the painting was owned in 1908 by the Baroness's grandson, Fernando Perrone di San Martino, of Turin, who was at that time offering it for sale. The subsequent history of this Lafayette replica of James Peale's painting has not been traced. See also John Hill Morgan and Mantle Fielding, *The Life Portraits of Washington and Their Replicas* (Philadelphia, 1931), pp. 128–129.

Oil painting by James Peale (1740–1831), approx. 56 x 75 cm. Maryland Historical Society, Baltimore.

Winter Quarters in Virginia November 1781 – June 1782

102 Freehand Map of Portsmouth, Virginia, and Environs

This map by the engineer Crublier d'Opterre was probably drawn in the autumn of 1781 or perhaps during the winter quarters of 1781–1782, when the French officers had leisure to inspect the country on the south side of the James River. Portsmouth had been seized by the British in October 1780 at the beginning of their invasion of Virginia. It served as their base until the end of July 1781, when the forces under Cornwallis were transported to Yorktown and Gloucester Point. Crublier d'Opterre's map shows, above the fortified city of Portsmouth, the position (dotted lines) of "Lord

Cornwallis's last camp." Across the river from Portsmouth are the "ruins of Norfolk." Norfolk had been burned by the Virginians early in 1776 to rid it of Tories and to deprive the royal governor, Lord Dunmore, of a shelter for his ships.

MS, 44.5 x 53 cm. (sheet); 32.5 x 40.5 (within border). Library of Paul Mellon, Upperville, Virginia, Crublier d'Opterre MS No. 10.

Although Portsmouth was no longer in enemy hands at the time of the Siege of Yorktown, it was nevertheless feared that an English fleet might attempt to slip into the Elizabeth River again. On 13 October 1781 Washington wrote to the commander of the Virginia militia in this vicinity: "It being a Matter of Importance that the Works erected at Portsmouth by the Enemy, should be destroyed, I have to request that you will immediately upon Receipt of this assemble the Militia in your Vicinity to effect that Purpose; let them be compleatly levelled and demolished, that no further use may be made of them." *Writings of GW*, XXIII, 216. The razing of the fortifications at Portsmouth was accomplished by the militia under the direction of Mathieu Dumas of Rochambeau's staff. Recalling this mission in his *Souvenirs* (I, 90–91), Dumas wrote: "This post, where Arnold had first taken refuge, had been well entrenched; and Lord Cornwallis, who had occupied it before moving to Yorktown, had extended and perfected the fortifications. I was sent in haste with a battalion of American militia to raze these works. I found them in excellent condition; the position was well chosen; the redoubts and redans, linked by deep trenches, were lined with very carefully made *fascinages*. All these works were fraised, palisaded, and surrounded with strong abatis. A very strong west wind having arisen, I took advantage of it in order to burn them, which greatly facilitated my operation. However, it was only after a week's work with my detachment and all the workers I could assemble that I finally completed this destruction."

Although Dumas does not date the operation precisely, it would appear to have taken place late in October or in early November 1781. Rochambeau's aide-de-camp, Von Closen, notes in his journal (p. 162), in early November, that "M. Dumas was sent to raze the works that Arnold had had constructed at Portsmouth. . . . he brought back a plan of them, of which I made a copy." The "Plan des Ouvrages de Portsmouth en Virginie," now in the Library of Congress, Rochambeau Map No. 53, is probably the plan referred to. Crublier d'Opterre's map reproduced here, though of different draftsmanship, is essentially the same. There is no specific evidence that Crublier d'Opterre participated in the demolition of the English works, but as an engineer he might well have done so. If not, he probably visited Portsmouth soon thereafter to cast a professional eye on the former English fortifications.

The building in the center of the town, shown with a steeple, presumably represents Trinity Church (built in 1762), still standing on this site at the corner of High and Court Streets. The streets have not been completed on the map. Those indicated by dotted lines represent: Court Street (left to right); High Street, branching off towards the top of map and continued by the Suffolk road; Queen Street, leading down to the waterfront at the bottom of the map. The "Q[uar]tier du General," on Court Street, designates the headquarters occupied by Cornwallis before his move to Yorktown. A "Camp des Nègres" (called "habitations de Negres" on Rochambeau Map No. 53) is shown across the creek, upper right. Throughout the war, whenever the opportunity offered, the English had recruited negro workers, often employing them, as here at Portsmouth, for work on fortifications. The recovery of such fugitive slaves (or compensation for their loss) was a matter of continuing concern to Virginia slave owners long after the end of the war.

Several maps of Portsmouth by British engineers are known; see, e.g., Christian Brun, *Guide to the Manuscript Maps in the William L. Clements Library* (Ann Arbor, 1959), Nos. 575, 577, 578, 579. Another plan of Portsmouth preserved among the Rochambeau maps (No. 52) appears to have been drawn, for intelligence purposes, while the English were still occupying the town. One of the objectives of the unsuccessful "Destouches expedition," March 1781, was the dislodgement of General Arnold from his base at Portsmouth. Later on, writing to de Grasse from Providence, 11 June 1781, Rochambeau had suggested that the Admiral's first action on the North American coast might be the destruction of the British base at Portsmouth; at that time he did not know that the enemy would subsequently retire to Yorktown. Doniol, v, 489–490.

MS, 44 x 57 cm. (sheet); 38 x 51 cm. (within border). Library of Paul Mellon, Upperville, Virginia, Crublier d'Opterre MS No. 11.

104 *Map of West Point on the York River at the Confluence of the Pamunkey and Mattaponi* [1781–1782]

Winter quarters for the artillery were established at West Point, also called Delaware, some 30 miles from Williamsburg. Lieutenant Clermont-Crèvecœur, of the Auxonne artillery, who spent the winter here, notes in his journal (p. 66) that he helped embark the heavy siege pieces at Yorktown, as well as the large artillery park. He also mentions that three artillery companies, plus the miners' company, were stationed at West Point under the command of M. de Chazelles. When the army moved northward in July 1782, two companies of artillery and the siege guns remained at West Point until they were transported up the Chesapeake Bay to Baltimore in mid-August. Cf. note to No. 130.

The map, by an unidentified cartographer, indicates various dwellings in the town and vicinity. Among the names are Bingham, Moore, and "Brackson," i.e., Braxton. "Dodley's Ferry" across the Mattaponi is Dudley's Ferry. Defensive works constructed by the French are shown on the following map.

MS, 33 x 37 cm. Library of Congress, Map Division, Rochambeau Map. No. 54. A similar map, entitled "Plan de West-Point du Sud," probably copied from this one, is in the Service Historique de la Marine, Fonds du Service Hydrographique, MS No. 2847, Cromot Dubourg's "Atlas," No. 7.

*105 Batteries at West Point
[in Virginia], at the
Head of York River*

Clermont-Crèvecœur (p. 66) notes that the point "was fortified and put into a state of defense only to protect the army's retreat in case of attack by a superior force. . . . The army could retire to this place and, with the aid of several redoubts . . . , defend it against superior forces." The legend of the map describes the batteries:

A.   [Battery] of six 24-pounders and four 16-pounders.
B.   Six 24-pounders and four 16-pounders.
C.   Two 8-inch howitzers and four 8-inch mortars.
D.   Seven 9- and 12-inch mortars.

MS, 31.5 x 41 cm. Library of Congress, Map Division, Rochambeau Map No. 55. There is a similar map in the Archives du Génie, 15–1–7, No. 31.

*106 Plan of Hampton [in
Virginia] to be used for
establishing the Winter
Quarters of Lauzun's
Legion, 1 November 1781*

The stream at the right, flowing south, is Hampton River. The other directional arrow, at the left of the map below the legend, is misleading (probably a mistake); the point indicates south, not the customary north. Directly below this arrow point is St. John's Episcopal Church. The two longest streets forming a cross are King Street (from top to bottom of map) and Queen Street (left to right). The numbers indicating available lodgings were presumably used for assigning quarters. The billeting list that might supply a key to these numbers is not preserved with the map and has not been found.

When steps were being taken to quarter his army early in November 1781, Rochambeau assured the local authorities that a barrack master approved by Governor Nelson and by General Washington would proceed in such a way as to cause minimum expense to the inhabitants and that necessary repairs to war-damaged houses would be made at the King's expense; cf. his letter to the Council of the City of Williamsburg, printed in Doniol, v, 584–585. According to Von Closen (p. 162), the winter quarters, into which the troops moved on 15–18 November, were assigned as follows: the Bourbonnais Regiment, seven companies of the Royal Deux-Ponts, part of the Auxonne artillery, as well as the General Staff, were quartered in Williamsburg. Three companies of the Royal Deux-Ponts were sent to Jamestown. The Soissonnais, with the grenadiers and chasseurs of the Saintonge, were at Yorktown (see No. 99). The Saintonge Regiment encamped at Halfway House (on the road from Yorktown to Hampton) and Back River. A detachment of 50 men and an artillery company was assigned to Gloucester. The rest of the artillery went to West Point at the head of York River (see No. 104). Finally, Lauzun's Legion took up quarters in Hampton, as confirmed by the present map.

The Lauzun Legion did not remain here at Hampton during the entire period of the "winter quarters." In early February 1782 Rochambeau sent the Legion under the command of General Choisy (Lauzun having returned temporarily to France) to an advanced position near the North Carolina border at the request of General Nathanael Greene, who feared the arrival of British reinforcements at Charleston. The Legion remained in the vicinity of Charlotte Courthouse until June, when it retired to Petersburg and eventually rejoined the main body of the army on its northward march. After the Legion's departure from Hampton a battalion of the Saintonge Regiment moved into quarters there; cf. Béville's "Ordre de marche" of 28 June 1782 (Library of Congress, Rochambeau Papers, Vol. 4, 469).

During the French "occupation" of Hampton the courthouse (serving Elizabeth City County) was used as a hospital. This is the unnumbered building shown on the map a bit to the left of King Street directly below the second "u" of "Lauzun" in the title. An Act of the General Assembly of the Commonwealth of Virginia (5 January 1782) empowered the justices of the peace for the County of Elizabeth City "to hold their sessions at such places in the said county as they may think proper, so long as the court-house in the town of Hampton shall be occupied by the troops of our allies, as a hospital." The names of several French soldiers who died in Hampton (including Carrette, Thouvenot, and Bourdet of the Saintonge Regiment) are mentioned in Bouvet, *Service de santé*, p. 94, and in Dawson, *Français Morts aux Etats-Unis*, pp. 60, 64, 65, 92.

MS, 39 x 31.5 cm. (41.5 x 35 cm. with blank margins). Princeton University Library, Berthier Papers, No. 28.

107 *Chain of Expresses between New Kent Courthouse, New Castle, and Lynch's Tavern, 1781*

Early in November, a few weeks after the capitulation of Yorktown, Washington's Continentals left Virginia and returned northward to winter quarters on the Hudson. The French army thus remained in an "intermediary position," as Rochambeau described it, between the Northern army and the Southern army in the Carolinas under the command of General Greene. In instructions to Colonel Timothy Pickering, dated Williamsburg, 4 November 1781, Washington had noted: "For the purpose of Communicating Intelligence, I have agreed with Count Rochambeau who remains here to establish a Chain of Expresses from hence to Philadelphia. You will take Measures to furnish your part of the Chain, which is to extend from the Bowling Green to Philadelphia; from the Bowling Green to this place [Williamsburg], extending towards Genl Greene, will be continued by Count Rochambeau." *Writings of GW*, XXIII, 331.

The diagram and related memoranda prepared by L.-A. Berthier (a good example of the kind of assignments he received as an assistant quartermaster-general) show the "part of the chain" maintained by the French. Instructions for the two hussars stationed at New Kent Courthouse, dated 9 November, specify that they will remain there night and day ready to relay dispatches between Williamsburg and Richmond or to the next post at New Castle; the tavernkeeper at New Kent [James Warren] will feed the men and supply forage for their horses ("2 gallons of oats and 17 bunches of cornstalks per day"). Agreements also recorded here by Berthier mention that the tavernkeeper at New Kent is to be paid 50 dollars a month, those at New Castle and at Lynch's Tavern 40 dollars.

Berthier was already familiar with this country, having traversed it when marching southward with the wagon train only a few weeks earlier; see Itinerary 6. New Castle, on the Pamunkey River, once a flourishing town, is now extinct. Lynch's Tavern (also known as "Head Lynch's Ordinary," from the name of the tavernkeeper, James Head Lynch) was near Reedy Creek about halfway between the Pamunkey and Mattaponi rivers along the road corresponding to present U.S. Route 301.

It evidently took the Americans some time to establish satisfactory service beyond Bowling Green to Philadelphia. Rochambeau, for example, complained to Governor Benjamin Harrison of Virginia that a month after Washington's departure from Virginia he had not received a single letter from him; cf. letters from Harrison to Rochambeau, 17 December, 21 December, and Harrison to Governor Thomas Sim Lee of Maryland, 21 December 1781, in H. R. McIlvaine, ed., *Official Letters of the Governors of the State of Virginia*, III (Richmond, 1929), 113, 116–117. In a letter addressed to Béville, French quartermaster-general, 5 December 1781, Richard Young reported from Fredericksburg: "If money cannot be obtain'd for the purpose of paying the Express Riders at the different posts [between Lynch's Tavern and Fredericksburg] it will be impossible to keep up a line of Communication. . . ." Manuscript Collections of Colonial Williamsburg, Miscellaneous Manuscripts. Writing from Philadelphia, 8 January 1782, Washington avowed to Rochambeau: "I am fearful that the Expresses between this place and Williamsburg are badly regulated, and I shall upon the return of the Quarter Master General from the North River endeavour to have things put in better train." *Writings of GW*, XXIII, 435.

MS, 3 pages (4th blank), 31 x 19.5 cm. Princeton University Library, Berthier Papers, No. 30. Several other memoranda relating to the expresses are in Berthier Papers, Nos. 32–37.

March Northward: Virginia, Baltimore, Philadelphia, the Hudson, Encampment at Crompond July - October 1782

Camp Plans

108 Plans of the Different Camps occupied by the Army under the Orders of the Comte de Rochambeau: Campaign of 1782

The following series of 45 maps depicts the army's camps on its march from Virginia to the Hudson and eventually to Boston. The cover sheet of the "cahier," reproduced here, is the same as the one for the 1781 southbound camps (No. 26) except for the heading "Amérique/ Campagne/ 1782." As with the earlier series, the maps are so oriented that the direction of the march (generally northward in 1782) is at the top of the sheet; thus the two series appear reversed in relation to each other. In instances where the army camped in 1782 on a site previously occupied in 1781 the cartographer has not repeated the map; the camp is merely recorded in the heading, with a cross-reference to the 1781 map. There are no detailed road maps for the 1782 marches, but the route is summarily shown on the comprehensive map of camps and marches (No. 162) with camp numbers corresponding to those of the present series. The route from Williamsburg to Spurrier's Tavern (19th camp, preceding the 20th camp at Baltimore) is described mile by mile in Itinerary 6, which records the march of the wagon train when it took this route in the opposite direction in 1781. Portions of the route through Virginia and Maryland can be traced in Christopher Colles, *A Survey of the Roads of the United States of America* (1789; facsimile, ed. Walter W. Ristow, 1961), Plates 59–80.

A second set of the 1782 camp maps, which once belonged to General Rochambeau, is in the Library of Congress, Map Division. There are a few minor variations, such as uncompleted place names, in the General's set.

The army moved northward from Williamsburg in four divisions, marching a day apart. The First Division, including the Bourbonnais Regiment, commanded by Major General Chastellux and led by Collot, left on 1 July; the Second Division, including the Royal Deux-Ponts, commanded by Comte Christian de Deux-Ponts and led by Cromot Dubourg, on 2 July; the Third Division, including the Soissonnais, commanded by Comte de Vioménil and led by his nephew Comte d'Ollonne, on 3 July; the Fourth Division, including the Saintonge, commanded by Comte de Custine and led by the younger Berthier (Charles-Louis), on 4 July. Meanwhile, the Lauzun Legion had left Petersburg (see note to No. 106) and proceeded via Kingsland Ferry, Richmond, North's Tavern on the Chickahominy, and Hanover Courthouse, to Littlepage's Bridge on the Pamunkey, at which point it became the vanguard of the army, preceding it by two days. The Legion was commanded by the Marquis de Choisy (Lauzun himself had not yet returned from France) and led by Dumas and the elder Berthier (Louis-Alexandre). The plan for the march is outlined in a document dated Williamsburg, 28 June 1782, signed by Béville, quartermaster-general: "Ordre de Marche pour porter l'armée Françoise aux ordres de M. le Cte. de Rochambeau de ses différens Quartiers en Virginie à George-town sur la Rive gauche du Potowmak où Elle doit rester jusqu'à nouvel ordre en 22 jours de marche y compris Quatre Séjours." Library of Congress, Rochambeau Papers, Vol. 4, 469–478. Rochambeau, who went ahead to confer with Washington in Philadelphia, did not personally accompany the army on the first stages of the march.

The march is briefly described in the journal of Clermont-Crèvecœur, who was with a company of the Auxonne artillery included in the Third Division (pp. 72ff.); and also, in more detail, in the journal of Verger, of the Deux-Ponts Regiment, Second Division (pp. 159ff.).

MS, 32 x 21 cm. Princeton University Library, Berthier Papers, No. 39. Rochambeau's set of these camp plans is recorded in Philip L. Phillips, *A List of Maps of America in the Library of Congress* (Washington, 1901), pp. 861–862. A somewhat similar series of the 1782 camps, but smaller in size, is in the

Huntington Library, MS 621, described above in the "Checklist of Journals," *s.v.* Soissonnais Regiment.

109 First Camp at Drinking Spring [in Virginia]

1–4 July 1782. The dates on this and the following maps are those of the arrival of the first of the four divisions. The camp was thus occupied on four successive days.

Drinking Spring, 8 miles northwest of Williamsburg, was along the road now known as U.S. Route 60. The camp ground was situated at present Norge in the vicinity of Our Savior Lutheran Church, where the small creek shown on the map can still be discerned.

MS, 32 X 21 cm. Princeton University Library, Berthier Papers, No. 39-1. Rochambeau's copy is in the Library of Congress, Map Division.

110 Second Camp Two Miles beyond Byrd's Tavern

2–5 July 1782. Eight miles from the previous camp. Byrd's (frequently written "Bird's") Tavern was earlier known as Doncastle's Ordinary and was situated about 2 miles south of present Barhamsville. Since the French camped 2 miles beyond the tavern (which is not shown on the map), this would seem to place their camp at Barhamsville. The road branching off to the right, not taken by the army, led to Ruffin's Ferry, which crossed the Pamunkey above West Point.

MS, 32 X 21 cm. Princeton University Library, Berthier Papers, No. 39-2. Rochambeau's copy is in the Library of Congress, Map Division.

111 Third Camp at Ratcliffe House

3–6 July 1782. Seven miles from Byrd's Tavern (i.e., 5 miles from the previous camp, which was 2 miles beyond the tavern). The much-corrected word "Rattelaffe" appears to be a copying error for "Ratcliffe." There was evidently some uncertainty about the correct form. This name is not filled in at all on the general map of camps and marches (No. 162). Verger in his journal writes it "Radelassen." It has been variously transcribed in printed versions of other French officers' journals: e.g., "Ratelof" (Blanchard) and "Ratilisse" (Vicomte de Rochambeau).

The name "Ratcliff" appears several times in the New Kent County Land Tax List for 1782 (earliest extant tax records for this county, Virginia State Library). "Ratcliffe"'s also appear in the Vestry Book of Blissland Parish, part of which coincided with the eastern part of New Kent County; C. G. Chamberlayne, ed., *The Vestry Book of Blisland (Blissland) Parish* (Richmond, 1935). Although the exact location of the Ratcliffe property shown here has not been determined, it was probably along the present secondary road that goes from Barhamsville, via Slatersville, to New Kent Courthouse. The stream shown on the map may perhaps be a portion of Beaverdam Creek. Cf. U.S. Geological Survey, Walkers Quadrangle.

MS, 32 X 21 cm. Princeton University Library, Berthier Papers, No. 39-3. A similar map is in Rochambeau's set, Library of Congress, Map Division.

112 Fourth Camp at Hartfield

4–7 July 1782. Seven and one half miles from the previous camp. The name "Hartfield," which should presumably read "Harfield," has disappeared from modern maps. A Michael Harfield appears in the New Kent County Tax List for 1782 (Virginia State Library), and Harfields are also mentions in the Vestry Book of St. Peter's Parish, part of which coincided with the western part of this county. Itinerary 6 describes the position near "Hartfield House" (the building shown here on a small round hillock) as a very poor campsite. It was located some 3 miles northwest of New Kent Courthouse (through which the army had marched on its way here), along the old road to New Castle. The creek flowing into the Pamunkey, shown here on the map, is perhaps Big Creek or White House Creek. Cf. U.S. Geological Survey, Tunstall Quadrangle. The site of "The White House," home of Martha Dandridge Custis at the time of her marriage to George Washington, is in this general region, as is the Pamunkey Indian Reservation across the river.

MS, 32 x 21 cm. Princeton University Library, Berthier Papers, No. 39–4. Another copy (formerly in the archives of General Rochambeau) is in the Library of Congress, Map Division.

113 Fifth Camp at New Castle

5–9 July 1782. Fifteen miles from the previous camp. There was an extra day's halt here for each of the divisions, so that two divisions were encamped here together on 6, 7, and 8 July, the Fourth Division only on the 9th. Itinerary 6, describing the wagon train's 1781 march, speaks of New Castle as "a small town with very few houses, situated on high ground. It is almost deserted. There are many plantations in the neighborhood." More than a half century later, when Benson J. Lossing visited it in December 1848, he described it as "once a flourishing village, but now a desolation, only one house remaining upon its site" (*Pictorial Field-Book of the Revolution* [New York, 1851], II, 225). With the decline of river traffic and the changing pattern of agricultural economy in this section of Virginia, New Castle has now wholly disappeared. It was situated a mile or so east of the present bridge over the Pamunkey on the Richmond-Tappahanock road (U.S. Route 360), where a state historical marker recalls Patrick Henry's "call to arms" at New Castle.

MS, 32 x 21 cm. Princeton University Library, Berthier Papers, No. 39–5. Rochambeau's copy is in the Library of Congress, Map Division.

114 Sixth Camp at Hanovertown

7–10 July 1782. Seven miles from the previous camp. Hanovertown (not to be confused with Hanover Courthouse, which was some 10 miles beyond, to the northwest) has, like New Castle, disappeared from modern maps. The French camp was a mile beyond the little town shown here, which had been laid out by vote of the Virginia Assembly in 1762 near Page's Warehouse. The small stream on the map is a tributary of the Pamunkey. The wagon train had camped here on 4 October 1781; see Itinerary 6, where it is recorded that Hanovertown and vicinity had suffered considerable damage from Cornwallis's raiders.

MS, 32 x 21 cm. Princeton University Library, Berthier Papers, No. 39–6. Rochambeau's copy is in the Library of Congress, Map Division.

*115 Seventh Camp at
[Little]Page's Bridge or
Graham's House*

8–11 July 1782. Ten miles from the previous camp. Littlepage's Bridge crossed the Pamunkey in the vicinity of Hanover Courthouse (not shown on the map). Graham's House was a mile or so beyond the river on the road (roughly present U.S. Route 301) leading north to Bowling Green. Itinerary 6 notes that the crossing of the Pamunkey was by a "wooden bridge." It was here at Littlepage's Bridge that the route of march of Lauzun's Legion (which had come from Petersburg and Richmond) joined that of the rest of the army. From here on the Legion formed the vanguard.

MS, 32 x 21 cm. Princeton University Library, Berthier Papers, No. 39-7. Rochambeau's copy is in the Library of Congress, Map Division.

*116 Eighth Camp at Burk's
Bridge or Kenner's
Tavern*

9–12 July 1782. Twelve miles from the previous camp. Burk's Bridge, which crossed the Mattaponi some 9 miles south of Bowling Green, was in Caroline County along present U.S. Route 301. John Burk was licensed as a tavernkeeper there. Although the wagon train did not camp at Burk's Bridge in 1781, the Itinerary describing its route notes that "a camp could be located in front of Burk's Bridge." "Kenner's Tavern" (the building to the left of the letter "K") is called "Kenner's Red House" on Colles's 1789 road map (Plate 72); the Itinerary (1781) refers to it only as "the red house."

MS, 32 x 21 cm. Princeton University Library, Berthier Papers, No. 39-8. Rochambeau's copy is in the Library of Congress, Map Division.

*117 Ninth Camp at
Bowling Green*

10–13 July 1782. Nine miles from the previous camp. Rochambeau's aide-de-camp Von Closen, who joined his regiment (Royal Deux-Ponts) here on 11 July, describes Bowling Green as "a small place where there is only one tavern and the residence of Mr. John Hoomes, a very wealthy person, where we danced in the evening" (p. 210). The road branching off to the right, as indicated on the map, led to Caroline Courthouse, which was some distance from the settlement at Bowling Green proper. A few years later the county seat was moved to Bowling Green, where the present county courthouse was erected on land provided for public use by John Hoomes. The wagon train had made its 10th camp here on 2 October 1781. See Itinerary 6, where it is noted: "Neither camp nor headquarters would be very well situated here. It is nevertheless better than any other campsite in this neighborhood."

MS, 32 x 21 cm. Princeton University Library, Berthier Papers, No. 39-9. Rochambeau's copy is in the Library of Congress, Map Division.

*118 Tenth Camp at Charles
Thornton's House*

11–14 July 1782. Eight and one half miles from the previous camp. The camp was on high ground beyond Charles Thornton's house on the road leading north to Fredericksburg and Falmouth. Some 2 miles beyond the campsite, but not shown on the map, was Todd's Ordinary (present Villboro, Caroline County) where, according to Von Closen (p. 210), the headquarters was located. "Charles" Thornton's house was evidently so designated in order to distinguish it from "Widow" Thornton's, another "fine house," 2 miles or so to the south and past which the army had marched on its way to its camp. Both Thornton houses are mentioned in the Itinerary (6) of the wagon train and are shown in Colles's *Survey*, Plates 70–71. When proceeding southward the wagon train had stopped to the east of the present route, at Colonel Dangerfield's plantation on the banks of the Rappahannock, as described in a fragment of Berthier's journal, Itinerary 6, n. 33.

MS, 32 x 21 cm. Princeton University Library, Berthier Papers, No. 39–10. Rochambeau's copy is in the Library of Congress, Map Division.

119 *Eleventh Camp at Falmouth*

12–16 July 1782. Fourteen miles from the previous camp. There was a "séjour," or extra day's rest here for each of the four divisions, so that two were in camp at the same time, as shown. The officers took advantage of the halt to make excursions in the vicinity. Clermont-Crèvecœur (p. 73) mentions a call on General Washington's mother in Fredericksburg (on the south bank of the Rappahannock, opposite Falmouth). Von Closen (pp. 210–211) speaks of visits to William Fitzhugh's house (Chatham) and to General Alexander Spotswood's estate at New Post. Blanchard ([1], p. 110) states that he set up and left at Falmouth a temporary hospital for 60 sick, who were later brought to Baltimore.

MS, 32 x 21 cm. Princeton University Library, Berthier Papers, No. 39–11. Rochambeau's copy is in the Library of Congress, Map Division.

120 *Ford at Falmouth across the Rappahannock River*

July 1782. According to Clermont-Crèvecœur (p. 73), the artillery used this ford, which was particularly bad. The infantry and the wagons, however, were ferried across; cf. Verger's journal, p. 159, and Von Closen, p. 210. The road at lower left, an alternate route from Fredericksburg to the ferry, is described here as "a very bad path, but shortening the distance over the main road by more than half."

MS, 17.5 x 26 cm. Princeton University Library, Berthier Papers, No. 19.

121 *Twelfth Camp at Peyton's Tavern*

15–17 July 1782. As explained in the heading, the First Division had camped on 14 July at "Garrot's" Tavern, 13 miles from the previous camp at Falmouth, but because of insufficient water there the divisions following continued 3 miles farther to camp here at Peyton's Tavern. Several of the officers' journals mention the hot weather and consequent importance of good spring water: e.g., Verger, p. 159. Peyton's Ordinary, as the tavern was also called, was a few miles north of Stafford (county seat of Stafford County, on present U.S. Route 1). The stream shown here is Aquia Run according to Colles, *Survey*, Plate 68.

MS, 32 x 21 cm. Princeton University Library, Berthier Papers, No. 39–12. Rochambeau's copy is in the Library of Congress, Map Division.

122 *Thirteenth Camp at Dumfries*

15–18 July 1782. Ten miles from the previous camp at Peyton's Tavern. Dumfries, county seat of Prince William County, on Quantico Creek (the stream shown here), was once a flourishing port; it was later eclipsed in this respect by Alexandria.

MS, 32 x 21 cm. Princeton University Library, Berthier Papers, No. 39–13. Rochambeau's copy is in the Library of Congress, Map Division.

123 *Fourteenth Camp at
Colchester*

16–19 July 1782. Ten miles from the previous camp at Dumfries. The town of Colchester, near the mouth of Occoquan Creek (east of present U.S. Route 1), was already in a state of decline when the French army camped nearby. Verger (p. 159) describes it as "almost deserted." The infantry was ferried across the Occoquan, but the artillery was obliged to use a ford 4 miles upstream. The road to the ford (*chemin du gué*) is indicated on the map. Chastellux describes a meeting here with General Daniel Morgan: "I was then at Colchester, where the first division of the troops had just arrived, after having crossed in boats a small river that flows near this town. The baggage train and the artillery had taken another route to reach a rather difficult ford. General Morgan met the baggage train when it was engaged in a narrow gorge, and finding that the wagoners were not managing very well, he stopped and showed them how they should drive their wagons. After having put everything in order, he called at my quarters and had dinner with me. The simplicity of his bearing and the nobility of his manners reminded me of those ancient Gallic or Germanic chiefs, who, when at peace with the Romans, came to visit them and offer assistance. He expressed great attachment to the French nation, and great admiration for the fine appearance of our troops. . . ." Chastellux (4), II, 581.

MS, 32 x 21 cm. Princeton University Library, Berthier Papers, No. 39–14. Rochambeau's copy is in the Library of Congress, Map Division.

124 *Fifteenth Camp at
Alexandria*

17–20 July 1782. Fifteen miles from the previous camp at Colchester. The road from Colchester, corresponding roughly to present U.S. Route 1, crossed Hunting Creek (not included on this map) before coming into the town. The two small creeks shown here have subsequently been filled in. The "Meeting house" is the Old Presbyterian Meeting House, built in 1774 and still standing on South Fairfax Street between Wolfe and Duke Streets. The army's camp seems to have been in the general vicinity of the present junction of Route 1 and the Mount Vernon Memorial Highway. George Grieve, who saw the French army in Alexandria, mentions that their camp was on the ground previously occupied in 1755 by General Braddock's army; see his description cited above, Verger's journal, n. 121.

On the way from Colchester to Alexandria several of the French officers had turned aside from the route to visit Mount Vernon, where Mrs. Washington was in residence. See, e.g., Von Closen, pp. 212–214, and Blanchard (1), p. 111. It was at this time that Colonel Custine (commanding the Saintonge Regiment) presented to Mrs. Washington a set of porcelain from his factory at Niderviller in Lorraine.

MS, 32 x 21 cm. Princeton University Library, Berthier Papers, No. 39–15. Rochambeau's copy is in the Library of Congress, Map Division. As an example of the slight variations between the two sets of maps, it may be noted that in this instance the words "Meeting house" have not been filled in on the Rochambeau copy.

125 Sixteenth Camp, a Mile and a Half beyond Georgetown

18–21 July 1782. Eight miles from the previous camp at Alexandria. Details concerning the ferries over the Potomac, which the army had crossed before reaching Georgetown (then in Maryland) on the east bank of the river, are given in the description of the wagon train's 1781 march in the opposite direction, in Itinerary 6. The stream shown here is a small segment of Rock Creek in what is now the city of Washington, D.C. The camp was located on high ground on the east bank of the creek, presumably in the vicinity of the present P Street Bridge, along the road from Georgetown to Bladensburg. In 1782 the District of Columbia was still in the future and L'Enfant's geometric grid had not yet been superimposed on the old road pattern. Cf. Colles, *Survey*, Plate 65.

The army had covered the route from Williamsburg to Georgetown—167 miles according to the mileage figures on the maps—in 18 days (2 of them halts) and 16 marches. The wagon train, when proceeding southward by forced marches over roughly the same route in September-October 1781, had covered it in 12 daily marches (no halts). Although the mileage estimates for the two marches do not exactly coincide, it would appear that the average daily march for the army in July 1782 was a bit over 10 miles, whereas that for the wagon train in 1781 had been over 16 miles a day.

MS, 32 x 21 cm. Princeton University Library, Berthier Papers, No. 39–16. Rochambeau's copy is in the Library of Congress, Map Division.

126 Seventeenth Camp at Bladensburg [in Maryland]

19–24 July 1782. Eight miles from the previous camp near Georgetown. Each division had an extra two-days' halt here. The stream is the Anacostia River. The road at the lower right, coming in from Annapolis, is the route by which the wagon train led by L.-A. Berthier had arrived on 23 September 1781. Although it only passed through Bladensburg without stopping to camp, the itinerary describing its route (Itinerary 6) notes that, if the army camped here, "headquarters would be well lodged on either side of the river, . . . there are fine campsites here, as well as pastures and forage."

MS, 32 x 21 cm. Princeton University Library, Berthier Papers, No. 39–17. Rochambeau's copy is in the Library of Congress, Map Division.

127 Eighteenth Camp at Snowden's Iron Works [Laurel, Maryland]

22–25 July 1782. Thirteen and a half miles from the previous camp at Bladensburg. Snowden's Iron Works was on the Patuxent River. Major Thomas Snowden's house, shown here, is "Montpelier," still standing on present State Route 197. Verger's journal (p. 160) designates the camp as "Rose's Tavern," also shown on the map.

MS, 32 x 21 cm. Princeton University Library, Berthier Papers, No. 39–18. Rochambeau's copy is in the Library of Congress, Map Division.

128 Nineteenth Camp at Spurrier's Tavern

23–26 July 1782. Nine miles from the previous camp at Snowden's Iron Works and 13 miles from the next camp at Baltimore. Spurrier's Tavern was near present Waterloo on U.S. Route 1. According to Von Closen (p. 215), the camp was "near Spurrier's Tavern . . . not far from Dorsay's house." At this point the army rejoined the route of its southbound march in September 1781. At that time it had reached Spurrier's Tavern when news of the arrival of La Villebrune's ships, with adequate transports, determined the march southeastward to Annapolis. Cf. No. 162 and notes to Nos. 80 and 82.

MS, 32 x 21 cm. Princeton University Library, Berthier Papers, No. 39–19. Rochambeau's copy is in the Library of Congress, Map Division.

129 Twentieth Camp at Baltimore

24 July–24 August 1782. During its month-long encampment here the army's positions were more extended than during the brief stop in Baltimore in September 1781; cf. Nos. 80 and 81. This time the camp stretched southward from a point near present Franklin and Paca Streets (left of map) to a point near Hanover and Lee Streets. The stream west of the camp (shown at bottom of map) flowing into Ridgeley's Cove was the Chatsworth Run, now lost beneath city pavements. Lauzun's Legion is shown in an advanced position on another height, in the vicinity of the present "old" Roman Catholic Cathedral (designed by Latrobe, dedicated in 1821).

Accounts of the sojourn in Baltimore are included in the journals of Clermont-Crèvecœur (pp. 73–76) and of Verger (pp. 160–161). Clermont-Crèvecœur notes that the camp was "on a charming site in the midst of woodland near the city, from which we enjoyed a most agreeable view."

When the army reached Baltimore, its subsequent destination was not generally known, though it was a matter of much speculation among all ranks. The decision to march north to join the Americans on the Hudson had been made at a conference between Rochambeau and Washington in Philadelphia, 19 July (cf. Clermont-Crèvecœur's journal, n. 155), and was subsequently confirmed in Washington's letter to Rochambeau, 16 August 1782 (*Writings of GW*, XXV, 26–28). "I am of opinion," Washington wrote from his headquarters at Newburgh, "that no good consequences can result from your remaining at Baltimore, but that many advantages may attend your marching forward and forming a junction with this Army."

When the army marched north—the First Division on 24 August—Rochambeau left behind the detachments under La Valette and Chazelles that had been transported there from Virginia, as well as a hospital. They remained until May 1783, when they returned directly to France. Thus several hundred French soldiers were in Baltimore for nine months or so longer.

MS, 32 x 21 cm. Princeton University Library, Berthier Papers, No. 39–20. Rochambeau's copy is in the Library of Congress, Map Division.

130 Baltimore, Harbor and Roadstead, 1782

This map, which repeats the preceding plan of the French encampment but places it within a larger frame of reference, can therefore be dated July-August 1782 and was probably also drawn by Berthier. It once belonged to General Rochambeau. Of particular interest is the depiction of Whetstone Point, showing batteries and a star-shaped fort there. Some years later, at the time of the undeclared "quasi-war" with France, these fortifications were improved and extended (1798–1800) under the direction of Major Anne-Louis Tousard, an émigré French artilleryman (who had earlier served with the Americans during the War of Independence), and were named for James McHenry, then secretary of war. Still later, during the War of 1812, Fort McHenry figured prominently in the defense of Baltimore; it was at the time of its bombardment by the British in September 1814 that Francis Scott Key wrote the words of "The Star-Spangled Banner." See Lee H. Nelson, *An Architectural Study of Fort McHenry* (Historic American Buildings Survey, Department of Interior, National Park Service, Eastern Office, Division of Design and Construction, Philadelphia, 1961); Harold I. Lessem and George C. Mackenzie, *Fort McHenry, National Monument and Historic Shrine*, National Park Service, Historical Handbook No. 5 (Washington, 1954, and subsequent editions).

Von Closen noted in his journal (p. 217) on 2 August 1782 that Rochambeau, who was expecting the siege artillery from Virginia, "intends to have it take a position called Whetstone Point, very like that at West Point [in Virginia], as you can see on the map of Baltimore." This reference suggests that Von Closen may have had in his personal collection a copy of the map reproduced here. The siege artillery that had been left at West Point (cf. Nos. 104 and 105) arrived by sea, under escort of the *Romulus*, on 19 August; cf. Clermont-Crèvecœur journal, p. 76. It remained in Baltimore until May 1783.

MS, 27.5 x 36.5 cm. Library of Congress, Map Division, Rochambeau Map No. 13.

131 *Twenty-first Camp at White Marsh Forge*

24–27 August 1782. Twelve and a half miles from the preceding camp in Baltimore. The army marched in four divisions, with Lauzun's Legion as vanguard, as far as Trenton. The camp at White Marsh Forge was some 3 miles northeast of the so-called White Marsh camp where the army had stopped on its way south in September 1781; see No. 79. The "Etang" shown on the map is a pond formed by a dam in Honeygo Run, which flows into White Marsh Run, where the forges (Nottingham Iron Works) were located. A tail-race from the pond to the forges is also shown. White Marsh Run is the head of Bird (or Back) River, which in turn flows into the Great Falls of the Gunpowder River.

MS, 32 x 21 cm. Princeton University Library, Berthier Papers, No. 39–21. Rochambeau's copy is in the Library of Congress, Map Division.

132 *Twenty-second Camp at Bush Town*

25–28 August 1782. Twelve and a half miles from the preceding camp at White Marsh Forge. The army had bivouacked here at Bush, in a slightly different position, in September 1781; cf. No. 78. The main road leading through the town is present State Route 7. The road branching off to the left is the "road to Bald Friar Ford" (present Maryland State Road 136). On this northward march the entire army proceeded directly to Lower Ferry, whereas the previous year the artillery and wagons had made a detour via Bald Friar Ford (see note to No. 77). The building shown at the right of the map is Bush Mill; the millrace can be traced from Bynum Run across the highway to the mill.

ms, 32 x 21 cm. Princeton University Library, Berthier Papers, No. 39–22. Rochambeau's copy is in the Library of Congress, Map Division.

133 *Twenty-third Camp at Lower Ferry*

26–30 August 1782. Twelve miles from the preceding camp at Bush. There was an extra day's halt here for each of the four divisions. In September 1781 the army had bivouacked on the west bank of the river (present Havre de Grace side), as shown on map, No. 77. This time the camp was on the east bank (present Perryville side). The entire army, including the artillery and wagons, was ferried across. Von Closen (then accompanying General Rochambeau, who was riding with the First Division) notes in his journal (pp. 227–228) that boats and "skows" had been sent on ahead from Baltimore. "Before crossing the river," he adds, "we had an excellent lunch at the house of the proprietor of the ferry, where we saw one of the pretty local girls—referred to thereafter in our conversation as *Miss Susquehanna*."

ms, 32 x 21 cm. Princeton University Library, Berthier Papers, No. 39–23. Rochambeau's copy is in the Library of Congress, Map Division.

134 *Twenty-fourth Camp at Head of Elk [in Maryland]*

28–31 August 1782. Fifteen miles from the preceding camp at Lower Ferry. The stream shown at right is Big Elk Creek. The entire army had been united here at Head of Elk the previous year when expecting to embark for transportation down the Chesapeake Bay. Cf. No. 76. The present map does not show the waterfront at Elk Landing, since it had no significance during the 1782 march. The slightly different locations of the two encampments can be determined by reference to the triangular road intersection shown on both maps.

ms, 32 x 21 cm. Princeton University Library, Berthier Papers, No. 39–24. Another copy of the map forms part of Rochambeau's set of the northbound camps, Library of Congress, Map Division. The words "Head-of Elk Bridge" do not appear on the Rochambeau copy.

135 *Twenty-fifth Camp at Newport [in Delaware]*

29 August–1 September 1782. Sixteen and a half miles from the preceding camp at Elkton, Maryland. The route from Elkton to Newport—the same taken in the opposite direction the previous year—is shown on the road map, No. 60. The Second Brigade had camped here in Newport in 1781 (cf. No. 59), but in a position differing slightly from the one shown on the present map of the 1782 encampment (by divisions). The main road, to the right of which the army camped, is present Market Street (State Route 4). The street intersecting this, at the top of the map, is State Route 41.

The next camp was at Chester, Pennsylvania. The army thus marched through Wilmington without camping there, as one brigade had done in 1781 (cf. No. 75). It may also be noted here that the Lauzun Legion, which remained in America after the rest of Rochambeau's army had departed, was quartered in or near Wilmington during the winter of 1782–1783. It embarked for France, with the detachments left at Baltimore, in

May 1783. The exact location of the Legion's cantonment in Wilmington has not been determined; no map of it has been found by the Editors.

MS, 32 x 21 cm. Princeton University Library, Berthier Papers, No. 39–25. Rochambeau's copy is in the Library of Congress, Map Division.

136 *Twenty-sixth Camp at Chester* [*in Pennsylvania*]

30 August–2 September 1782. Fifteen miles from the preceding camp at Newport, Delaware. The camp was to the northeast of the town of Chester, along the road to Philadelphia, on high ground between the two streams shown here: Ridley Creek at the bottom of the map, and Crum Creek at the top. This is in the general vicinity of the present Baldwin Locomotive Works. The 1781 camp had been southwest of Chester; cf. Nos. 58 and 74.

MS, 32 x 21 cm. Princeton University Library, Berthier Papers, No. 39–26. Rochambeau's copy is in the Library of Congress, Map Division.

137 *Twenty-seventh Camp at Philadelphia*

31 August–4 September 1782. Sixteen miles from the preceding camp near Chester. The four divisions, preceded by Lauzun's Legion as a vanguard, marched on successive days through the city to their camp on its northern outskirts; the previous year the camp had been on the banks of the Schuylkill near the present Market Street Bridge (cf. No. 73). There was at least one extra day's halt here for each of the divisions. The map shows three regiments and three artillery units, as well as Lauzun's cavalry (yellow and white), in camp at the same time. The First Division (including the Bourbonnais Regiment) resumed its march northward on 2 September.

The camp ground was along the eastern side of the "Chemin de German Town," indicated on the map as a continuation of Second Street. It was on high ground north of Cohocksink Creek, the larger of the two streams shown, with a dike ("Digue") across its mouth. The smaller stream, marking the northern limit of the regular street grid, is Pegg's Run, also known as Conoquonoque Creek. Both streams have long since been obliterated. The French camp was thus in the general vicinity of the junction of present North Second Street and Germantown Avenue. An interesting comparison can be made between this 1782 camp plan and John Hills's "Plan of the City of Philadelphia" (engraved and published, 1797). The Hills plan, on which the locality is called "Bath," shows that streets had been laid out and many houses constructed there during the postwar years.

The army resumed its march northward by the road designated here as "Chemin de Read-Lyon's Tavern" (Frankford Avenue). The stay in Philadelphia, with its attendant festivities, is described in the journals of Clermont-Crèvecœur (pp. 77–78) and Verger (pp. 162–163).

MS, 32 x 21 cm. Princeton University Library, Berthier Papers, No. 39–27. Rochambeau's copy is in the Library of Congress, Map Division.

138 *Thirty-first Camp at Somerset Courthouse* [*Millstone, New Jersey*]

8–9 September 1782. Fourteen miles from the preceding camp at Princeton. The camp ground at Somerset Courthouse was in a slightly different location from that of 1781, as can be seen by comparison with maps Nos. 53 and 68. This time two regiments were placed on the bank of the Millstone, east of the road and opposite the church. The main road shown here is present State Route 533; the second (from the top) of the three roads crossing the Millstone and leading to New Brunswick is approximately present State Route 514.

As indicated in the heading, no new maps for the preceding camps at Red Lion Tavern (28th), Trenton (29th), and Princeton (30th) are included in this series, the army having camped in the same positions as in 1781; cf. Nos. 72, 70, and 69. On the present march, after leaving Trenton, the army marched northward through New Jersey by brigades: the First included the Bourbonnais and Royal Deux-Ponts regiments, the Second, the Saintonge and Soissonnais. Covering the main corps on its right, the Lauzun Legion, commanded by Colonel Robert-Guillaume Dillon, took a route farther to the east, proceeding in seven marches via (1) Kingston, (2) New Brunswick, (3) Scotch Plains, (4) Chatham, (5) The Forks (Two Bridges), (6) Paramus, and (7) Kakiat (New Hempstead, New York) before joining up with the army at Haverstraw prior to crossing the Hudson at King's Ferry. See the general map of camps and marches, No. 162, for the two routes. At this time the enemy still occupied New York, and there were rumors of reinforcements arriving there. See Von Closen's journal, p. 234, and Verger's journal, n. 145.

MS, 32 x 21 cm. Princeton University Library, Berthier Papers, No. 39-28/31. Rochambeau's copy is in the Library of Congress, Map Division.

139 *Thirty-second Camp at Bullion's Tavern* [*Liberty Corner*]

9–10 September 1782. Thirteen miles from the preceding camp at Somerset Courthouse (Millstone). The same route had been taken in the opposite direction in 1781. See No. 53 and also No. 67 for the 1781 camp at Bullion's Tavern. The locations of the two encampments differ slightly. The pattern of roads shown on the map can readily be recognized in the present village of Liberty Corner. The "chemin de Somerset-Court-house," lower right, is present State Route 525, coming into Liberty Corner over Second Watchung Mountain from Martinsville. The road to Whippany (the next day's destination), upper left, is the road from Liberty Corner to Lyons and Basking Ridge. Cf. the map, "Points of Interest, Liberty Corner," in *Historical Booklet of Bernards Township, N.J., published to commemorate the Bicentennial, 1760–1960* (Basking Ridge, N.J., 1960), pp. [62–63].

MS, 32 x 21 cm. Princeton University Library, Berthier Papers, No. 39-32. Rochambeau's copy is in the Library of Congress, Map Division.

140 *Thirty-fourth Camp at Pompton Meetinghouse* [*Pompton Plains*]

12–13 September 1782. Fifteen miles from the previous camp at Whippany, where each of the two brigades had remained an extra day. No new map of the Whippany camp was included in this series, since the camp was in the same position in 1781; see No. 66.

There had also been a camp at Pompton Plains the previous year (No. 65), but since the present camp is in a slightly different position, there is a new map. Comparison of the two maps and reference to the "Meetinghouse," shown on both, indicate that the greater part of the troops camped this time on the eastern side of the main road. In both instances, as indicated by the points on the symbols for regiments, the camp "faces" the enemy, who occupied Manhattan and Staten Islands to the eastward. This 1782 map includes a larger area than the earlier one, extending northward to the bridges across the river at the top of the sheet. (The two branches of the Pompton are called the Pequannock and Wanaque on modern maps.) An advance unit is shown here near the river crossing, where a small work protecting a strategic point in the road communication system is situated. The road branching off to the left (labeled upside down) went to Ringwood and thence, via The Clove, to New Windsor, which is on the Hudson above West Point. The road here designated as "Chemin de Suffrantz" went to present Pompton Lakes (Passaic County), then through the Ramapo Valley (present U.S. Route 202) to Suffern, New York, the next camp. This route is shown on map, No. 50, and is described in Itinerary 3.

MS, 32 x 21 cm. Princeton University Library, Berthier Papers, No. 39–33/34. Rochambeau's copy is in the Library of Congress, Map Division.

141 *Thirty-fifth Camp at Suffern [in New York]*

13–14 September 1782. Fifteen miles from the preceding camp at Pompton Plains. The stream is the Ramapo River. The previous year's camp at Suffern is shown above on map, No. 64, which appears reversed in relation to the present one, it being the cartographer's practice to orient his map with the direction of the march at the top of the sheet.

MS, 32 x 21 cm. Princeton University Library, Berthier Papers, No. 39–35. Rochambeau's copy is in the Library of Congress, Map Division.

142 *Thirty-sixth Camp at Haverstraw*

14–16 September 1782. Fifteen and a half miles from the preceding camp at Suffern. The First Brigade remained here for three days, the Second Brigade for two, before crossing the Hudson at King's Ferry on 17 September. The First Brigade camped on the site already used the previous year (cf. No. 63) north of Cedar Pond Brook, in what is now the village of Stony Point. The Second Brigade camped farther south, along the road leading from the village of Haverstraw to "Smith-house." This was the house of Joshua Hett Smith, later known as "Treason House," where Arnold and André spent the night of 21–22 September 1780; the site is now occupied by the New York State Rehabilitation Hospital (West Haverstraw). The stream at the far right of the map is Minisceongo Creek.

MS, 32 x 21 cm. Princeton University Library, Berthier Papers, No. 39–36. Rochambeau's copy is in the Library of Congress, Map Division.

143 *Thirty-seventh Camp at Peekskill*

17–23 September 1782. Nine and a half miles from the preceding camp at Haverstraw. The entire army is shown in camp here (Lauzun's Legion, at right, nearest the Hudson) on hillocks to the south of the village of Peekskill. The site is in the southern part of the now-populated part of Peekskill. The small stream at top of map (south) is Dickey Brook; the single peak beyond it, Blue Mountain. For its relationship to the larger general area, see No. 146 and also maps of the 1781 campaign, Nos. 48 and 62. On the way to its camp here at Peekskill the French army had crossed the

Hudson at King's Ferry (Stony Point to Verplanck's Point) and then marched past the American camp, which was closer to the ferry landing. The French halted at Peekskill for a week before proceeding on 24 September, eastward and farther inland, to their next camp at Hunt's Tavern (also referred to as the Crompond encampment). Accounts of the stop at Peekskill, including the review by General Washington, are in the journals of Clermont-Crèvecœur (pp. 78–79) and of Verger (pp. 165–167).

According to a "Plan du Camp de Pisk-Kill" in Cromot Dubourg's "Atlas," No. 8 (Service Historique de la Marine, Fonds du Service Hydrographique, MS No. 2847), Washington's army had occupied a position on these same heights in "1780" (presumably an error for 1781).

MS, 32 x 21 cm. Princeton University Library, Berthier Papers, No. 39-37. Rochambeau's copy (on which "North-River" is not so labeled and the directional arrow is missing) is in the Library of Congress, Map Division.

144 *Encampment of the American Army at Verplanck's Point on the North River in 1782, and the Reception of the French Army on their Return from Virginia, by John Trumbull*

The American painter John Trumbull included this scene in the background of a portrait of General Washington that he painted in 1790 for presentation to Martha Washington. According to Trumbull's own note accompanying the painting: "Stoney Point & part of the Highlands, and a glimpse of the North River at the place where the Troops of France crossed are seen in the distance." The Stony Point peninsula, crowned by a fort, rises at the far left. Below this, protecting the eastern terminus of King's Ferry at Verplanck's Point, is Fort Lafayette, also flying the American flag. The tents of the American encampment stretch to the right, while the French army, colors flying, can be discerned marching toward its camp at Peekskill. General Washington would seem to be standing on the eminence where the camp was situated. Cf. Nos. 143 and 146.

Although Trumbull did not paint this canvas until 1790, he presumably based the background scene, according to his practice, on earlier sketches made on the spot. The artist is known to have visited the encampment in the autumn of 1782 and to have made sketches (now unlocated), which he could have consulted when completing the portrait. See Trumbull, *Autobiography*, ed. Theodore Sizer (New Haven, 1953), pp. 81–82; Sizer, *The Works of Colonel John Trumbull*, rev. edn. (New Haven, 1967), pp. 82, 118–119, Figs. 92–93; Verger's journal, n. 151.

Detail of oil painting by John Trumbull (1756–1843). Dimensions of the whole are 76 x 51 cm. Signed, lower right, "J. Trumbull 1790." Courtesy of The Henry Francis du Pont Winterthur Museum.

145 *Thirty-eighth Camp at Hunt's Tavern*

24 September–21 October 1782. Eight miles from the preceding camp at Peekskill. The army had already camped here the previous year, as shown on map, No. 61. The road running from the bottom to the top of the sheet (south) is Crompond Road, present State Route 35 (U.S. 202) in the town of Yorktown, New York. The lower of the two roads leading into it from the right is present Baldwin Road. Hunt's Tavern (not so labeled on this map) is the house situated at this junction. The road leading off at this

point to the left (which the army would eventually take when resuming its march to Salem Center) is present Hallock's Mill Road. An outlet of Crom Pond (the larger of the two "Etangs") curves around the high ground where part of the army camped behind the tavern and then crosses Hallock's Mill Road. The "Q^ier G^al" (Quartier Général), i.e., Rochambeau's Headquarters, was situated here in Samuel Delavan's house. For the story of Delavan's claims against the General, see Verger's journal, n. 158. The position of the "Hunt's Tavern camp" within the general "Crompond" area is shown on the next map.

MS, 32 x 21 cm. Princeton University Library, Berthier Papers, No. 39–38. Rochambeau's copy is in the Library of Congress, Map Division. Another, less accurate version of this map appears in Cromot Dubourg's "Atlas," No. 9 (Service Historique de la Marine, Fonds du Service Hydrographique, MS No. 2847), where it is entitled "Plan de Crompond Occupé par l'Armée Française depuis le 24. 7bre. Jusqu'au 22. 8bre. 1782." In the lower left corner there is a vignette representing truncated and cracked columns, perhaps intended to symbolize the breaking up of the allied army.

146 Position of the French and American Armies at King's Ferry, Peekskill, Crompond and Hunt's Tavern, from 17 September to 20 October 1782

This large map, which once formed part of Rochambeau's personal archives of his American campaigns, was probably surveyed and drawn by L.-A. Berthier, perhaps with the assistance of his brother Charles-Louis. Like its counterparts for Rhode Island (No. 7), Philipsburg (No. 46), and Virginia (No. 91), it marks one of the longer encampments, when there was time to extend field observations beyond the immediate vicinity of the camp or route of march.

Several of the smaller maps are here placed in a broader context. At the upper left is King's Ferry (cf. No. 62) and the American camp there; midway across the top of the sheet is the Peekskill camp (cf. No. 143); farther to the right and lower down is the Hunt's Tavern camp (cf. Nos. 61 and 145). The route traversing the whole area is also shown on the 1781 road map (No. 48) and is described in Itinerary 3.

This map, furthermore, supplies certain information not found elsewhere. For example, the distribution of the regiments at the Hunt's Tavern camp is indicated: the Soissonnais Brigade (Soissonnais and Saintonge regiments) to the east of the main road, the Bourbonnais Brigade (Bourbonnais and Royal Deux-Ponts regiments) to the west. Lauzun's Legion is shown in a forward position along the road to Pines Bridge, the key crossing over the Croton River (present Hanover Street, from Yorktown Heights to Croton Heights). This is the last map on which the Legion appears. When the rest of the army marched eastward for eventual embarkation at Boston, the Legion returned southward to winter quarters in Wilmington, Delaware, where it remained until May 1783.

A note, upper right, points out that "Green indicates woods, which were cut [for firewood] around the camps."

MS, 63 x 96 cm. (sheet measurement). Library of Congress, Map Division, Rochambeau Map. No. 33.

March from Crompond to Hartford, Providence, and Boston October – November 1782

Camp Plans

---

147 *Thirty-ninth Camp at Salem* [*Salem Center, Westchester County, New York*]

22–23 October 1782. Thirteen and a half miles from the Hunt's Tavern (Crompond) camp. The route from Hunt's Tavern via Hait's (or Haight's) Tavern (Somers) and Dean's Bridge (Purdys), to Salem is described (in reverse) in the 1781 "Itinerary from Providence to the Camp at Philipsburg." This portion of the route had not, however, been taken in 1781, because of the change in itinerary; see note to map, No. 24. Thus the army marched over this road for the first time in 1782. From here to Providence, Rhode Island, the march was by brigades: the Bourbonnais Brigade (including the Bourbonnais and Royal Deux-Ponts regiments) a day ahead of the Soissonnais Brigade (including the Soissonnais and Saintonge regiments).

The locality here designated as "Salem" is now known as Salem Center, which is in the town of North Salem, Westchester County, New York, near the Connecticut line. The stream at the right of the map is the Titicus River (its enlargement into the Titicus Reservoir now begins at approximately the point shown at the bottom of the map). The road running parallel to the river is present State Route 116. The two roads branching off to the right and leading to Bedford correspond roughly to present Turk Hill Road and June Road.

The building on the left-hand side of the road in the center of the map (to the right of the letters "em" in "Salem") is the manor house built *ca.* 1773 by the Loyalist Stephen Delancey. During the Revolution it was confiscated by the patriots and used as a courthouse and jail. From 1790 to 1884 it was occupied by the North Salem Academy and since that time has been the Town Hall for the town of North Salem. See Fred C. Warner, "Famous Landmark Restored, Restoration of North Salem's Town Hall," *The Westchester Historian* (Westchester County Historical Society), XXXIV, No. 1 (Jan.–March 1958), 10–12.

MS, 32 x 21 cm. Princeton University Library, Berthier Papers, No. 39-39. Rochambeau's copy is in the Library of Congress, Map Division.

148 *Fortieth Camp at Danbury* [*in Connecticut*]

23–24 October 1782. Eleven miles from the preceding camp at Salem Center, New York. When marching to Danbury the army passed through Ridgebury where it had camped the previous year (cf. No. 37); henceforth it followed, in the opposite direction, the route already taken in 1781. The road from Ridgebury to Danbury is shown on map, No. 23.

The road at the lower right coming in from the previous camp at Salem is present West Wooster Street, which joins Main Street at right angles. The "Meeting house" shown at this point is the Congregational Church, no longer standing; its site was near the present County Courthouse. The route went right to the foot of Main Street, then left into South Street. The second "Meeting house" shown here is the early Episcopal Church, which has also disappeared from this site. A bit farther along, a road (approximately present Coal Pit Hill Road) branches right (south) to Stratford and Newtown. Beyond this junction, on high ground to the north of the road, two regiments camped. The artillery was farther forward near the bank of the Simpaug, a small tributary of the Still River. After crossing the brook the route (corresponding to present Shelter Rock Road) led on towards Newtown, as shown on map, No. 23.

The "hôpital" in the lower part of the map was a military hospital maintained by the Americans, which local tradition places in the "Hoyt House" on present Park Avenue.

MS, 32 x 21 cm. Princeton University Library, Berthier Papers, No. 30–40. Rochambeau's copy is in the Library of Congress, Map Division.

149 Forty-fourth Camp at Farmington

28–29 October 1782. Thirteen miles from the preceding camp at Barnes's Tavern (in Marion). On the march from Danbury to Farmington the army had camped at Newtown (41st camp, 24–26 October 1782), Break Neck (42nd camp, 26–27 October), and Barnes's Tavern (43rd camp, 27–28 October), but no new maps are included in the present series since the positions were the same as those occupied on the 1781 southward march. Cf. Nos. 36, 35, and 34. The route is shown on Nos. 23, 22, 21, and 20.

The army had camped in Farmington the previous year during its southward march, but the campsite had then been south of the village, as shown on No. 33. The 1782 camp was in a different location, more in the village, as shown on the present map. The brook at the bottom of the map, flowing westerly under the road to join the larger stream (Pequabuck), is Diamond Glen Brook. Beyond the brook, when proceeding north along Main Street, is a road leading west, corresponding to present Meadow Road. The camp of the infantry regiments would thus have been roughly along the line of present Garden Street; the artillery and wagons camped east of Main Street along Hatter's Lane.

The general street plan of Farmington, as shown here, has changed little over the years. Many of these houses still stand. The building enclosed in a small square in the upper part of the map is the Congregational Church, built in 1772–1773 by Judah Woodruff.

MS, 32 x 21 cm. Princeton University Library, Berthier Papers, No. 39–41/44. Rochambeau's copy is in the Library of Congress, Map Division.

150 Field Sketch for Map of Camp at Farmington

This rough pencil sketch of Farmington appears on the verso of a memorandum noting the timetable and distances for the march of the two brigades from Hunt's Tavern to East Hartford, 22–31 October 1782. It provides an unusual example (the only one known to the Editors) of Berthier's rapid on-the-spot notations that he later worked up into finished maps.

Other such field sketches were presumably made day by day as a cumulative record of the camps and marches of the army. The training of the topographical engineers emphasized quick and accurate observation in circumstances that precluded the use of regular surveying instruments. A standard textbook, Dupain de Montesson's *L'Art de lever les plans*, in a section entitled "Des reconnaissances militaires, ou faites à vue" (2nd edn., 1775, pp. 176–178), discusses such a situation. The reconnoiterer must then count his own paces, or his horse's, to determine distances from point to point along the road. As he proceeds he must observe and note roughly on his paper "rivers, brooks, canals, bridges, fords, ravines, swamps, mountains, woods, wayside shrines, mills, gallows, and anything else he meets up with." He must sight such distant landmarks as towers, belfries, and windmills in order to establish the direction of the road. And, if time allows, he should also go up into some high building and sketch the surrounding country.

MS, 18 x 35 cm. Princeton University Library, Berthier Papers, No. 40.

151 *Forty-fifth Camp at East Hartford*

29 October–5 November 1782. Twelve and a half miles from the preceding camp at Farmington. Owing to the extra *séjour*, or halt, the entire army was encamped here together, as shown, from 30 October through 4 November. The camp was east of the village and of the Hockanum River, on either side of the road to Bolton Center. When the army stopped here the previous year, only one regiment (Soissonnais) camped in this position. The other regiments had been west of the village closer to the banks of the Connecticut in an area not included on the present map; cf. No. 32.

It was here at East Hartford that Rochambeau announced that the army would march to Boston and embark there for the West Indies. Many had hitherto supposed that they would remain in winter quarters at Hartford; cf. Clermont-Crèvecœur's journal, p. 81. See also Von Closen, pp. 263–264, and Chastellux (4), II, 477.

Dr. Ezra Stiles, journeying westward with his wife, met up with the French army at this time. He noted in his diary (4 November) that he saw the First Division at Bolton (where General Rochambeau visited him at the Reverend Mr. Colton's house), and then, on 5 November, when proceeding from Bolton to East Hartford: "Met & passed the 2d Div. of French Army, probably 1500 men. The whole sd. to be 4000, I judge 3000. We stopt our chaise near half an hour in passing the Troops, & afterwards above half an hour in passing 2 Divisions of Wagons, I judge 200. Some of them sd. they had 500 Waggons for whole Army...." *The Literary Diary of Ezra Stiles*, ed. Franklin B. Dexter (New York, 1901), III, 45.

MS, 32 x 29 cm. Princeton University Library, Berthier Papers, No. 39-45. Rochambeau's copy is in the Library of Congress, Map Division.

152 *Forty-sixth Camp, Two Miles beyond Bolton Meetinghouse*

4–5 November 1782. Fourteen miles from the preceding camp at East Hartford. In June 1781 the army had camped near Bolton Meetinghouse (present Bolton Center), as shown on Nos. 17 and 31. This time the camp was 2 miles beyond the meetinghouse (i.e., southeastward) in a position that appears to be near the Hop River and one of its small tributaries. This would be in the southwestern corner of the present town of Coventry, or northwestern corner of the present town of Andover (incorporated separately in 1848), along present U.S. Route 6.

MS, 32 x 29 cm. Princeton University Library, Berthier Papers, No. 39–46. Rochambeau's copy is in the Library of Congress, Map Division.

153 Forty-seventh Camp at Windham

5–7 November 1782. Sixteen and a half miles from Bolton. There was an additional day's stop here. The camp was east of the village on either side of the road leading to Canterbury (present State Route 14). The previous year the army had camped west of the village on the banks of the Shetucket; cf. Nos. 16 and 30.

No artillery units are shown on the map. Von Closen (p. 263) notes that the artillery obtained permission to march as far as Providence one day in advance of the First Brigade. See also Clermont-Crèvecœur's journal, p. 81.

MS, 32 x 29 cm. Princeton University Library, Berthier Papers, No. 39–47. Rochambeau's copy is in the Library of Congress, Map Division.

154 Forty-eighth Camp at Canterbury

7–8 November 1782. Ten miles from the preceding camp at Windham. The stream at the bottom of the map is the Little River. The campsite is on high ground south of the road (present State Route 14) before reaching "Westminster Meeting," the building shown to the left of a small triangular bulge in the road. The rebuilt eighteenth-century church still stands on this spot. The "Meeting-house" shown at the top of the map in the village of Canterbury proper is on the site of the present Congregational Church (built in 1805). Although the army had passed along this route in June 1781, it did not then camp at Canterbury; cf. No. 16.

MS, 32 x 29 cm. Princeton University Library, Berthier Papers, No. 39–48. Rochambeau's copy is in the Library of Congress, Map Division.

155 Forty-ninth Camp at Voluntown [Sterling Hill, Connecticut]

8–9 November 1782. Ten miles from the preceding camp at Canterbury. "Walen-Town," i.e., Voluntown, here refers to the present village of Sterling Hill in the town of Sterling, Windham County, Connecticut, and not to the present village of Voluntown in the town of that name, New London County, some nine miles to the south. In 1782 the town of Voluntown included territory that was later, in 1794, incorporated separately as the town of Sterling.

The army had passed through Voluntown but had not camped there in June 1781, as shown on the road map, No. 15. Dorrance's Tavern (still standing) is the building just above the letter "w" in "Town." General Chastellux in his *Travels* recorded much information about the tavern-keeper, Samuel Dorrance, and his family; see Chastellux (4), Index. The army's 1782 camp was in the fields east of the tavern on the north side of the road (present State Route 14-A).

MS, 32 x 29 cm. Princeton University Library, Berthier Papers, No. 39–49. Rochambeau's copy is in the Library of Congress, Map Division.

156 *Fifty-second Camp at Providence*

13 November–4 December 1782. Proceeding from Voluntown (Sterling Hill) the army made its next (50th) camp at Waterman's Tavern on the site occupied the previous year (cf. Nos. 14 and 28) and then, upon reaching Providence, camped again (51st camp) on the western outskirts of the town, as it had done in June 1781 when beginning the march to the Hudson (cf. Nos. 14 and 27).

After pausing for three days on the former camp ground the two brigades marched through Providence to another site north of town, as shown on the present map. According to Von Closen (p. 267), the move was determined by the landowner's refusal to agree to the cutting of wood on his property. The new camp, described by Verger as "barracks in a wood" (p. 169), was on the farm of Jeremiah Dexter, overlooking the Boston road, in what was then North Providence. Present Camp Street and Rochambeau Avenue are in the vicinity. An account of the "French Encampment in North Providence" in Stone, *French Allies*, pp. 309–327, includes a map of the vestiges of the camp and huts as platted in 1865. Further documents from the state and town records, including Dexter's claims for damages and their settlement, are printed in Howard W. Preston, *Rochambeau and the French Troops in Providence* (Providence, 1924), pp. 18–23. See also Forbes and Cadman, I, 167–174.

The troops remained here in North Providence until Vaudreuil's ships at Boston were ready to receive them. They left successively in four divisions: Bourbonnais on 1 December, Soissonnais on the 2nd, Saintonge on the 3rd, and Royal Deux-Ponts on the 4th. The artillery, however, had left Providence for Boston a fortnight earlier (16–17 November), "because of the large amount of matériel to be embarked" (cf. Clermont-Crèvecœur's journal, p. 81).

The inclusion of a stretch of the "Pattukey River" (i.e., the Pawtucket, now called the Seekonk), upper right of the map, is a reminder that a French vessel, the *Fantasque*, was anchored here. As noted by Verger (p. 169), a detachment commanded by M. d'Espeyron, major of the Soissonnais Regiment, comprising one company from each of the four regiments, was embarked on the *Fantasque*, also used as a hospital ship. This vessel, which was in bad repair, did not join Vaudreuil's fleet as planned and remained here until early February 1783. Thus French soldiers were to be seen in Providence for another two months after the departure of the main corps of the army.

It was at Providence that General Rochambeau took leave of his army and handed over the command to Baron de Vioménil.

MS, 32 x 29 cm. Princeton University Library, Berthier Papers, No. 39–50/52. Rochambeau's copy is in the Library of Congress, Map Division.

157 *Fifty-third Camp at Wrentham [in Massachusetts]*

1–4 December 1782. Sixteen miles from the preceding camp at North Providence. The camp ground lay between Lake Archer (the "Etang" at the left of the map) and Main Street, near present State Route 1-A, the old road from Providence to Boston.

158 Fifty-fourth Camp at Dedham

2–5 December 1782. Sixteen miles from the preceding camp at Wrentham. The road from Wrentham coming in at the lower left of the map crosses a small stream (Lowder Brook) before joining another road, which in turn leads to the "Meeting House" (Congregational Church) on Dedham Common. The river at the top of the map is the Charles. The camp was southeast of present St. Paul's Church on ground lying between present Court, School, Washington, Worthington, and Richards Streets. For further identification of the houses, see Albert A. Folsom, "Camp of the French Army, Dedham, 1782," *The Dedham Historical Register*, XII, No. 1 (Jan. 1901), 8–10.

Pages from the manuscript diary of a Dedham resident, Dr. Nathaniel Ames, noting the passage of the French artillery on 17 November and of the four infantry regiments on 2, 3, 4, and 5 December, are reproduced in Forbes and Cadman, I, 178.

MS, 32 x 29 cm. Princeton University Library, Berthier Papers, No. 39–54/55. Rochambeau's copy (lacking directional arrow for the river and the designation "Meeting House") is in the Library of Congress, Map Division.

Embarkation at Boston and at Portsmouth, New Hampshire December 1782

Although the preceding map notes a "55th camp at Boston," no plan of it is included in this series and probably none was drawn. This apparent lacuna may be explained by the fact that there was no "camp," strictly speaking, in Boston. Arriving in succession on 3, 4, 5, and 6 December, the troops were immediately embarked on the ships lying in the harbor, as noted in several of the officers' journals. Verger, sublieutenant of the Royal Deux-Ponts, the last regiment to reach Boston, further states that the wind was too strong to launch the boats, so that "we spent the night in warehouses along the wharves," embarking only the next morning (7 December); cf. his journal, p. 170.

Only the higher-ranking officers were lodged in town, where most of them remained until 21 December. The Selectmen of Boston had previously been directed by the Governor and Council of Massachusetts (7 November 1782) "to provide convenient quarters for the general officers and staff of the French Army," the expenses to be charged eventually to the United States government.

Vaudreuil's fleet did not finally set sail from Boston until 24 December 1782.

159 Plan of a Part of the Roadstead of Boston, showing the State of its Defenses

This map showing Vaudreuil's fleet at anchor in the outer harbor was presumably drawn in the late summer or early autumn of 1782, before the arrival of the army in November and December. Vaudreuil's fleet (the remnant of the larger fleet under de Grasse that had been defeated by the English in the Battle of the Saints, 12 April 1782) reached Boston early in August. The 74-gun *Magnifique* was wrecked off Lovell's Island when entering the harbor; cf. Clermont-Crèvecœur's journal, n. 151. The wrecked ship is indicated on the map by the reference number "16."

Upon receiving news of Vaudreuil's imminent arrival, Rochambeau (who was then in Baltimore, 2 August) sent General Choisy with two engineers and three artillery officers to Boston to inspect the defenses there; cf. Von Closen (who accompanied them), pp. 216–217, and Clermont-Crèvecœur's journal, pp. 73–74. The present map was probably drawn at that time, perhaps by one of the engineers.

Islands and other natural features are identified in the legend: Nantasket peninsula (Hull) at far right (a), Pullen Point at upper left (p), Governor's Island (n), Apple Island (o), Deer Island (q), Castle William (m), Thompson's Island (l), Spectacle Island (k), Long Island, serving as a camp for convalescents (i), Rainsford Island (h), Nick's Mate (g), Gallop's Island (e), George's Island (D), Lovell's Island (f), Peddock's Island (b).

Shown to the west of Long Island (in King's, now President, Roads) are the ships: *Neptune* (17), *Hercule* (18), Vaudreuil's flagship *Triomphant* (19), *Duc de Bourgogne* (20), *Souverain* (21). East of Rainford Island (in Nantasket Roads) are: the *Couronne* (9), *Northumberland* (10), *Brave* (11), *Citoyen* (12). Only ships of the line are shown. The *Bourgogne*, *Auguste*, and *Pluton* are missing, since they had gone (14 August) to Portsmouth, New Hampshire, for repairs. The *Bourgogne* left Portsmouth on 24 October to rejoin the rest of the fleet at Boston.

Defensive works at Hull are indicated by the figures 1–8.

MS, 24 x 50 cm. Library of Congress, Map Division, Rochambeau Map No. 14. A 4-page memorandum discussing the defenses of Boston Harbor accompanies the map. A similar map is in the Archives du Génie, 15–1–7, pièce No. 30.

160 Plan of the City and Harbor of Portsmouth in New Hampshire, by Crublier d'Opterre

This map has been preserved among the papers of Crublier d'Opterre, captain in the Royal Corps of Engineers. According to the embarkation lists in Cromot Dubourg ([2], p. 29) "Dopterre" was among the officers assigned to the *Auguste*, which sailed from Portsmouth on 29 December 1782.

In August 1782 three ships, detached from the Marquis de Vaudreuil's fleet at Boston, had come to Portsmouth for refitting: the *Auguste* (commanded by the Marquis's brother, the Comte de Vaudreuil), *Pluton* (Albert de Rions), and *Bourgogne* (Champmartin). The latter, her repairs completed, had returned to Boston in late October, but the others remained in Portsmouth until the end of the year. These ships were garrisoned with detachments from various army regiments; the *Auguste*, for example, had men from the Viennois. Still other such troops—some 600 men—were transferred from the ships at Boston to Portsmouth early in October. These were placed under the command of the Vicomte de Fleury, whom Rochambeau had sent eastward from Peekskill when it was rumored that the English fleet might attempt an attack on Boston or Portsmouth. See Von Closen, p. 242. Following Fleury's arrival, the defenses of Portsmouth were improved. For example, Fort Washington on Pierce's Island close to the town (shown on the present map) was redesigned and strengthened. Farther eastward (right half of map) the French remounted a battery of 12-pounders on the lower tip of Newcastle or Great Island; 300 men of the Armagnac Regiment were stationed ashore at Newcastle.

Other French maps of Portsmouth dating from this period have survived. Among the Rochambeau maps in the Library of Congress are a "Croquis de la rade de Portsmouth, Position de la flotte française," drawn by Von Closen in October 1782 (No. 16) and a "Plan du Port de Portsmouth, levé à vue, 1782," showing the defensive works (No. 16½). A "Plan de la Rivière de Piscataqua depuis son Embouchure Jusqu'à la Ville de Portsmouth" (two versions, one with legend in English) is among the Service Hydrographique de la Marine maps, 135–4–2, now deposited in the Bibliothèque Nationale, Département des Cartes et Plans. Although the draftsmanship is entirely different, there is a close relationship between the Service Hydrographique map and the Crublier d'Opterre map reproduced here. Further material on the French in Portsmouth and the circumstances under which the maps were prepared will be found in the journals of the Comte de Vaudreuil, Von Closen, and Chastellux (4).

MS, 81 x 112 cm. Library of Paul Mellon, Upperville, Virginia, Crublier d'Opterre MS No. 9.

161 City of Portsmouth, New Hampshire, Detail from Crublier d'Opterre's Map

At the upper part of the map, north of the town, is Rising Castle Island (now Badger's Island, over which present U.S. Route 1 passes via the Memorial Bridge from Portsmouth to Kittery, Maine). Shipyards are indicated here, as well as a "retraite pour les bois de construction," i.e., a storage depot for masts and other timber, which were floated down the Piscataqua from forests higher upstream. The Comte de Vaudreuil notes in his journal (*Neptunia*, No. 49, p. 41) that, in anticipation of the French navy's needs, arrangements had been made the previous year for assembling masts at Portsmouth.

The Continental 74-gun ship *America*, originally intended for John Paul Jones but subsequently presented by Congress to the French as a replacement for the ill-starred *Magnifique*, was launched on 5 November 1782 from the Rising Castle shipyards. However, *America* (now commanded by Macarty de Macteigue, formerly of the *Magnifique*) was not ready to put to sea until the summer of 1783. Thus there were French sailors and soldiers (including some of their sick) in Portsmouth for six months or more after the departure of the *Auguste* and *Pluton*.

Detail, actual size, from the map by Crublier d'Opterre, described in preceding note.

*162 General Map of the
Camps and Marches of
the French Army
commanded by General
Rochambeau, 9 June 1781
to 1 December 1782*

The complete title, as it appears on another version of this map, is: "Carte générale des camps et marches des troupes françaises sous les ordres du Lieutenant General Comte de Rochambeau, de Rhode Island à York en Virginie, et des Camps occupés au retour de l'armée française de York à Boston: du 9 Juin 1781, au 1er. Décembre 1782."

This general map recapitulates and presents in a broader perspective the detailed maps of roads and campsites reproduced above. The numbers here designating the camps correspond to those on the separate maps.

Legend

Along the *yellow* line extending from Providence, Rhode Island, to Annapolis, Maryland, and thence down Chesapeake Bay to Williamsburg and Yorktown, Virginia, are camps Nos. 1–40, 10 June–30 September 1781. See Nos. 26ff., above.

The *green* line extending from Scott's House southward to Williamsburg shows the overland march of the wagon train by means of *red* rectangles labelled in *red* "1e–14e Marches." There are no detailed maps for this march, but see Itinerary 6.

The *red* line, running roughly parallel to the yellow line from Lebanon, Connecticut, to Bedford and Philipsburg, New York, represents the flanking march of Lauzun's Legion (1781), with camps numbered 1–8. There are no detailed maps for this march.

The camps of the 1782 return march from Williamsburg to Spurrier's Tavern (*green* rectangles numbered 1–19) are also along the *green* line, and then continue (*green* rectangles numbered 20–55) along the *yellow* line to Boston. See Nos. 108ff. above. The points on the symbol for camps generally indicate the direction of the march.

The camps tinted *red*, numbered 1–7, represent the flanking march of Lauzun's Legion north through New Jersey in 1782. There are no detailed maps for this march.

Several versions of this map are extant. (1) General Rochambeau's copy (now in the Library of Congress) is the one reproduced here. (2) Another copy, of the same dimensions and draftsmanship, once belonging to L.-A. Berthier, is preserved at the Château de Grosbois—which suggests that the map may plausibly be attributed to Berthier. (3) Another copy (with the stamp of the "Dépôt de la Guerre") is in the Bibliothèque du Ministère des Armées "Terre," Paris, L.I.D. 173. Similar maps, *but showing only the 1781 camps and marches*, are: (4) Bibliothèque du Ministère des Armées "Terre,"

Paris, L.I.D. 6; (5) Bibliothèque du Génie, MS A 224, "Atlas de la Guerre d'Amérique," fol. 67; (6) Service Historique de la Marine, Fonds du Service Hydrographique, MS 2847, Cromot Dubourg's "Atlas," No. 2. Finally, (7), a reduced engraved version of the complete map, without title or explanatory legend, appears as an unnumbered folding plate in François Soulès, *Histoire des Troubles de l'Amérique Angloise*, 4 vols. (Paris, 1787), IV. A separate copy of this engraving is among the Rochambeau maps, Library of Congress, No. 64. Another copy of the engraving, in the Bibliothèque du Ministère des Armées "Terre," Paris, L.I.D. 173bis, has a title and explanatory legend added in manuscript (as if prepared for the engraver).

MS, 44 x 169 cm. Library of Congress, Map Division, Rochambeau Map No. 65.

The map entitled "Marche de l'armée française de Providence à la rivière du Nord, 1781" (3 sheets, Library of Congress, Rochambeau Maps Nos. 42–44) may also be recorded here. Although related to the "General Map of Camps and Marches," it is actually an entirely different map. It shows the route of the 1781 march from Providence to the Hudson as originally planned, but not as actually accomplished. The camps beyond Ridgebury, at Crompond and Peekskill, are indicated, whereas this portion of the route was not covered in 1781 because of a change in itinerary; cf. Clermont-Crèvecœur's journal, n. 31. The map must therefore have been prepared in advance of the actual march (perhaps by Béville or Mathieu Dumas) and was probably intended to accompany the "Plan for marching the army from Providence to King's Ferry . . ." (Itinerary 1).

The West Indies and Venezuela Sea Campaign in the Caribbean January - May 1783

163 Map of the Gulf of Mexico

This map showing the Caribbean and West Indies sets the stage for the last campaign of Rochambeau's expeditionary forces—what they called the "campaign of 1783" or "sea campaign." The army—then under Baron de Vioménil, Rochambeau having relinquished his personal command—sailed from Boston (or Portsmouth, New Hampshire) at the end of the year 1782 in the ships of Vaudreuil's fleet. The original plan called for a rendezvous with Spanish forces at Puerto Cabello on the coast of Venezuela, which was to be the springboard for a joint French-Spanish attack on the British island of Jamaica. Although the French reached Puerto Cabello in February 1783, the proposed expedition against Jamaica never took place. Preliminary peace treaties with Great Britain had been signed in Paris by France and

Spain on 20 January 1783; pending the signature of the definitive treaties in September, hostilities ceased early in April. Thus, after two months or so at Puerto Cabello, Rochambeau's army sailed north to Saint-Domingue and thence home to France, reaching Brest again in June 1783, after an absence of three years. Although Rochambeau's forces saw no military action during their final campaign, it was filled with incidents and personal adventures for the campaigners. All three of the journals published above in Volume 1 describe the Caribbean cruise in some detail.

The engraved map reproduced here, published in 1787, is a simplified version of one previously published in Bellin's *Description Géographique des Isles Antilles possédées par les Anglois* (Paris, Didot, 1758). Since it was specifically designed to illustrate a history of the war of 1775–1783, it can appropriately serve again in the present publication. The key points to be noted are: the Spanish island of Puerto Rico, the Dutch island of Curaçao, Puerto Cabello on the Spanish Main, and The French Cape ("Le Cap Fran-çois"), metropolis of the French colony of Saint-Domingue. Although Vaudreuil's fleet did not touch at Martinique during the campaign of 1783, Berthier, as related in his journal, visited this French island in the summer of 1780 when on his way to join Rochambeau's army in Newport.

Engraving, 20 x 29.5 cm. [Odet Julien Leboucher], *Histoire de la dernière guerre entre la Grande-Bretagne, et les Etats-Unis de l'Amérique, la France, l'Espagne et la Hollande, depuis son commencement en 1775 jusqu'à sa fin en 1783, Ornée de Cartes géographiques et marines* (Paris, Brocas, 1787), folding map, between pp. 70 and 71. Princeton University Library.

164 *Fort Royal, Island of Martinique*

This view, drawn by the marine artist Nicolas Ozanne (1728–1811) and engraved by his sister Jeanne-Françoise Ozanne (1734–1795), can be dated 1780. Berthier, who visited Fort Royal that same year, describes it as "the Gibraltar of the Windward Islands." The places shown on Du Perron's map (opposite) can also be distinguished here: the fort itself projecting into the bay, with the town on the left and the carénage on the right. Fort Bourbon is on the heights at the right. The Pitons du Carbet loom in the background. Fort Royal is today known as Fort-de-France, the *chef-lieu* of Martinique, now an overseas department of France. The city extends on either side of the old fort (Saint-Louis), remains of which still survive.

Another member of the Ozanne family, Pierre Ozanne (1737–1813), called "Ozanne le cadet," accompanied d'Estaing's fleet in 1778–1779 and made a series of drawings that graphically illustrate that campaign. These drawings, which are now scattered in several repositories and of which there are several sets, are listed (A 11 c [1–37]), with some omissions, by J. Vichot in his *L'Oeuvre des Ozanne*, an illustrated *catalogue raisonné* published serially in *Neptunia*, No. 87 (Summer 1967), and subsequent issues.

Engraving, 21 x 34.7 cm. (plate line). Princeton University Library. Cf. Vichot, *L'Oeuvre des Ozanne*, B 5 b (2). The drawing from which the engraving was made is in the Louvre, Cabinet des Dessins.

165 Map of the Island of Martinique

When on his way to join Rochambeau's army in Newport Berthier first went to Martinique, as related in his journal (pp. 228ff.). The localities mentioned in his narrative are shown on this map from Bellin's *Petit Atlas Maritime*. Far left, near the western tip of the island, is an offshore rock called "La Perle," and another called "Le Prêcheur." Along the coast is Bourg du Prêcheur (now known as Prêcheur), where Berthier and his brother were put ashore on 4 August 1780. They were next taken along the coast in a pirogue, or canoe, to Saint-Pierre, then the largest town on the island. Saint-Pierre was subsequently destroyed by the eruption of Mount Pelée in 1902 and is today largely a ruin (referred to in tourist publicity as the Pompei of the New World). From Saint-Pierre the Berthier brothers were again rowed down the coast to Fort Royal, the French military stronghold. Here on 30 August they sailed on the frigate *Gentille* for The French Cape and eventually reached Newport, Rhode Island, on 30 September 1780.

Engraving, 21.5 x 34.5 cm. Jacques-Nicolas Bellin, *Le Petit Atlas Maritime* (Paris, 1764), Vol. 1, Plate 91. Princeton University Library.

166 Bay of Fort Royal [Fort-de-France], Martinique Map by Du Perron, 1781

The map reproduced here was drawn in June 1781 by Joachim du Perron, then serving in the ship's garrison of the *Languedoc* in de Grasse's fleet. He was soon afterwards to participate in the "Chesapeake Expedition" and Siege of Yorktown. Other examples of maps by Du Perron are reproduced as Nos. 3, 84, and 90.

"E" designates the town of Fort Royal (now called Fort-de-France). "A" is Fort Royal itself, on a small peninsula projecting into the Bay. Overlooking it, higher up ("B" on the map) is Fort Bourbon, which had been built more recently, during the interval between the Seven Years' War and the War of American Independence. "K" is a sheltered cove where ships were careened. "G" is the anchorage for merchantmen, "F" for warships. Batteries at "C" (Pointe aux Nègres) and at "D" (Ilet à Ramier) defended the entrance to the Bay. The zigzag dotted line represents the course taken by warships to reach their anchorage.

Martinique, or "Martinico," as the Americans often called it, remained in French possession throughout the war. Saint-Pierre and Fort Royal were familar ports of call to North American traders and ships of the Continental Navy. William Bingham of Philadelphia was stationed here as agent of the Continental Congress for a considerable period during the war.

MS, 35 x 24 cm. (page measurement). Princeton University Library, in manuscript journal of Joachim du Perron, comte de Revel, facing p. 37. Hitherto unpublished; not reproduced in printed version of the journal.

167 Island of Curaçao, with Inset of Fort Amsterdam [Willemstad]

Although no manuscript maps of Curaçao drawn by French officers who visited the Dutch island in 1783 have been located, this engraved map from Bellin's *Petit Atlas Maritime* was probably familar to many of them. The ships of Vaudreuil's fleet, with Rochambeau's army aboard, passed Curaçao on their way to Puerto Cabello; several of them (including the *Neptune*,

Couronne, and *Hercule*) remained in the harbor at Fort Amsterdam (Willemstad) for several weeks in February 1783. Clermont-Crèvecœur, who was on the frigate *Amazone*, gives a description of Curaçao in his journal (pp. 90–91). It was here, too, that Berthier's younger brother Charles-Louis (embarked on the *Neptune*) lost his life in a duel; see Berthier's journal, pp. 260–266 and notes. Another map of Curaçao (more nearly contemporary with the French visit, but not substantially different from Bellin's map) serves as the frontispiece to J. H. Hering's *Beschryving van het Eiland Curaçao* (Amsterdam, 1779; facsimile reprint, Aruba, 1969): "Kaart van het Eiland Curaçao," with inset of "De Haven en 't Kasteel van Curaçao," engraved by Ad. Krevelt, 1779. The street pattern of the town as depicted here, as well as the outlines of Fort Amsterdam, are readily recognizable in the present city of Willemstad, Netherlands Antilles.

Engraving, 21.5 x 17 cm. Jacques-Nicolas Bellin, *Le Petit Atlas Maritime* (Paris, 1764), Vol. II ("L'Amérique Méridionale"), Plate 26. Princeton University Library.

168 *Northern Coast of Venezuela*

The coast of Venezuela, shown here on maps from Bellin's *Petit Atlas Maritime*, marked the southern limit of the American campaigns of Rochambeau's army. Vaudreuil's fleet reassembled at Puerto Cabello with considerable difficulty and only after various tribulations, which are vividly authenticated in the three journals published in Volume I. The French navigators found themselves in unfamiliar waters, and the available charts were far from adequate.

At the upper left of the map are the Dutch islands of Aruba, Curaçao, and Bonaire. One of the French ships, the 74-gun *Bourgogne* commanded by Champmartin (not to be confused with the *Duc de Bourgogne*), with troops from the Bourbonnais Regiment aboard, was wrecked off Punta Uvero on the Venezuelan coast (the Spanish Main) during the night of 3–4 February 1783. This spot, not named on the Bellin map reproduced here, was approximately due south of "Petit Curaçao," a bit above Bellin's "Pointe Rivelate." The French accounts of 1783 refer to it as "Pointe de Lubero" (Coriolis), "Pointe d'Ubero" (Désandroüins), or, less precisely, as the Coro coast (Vaudreuil); the present designation is Punta del Ubero or Punta Uvero. See Clermont-Crèvecœur journal, nn. 186–188.

Puerto Cabello (see next map) was in the Golfo Triste, which the French soldiers and sailors thought appropriately named, for it appeared to them a sad, sorry, and forbidding land. During the two months' stay here only a few of the more favored officers (including Berthier) were able to visit the "paradise" beyond the coastal mountain barrier. Berthier traveled overland from Puerto Cabello to Caracas ("Leon de Caracas" on the map) via Valencia, Maracay, and Victoria, while others sailed along the coast in small craft to La Guaira and thence went on muleback up to the capital city.

Engravings, 21 x 30 cm.; 20 x 29.5 cm. "Carte des Provinces de Cartagene, Se. Marthe et Venezuela," Jacques-Nicolas Bellin, *Le Petit Atlas Maritime* (Paris, 1764), Vol. II ("L'Amérique Méridionale"), Plate 17; "Carte des Provinces de Caracas, Comana, et Paria," *ibid.*, Plate 23. Princeton University Library.

169 Plan of Puerto Cabello

Maps of Puerto Cabello were probably drawn by some of the French officers during the sojourn there in February and March 1783, but since none has been found by the Editors, this engraved map from Bellin's *Petit Atlas Maritime* (with which they were certainly acquainted) can serve to illustrate their descriptions of the town, harbor, and military works. Clermont-Crèvecœur, Verger, and Berthier all comment at length on Puerto Cabello in their journals. Another more detailed engraved map of a somewhat later date ("Plan de la Rade et de la Ville de Porto Cabello dans l'Amérique Méridionale," engraved by J.-B. Tardieu) is included in François R. J. de Pons, *Voyage à la partie orientale de la Terre-Ferme dans l'Amérique Méridionale . . .*, 3 vols. (Paris, 1806), III, between 128 and 129. Both Bellin's *Atlas* and Pons's *Voyage* contain maps of La Guaira, the port farther to the east, which also figures in the French journals of 1783.

Engraving, 21 x 17 cm. Jacques-Nicolas Bellin, *Le Petit Atlas Maritime* (Paris, 1764), Vol. II, Plate 24. Princeton University Library.

170 Plan of the City of Caracas

According to his journal (p. 270), Berthier drew a view of Caracas when he was there in March 1783. In lieu of the drawing, missing from the Princeton manuscript of his journal, this engraved plan, by another Frenchman who was in Caracas two decades later, shows the city substantially as it was when Rochambeau's officers were entertained there by their Spanish allies. The map tallies closely with Berthier's description (pp. 270–271). The street pattern has survived in the heart of the present capital of Venezuela. The "Grande Place," "a" on the map, is now called Plaza Bolivar.

Engraving, 21 x 27 cm. "Plan de la Ville de Caracas," by F. de Pons, engraved by J.-B. Tardieu. Folding plate in François R.J. de Pons, *Voyage à la partie orientale de la Terre-Ferme dans l'Amérique Méridionale, fait dans les années 1801, 1802, 1803 et 1804*, 3 vols. (Paris, 1806), III, between 62 and 63. Princeton University Library.

171 Island of Saint-Domingue

The dotted line through the middle of the map marks the boundary between the French part of the island to the west (now the French-speaking Republic of Haiti) and the Spanish part to the east (now the Spanish-speaking Dominican Republic). Saint-Domingue, at the time of the American Revolution, was France's largest and most prosperous colony and thus played an important role in the war. It was from Saint-Domingue, for example, that de Grasse's fleet and Saint-Simon's army set sail for the decisive junction of allied forces at Yorktown in 1781.

The largest city was "Le Cap" or "Le Cap François" (also spelled "Français") on the northern coast, known to Americans of the time as "The French Cape" and today as Le Cap Haïtien. The second city in size was Port-au-Prince on the western coast of the island. After its sojourn at Puerto Cabello in Venezuela, Rochambeau's army sailed for The French Cape and remained in port there for several weeks in April 1783 before returning home to France. Verger's journal describes the route taken by most of the ships, around the eastern end of the island and thence along its northern coast to The Cape. The frigate *Amazone*, with Clermont-Crèvecœur's detachment of the Auxonne artillery aboard, took a variant route. The frigate had as passengers the Comte de Ségur, accompanied by Berthiers and others. After landing Ségur and his party at Jacmel on the southern coast, the *Amazone* continued her route around the western end of the island (Cape Tiburon, Cape Saint-Nicolas) to The Cape. Berthier describes in his journal (pp. 280ff.) his overland journey from Jacmel to Léogane, Port-au-Prince, and the Ségur plantation in the Cul-de-Sac plain. After this excursion he rejoined the army at The Cape (which he had already visited briefly in September 1780 when on his way to Newport).

Engraving, 20 x 35 cm. Jacques-Nicolas Bellin, *Le Petit Atlas Maritime* (Paris, 1764), Vol. 1, Plate 66. Princeton University Library.

172 Jacmel Bay, Saint-Domingue

This view by Ozanne, engraved by Nicolas Ponce, though not published until 1791, was drawn in the 1780's. Jacmel was the chief port on the southern coast of French Saint-Domingue. Berthier, who landed there on 12 April 1783, mentions in his journal the batteries defending the anchorage. A plan of the town of Jacmel is also included in the set of engravings (Plate 29) from which this view is taken.

Engraving, 9 x 14 cm., by Nicolas Ponce after Nicolas Ozanne. Moreau de Saint-Méry, *Recueil de vues des lieux principaux de la Colonie Françoise de Saint-Domingue, gravées par les soins de M. Ponce . . . accompagnées de cartes et plans de la même Colonie, gravés par les soins de M. Phélipeau, Ingénieur-Géographe* (Paris, 1791), Plate 12, No. 20. Princeton University Library (gift of Norman Armour). Cf. Vichot, *L'Oeuvre des Ozanne*, B 5 e (9) No. 20.

173 Cape and Môle Saint-Nicolas, Saint-Domingue

Cape Saint-Nicolas and the port called Môle Saint-Nicolas (or simply "Le Môle") were on the northwestern tip of the island. Clermont-Crèvecœur notes in his journal the difficulties experienced by the frigate *Amazone* in rounding Cape Saint-Nicolas because of the strong headwinds in the Windward Passage between Cuba and Saint-Domingue. A map of the bay and town of Môle Saint-Nicolas, corresponding to this view, will also be found in Moreau de Saint-Méry's *Recueil* (Plate 23).

Engraving, 17 x 22.5 cm., by Nicolas Ponce after Nicolas Ozanne. Moreau de Saint-Méry, *Recueil de vues* (Paris, 1791), Plate 8, No. 10. Princeton University Library. Cf. Vichot, *L'Oeuvre des Ozanne*, B 5 e (9) No. 10.

174 The French Cape, Saint-Domingue

This view of the largest city in the French colony of Saint-Domingue was apparently drawn on the spot in 1780 by Pierre Ozanne, then redrawn by his brother Nicolas, and finally engraved by their sister Jeanne-Françoise. It was issued as a sequel to Gouaz's series of the great French ports. The three journals published in Volume 1 all describe The French Cape, where Rochambeau's army stopped in April 1783 before resuming its homeward voyage to Brest. Berthier also visited The Cape on his way to Rhode Island in 1780.

Engraving, 21 x 35 cm. (plate line). Princeton University Library. Cf. Vichot, *L'Oeuvre des Ozanne*, B 5 e (1). The drawing by Pierre Ozanne, from which this engraving derives, is in the Louvre, Cabinet des Dessins.

175 *View of Port-au-Prince, Saint-Domingue*

Berthier in his journal (p. 281) gives a rather unflattering description of Port-au-Prince. "The port," he noted, "posesses neither quay nor dry-dock, which renders the waterfront muddy and ill-smelling. The defensive works are of little consequence and can be ignored." At this time Port-au-Prince, though technically the administrative capital of the colony, was considerably smaller than The French Cape, which had assumed the role of wartime capital. A city plan of Port-au-Prince is also included in the *Recueil* (Plate 19), from which our view is taken.

Engraving, 19 x 33 cm., by Nicolas Ponce after Pérignon. Moreau de Saint-Méry, *Recueil de vues* (Paris, 1791), Plate 5. Princeton University Library.

176 *Plan of the City of The French Cape*

This detail from a still more extensive plan of The French Cape and its environs, dated 1786, shows only the central part of the city. Berthier, who was here in September 1780 and again in April 1783, thought of it as "the Paris of our colonies . . . extremely well built and inhabited by very wealthy people," albeit "the most dissolute city I have yet seen and the most dishonest." The journals of Clermont-Crèvecœur (pp. 97ff.) and of Verger (pp. 176ff.) describe the city at some length. The building squares, and fountains mentioned by them can be located on this plan. Moreau de Saint-Méry's *Recueil*, from which the plan is taken, also includes views of the city and its monuments (Plates 1, 2, 3, 6, 14) as they appeared during the last years of the Old Regime. During the French Revolution the colony was wracked by fierce civil struggles and was finally lost to France, in spite of the attempt to recover it during the Consulate (Leclerc's expedition). In June 1793, only a decade after the visit of Rochambeau's army, The French Cape was the scene of a great holocaust. "For four days and nights," wrote one of the refugee colonists, "we watched the fire consume this rich and famous city, the glory of the French colonies. . . . We were stupefied at the sight of the immense clouds of black smoke that rose by day; at night we were awed by the flames that, striking the bold promontory that overhangs the town, lit up with reflected light the whole vast immensity of the Plain." J. F. Carteau, *Soirées Bermudiennes, ou Entretiens sur les Evénemens qui ont opéré la Ruine de la Partie française de l'île St.-Domingue* (Bordeaux, 1802), p. 4.

Engraving, 42.5 x 60 cm. (complete map). "Plan de la Ville du Cap François et de ses Environs, dans L'Isle St. Domingue," Moreau de Saint-Méry, *Recueil de vues* (Paris, 1791), Plate 18. Princeton University Library.

177 *The "Débouquements" of Saint-Domingue*

The many small islands and reefs lying north of Saint-Domingue, forming the eastern continuation of the Bahamas, were a perennial hazard to navigators, as well as the scene of raids and counterraids during the War of American Independence. Charting the *débouquements*, or passages, through these islands had long been a concern of the hydrographic service of the French navy. The map reproduced here, for example, is from a volume entitled *Description des Débouquemens qui sont au nord de l'Isle de Saint-Domingue*, printed by the French navy in 1773. In this mariners' guide (which also includes many detailed charts of the various islands) it is noted

(p. 2) that the French terms *débouquer*, *débouquement*, etc., came from the Spaniards, the first navigators of these waters, who named the passages and narrow entrances *boca*, i.e., *bouche* (mouth) in French. The verb *débouquer* thus came to mean "to go out through a mouth or narrow passage." French mariners also used the verb *embouquer* for "enter." Another elaborate description of "Les Débouquements" (including mention of notable shipwrecks) is found in Moreau de Saint-Méry's *Description de la Partie Française de l'Isle Saint-Domingue*, ed. Maurel et Taillemite (1958), III, 1409–1421.

Rochambeau's homeward-bound army, after leaving The French Cape and before reaching the open sea, sailed through these *débouquements*, as noted above in Verger's journal (p. 179). Islands such as The Turks gave them one of their last glimpses of the New World.

Engraving, 20.3 x 28.3 cm. *Description des Débouquemens qui sont au nord de l'Isle de Saint-Domingue* (Versailles, Imprimerie du Département de la Marine, 1773), Plate 1. Princeton University Library (gift of Norman Armour).

1 BREST, ENTRANCE TO THE PORT, BY LOUIS-NICOLAS VAN BLARENBERGHE, 1776

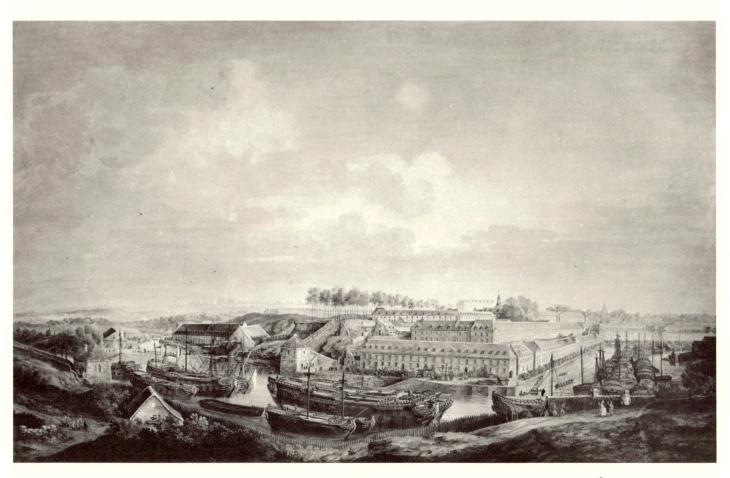

2 BREST, THE INNER PORT, BY LOUIS-NICOLAS VAN BLARENBERGHE, 1776

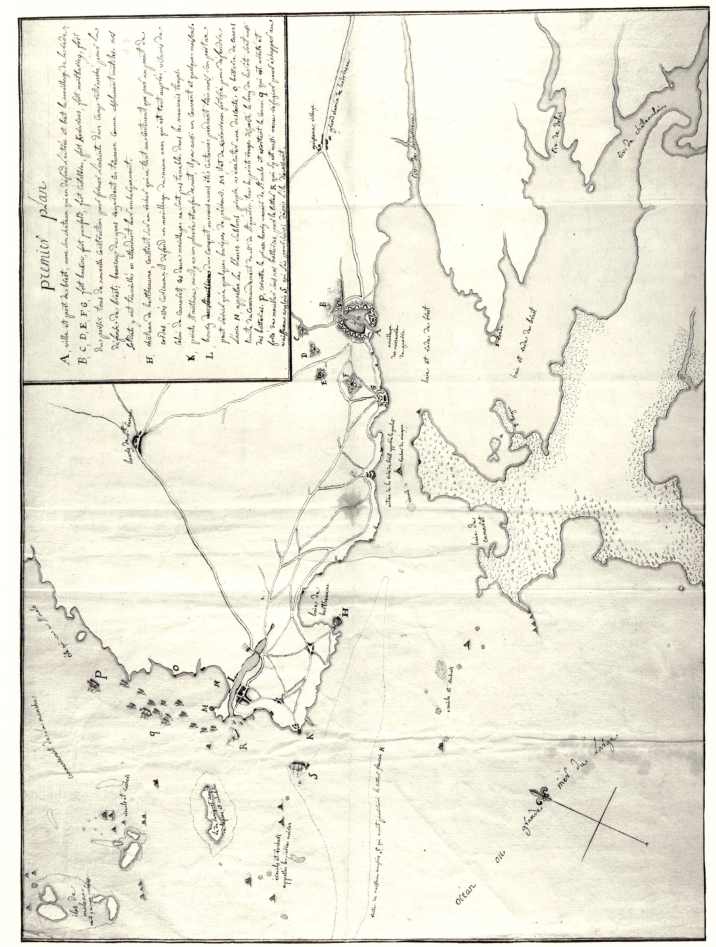

3 BREST AND ENVIRONS, MAP BY DU PERRON, 1780

4 PLAN OF NEWPORT AND VICINITY SHOWING THE CAMP OCCUPIED BY THE COMTE DE ROCHAMBEAU, WITH
THE ANCHORAGE OF THE WARSHIPS AND TRANSPORTS COMMANDED BY THE CHEVALIER DE TERNAY, BY MATHIEU DUMAS, JULY 1780

NEWPORT

blue
rock

Dyers
point

Convoi

Port

Goat Island

Rose Island

rock
ledge

RADE

Brenton's
point

Brentons Cove

East
ferry

Dumpling Rocks

L'ISLE DE

RÉE DE LA RADE

Castle
hill

5   CAMP OF THE FRENCH ARMY NEAR NEWPORT, RHODE ISLAND, MAP BY CRUBLIER D'OPTERRE

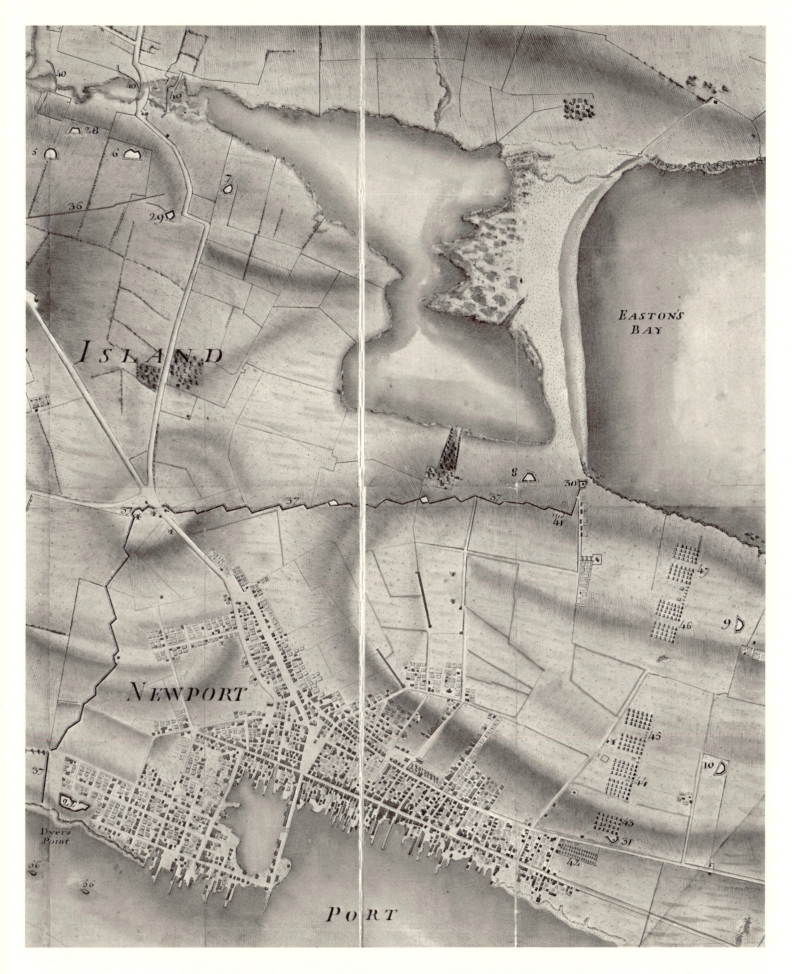

6 POSITION OF THE FRENCH ARMY AROUND NEWPORT, 1780

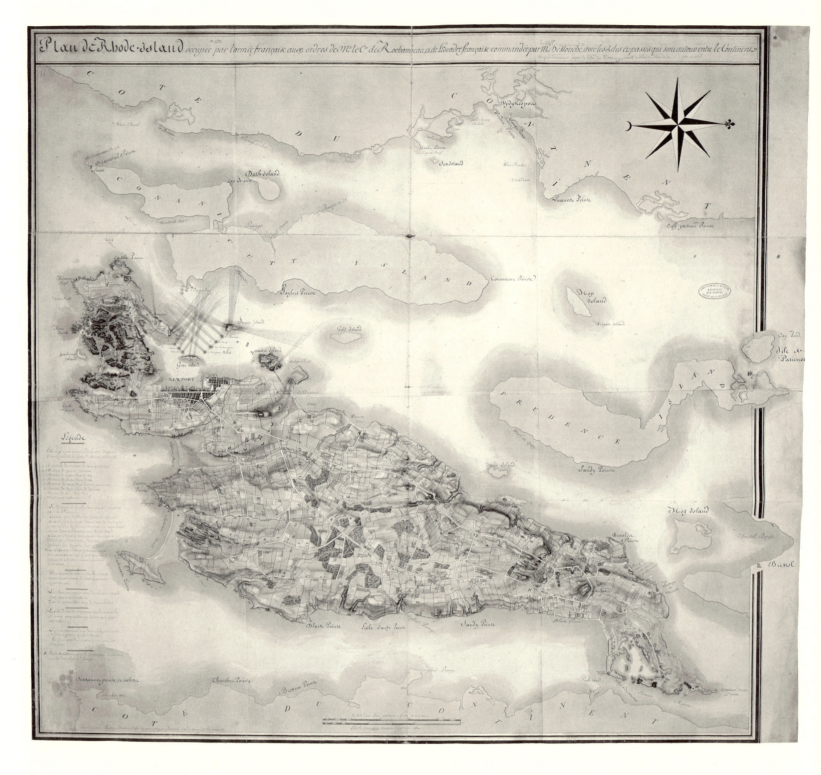

7   PLAN OF RHODE ISLAND OCCUPIED BY THE FRENCH ARMY UNDER THE ORDERS OF THE
COMTE DE ROCHAMBEAU, AND OF THE FRENCH FLEET COMMANDED BY M. DESTOUCHES,
WITH THE ISLANDS AND CHANNELS BETWEEN IT AND THE MAINLAND,
BY L.-A. AND C.-L. BERTHIER

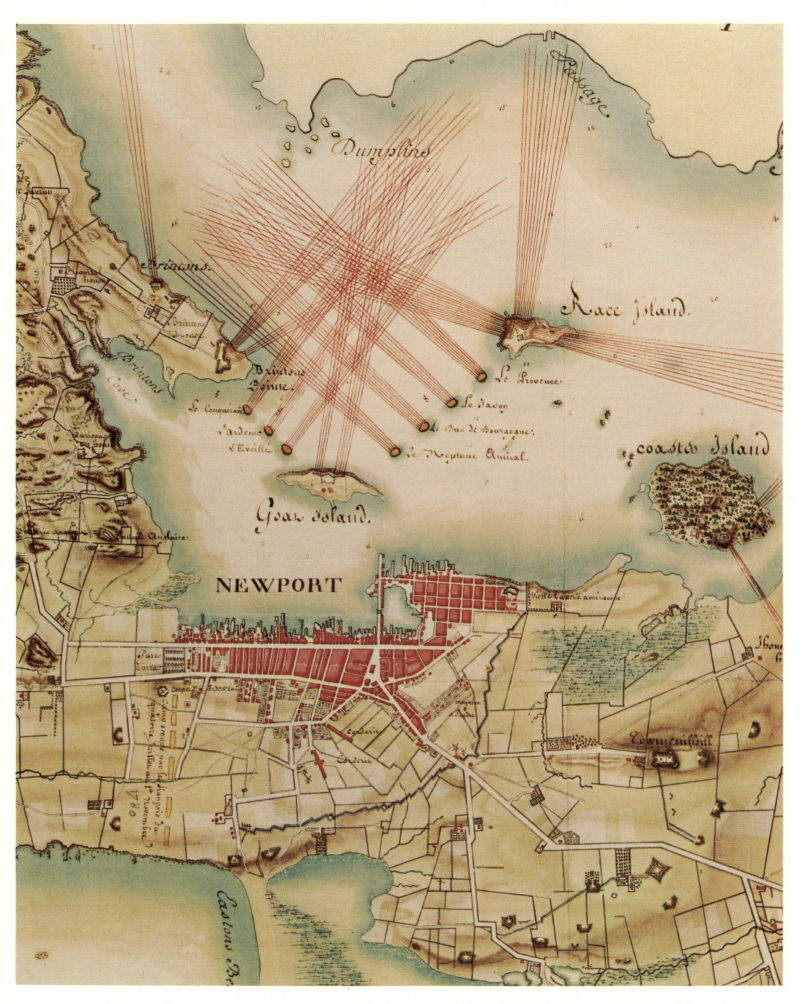

8   NEWPORT AND HARBOR. DETAIL FROM THE BERTHIER BROTHERS' PLAN OF RHODE ISLAND

9 NEIGHBORHOOD OF NEWPORT. DETAIL FROM THE BERTHIER BROTHERS' PLAN OF RHODE ISLAND

10　"CARTE DES CHASSES DU ROI," DETAIL SHOWING CHÂTEAU DE GROSBOIS

11   VIEW OF THE CITY, HARBOR, AND ROADSTEAD OF NEWPORT [MARCH–APRIL 1781]

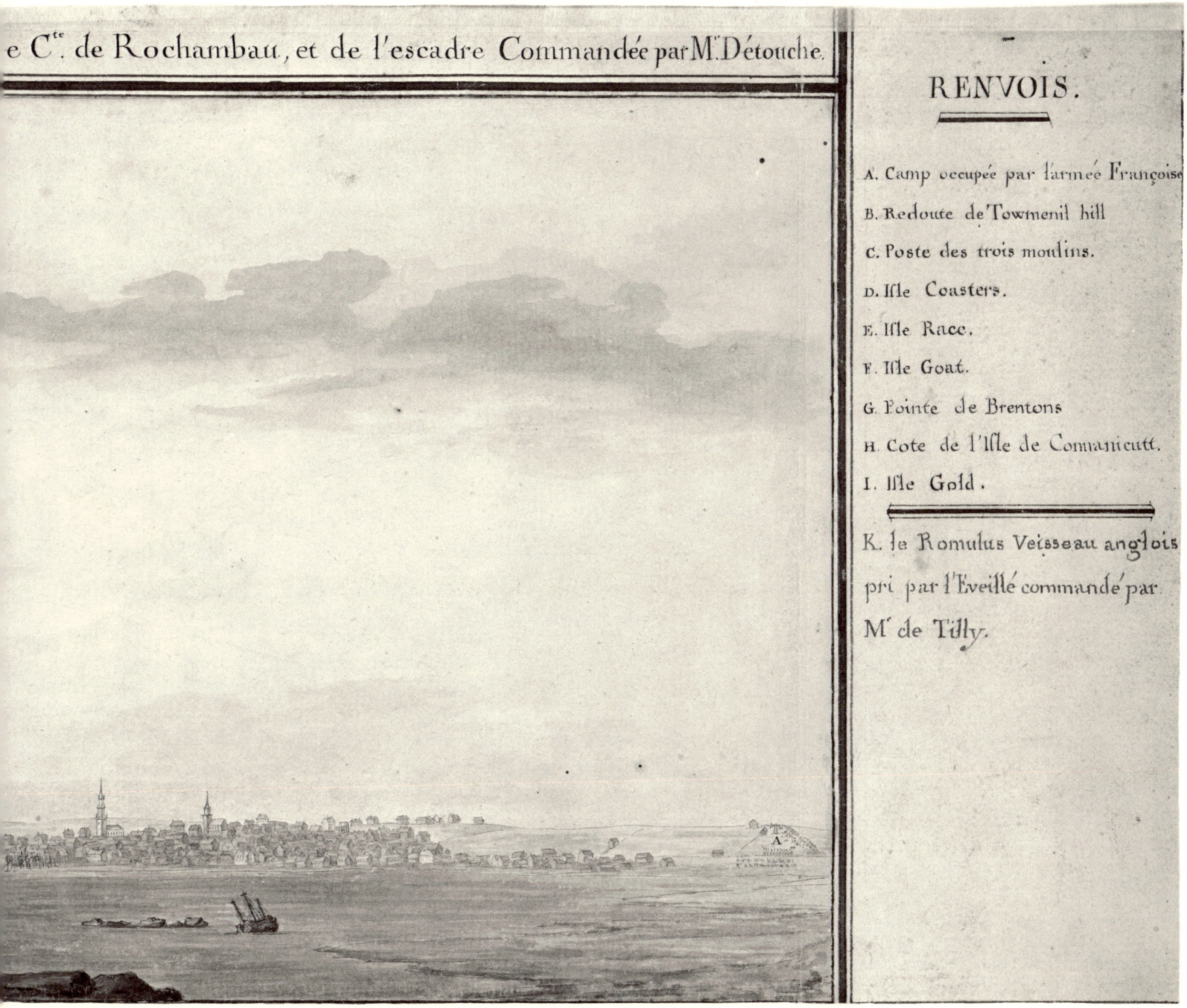

e C.te de Rochambau, et de l'escadre Commandée par M. Détouche.

RENVOIS.

A. Camp occupée par l'armée Françoise

B. Redoute de Towmenil hill

C. Poste des trois moulins.

D. Isle Coasters.

E. Isle Race.

F. Isle Goat.

G. Pointe de Brentons

H. Cote de l'Isle de Connanicutt.

I. Isle Gold.

K. le Romulus Veisseau anglois pri par l'Eveillé commandé par M. de Tilly.

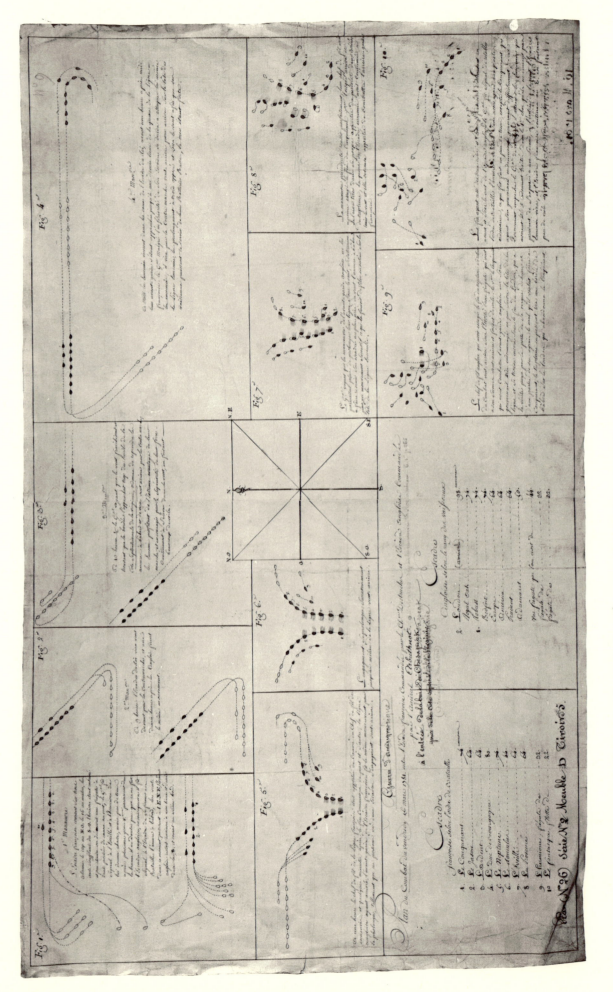

12 ENGAGEMENT OF 16 MARCH 1781, BETWEEN THE FRENCH SQUADRON COMMANDED BY DESTOUCHES AND
THE ENGLISH SQUADRON COMMANDED BY ARBUTHNOT, AT THE ENTRANCE TO THE CHESAPEAKE BAY

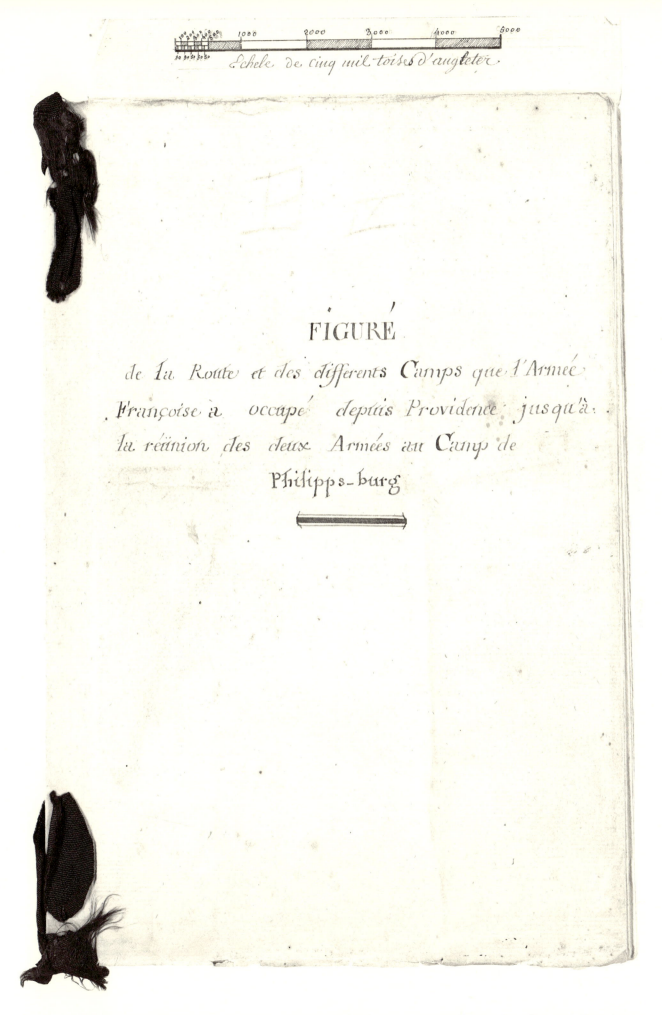

FIGURÉ

de la Route et des differents Camps que l'Armée
Françoise à occupé depuis Providence jusqu'à
la réünion des deux Armées au Camp de
Philipps-burg

13 FIGURATION OF THE ROUTE AND OF THE DIFFERENT CAMPS OCCUPIED BY THE FRENCH ARMY
FROM PROVIDENCE TO THE JUNCTION OF THE TWO ARMIES AT THE PHILIPSBURG CAMP, 1781

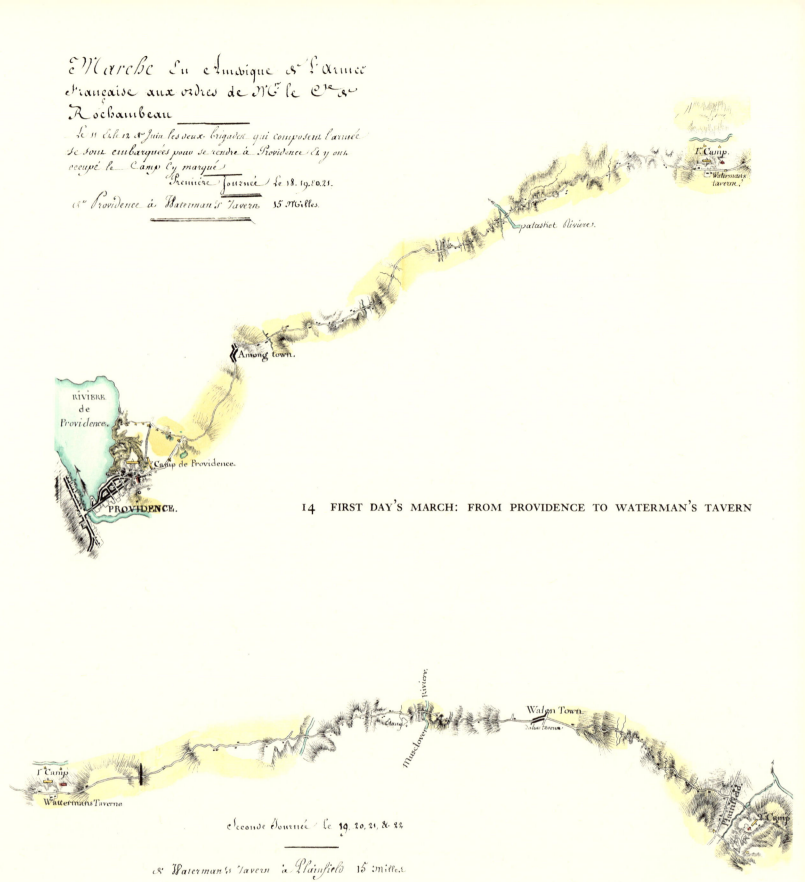

Marche en Amérique de l'armée française aux ordres de Mgr le Cte de Rochambeau

Le 11 et le 12 de Juin les deux brigades qui composent l'armée se sont embarquées pour se rendre à Providence et y ont occupé le Camp cy marqué

Première Journée le 18. 19. 20. 21.

de Providence à Waterman's Tavern 15 Milles.

RIVIERE de Providence.

Camp de Providence.

PROVIDENCE.

Among town.

patasket Rivieres.

1er Camp.

Watermans taverne.

14   FIRST DAY'S MARCH: FROM PROVIDENCE TO WATERMAN'S TAVERN

1er Camp

Watermans Taverne

Musclover

Riviere

Etang

Watun Town

Dalois tavern

Plainfield

2e Camp

Seconde Journée le 19. 20. 21. & 22

de Waterman's Tavern à Plainfield 15 milles.

15   SECOND DAY'S MARCH: FROM WATERMAN'S TAVERN TO PLAINFIELD [IN CONNECTICUT]

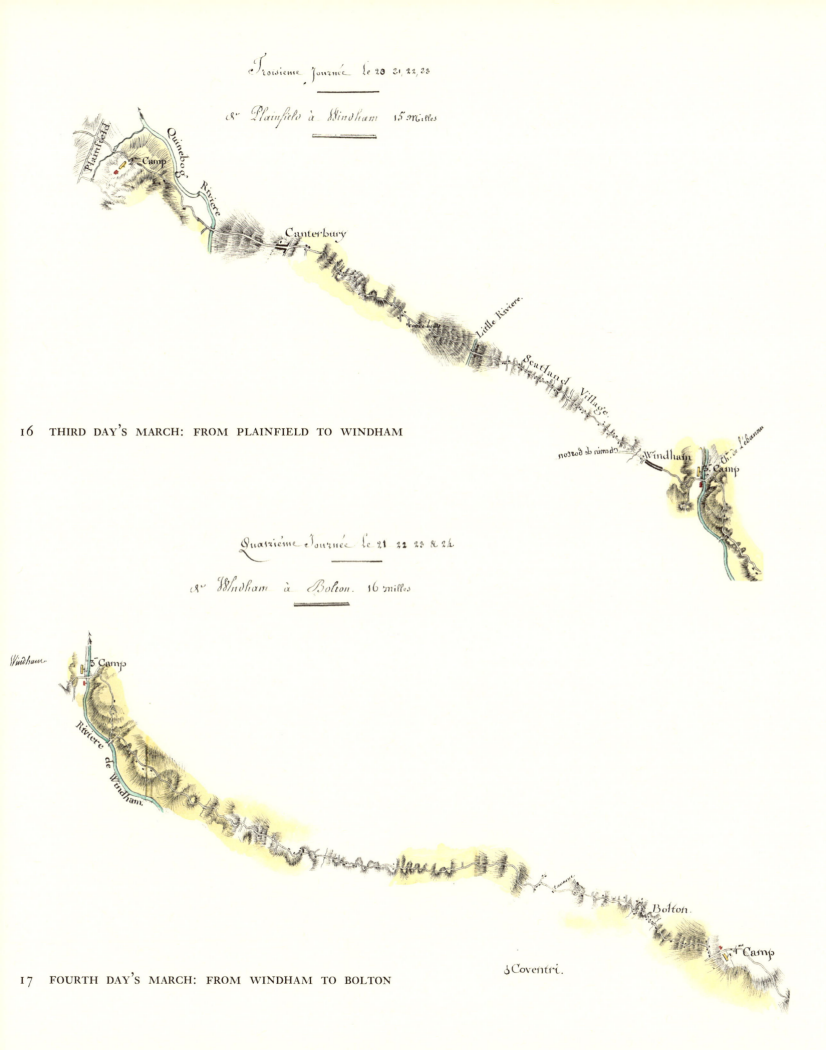

Troisieme Journée le 20 21, 22, 23

8ᵉ Plainfield à Windham 15 Milles

Plainfield

Quinebog Riviere

2ᵈ Camp

Canterbury

Litlle Riviere.

Scotland Village.

Chemin de boston

Windham

3ᵉ Camp

Ch. de l'Hanau

16 THIRD DAY'S MARCH: FROM PLAINFIELD TO WINDHAM

Quatrieme Journée le 21 22 23 & 24

8ᵉ Windham à Bolton. 16 milles

Windham

3ᵉ Camp

Rivière de Windham.

Bolton.

4ᵉ Camp

Coventri.

17 FOURTH DAY'S MARCH: FROM WINDHAM TO BOLTON

Cinquieme Journée Le 22. 23. 24 et 25.
Le regem.t 8.e Bourbonnois séjourna le 23 et le 24
Deux Ponts le 24 et le 25. Soissonnois le 15 et le 26
Saintonge le 26 et le 27. L'armée continua sa
marche dans le meme ordre

8.e Bolton à East. d'Hartford. 12 milles ½

18   FIFTH DAY'S MARCH: FROM BOLTON TO EAST HARTFORD

19   SIXTH DAY'S MARCH: FROM EAST HARTFORD TO FARMINGTON

Septieme Journée   Le 26 27, 28 & 29

de Farmington à   Boron's Tavern   13 milles

20   SEVENTH DAY'S MARCH: FROM FARMINGTON TO BARNES'S TAVERN

Huitieme Journée   Le 27 28 29 30

de Baron's Tavern à   Break neck 13 milles

21   EIGHTH DAY'S MARCH: FROM BARNES'S TAVERN TO BREAK NECK

Neuvieme Journée le 28, 29, 30, & 1.

Le regim.t S.t Bourbonnois séjourna le 29, 30,

Deux-Ponts, 30, ;., Et la brigade partit Dans la nuit du 30 au 1

Soissonnois Séjourna le 1 Saintonge point

Et la brigade partit le 1.er

8.e Break neak à New-Town 55 Milles.

22   NINTH DAY'S MARCH: FROM BREAK NECK TO NEWTOWN

Onzieme Journée le 3

La route fut changée. Nous laissames Crampond
à droite où L'armée devait passer, Et Nous fumes
à Nord castel où nous Campames Et Séjournames
Les 4 Et 5.

8.e Ridgebury à Nord castel 22 Milles.

24   ELEVENTH DAY'S MARCH: FROM RIDGEBURY [IN CONNECTICUT] TO NORTH CASTLE [IN NEW YORK]

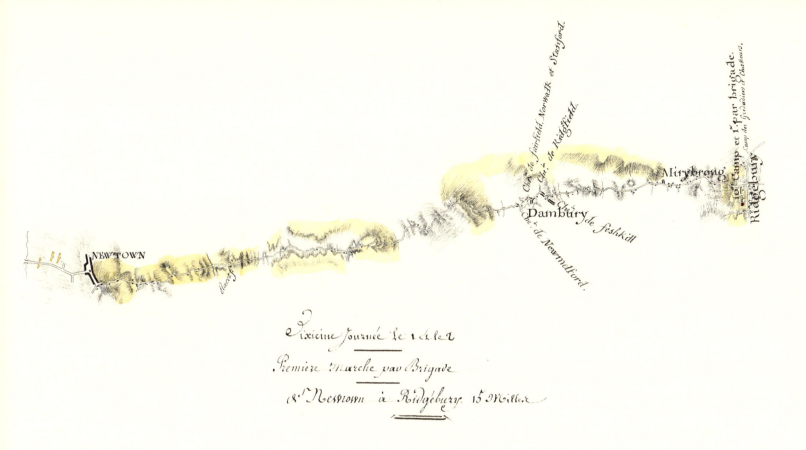

Dixieme Journée le 1 ch.le 2

Première Marche par Brigade

8.ᵉ Newtown à Ridgebury 15 Milles

23 TENTH DAY'S MARCH: FROM NEWTOWN TO RIDGEBURY

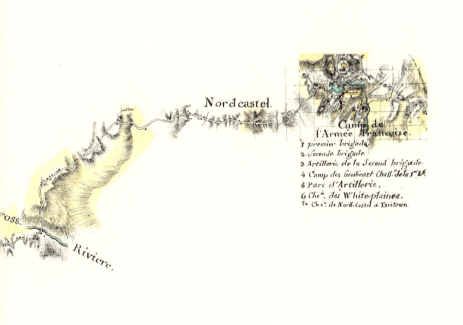

Nordcastel.

Camp de
l'Armée Françoise.
1 premier brigade.
2 Seconde brigade.
3 Artillerie de la Second brigade.
4 Camp des Grediezet Chaß. de la 1.ʳᵉ bᵉ.
5 Parc d'Artillerie.
6 Chᵉ. des White-plaines.
5+ Chᵉⁿ. de North-Castel a Taritown.

Camp de
l'Armée Françoise.
1 premier brigade.
2 Seconde brigade.
3 Artillerie de la Second brigade.
4 Camp des Grediezet Chaß. de la 1.ʳᵉ bᵉ.
5 Parc d'Artillerie.
6 Chᵉⁿ. des White-plaines.
5+ Chᵉⁿ. de North-Castel a Taritown.

NORTH CASTLE CAMP

DETAIL FROM NO. 24

Douzième Journée le 6

Marche par armée et reunion
des deux armées le 6 Juillet 1781
au Camp de Philipp's burg.
occupant la position cy marquée.

de Nord castel a Philip's burg 22 milles

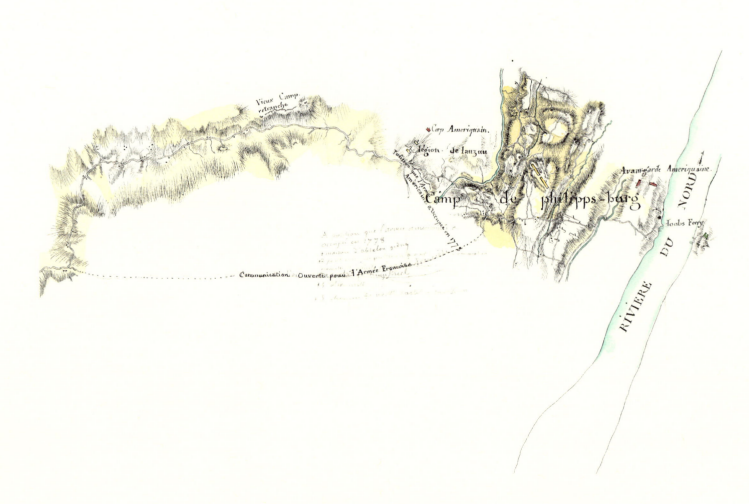

25   TWELFTH DAY'S MARCH: FROM NORTH CASTLE TO PHILIPSBURG

Amerique
Campagne
1781

Plans

des differents camps occupés
par L'Armée aux ordres de
M: Le Comte de Rochambeau

🟥 Artillerie

🟨 Troupes françaises

🟩 Troupes Americaines

🟨 Les Troupes pointillées avec une teinte jaune marquent l'emplacement
occupé par les regiments de royal Deux ponts et Saintonge
ayant Campés la Campagne 1782 par Brigade dans les
mêmes endroits ou ils Campèrent par regiments la Campagne
1781.

Bois

Eaux.

26 PLANS OF THE DIFFERENT CAMPS OCCUPIED BY THE ARMY UNDER THE ORDERS OF
THE COMTE DE ROCHAMBEAU: CAMPAIGN OF 1781

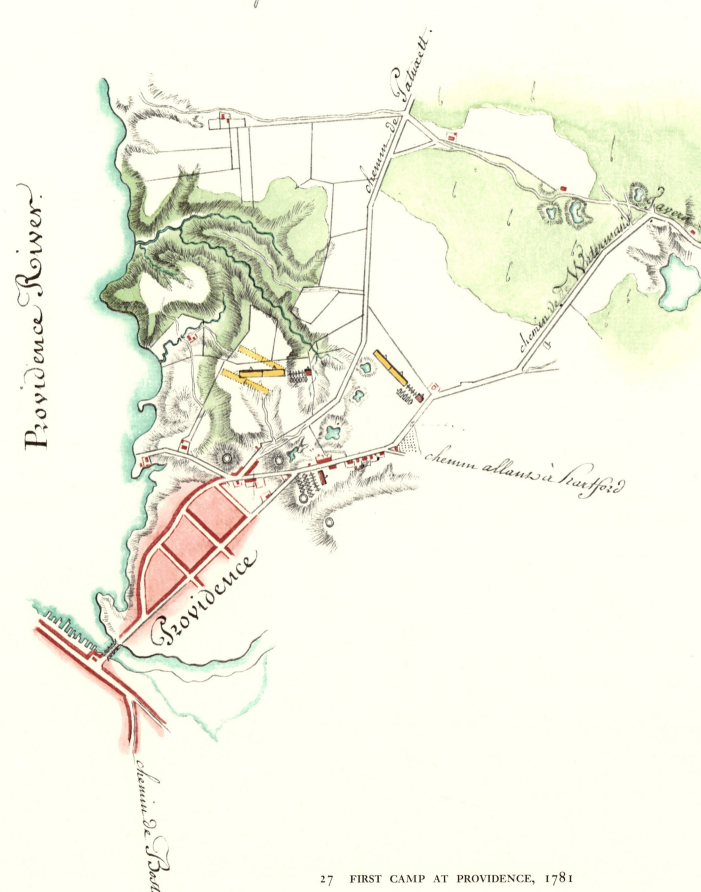

1.er Camp à *Providence* le 10 & 11 Juin, 30 miles de Newport.

cette Marche s'est faite pareau.

Providence River.

chemin de Patuxett

chemin de Mr Waterman's Tavern

chemin allant à Hartford

Providence

chemin de Boston

27 FIRST CAMP AT PROVIDENCE, 1781

2.ᵉ Camp à **Waterman's Tavern** le 18 Juin, quinze miles de Providence.

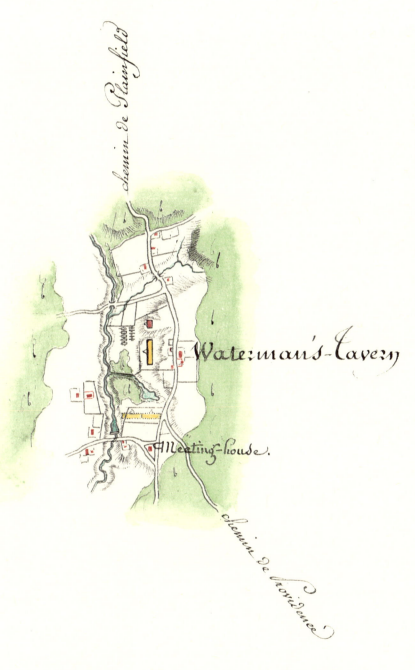

28 SECOND CAMP AT WATERMAN'S TAVERN, 1781

3.ᵉ Camp à **Plainfield**, le 19 Juin, 16 miles de Waterman's Tavern.

29 THIRD CAMP AT PLAINFIELD [IN CONNECTICUT], 1781

4.ᵉ Camp à *Windham*, le 20 Juin, 15 miles de Plainfield.

chemin de Lebanon.

chemin de Bolton.

Windham

River

chemin de Marshfield à 8.ᵐ

chemin de Lebanon à 6.ᵐ

Windham

chemin de Plainfield

30   FOURTH CAMP AT WINDHAM, 1781

5.ᵉ Camp à *Bolton*.

le 21. Juin, 16 miles de Windham.

chemin de East hartford

meeting house

chemin de Boston

Bolton.

Tavern.

chemin de Windham

31   FIFTH CAMP AT BOLTON, 1781

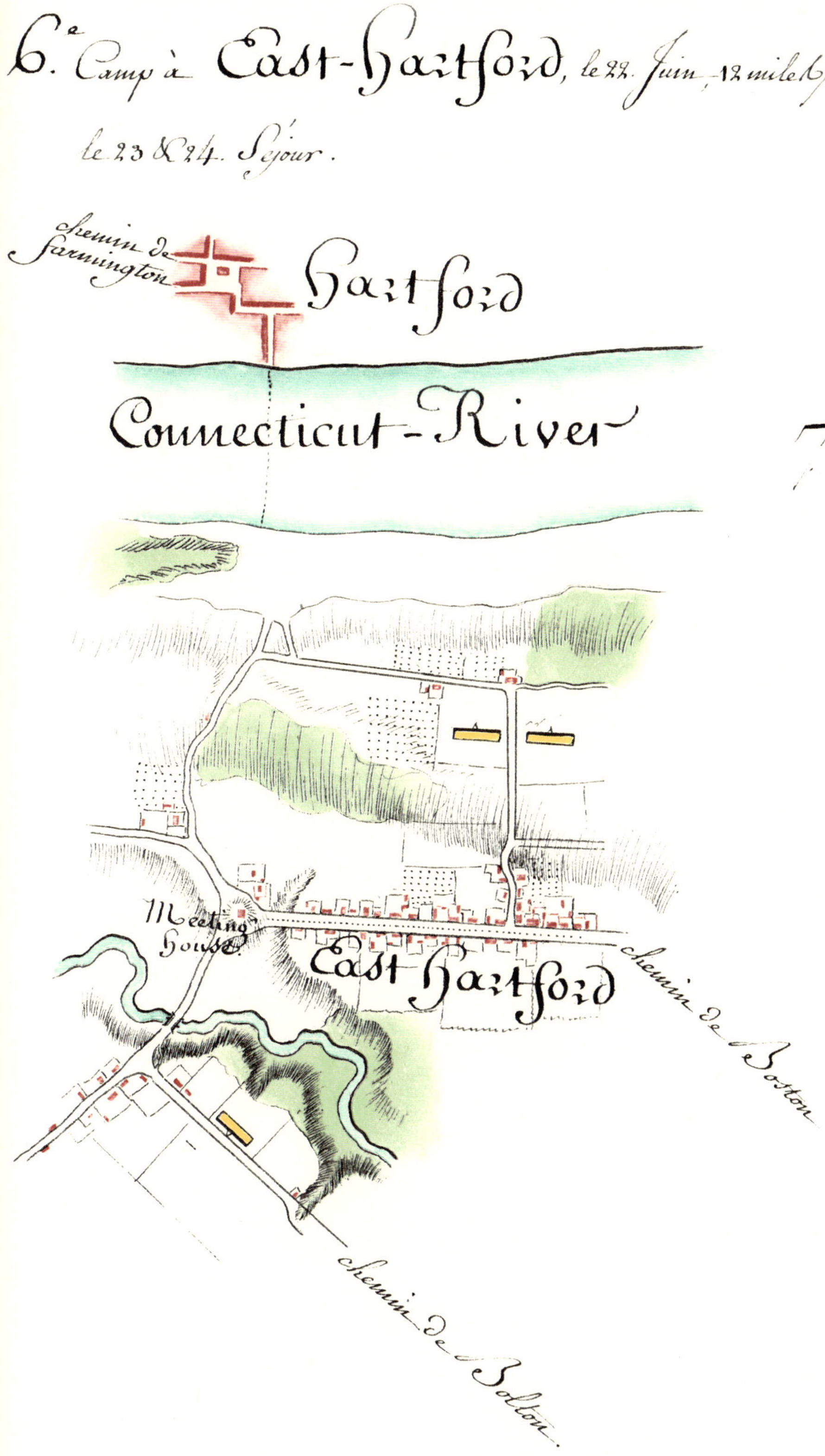

6.ᵉ Camp à **East-Hartford**, le 22 Juin, 12 miles 1/2 de Bolton,

le 23 & 24. Séjour.

chemin de farmington

Hartford

Connecticut-River

Meeting House

East Hartford

chemin de Boston

chemin de Bolton

32 SIXTH CAMP AT EAST HARTFORD, 1781

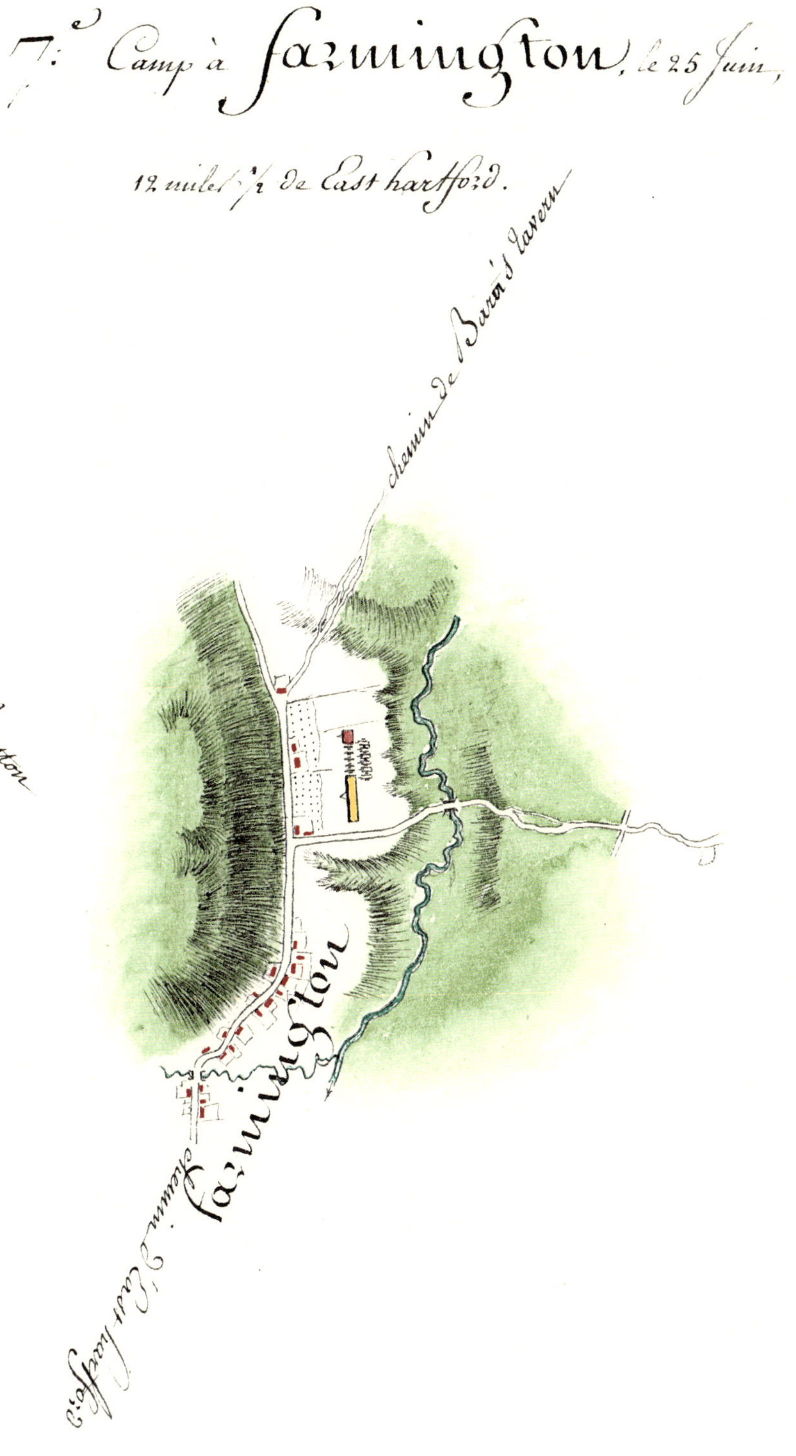

7.ᵉ Camp à **farmington**, le 25 Juin,

12 miles 1/2 de East hartford.

chemin de Buzn's Tavern

chemin de East hartford

farmington

33 SEVENTH CAMP AT FARMINGTON, 1781

8.ᵉ Camp à Barn's Tavern, le 26. Juin, 13. miles de Farmington.

9.ᵉ Camp à Break-Neck,

le 27. Juin, 13 miles de Barn's-Tavern.

34 EIGHTH CAMP AT BARNES'S TAVERN, 1781

35 NINTH CAMP AT BREAK NECK, 1781

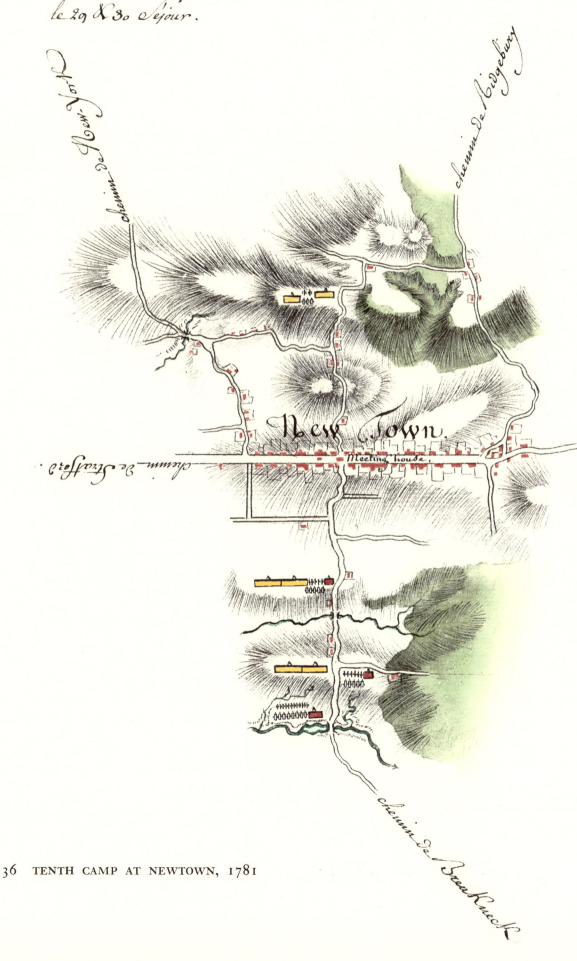

10.ᵉ Camp à New-Town le 28. Juin, 15 miles de Break-Neck;
le 29 & 30 Séjour.

chemin de New-York

chemin de Ridgebury

New Town.

chemin de Stratford

Meeting house.

chemin de Break-Neck

TENTH CAMP AT NEWTOWN, 1781

11. Camp à *Ridgebury*, le 1. Juillet, 15. miles de New-Town.

37 ELEVENTH CAMP AT RIDGEBURY [IN CONNECTICUT], 1781

12.° Camp à Bedford le 2 Juillet, 14 miles de Ridgebury, manque, n'ayant pas été figuré.

13.° Camp à North-Castle le 3 Juillet, 5 miles de Bedford, le 4. Séjour.

38   THIRTEENTH CAMP AT NORTH CASTLE [MOUNT KISCO, NEW YORK], 1781

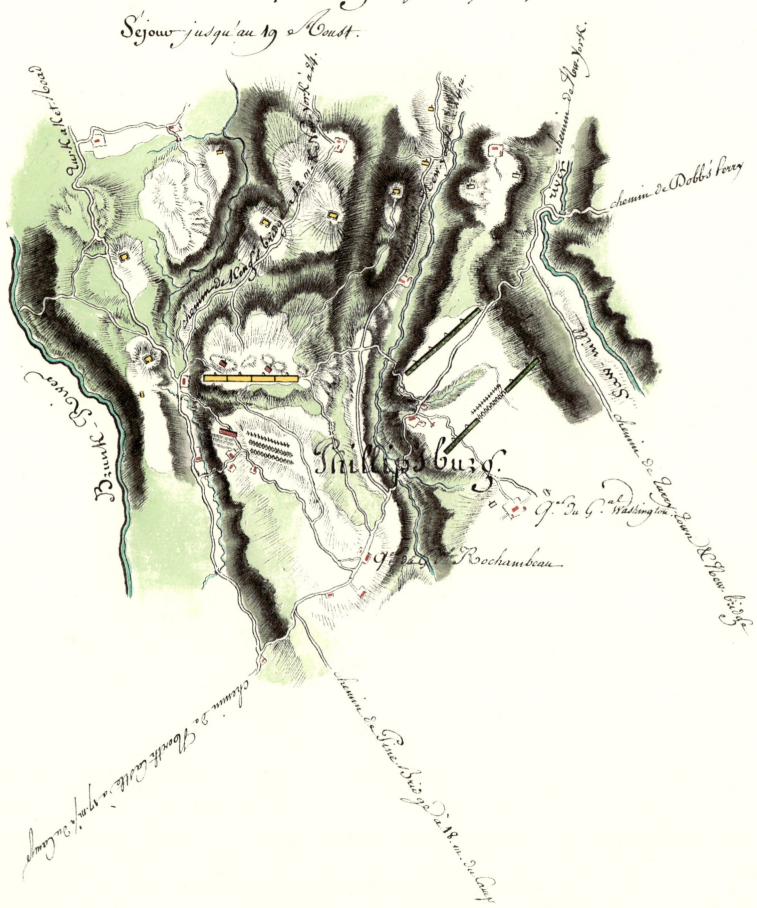

14. Camp à **Phillipsburg**, le 5 Juillet, 17 miles ½ de North-Castle
Séjour jusqu'au 19 Aoust.

Phillipsburg.

chemin de Dobb's ferry

Qg. du Gal Washington

Qg. de Mr de Rochambeau

40 POSITION OF THE AMERICAN AND FRENCH ARMY AT PHILIPSBURG . . .
FROM 6 JULY 1781

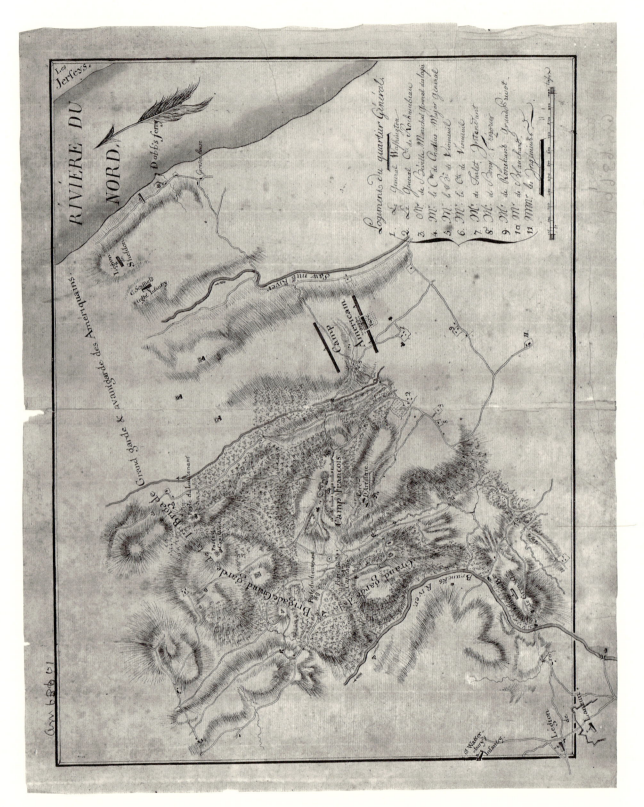

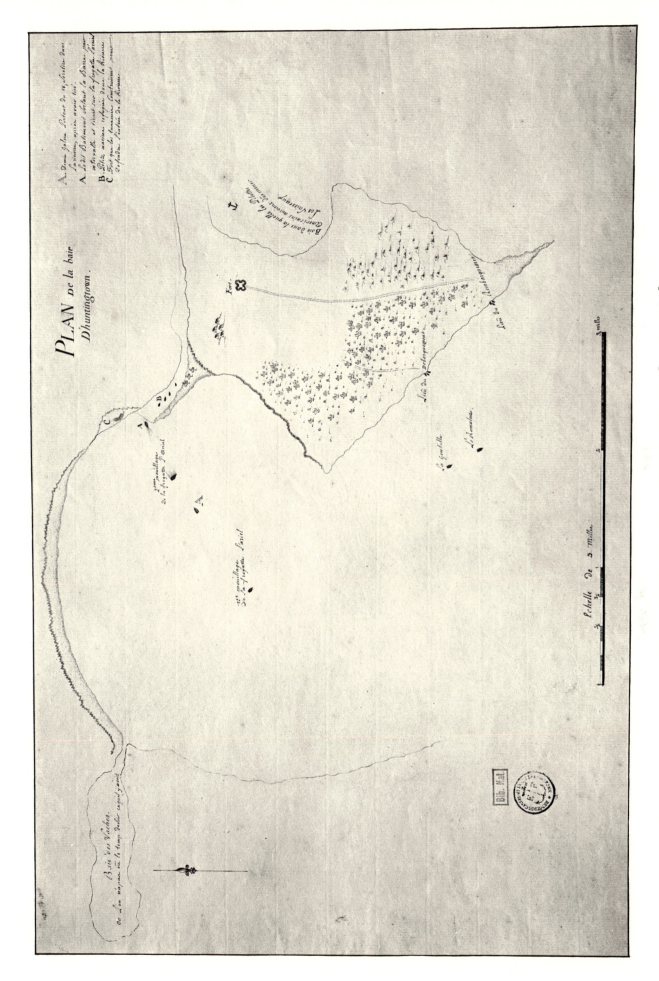

42   PLAN OF HUNTINGTON BAY, LONG ISLAND [JULY 1781]

1781

Reconnoissance des Ou...
du nord de l'Isle de Newyor...
dont on a déterminé Géometriquemen...
les principaux points
le 22 et le 23 juillet.

A. fort Washington.
B. fort laurel hill.
C. fort Tryon.
D. ligne continuë d'un travers a l'autre de...
F. Batteries.
G. abattis.
H. anciennes Batteries faites par les Am...
I. Redoute de Coxhill.
K. Redoute de kings brigde ou fort charle...
L. Redoute N.º 8.
M. ancien fort d'independance détruit.
N. ancienne Redoute détruite.

ECHELLE de 600 Toises

43 RECONNAISSANCE OF THE WORKS ON THE NORTHERN PART OF
THE ISLAND OF NEW YORK, THE PRINCIPAL POINTS OF WHICH
WERE DETERMINED GEOMETRICALLY, 22 AND 23 JULY 1781

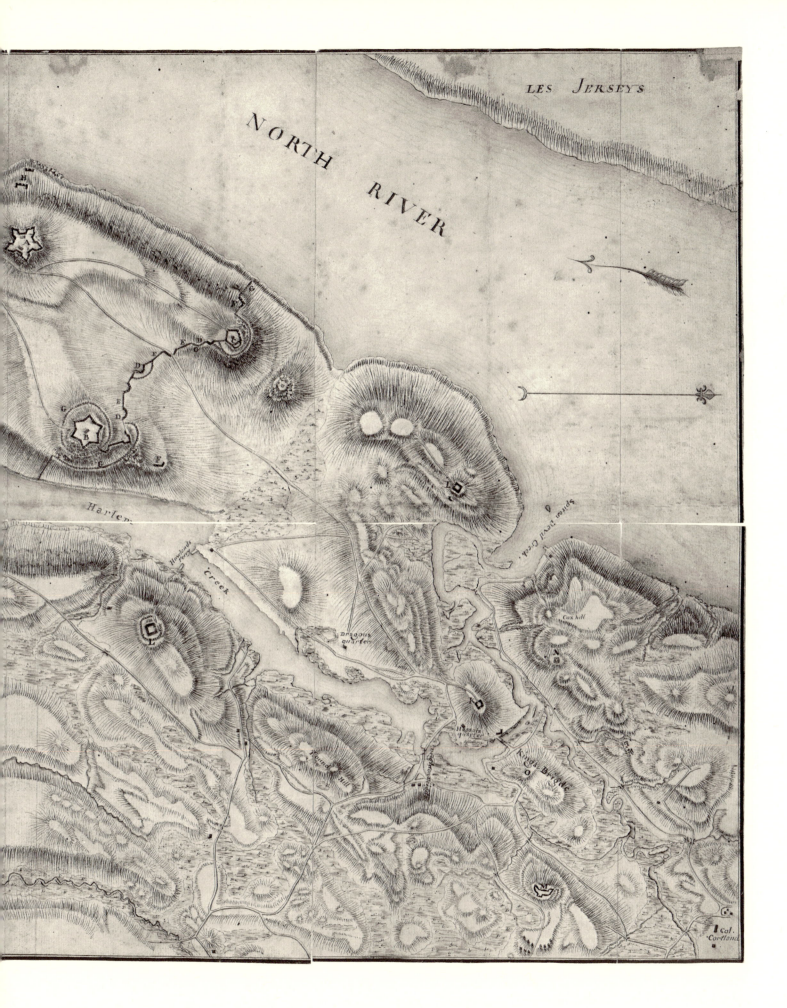

LES JERSEYS

NORTH RIVER

Harlem

Creek

Spuyt Devil Creek

Howlands ferry

Dragoons quarter

Cox hill

Found hill

Hussars quarter

Kings Bridge

Col. Cortland

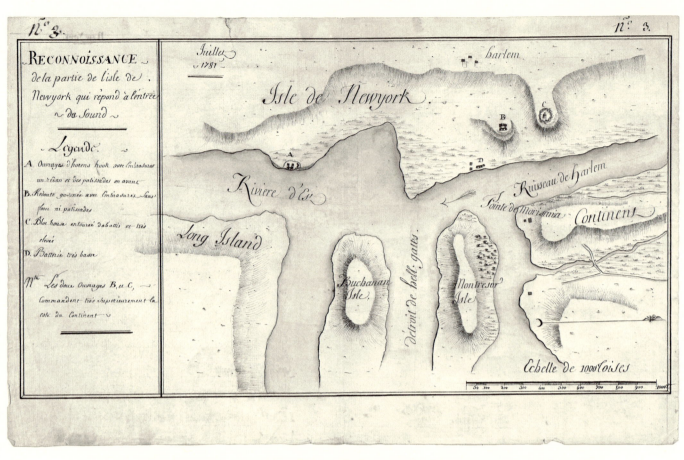

44   RECONNAISSANCE OF THE PART OF THE ISLAND OF NEW YORK THAT FACES
THE ENTRANCE OF THE SOUND [22–23 JULY 1781]

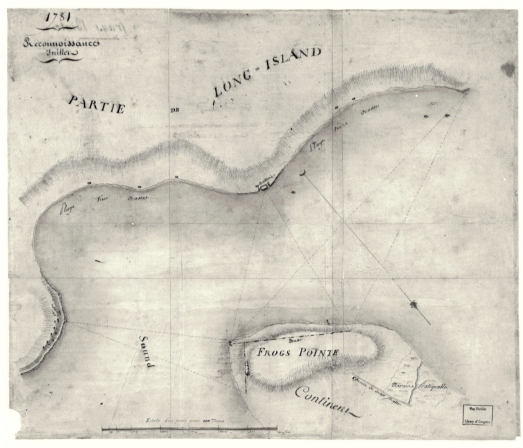

45   THROGS NECK RECONNAISSANCE, 23 JULY 1781

47   SKIRMISH AT MORRISIANA, 22 JULY 1781. PAINTING BY ALBRECHT ADAM, CA. 1825,
DEPICTING VON CLOSEN RECOVERING HIS HAT, WITH WASHINGTON, ROCHAMBEAU,
AND STAFF OBSERVING BRITISH WORKS ON MANHATTAN ISLAND

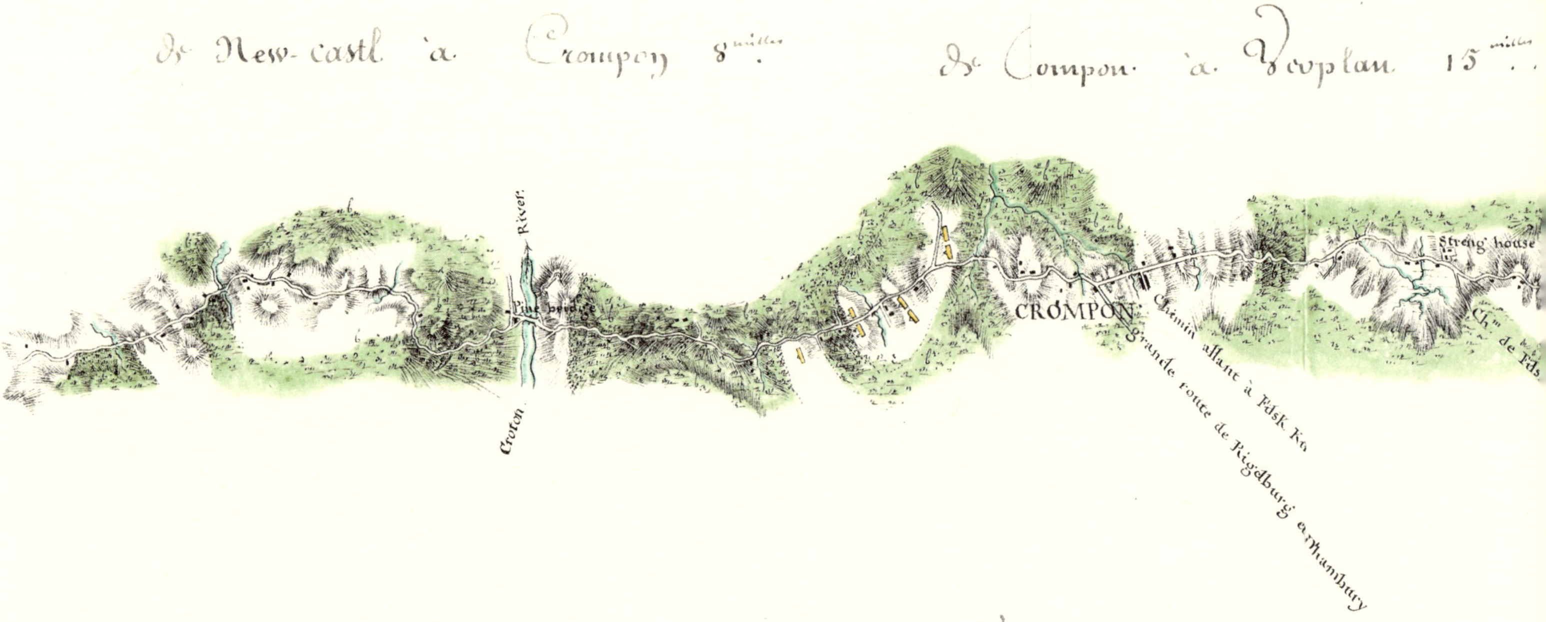

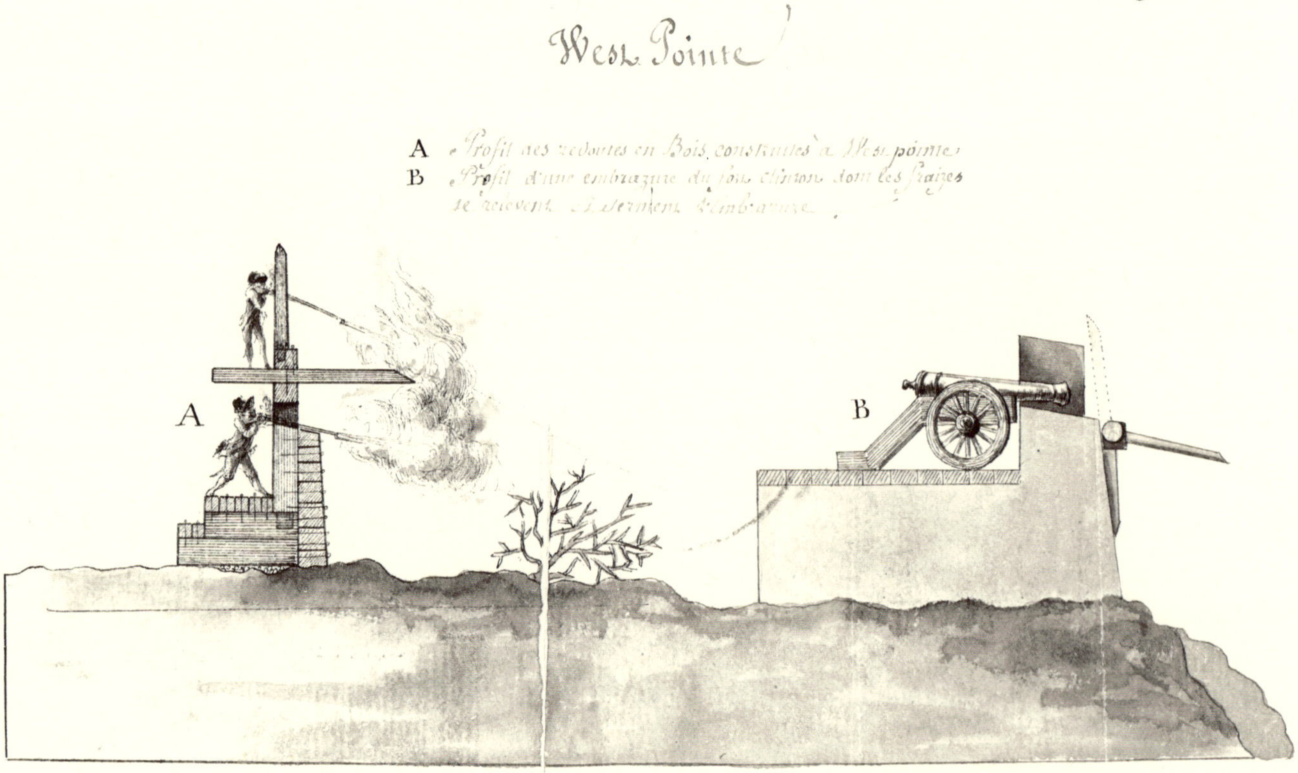

De New-castl `a Crompon 8 milles

De Compon `a Youplan 15 milles

River.

Pine pond

Croton.

CROMPON

Chemin allant `a Fisk Kn

Grande route de Rigdburg et Chambury

strag' house

West Pointe

A — Profil des redoutes en Bois construites `a West pointe

B — Profil d'une embrazure du fort clinton dont les Faces se relevent `a l'ermtere l'embrazure

A

B

48   MARCH FROM NEWCASTLE, VIA PINES BRIDGE AND CROMPOND, TO KING'S FERRY AND
STONY POINT, INCLUDING A PLAN OF WEST POINT

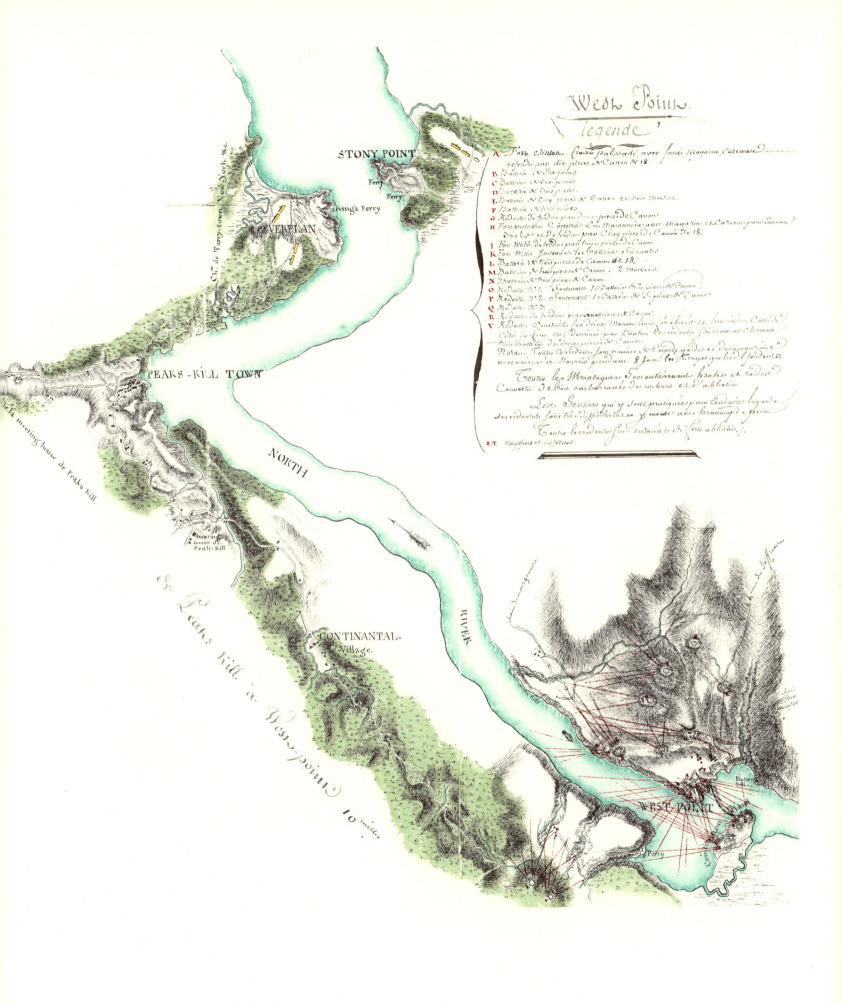

West Point

Stony Point

Ferry
Ferry
King's Ferry

VERPLAN

Ch. de Tarytown New-York &c.

PEAKS-KILL TOWN

de la meeting house de Peaks Kill.

NORTH

RIVER

meeting house de Peaks Kill

CONTINANTAL-Village.

de Peaks Kill a West point

10 milles.

WEST POINT

Ferry

Haver ſtrow.

Chᵐ de Chak=town

Lower road grand Chᵐ de l'Etat des Jers

Chᵐ de Sufferen's hameaux

meeting house

La taverne

Keyſt place

SUFFANS

Chᵐ de New Windſor par le gluve

Dᵉ Haver-ſtrow. à Suffrans. 16ᵐⁱˡˡᵉˢ

49   MARCH FROM HAVERSTRAW TO SUFFERN

Dᵉ Suffrans à Pompton 12ᵐⁱˡˡᵉˢ

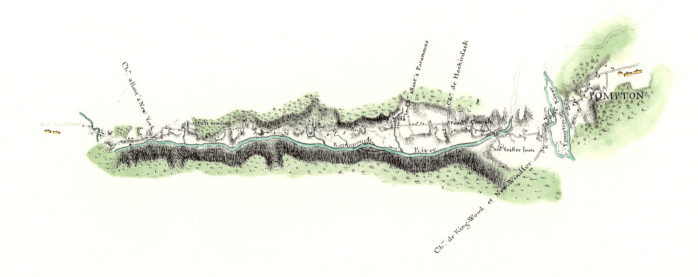

Chᵐ allant à New York

Buſtoſt moulin

Chᵐ allant à Paramus

Chᵐ de Hackinſack

Vander Church

Komopough River

Chᵐ de King-Wood et New-Windſor

buſt cattler houſe

POMPTON

50   MARCH FROM SUFFERN [IN NEW YORK] TO POMPTON [IN NEW JERSEY]

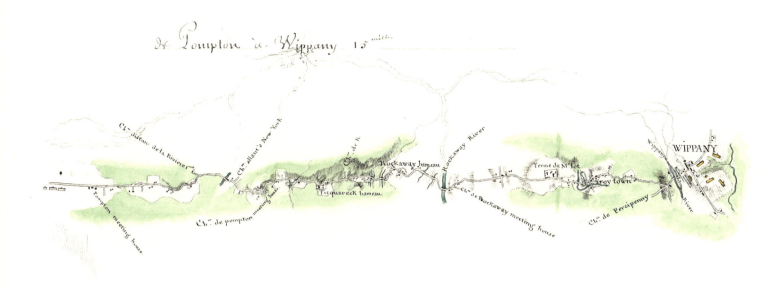

51   MARCH FROM POMPTON TO WHIPPANY

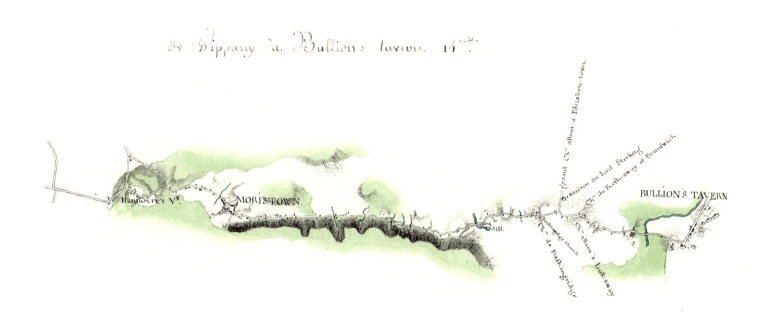

52   MARCH FROM WHIPPANY TO BULLION'S TAVERN

53 MARCH FROM BULLION'S TAVERN TO SOMERSET COURTHOUSE

de Summerset court house à Prince-town 13.ᵐⁱˡˡ

54 MARCH FROM SOMERSET COURTHOUSE TO PRINCETON

De Prince-town à Trenton 12 m. ½

55   MARCH FROM PRINCETON TO TRENTON

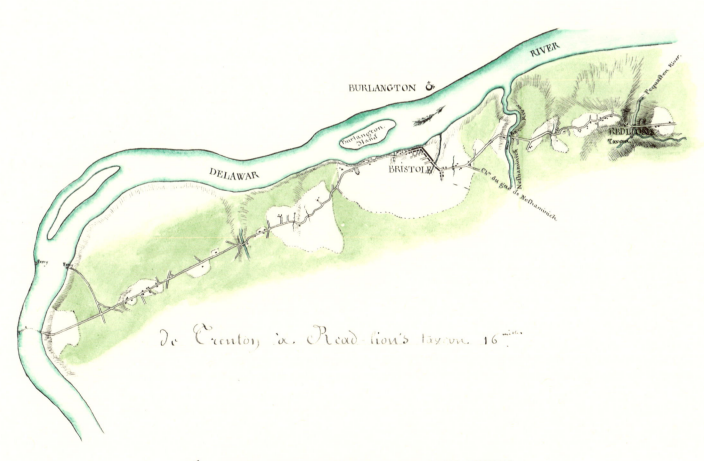

De Trenton à Read-lion's tavern 16 m.

56   MARCH FROM TRENTON TO RED LION TAVERN

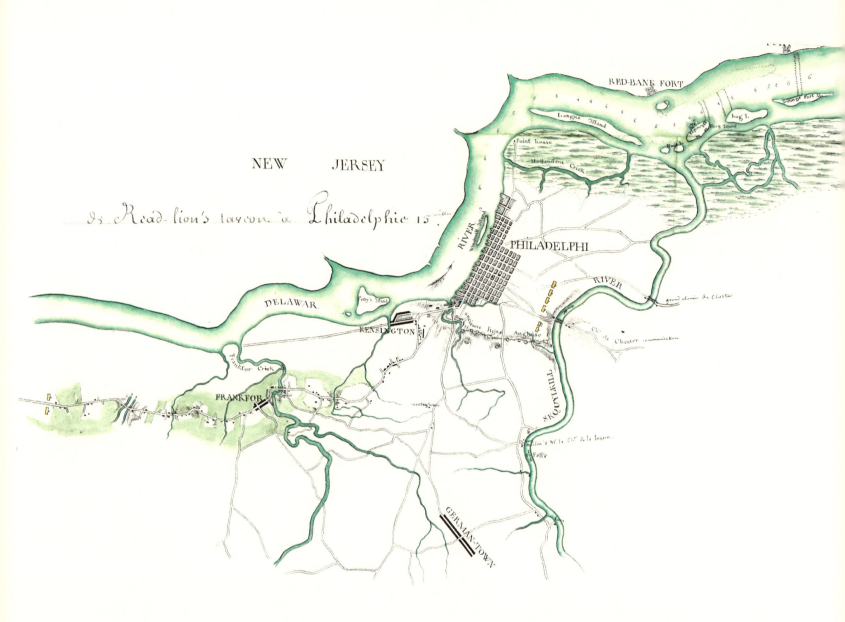

57   MARCH FROM RED LION TAVERN TO PHILADELPHIA

Dr Philadelphie à Chester 16.

DELAWAR RIVER

CHESTER

DARBY

58   MARCH FROM PHILADELPHIA TO CHESTER

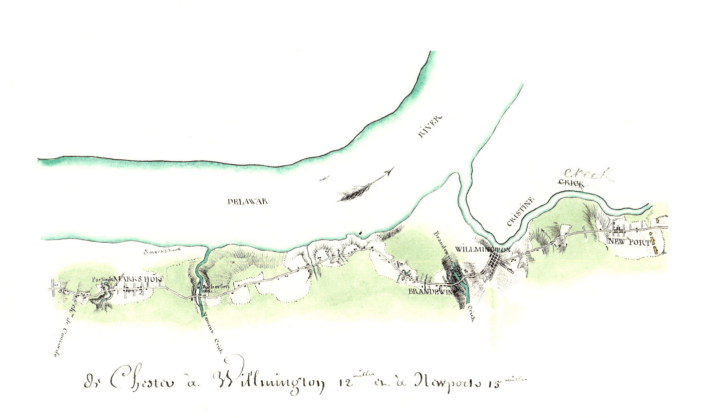

RIVER

DELAWAR

CRISTINE

CREEK

CRICK

CRICK

NEW PORT

WILLMINGTON

BRANDEWIN

MARKS HOK

Dr Chester à Willmington 12 milles et à Newports 15 milles

59   MARCH FROM CHESTER [IN PENNSYLVANIA] TO WILMINGTON
AND TO NEWPORT [IN DELAWARE]

Dr Newport a. head-of-Elk, 16. milli ½.

60   MARCH FROM NEWPORT [IN DELAWARE] TO HEAD OF ELK [IN MARYLAND]

[The series of Camp Plans,
interrupted with No. 39,
continues with No. 61]

15, Bivouac à North-Castle, le 19. Aoust, 17. miles ½ de Phillip'sburg.
Le 20. Séjour.

16e Camp à Huntz-Tavern le 21. Aoust, 8. miles de North-Castle.

61   SIXTEENTH CAMP AT HUNT'S TAVERN, 1781

17.ᵉ Camp à **King's ferry** ou **Verplank** le 22. Aoust, 14 mile.b de huntz-tavern. Le 23. Séjour.

Tapan's-Sea

Stony Point

chemin De Suffrantz

Ferry

chemin à New-Burg

King's ferry

Verplank

North-River

chemin De Peek's Kill

62   SEVENTEENTH CAMP AT KING'S FERRY, OR VERPLANCK, 1781

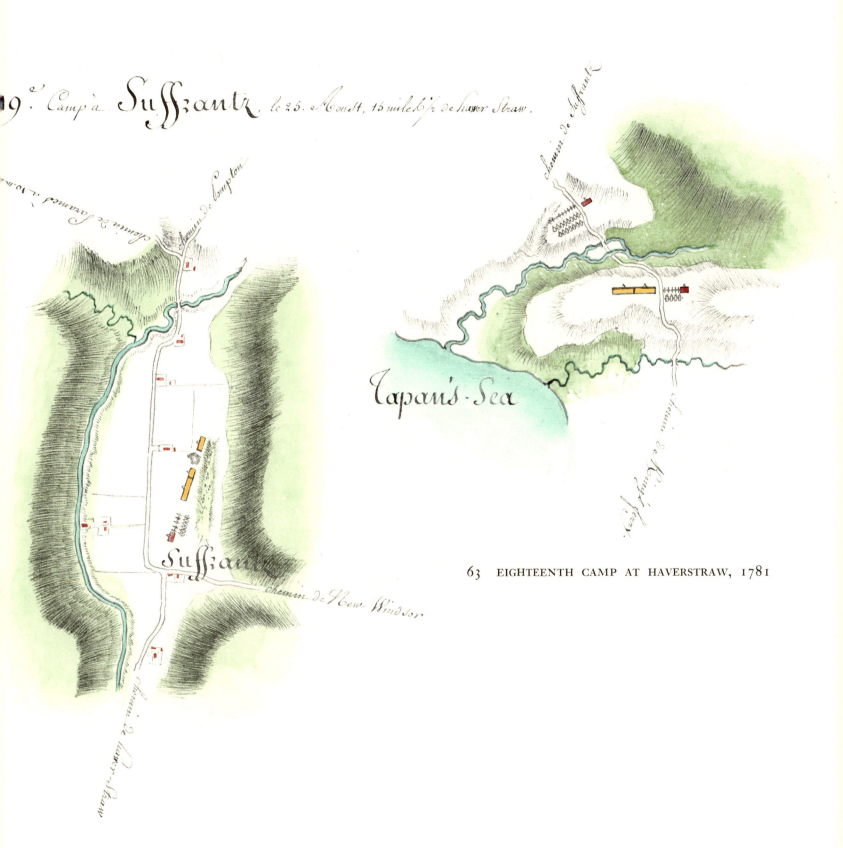

18.e Camp à Haver-Straw le 24. Aoust, 2 miles du ferry.

19.e Camp à Suffrantz le 25. Aoust, 15 miles ½ de haver Straw.

Japan's Sea

63   EIGHTEENTH CAMP AT HAVERSTRAW, 1781

64   NINETEENTH CAMP AT SUFFERN [IN NEW YORK], 1781

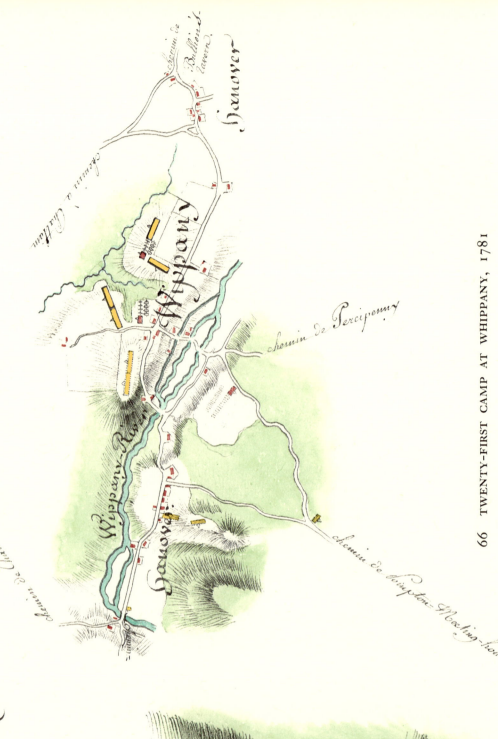

21.ᵉ Camp à Wippany, le 27. Août, 15 mile. 6 de Pompton-Meeting-house.
Le 28. Séjour.

20.ᵉ Camp à Pompton-Meeting-house.
le 26. Août, 15 mile. 6 de Suffrantz.

66   TWENTY-FIRST CAMP AT WHIPPANY, 1781

65   TWENTIETH CAMP AT POMPTON
        MEETINGHOUSE [IN NEW JERSEY], 1781

23ᵈ. Camp à Sommerset - Court - House. à 30. Court, 15 miles 68.

à Sullion's Tavern.

22ᵈ. Camp à Bullion's Tavern à 23 Court, 16 miles de Whippany.

68 TWENTY-THIRD CAMP AT SOMERSET
COURTHOUSE [MILLSTONE], 1781

67 TWENTY-SECOND CAMP AT BULLION'S TAVERN [LIBERTY CORNER], 1781

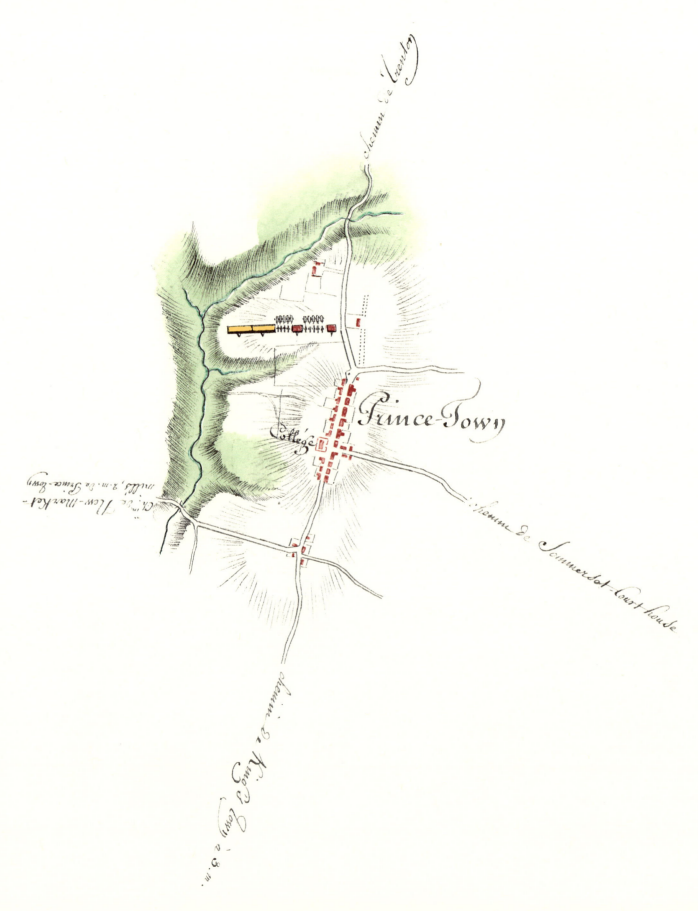

Prince-Town

College

chemin de Trenton

chemin de Sommerset-Court-house

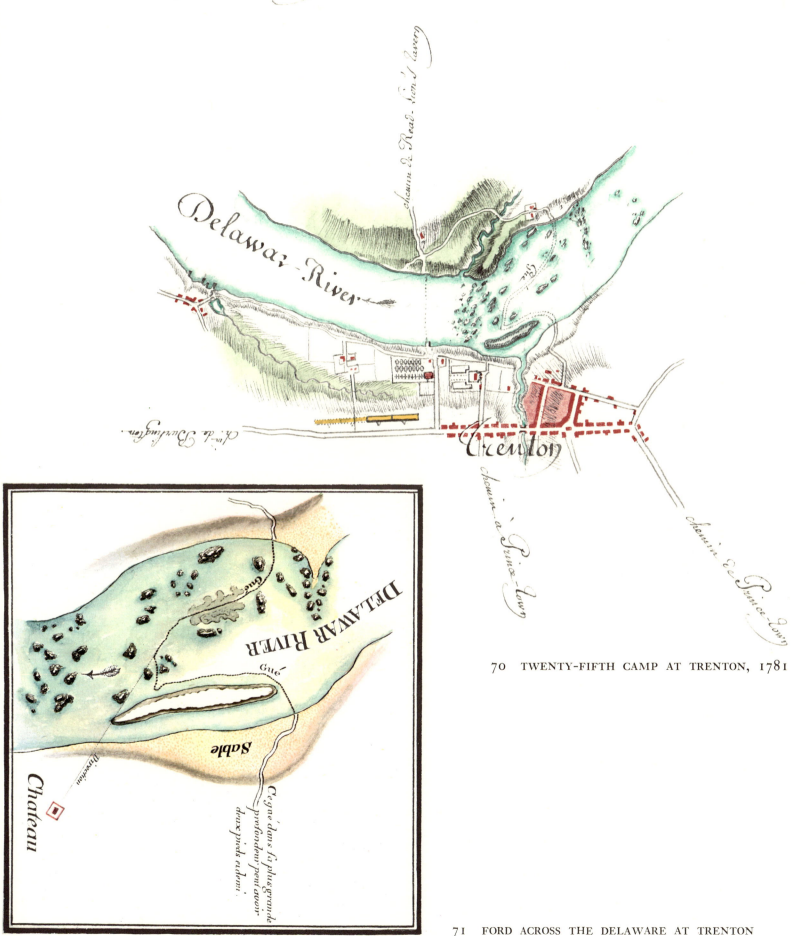

25. Camp à *Trenton*, le 1er Septembre, 12 miles ½ de Princetown.

Delawar-River

chemin de Real-Sem d'Asery

Trenton

dm. de Burlington

chemin à Prince-town

chemin de Prince-Town

70   TWENTY-FIFTH CAMP AT TRENTON, 1781

DELAWAR RIVER

Gué

Sable

Ce gué dans sa plus grande
profondeur peut avoir
deux pieds d'eau.

Direction

Chateau

71   FORD ACROSS THE DELAWARE AT TRENTON

26.ᵉ Camp à Read-Lion's Tavern le 2. Septembre 17 miles de Trenton.

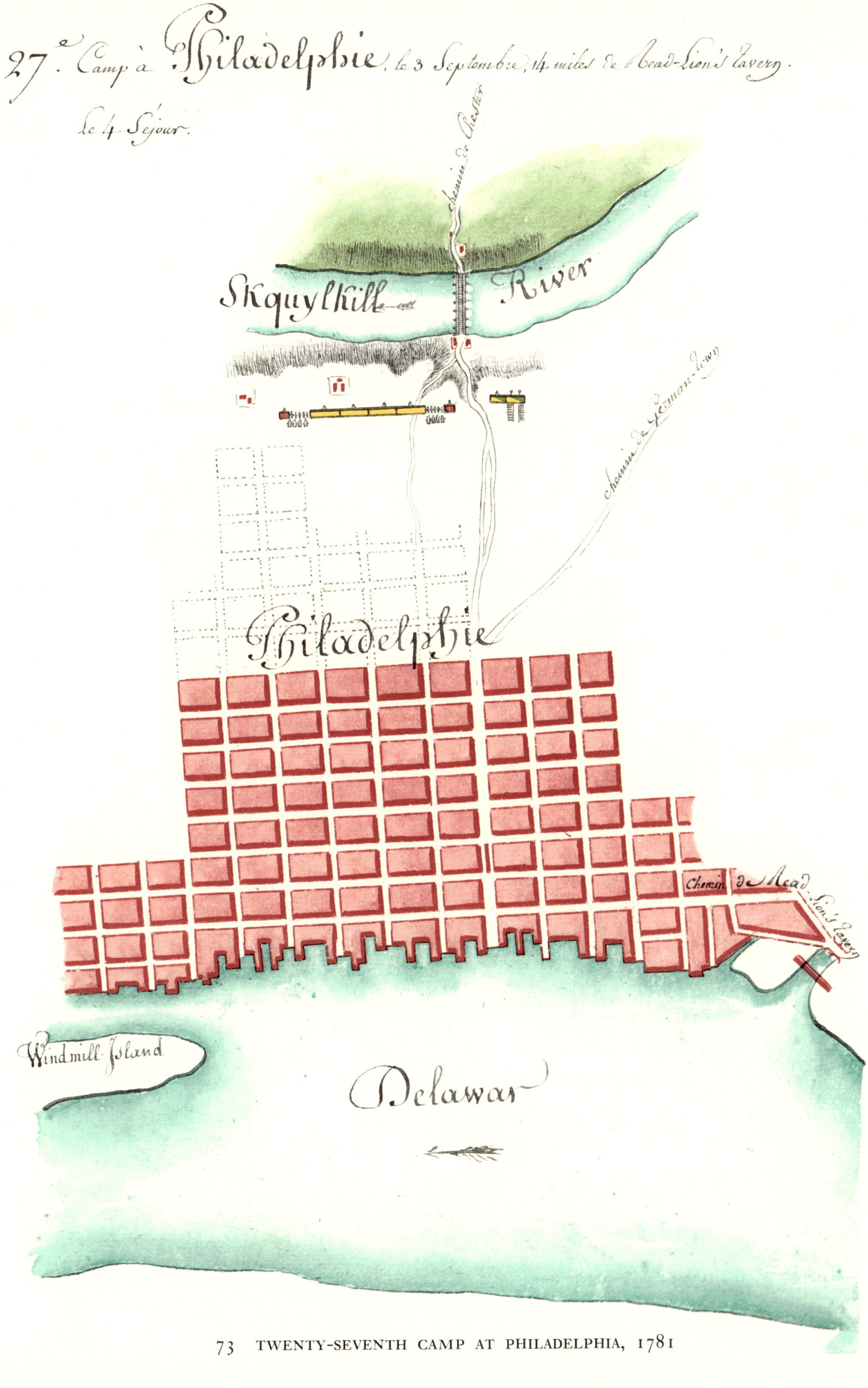
27.e Camp à Philadelphie, le 3 Septembre, 14 miles de Mead-Lion's tavern.
Le 4 Séjour.
chemin de Chester
Skquylkill River
chemin de German-town
Philadelphie
Chemin de Mead-Lion's tavern
Windmill-Island
Delawar

73 TWENTY-SEVENTH CAMP AT PHILADELPHIA, 1781

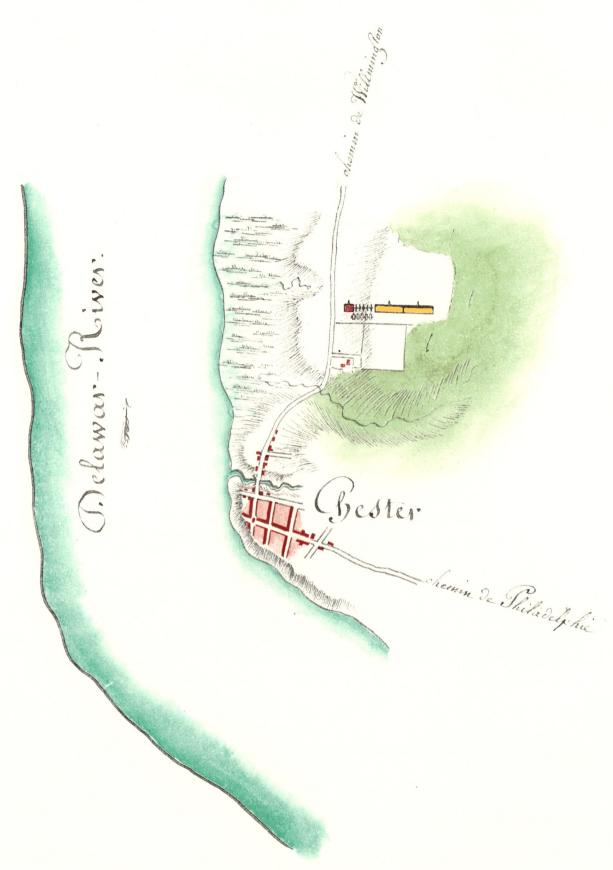

28.ᵉ Camp à **Chester**, le 5 Septembre, 16. miles de Philadelphie

Delawar - River.

chemin de Wilmington

Chester

chemin de Philadelphie

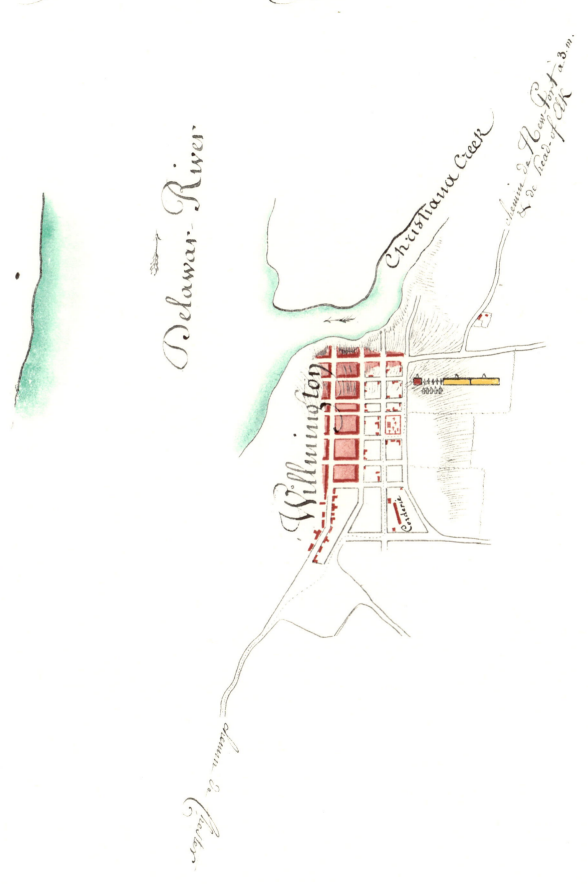

75   TWENTY-NINTH CAMP AT WILMINGTON [IN DELAWARE], 1781

30ᵉ Camp à Head-of-Elk, le 7. Septembre, 20 mile de Willmington.

le 8. Sejour.

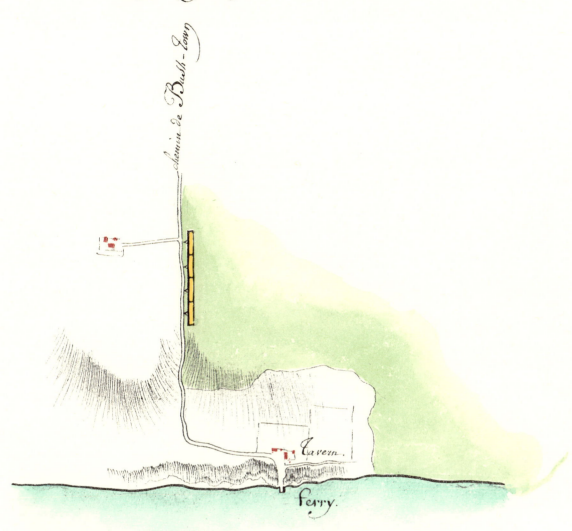

Susquehannah, ou ⟵ *Susquehanock-River.*

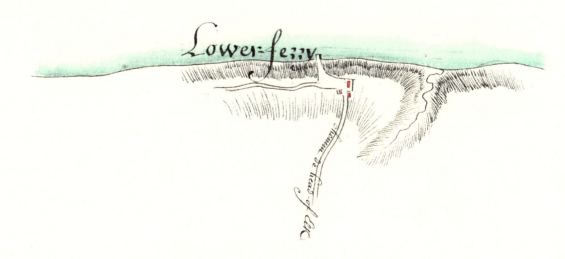

77 BIVOUAC AT LOWER FERRY, 1781

32, Bivoüac à Bush-Town, où Hartford le 10. Septembre, 12 miles de Lower-ferry.

33.ᵉ Camp à White Marsh le 11. Septembre, 15 miles de Bush-Town,

Bush-Town

78   BIVOUAC AT BUSH TOWN, OR HARFORD, 1781

79   THIRTY-THIRD CAMP AT WHITE MARSH, 1781

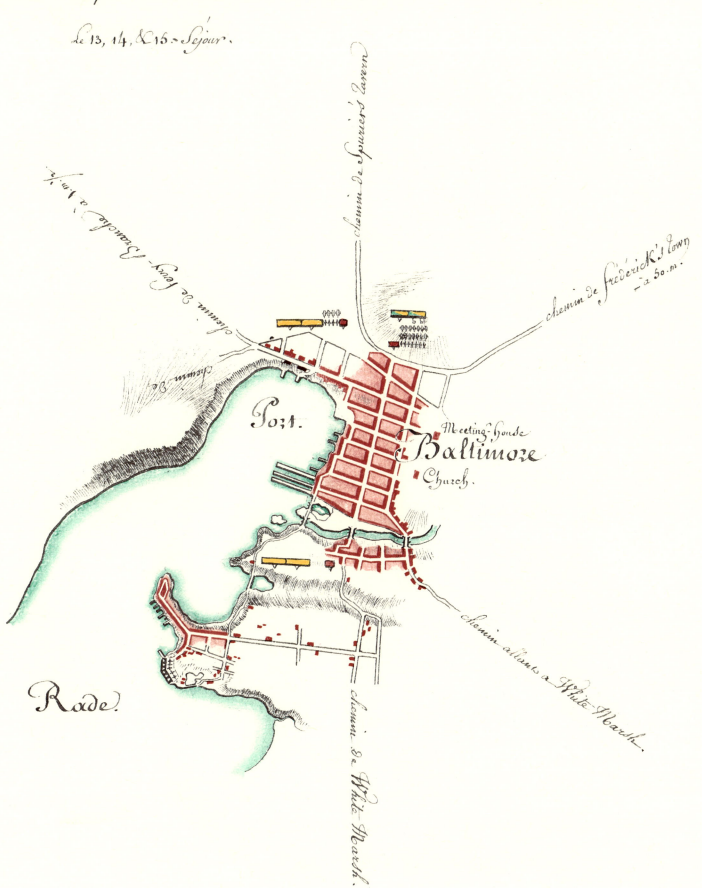

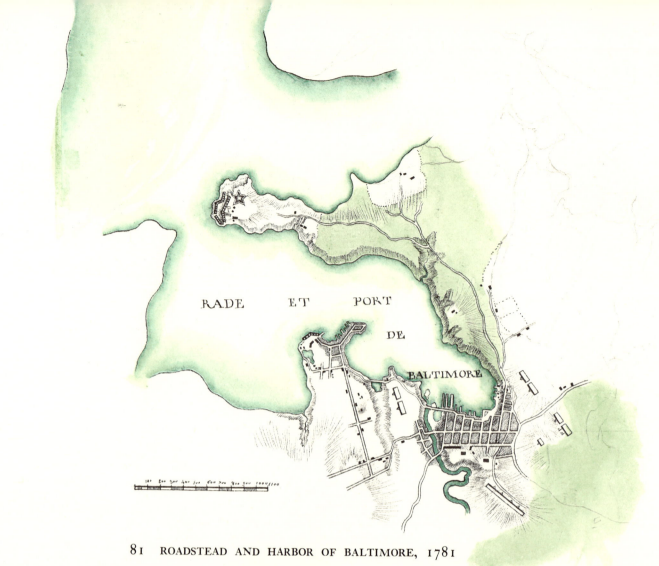

81 ROADSTEAD AND HARBOR OF BALTIMORE, 1781

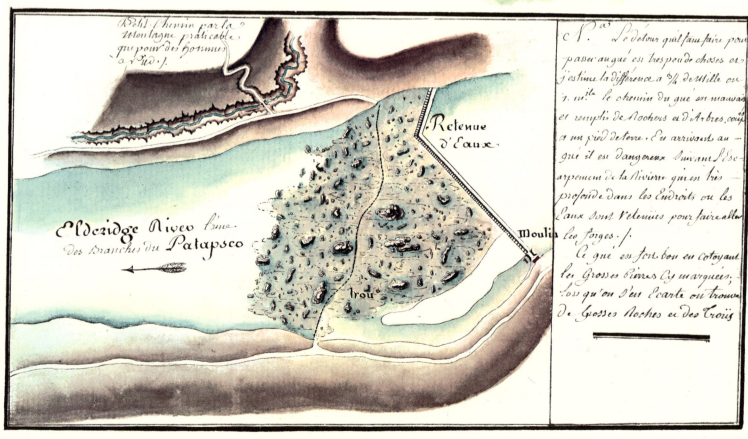

82 FORD ACROSS THE ELKRIDGE RIVER

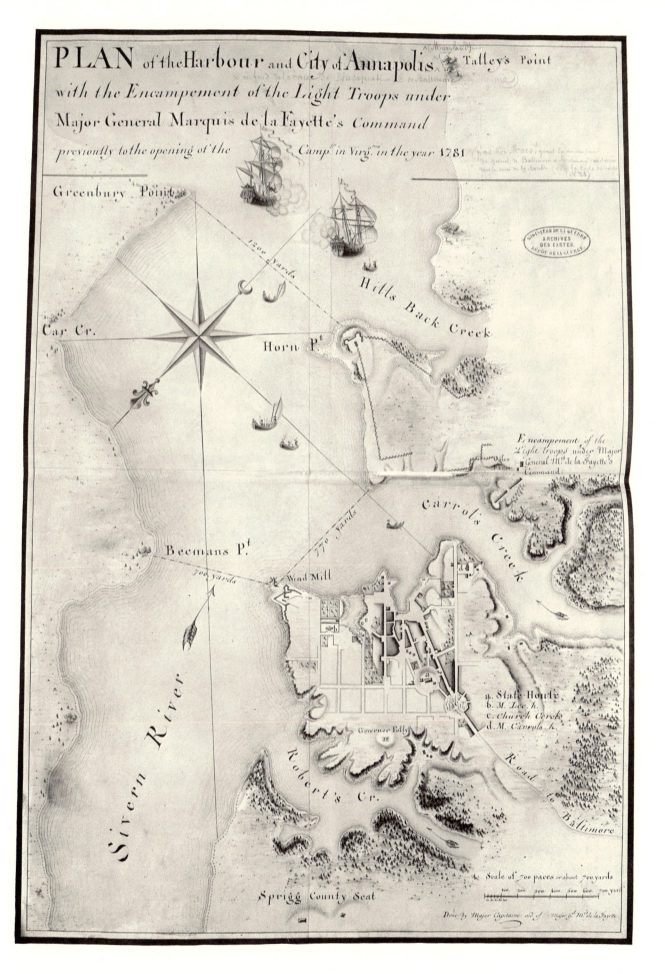

83 PLAN OF THE HARBOUR AND CITY OF ANNAPOLIS . . . [MARCH—APRIL 1781]

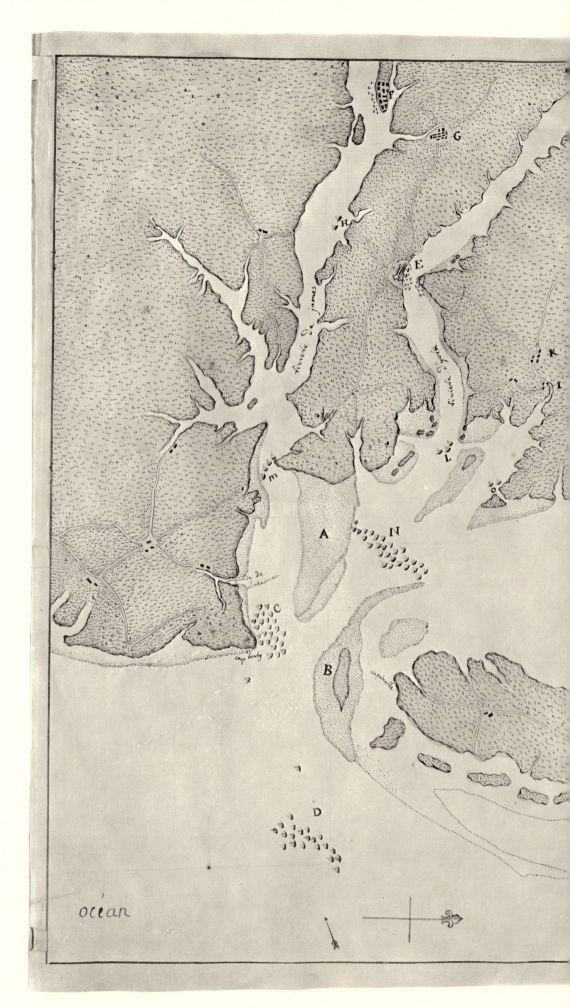

Expédition De chesapeack

anc de sable appellé horse-shoe. B, autre banc de sable nommé midle-ground. ces deux bancs ne sont couverts que de cinq
à six pieds d'eau, et celui de midle ground assèche quelquefois. ils ne laissent entre eux qu'un étroit canal, seul passage
pour entrer dans la baie avec des vaisseaux. C, premier mouillage de l'armée françoise a son arrivée dans la baie, et lorsque
elle apperçut le 5 septembre. l'armée ennemie D, qui venoit a elle. E, postes d'york et gloucester, retranchés et occupés
par le lord cornwalis, et sous lesquels étoient mouillés le charon de 50 canons, la guadeloupe de 24 canons, et plus de 60 batimens
marchands. F ville de jams town, lieu du débarquement de mté de st simon. G, ville de williamsbourg ancienne capitale
de la virginie, et lieu de la réunion des armées combinées, H lieu de débarquement de l'artillerie. I, lieu du débarquement
de mté De choisy. K, village du court-house, lieu de leur premier campement. L, trois vaisseaux ou frégattes françoises, qui
bloquoient la rivière d'york. M, quatre vaisseaux ou frégattes françoises, bloquant la rivière james, et chargés d'en défendre l'entrée.
N, second mouillage de l'armée françoise ┤ échelle de 5 lieues ├ entre les deux bancs pour en défendre le passage.
O, corvettes françoises en station le long de la côte pour arrêter tous les petits batteaux, qui en faisant la terre auroient pu échapper aux vaisseaux

Virginie

maryland

Rivière patowmak

de La baie de chesapeack.

Virginie

maryland

35. Camp à Spurier's Tavern, le 16. Septembre, 14 miles de Baltimore, manque.

36. Camp à Scott's House, le 17. Septembre, 16 miles de Spurier's Tavern, manque.

37. Camp à Annapolis, le 18 Septembre, 6 miles de Scott's house, manque.

Le 19 & 20. Séjour pendant lequel temps on embarqua l'Artillerie, les vivres & les Equipages, & le 21. les troupes ayant commencé à s'embarquer à 7 heures du matin, la flotte mit à la voile à 1 heure pour descendre la Baye de Chésapeak, & arriva le 24 dans la Rivière de James au point où elle devait débarquer, appelé Arche's Hupe, 1 mile au dessus de l'embouchure de Collège Creek.

38. Camp à Arche's-Hupe le 25 Septembre.

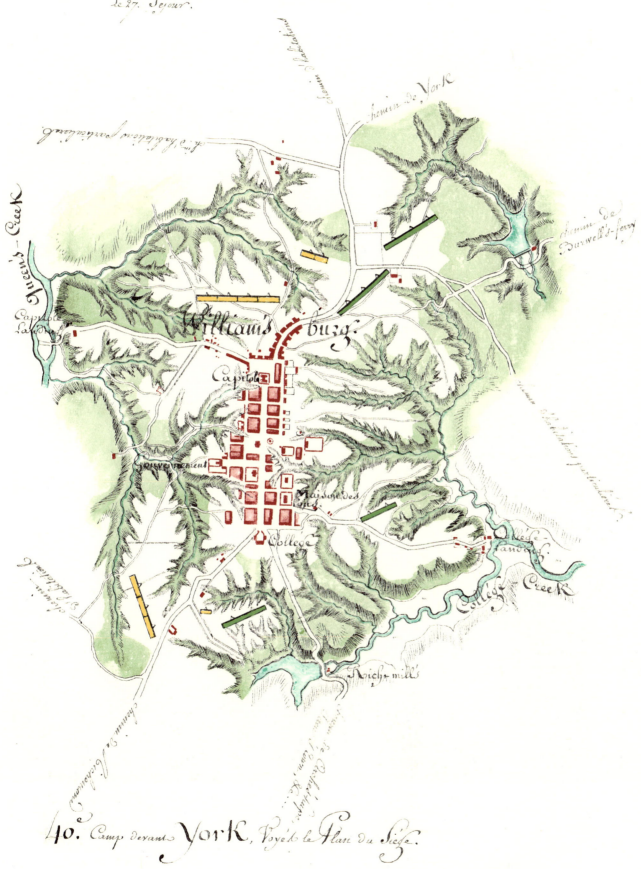

39. Camp à Williamsburg le 26. Septembre, 7. miles de Arche's hope.

le 27. Séjour.

40. Camp devant York, Voyé le Plan du Siège.

Plan figuré à vue du siege d'York

87 PLAN OF THE SIEGE OF YORK, BY L.-A. AND C.-L. BERTHIER

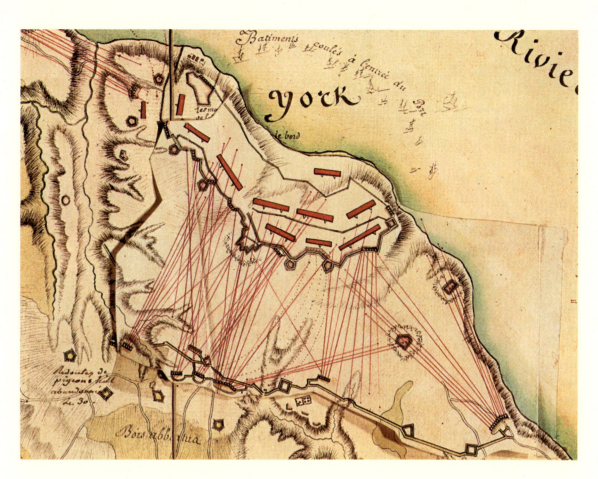

88 FIRST PARALLEL. DETAIL FROM THE BERTHIER BROTHERS' PLAN

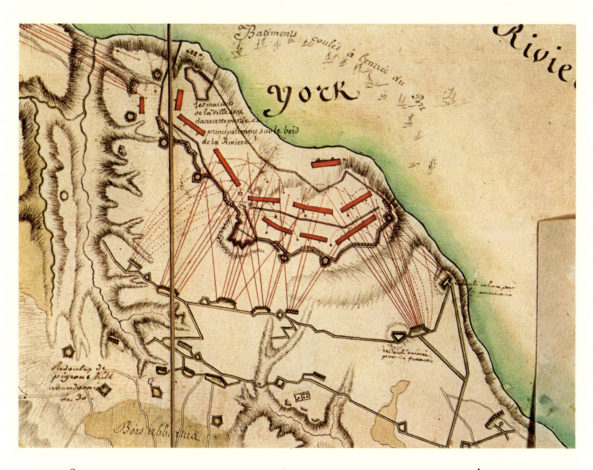

89 SECOND PARALLEL. DETAIL FROM THE BERTHIER BROTHERS' PLAN

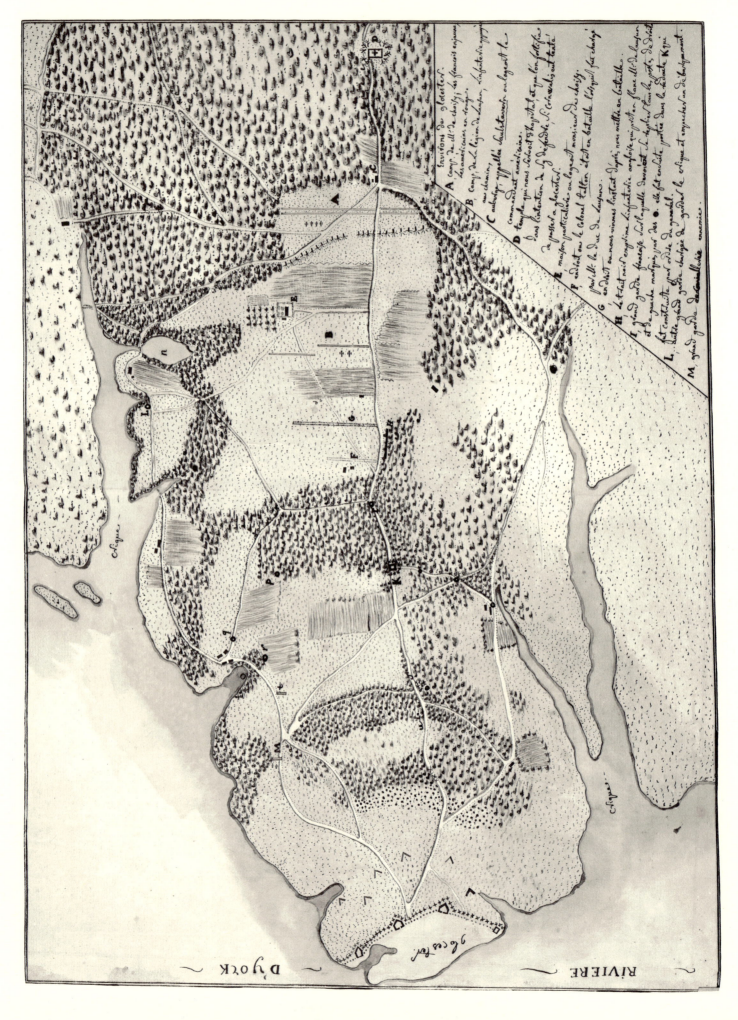

91   ENVIRONS OF WILLIAMSBURG. DETAIL FROM UNFINISHED MAP

92   THE SIEGE OF YORKTOWN, BY LOUIS-NICOLAS VAN BLARENBERGHE, 1784

93   ROCHAMBEAU AND HIS OFFICERS. DETAIL FROM VAN BLARENBERGHE'S "SIEGE," 1784

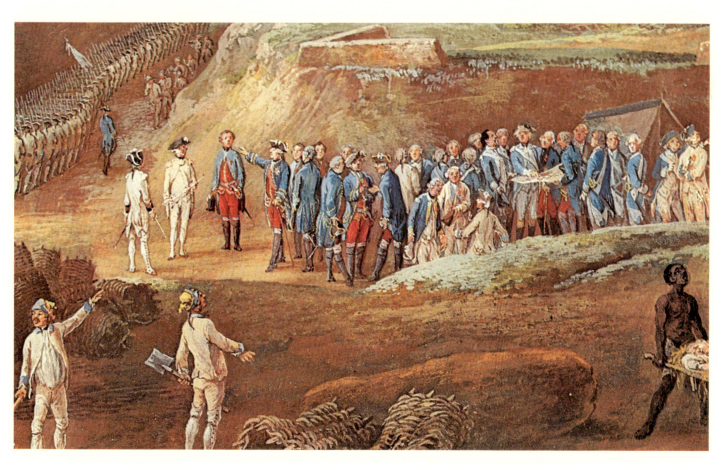

94   ROCHAMBEAU AND HIS OFFICERS. DETAIL FROM VAN BLARENBERGHE'S "SIEGE," 1786

95　THE SURRENDER OF YORKTOWN, BY LOUIS-NICOLAS VAN BLARENBERGHE, 1785

96   BRITISH TROOPS GROUNDING THEIR ARMS. DETAIL FROM
VAN BLARENBERGHE'S "SURRENDER," 1785

97   THE GARRISON OF YORK MARCHING OUT TO THE SURRENDER FIELD.
DETAIL FROM VAN BLARENBERGHE'S "SURRENDER," 1786

Vue d'Yorck

98   VIEW OF YORK, 1781

Plan d'york town pour servir a l'Etablissement du Quartier d'hyver du Regiment de Soissonnois; et des Grenadiers et Chasseurs de St Onge le 12 9bre 1781.

YORK   RIVER

99   PLAN OF YORKTOWN TO BE USED FOR ESTABLISHING THE WINTER QUARTERS OF THE
SOISSONNAIS REGIMENT; AND OF THE GRENADIERS AND CHASSEURS OF THE
SAINTONGE REGIMENT, 12 NOVEMBER 1781

100 PROFILE OF YORKTOWN

FORTIFICATIONS

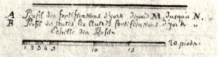

101 GENERALS OF THE FRENCH AND AMERICAN ARMIES AT YORKTOWN AFTER THE SURRENDER,
BY JAMES PEALE

Virginie

Figuré avüe de Portsmouth à dot Environs

Jamea River

Elisabeth River

Echelle N. 4 miles

102   FREEHAND MAP OF PORTSMOUTH, VIRGINIA, AND ENVIRONS

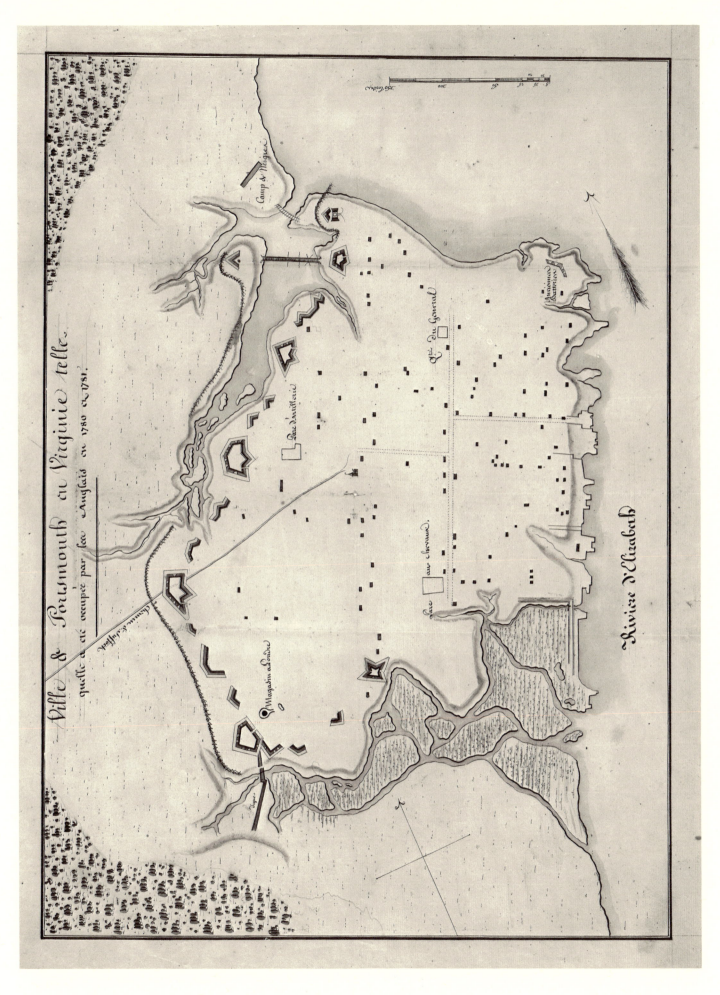

104   MAP OF WEST POINT ON THE YORK RIVER AT THE CONFLUENCE OF
THE PAMUNKEY AND MATTAPONI [1781–1782]

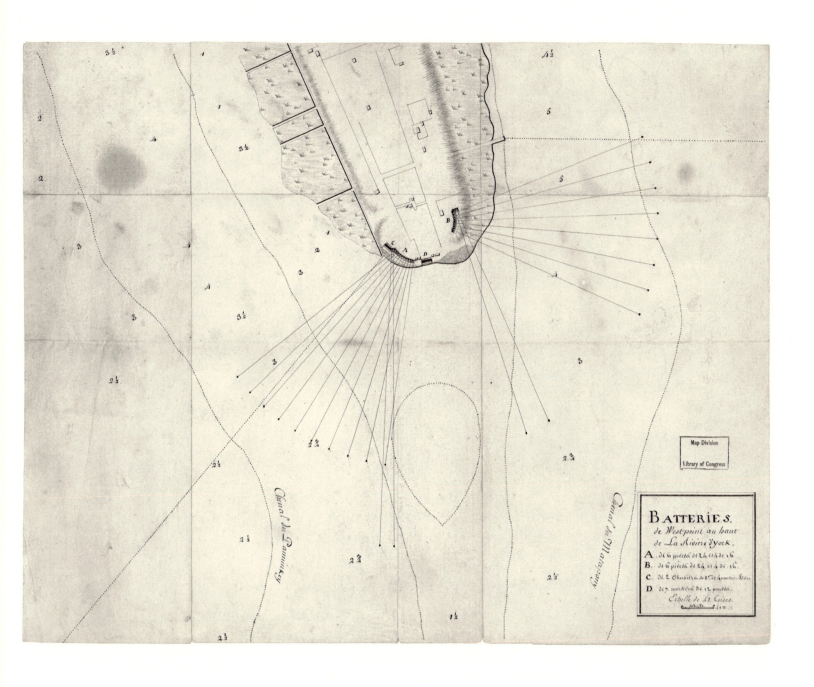

BATTERIES.
de West-point au haut
de La Rivière d'york.
A. de 6 pièces de 24 et 4 de 16.
B. de 6 pièces de 24 et 4 de 16.
C. de 2 Obusiers de 8 et 4 mortiers à la...
D. de 7 mortiers de 12 pouces.
Echelle de 42 toises.

105   BATTERIES AT WEST POINT [IN VIRGINIA] AT THE HEAD OF THE YORK RIVER

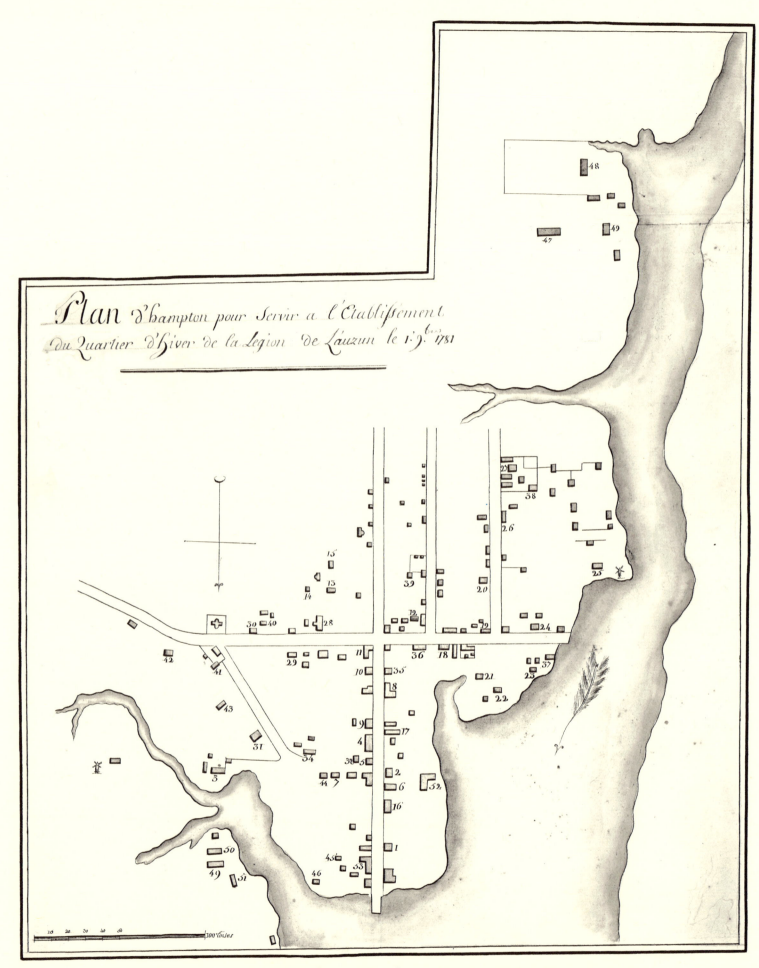

Plan d'hampton pour Servir a l'Etablissement
du Quartier d'Hiver de la Legion de Lauzun le 1.9.bre 1781

106 PLAN OF HAMPTON [IN VIRGINIA] TO BE USED FOR ESTABLISHING THE
WINTER QUARTERS OF LAUZUN'S LEGION, 1 NOVEMBER 1781

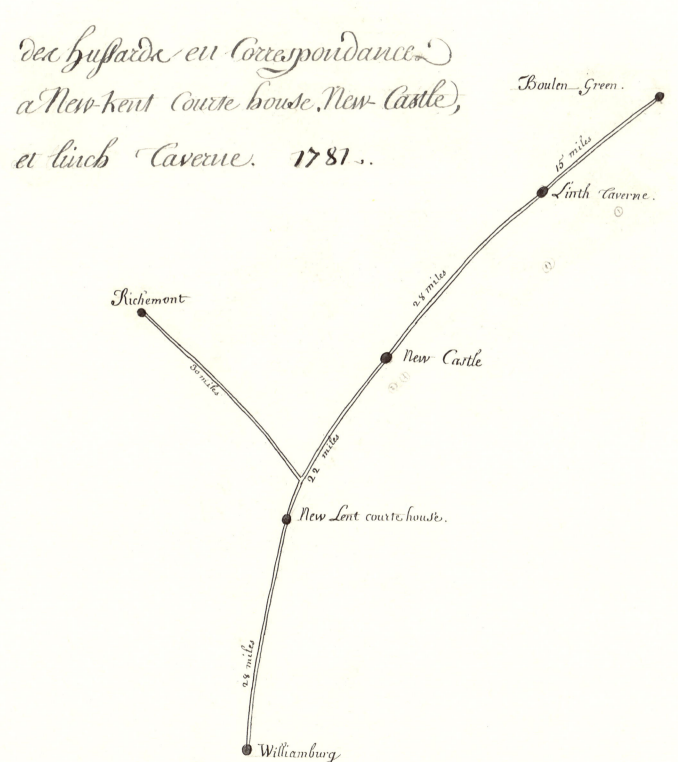

Établissement

des hussards en Correspondance
a New-Kent Courte house. New-Castle,
et linch Caverne. 1781.

Boulen Green.

15 miles

Linth Caverne.

28 miles

Richemont

30 miles

New Castle

22 miles

New Lent courte house.

28 miles

Williamburg

107A   CHAIN OF EXPRESSES BETWEEN NEW KENT COURTHOUSE,
NEWCASTLE, AND LYNCH'S TAVERN, 1781

Armée de
Mr le Cte de
Rochambeau

Amerique
Septentrionale

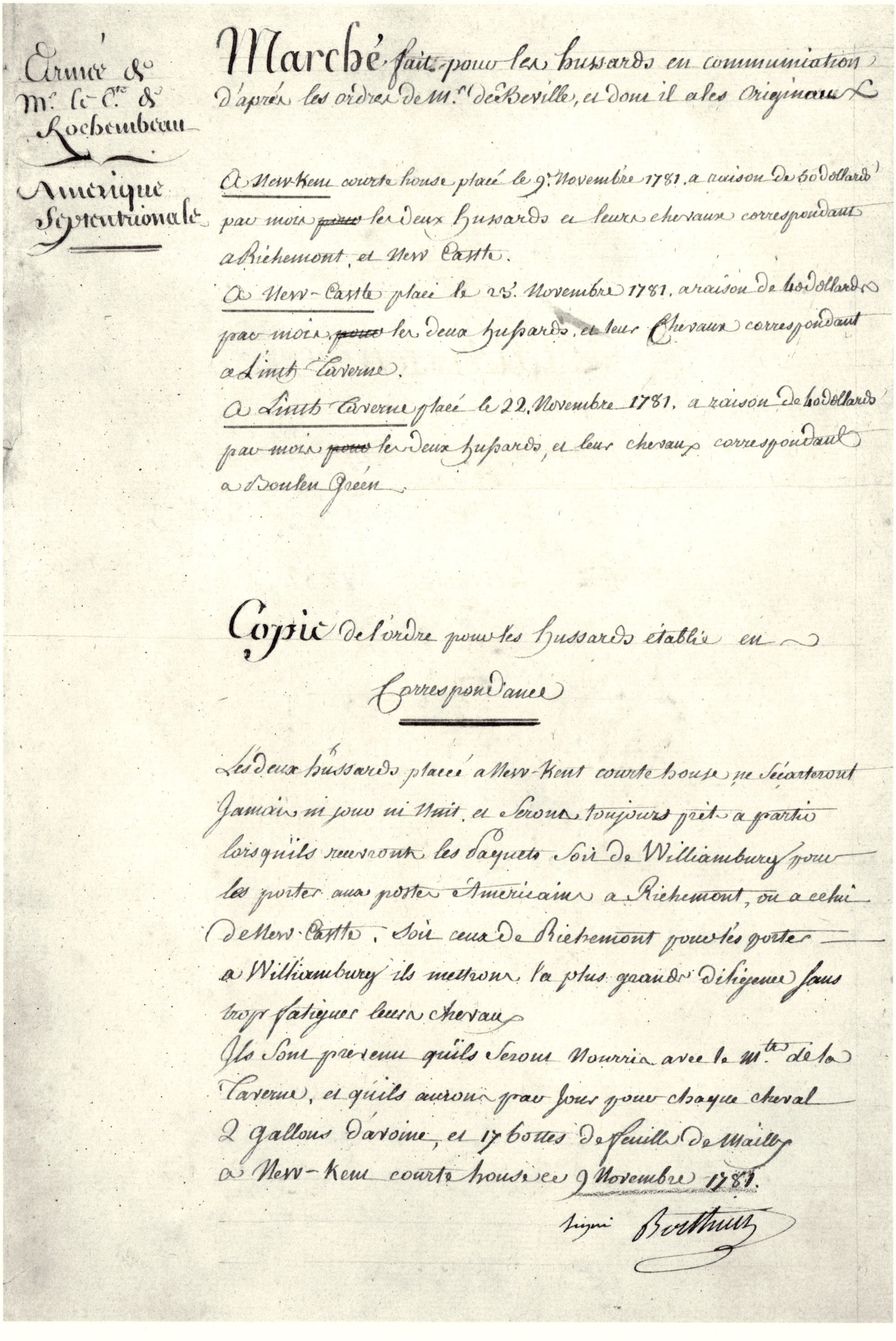

Marché fait pour les hussards en communication d'après les ordres de Mr de Beville, et dont il a les Originaux

A New Kent courte house placé le 9. Novembre 1781. a raison de 60 dollards par mois ~~pour~~ les deux hussards et leurs chevaux correspondant a Richemont, et New Castle.

A New-Castle placé le 25. Novembre 1781. a raison de 60 dollards par mois ~~pour~~ les deux hussards, et leurs Chevaux correspondant a Limt Taverne.

A Limb Taverne placé le 22. Novembre 1781. a raison de 60 dollards par mois ~~pour~~ les deux hussards, et leur chevaux correspondant a Boulen Green.

Copie de l'ordre pour les hussards établie en Correspondance

Les deux hussards placé a New-Kent courte house ne Séparteront jamais ni jour ni Nuit, et Seront toujours prêt a partir lorsquils recevront les paquets Soit de Williamburg pour les porter aux postes Américains a Richemont, ou a celui de New-Castle. Soit ceux de Richemont pour les porter a Williamburg ils mettront la plus grande diligence sans trop fatiguer leurs chevaux.

Ils Sont prevenu quils Seront Nourris avec le Mtre de la Taverne, et quils auront par jour pour chaque cheval 2 gallons d'avoine, et 17 bottes de feuille de Maïs

a New-Kent courte house ce 9 Novembre 1781.

signé Berthier

107B ORDERS SIGNED BY BERTHIER, 9 NOVEMBER 1781, CONCERNING THE CHAIN OF EXPRESSES

Amérique
Campagne
1782.

Plans

des différents camps occupés
par l'armée aux ordres de
M^r le Comte de Rochambeau.

■ Artillerie

▬ Troupes françaises

▬ Troupes Américaines

▬ Les Troupes pointillées avec une teinte jaune marquent les
Emplacements occupés par les Reg^{ts} de royal Deux ponts
et Saintonge ayant campés la Campagne 1782. par Brigade
dans les mêmes endroits où ils Camperent par régiment
la Campagne 1781.

Bois

Eaux.

PLANS OF THE DIFFERENT CAMPS OCCUPIED BY THE ARMY UNDER THE ORDERS OF
THE COMTE DE ROCHAMBEAU: CAMPAIGN OF 1782

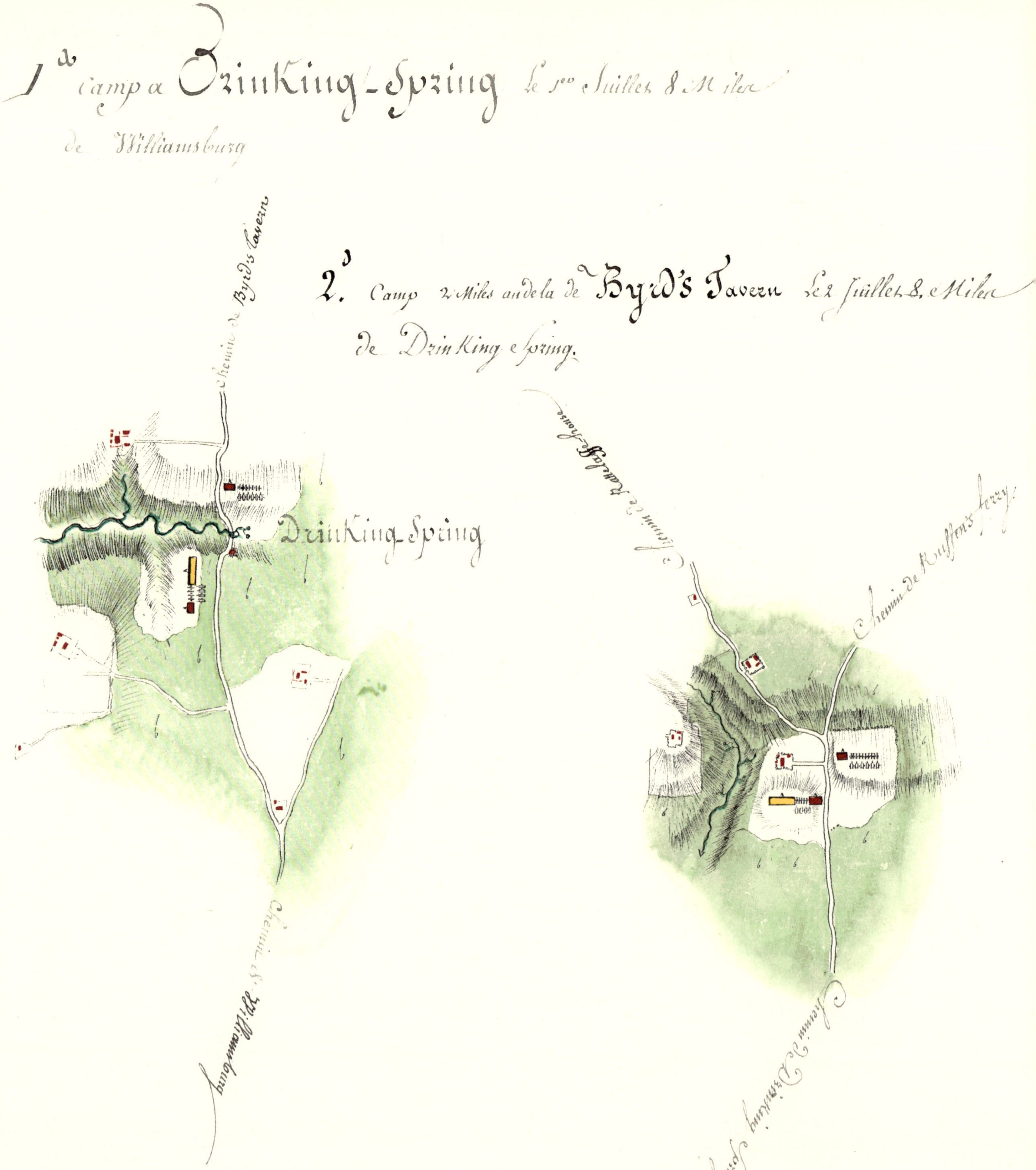

1ᵈ camp a *Drinking-Spring* le 1ᵒ Juillet 8 Miles
de Williamsburg

2ᵈ Camp 2 Miles au dela de *Byrd's Tavern* le 2 Juillet 8. Miles
de Drinking Spring.

Chemin de Byrd's Tavern

Drinking Spring

Chemin de Williamsburg

Chemin de Rasselet house

Chemin de Ruffins ferry

Chemin de Drinking Spring

109   FIRST CAMP AT DRINKING SPRING
[IN VIRGINIA], 1782

110   SECOND CAMP, TWO MILES
BEYOND BYRD'S TAVERN, 1782

3ᵉ Camp à *Rattelaffe House* le 3 Juillet . 7 Miles
de *Byrda Cavern*.

Rattelaffe house.

4ᵉ Camp à *Hartfield*. le 4 Juillet
7 Miles ½ de *Rattelaffe house*.

Hartfield

111   THIRD CAMP AT RATCLIFFE HOUSE, 1782

112   FOURTH CAMP AT HARTFIELD, 1782

5 Camp à New Castle 1 Miles en deça de la ville

Le 5 Juillet 15. Miles de Hartfield.

Le 6. Sejour.

New Castle.

6e Camp à Hannover Town Un Miles au de là de la Ville

Le 7 Juillet 7 Miles de New Castle.

Hannover Town.

113   FIFTH CAMP AT NEWCASTLE, 1782

114   SIXTH CAMP AT HANOVERTOWN, 178

7. Camp à Peage's Bridge ou Graham's house
Le 8 Juillet 10 Miles de Hannover Town

8e Camp à Burck bridge ou Kenner's Tavern
Le 9 Juillet 12 Miles de Peage Bridge

Chemin De Burck bridge.

Graham's house

Chemin de Bowlinggreen

Kenner's Tavern

Pamunkey R.
Peage's Bridge

Chemin De Hannover Town

River

Mattapony

Burck bridge

Chemin de Peage bridge.

115   SEVENTH CAMP AT [LITTLE] PAGE'S
BRIDGE OR GRAHAM'S HOUSE, 1782

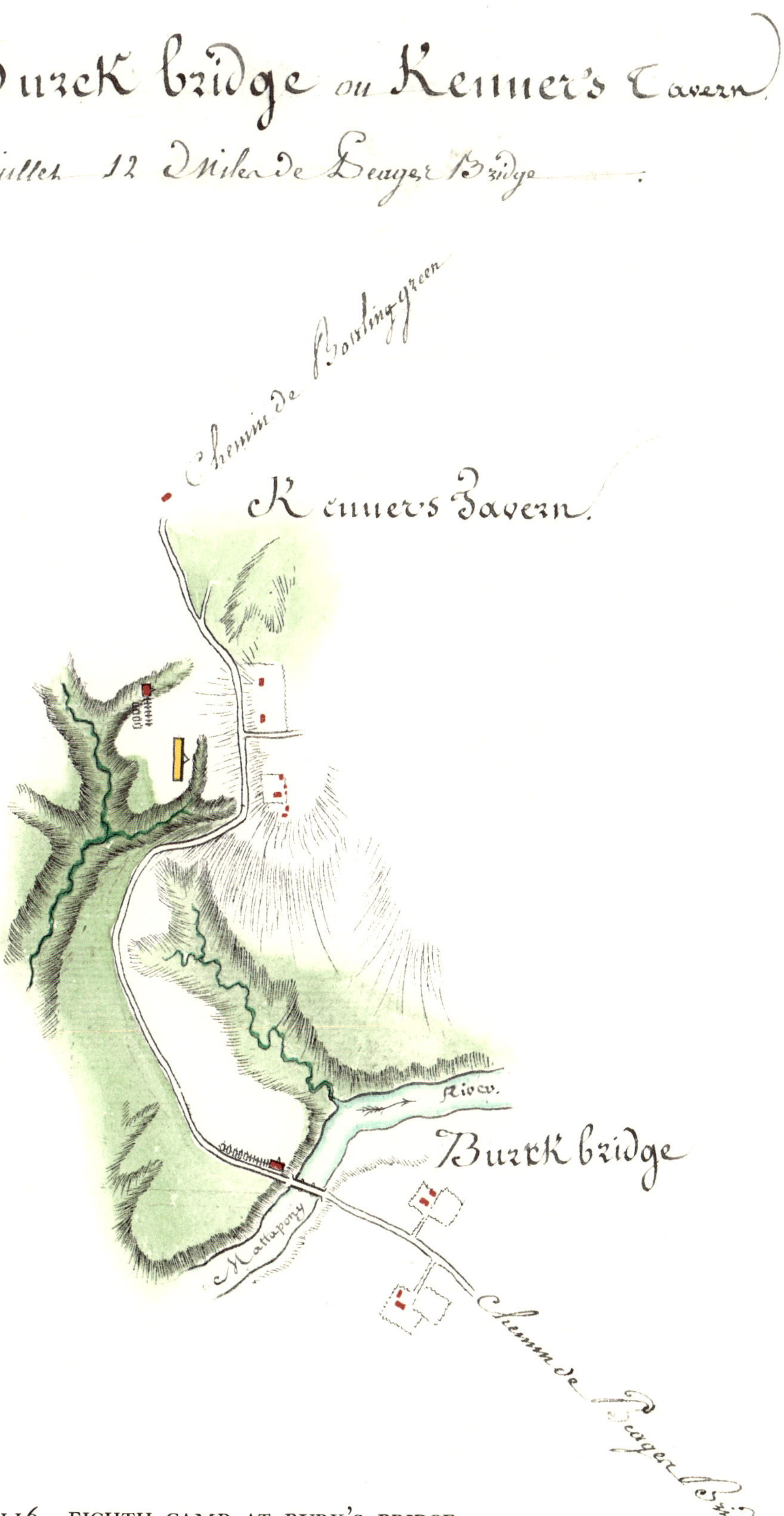

116   EIGHTH CAMP AT BURK'S BRIDGE
OR KENNER'S TAVERN, 1782

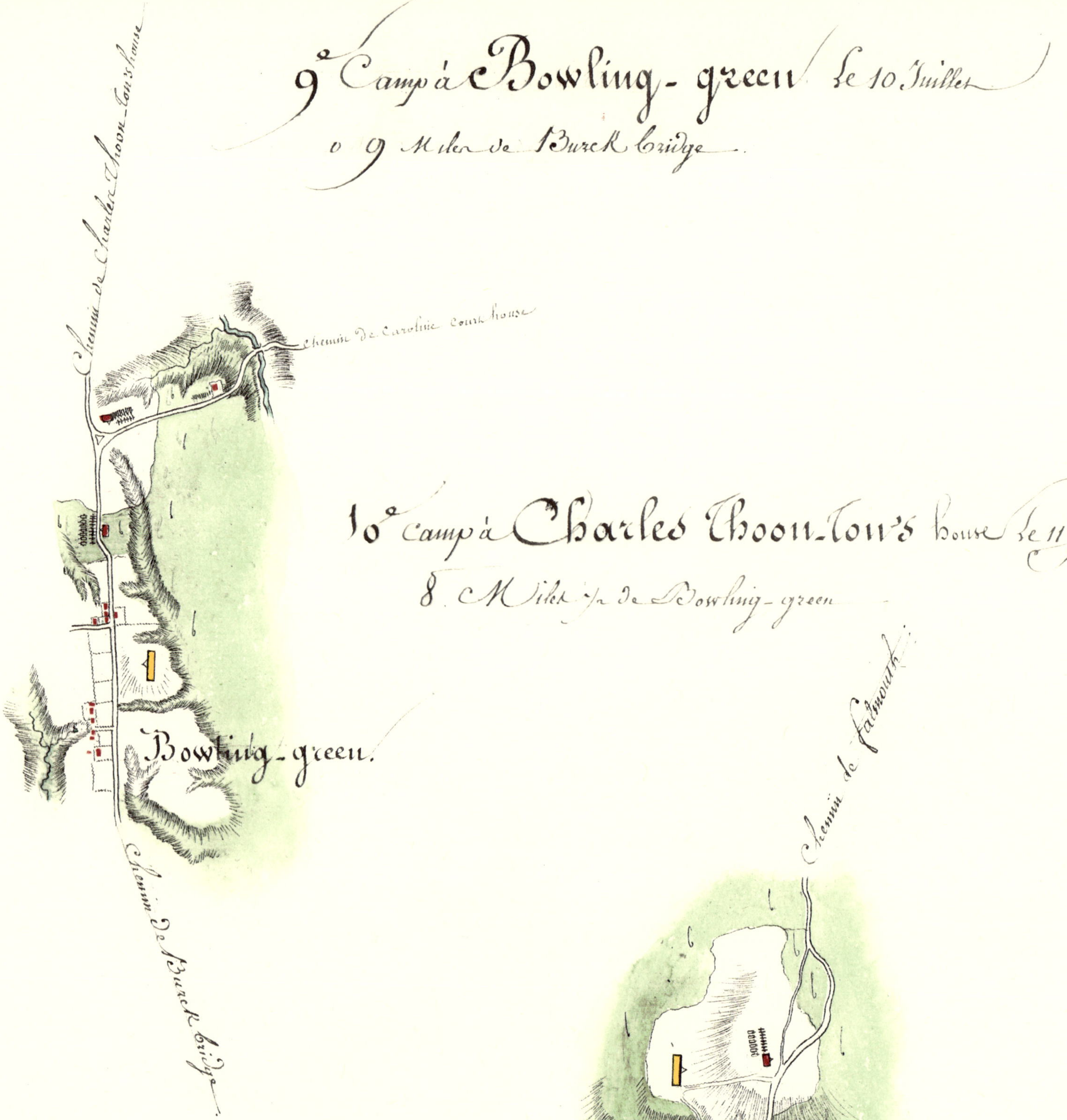

9e Camp à Bowling-green le 10 Juillet
a 9 Miles de Burck bridge
Chemin de Charles Thoon-Ton's house
Chemin de Caroline Court house
Bowling-green.
Chemin de Burck bridge

117 NINTH CAMP AT BOWLING GREEN, 1782

10e camp à Charles Thoon-Ton's house le 11 Juillet
8 Miles ½ de Bowling-green
Chemin de Falmouth
Charles Thoon-Ton's house.
Chemin de Bowling-green

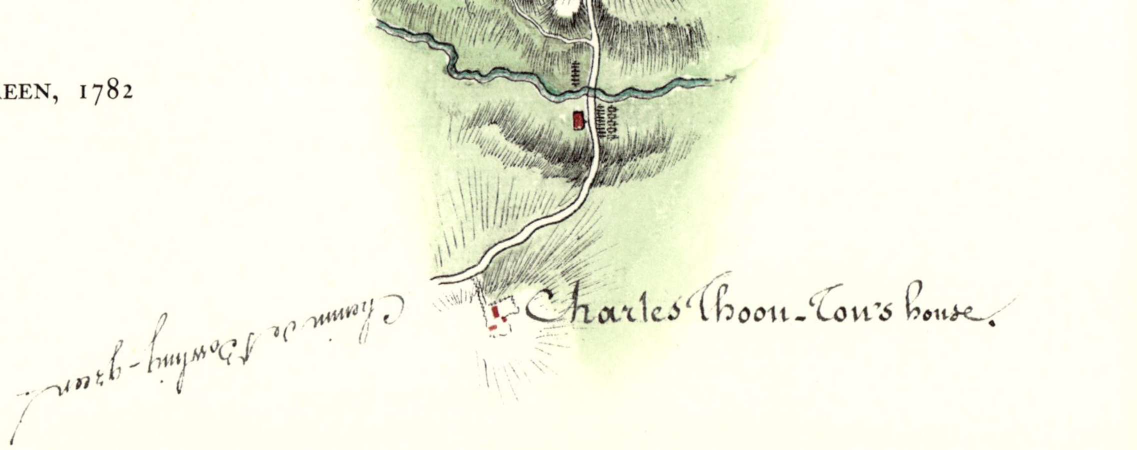

118 TENTH CAMP AT CHARLES THORNTON'S HOUSE, 1782

Falmouth!

Rappahanok. R.

119 ELEVENTH CAMP AT FALMOUTH, 1782

GUÉ DE FALMOUTH

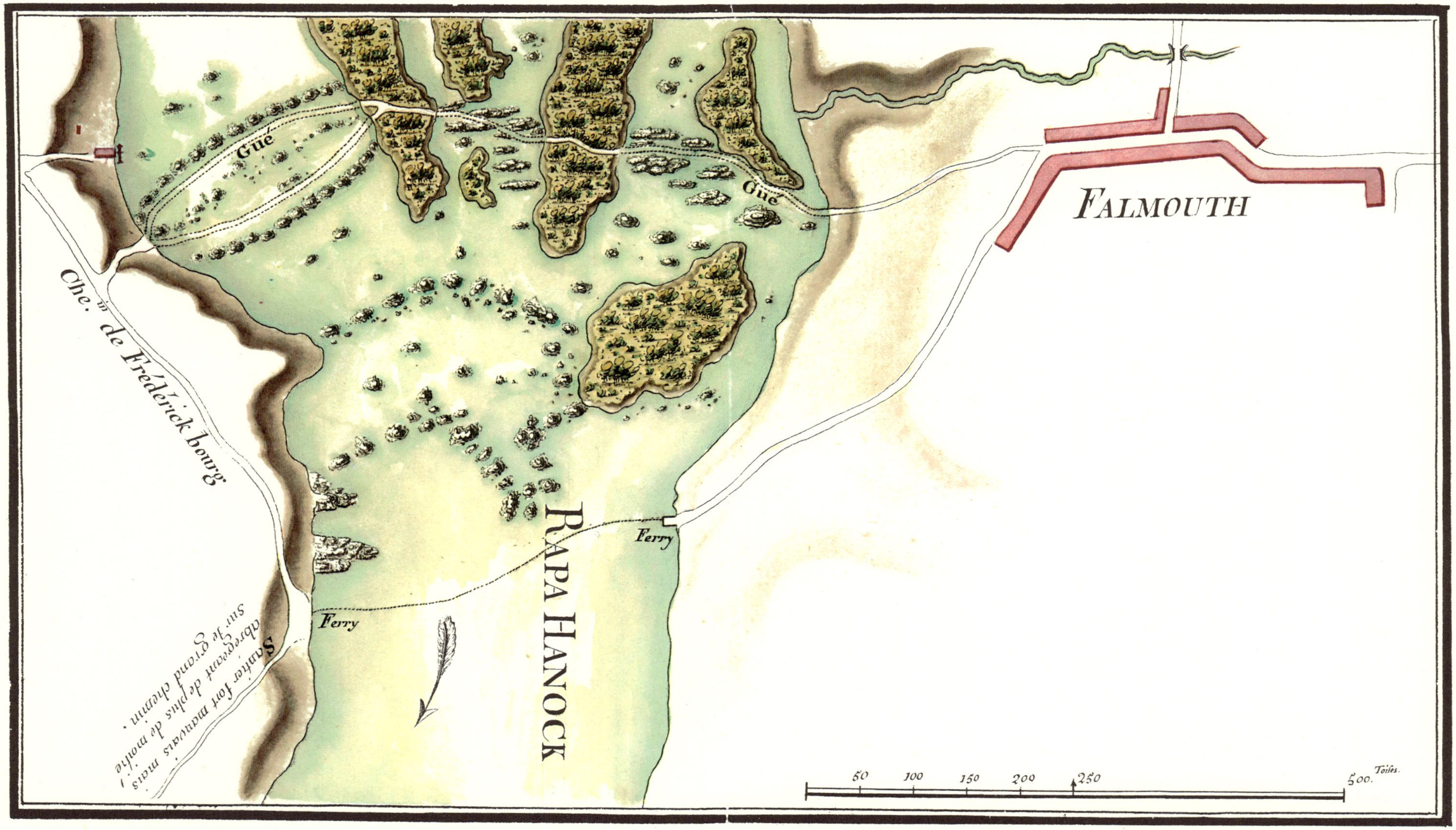

FALMOUTH

RAPA HANOCK

Gué

Gué

Ferry

Ferry

Chem. de Fréderick bourg

Sentier fort mauvais mais
abregeant de plus de moitie
sur le grand chemin.

Toises.

50   100   150   200   250   500.

120   FORD AT FALMOUTH ACROSS THE RAPPAHANNOCK RIVER

12ᵉ Camp à Garrots tavern le 14 Juillet 13 M iles de falmouth (Les Eaux
n'étant pas assez abondantes, les Divisions Suivantes Campèrent trois miles
plus loin à Peyton's tavern.)

Chemin de Dumphries

Peyton's Tavern.

Chemin de falmouth.

13. Camp à Dumphris Le 15 Juillet 10. Miles
de Peyton's Tavern & 13 de Garrots tavern.

Chemin de Colchester

Dumphris.

121   TWELFTH CAMP AT PEYTON'S TAVERN, 1782

122   THIRTEENTH CAMP AT DUMFRIES, 1782

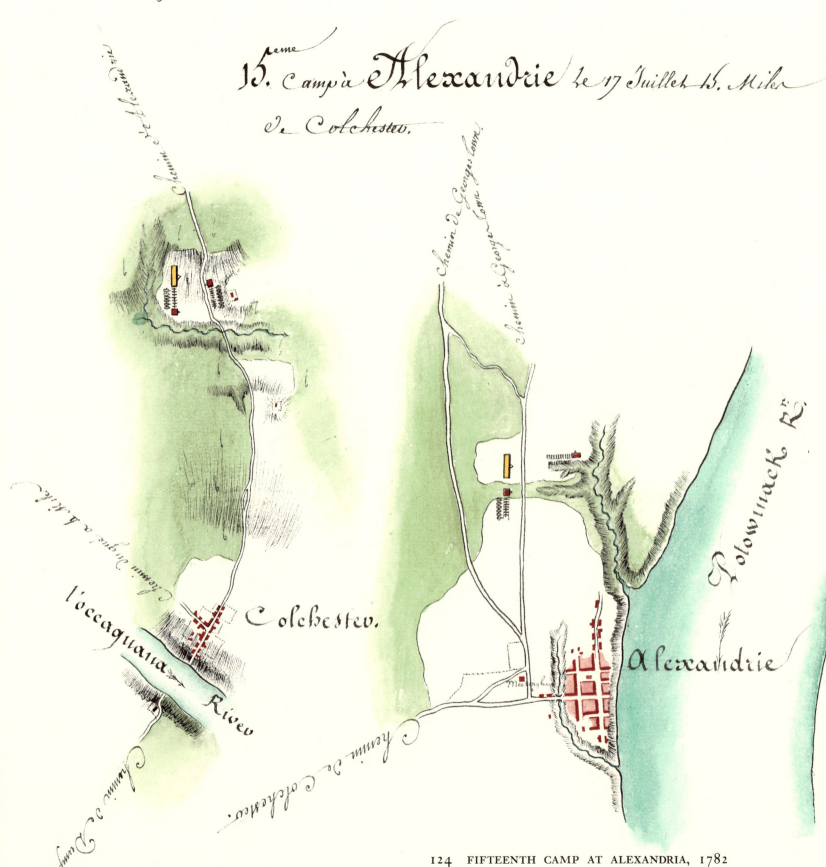

14 Camp à Colchester le 16 Juillet 10 Milles de Dumphrie

15.eme Camp à Alexandrie le 17 Juillet 15. Miles de Colchester.

Chemin de Alexandrie

Chemin de Georges Town

Chemin de Georges

Potowmack R.

l'occaguana River

Colchester.

Chemin de Colchester

Meeting house

Alexandrie

Chemin de Dumphrie

123 FOURTEENTH CAMP AT COLCHESTER, 1782

124 FIFTEENTH CAMP AT ALEXANDRIA, 1782

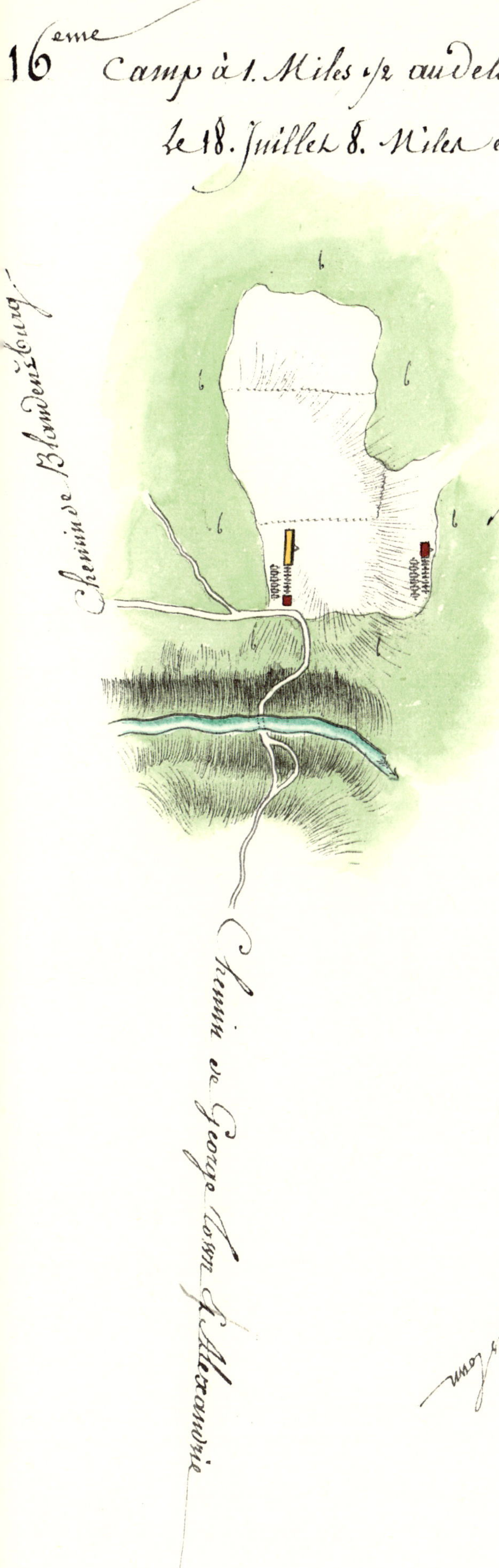

16ᵉᵐᵉ Camp à 1. Miles ½ au delà de Georges Town:
Le 18. Juillet 8. Miles d'Alexandrie

17ᵉᵐᵉ Camp à Blandensburg
Le 19 Juillet   8. Miles de Georges Town.
Le 20, et 21. Séjour.

Chemin de Blandensbourg

Chemin de George town d'Alexandrie

Chemin von Warss

Chemin de Georgetown

Blandensburg

Chemin d'Anapolis

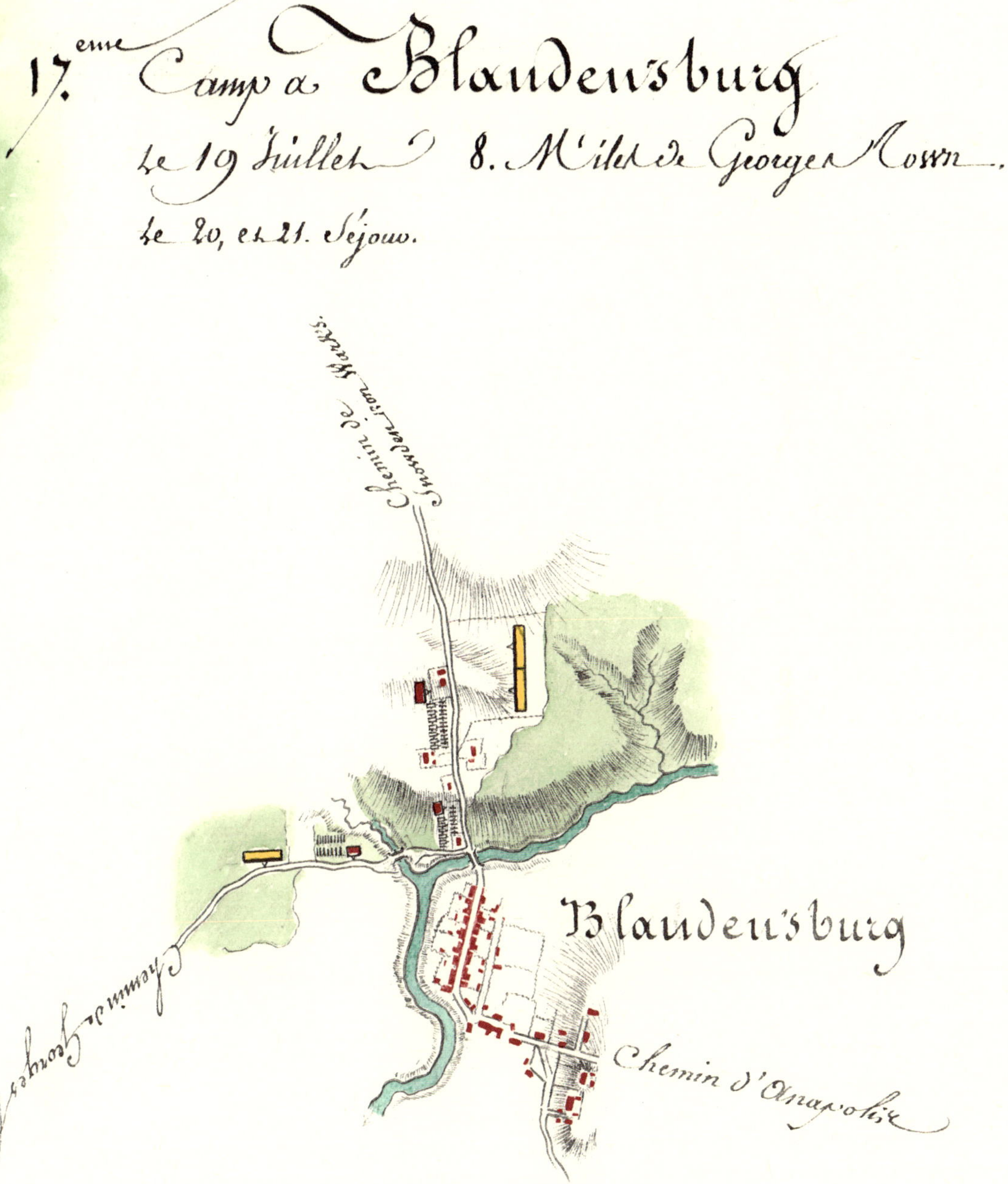

126 SEVENTEENTH CAMP AT BLADENSBURG [IN MARYLAND], 1782

125 SIXTEENTH CAMP, A MILE AND A HALF
BEYOND GEORGETOWN, 1782

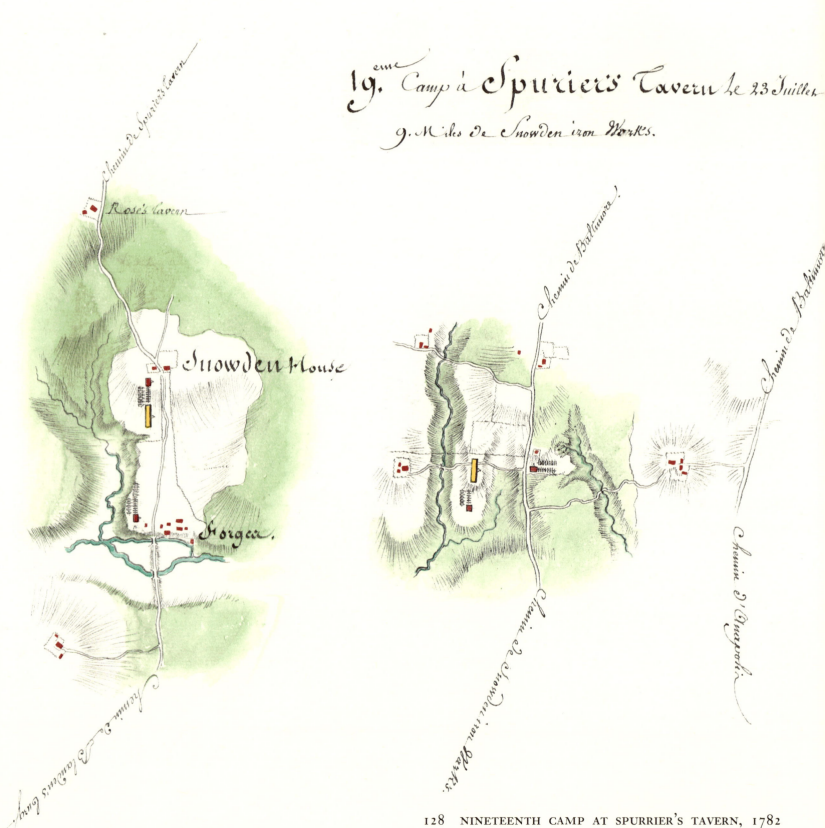

18eme Camp à Snowden-iron-Works. Le 22 Juillet

13 Miles f. de Blandensbury.

19eme Camp à Spurrier's Tavern Le 23 Juillet

9. Miles de Snowden iron Works.

Chemin de Spurriers Tavern

Rose's tavern

Snowden House

Forgee.

Chemin de Baltimore

Chemin de Baltimore

Chemin D'Annapolis

Chemin De Snowden iron Works.

128   NINETEENTH CAMP AT SPURRIER'S TAVERN, 1782

127   EIGHTEENTH CAMP AT SNOWDEN'S
IRON WORKS [LAUREL, MARYLAND], 1782

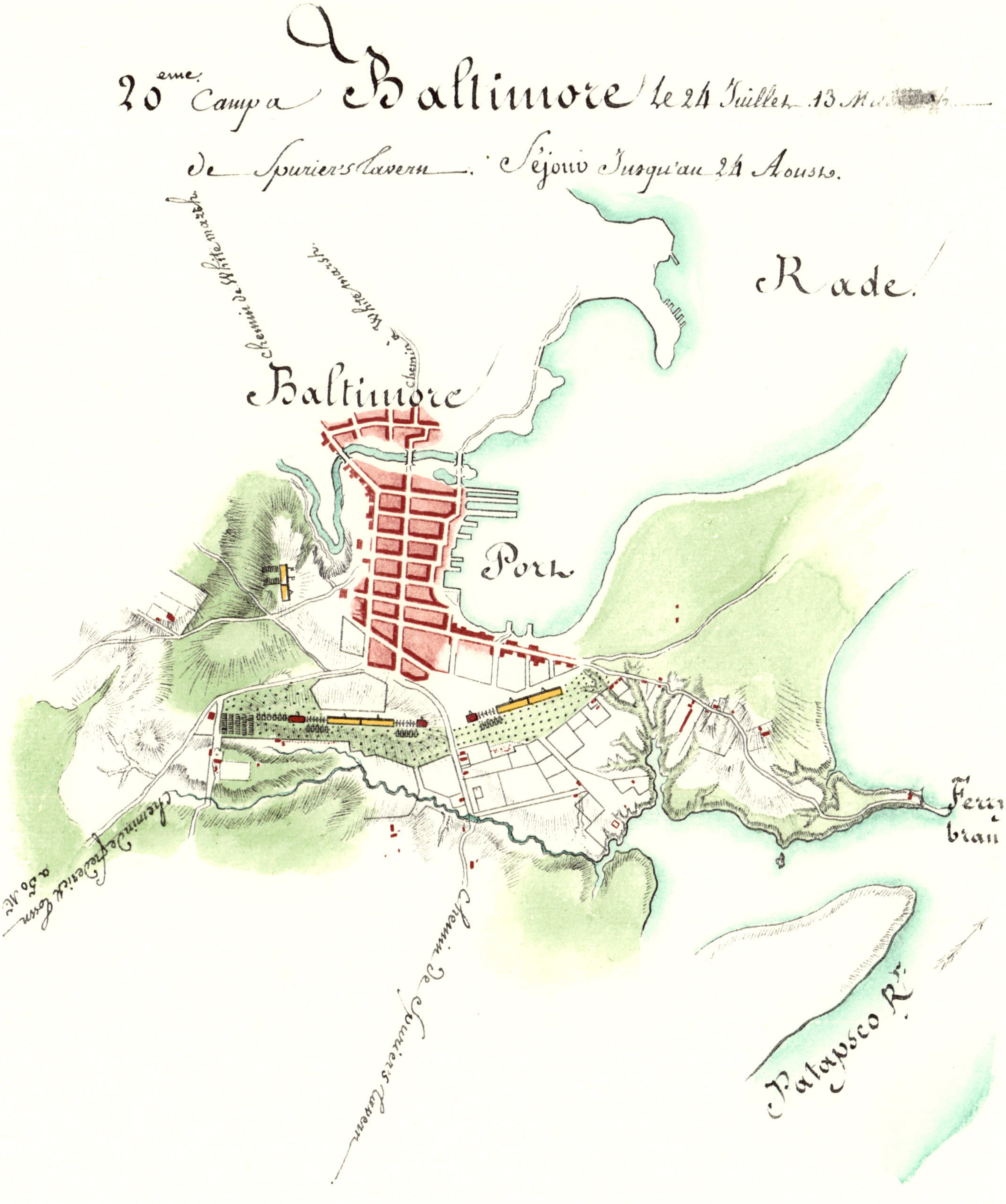

20eme Camp a Baltimore le 24 Juillet. 13 Mille.

de Spuriers tavern ——— Séjour Jusqu'au 24 Aoust.

Rade.

Baltimore

Port

Chemin de Whitemarsh

Chemin de Whitemarsh

Chemin de frederick Town a 50 M.

Chemin de Spuriers tavern

Ferry bran

Patapsco R.

129   TWENTIETH CAMP AT BALTIMORE, 1782

BALTIMORE

Ch. de White Marsh

PORT   ET

RADE   DE

Bat

FERRY

BRANCHE

Ferry

2 1/2

2 1/2

2 1/2

2 1/2

1/2

P A T A P S

2

1/2

P

2

Ferry

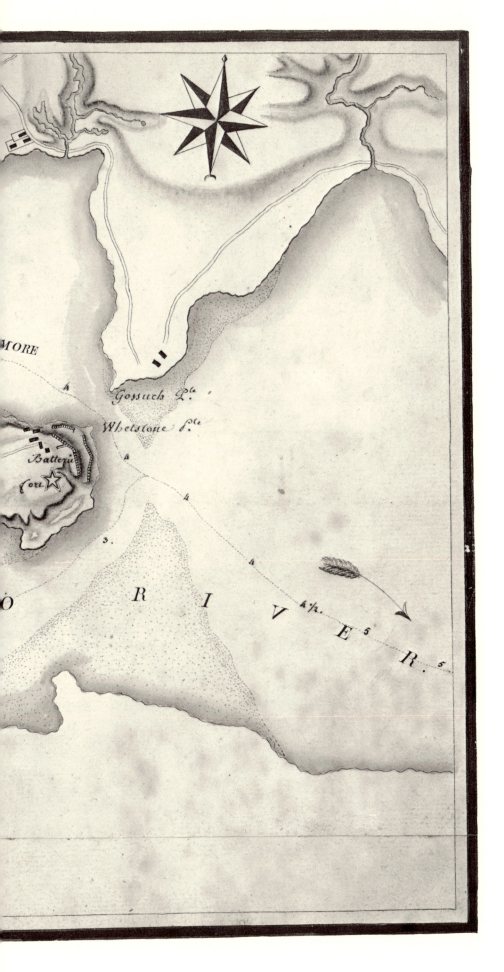

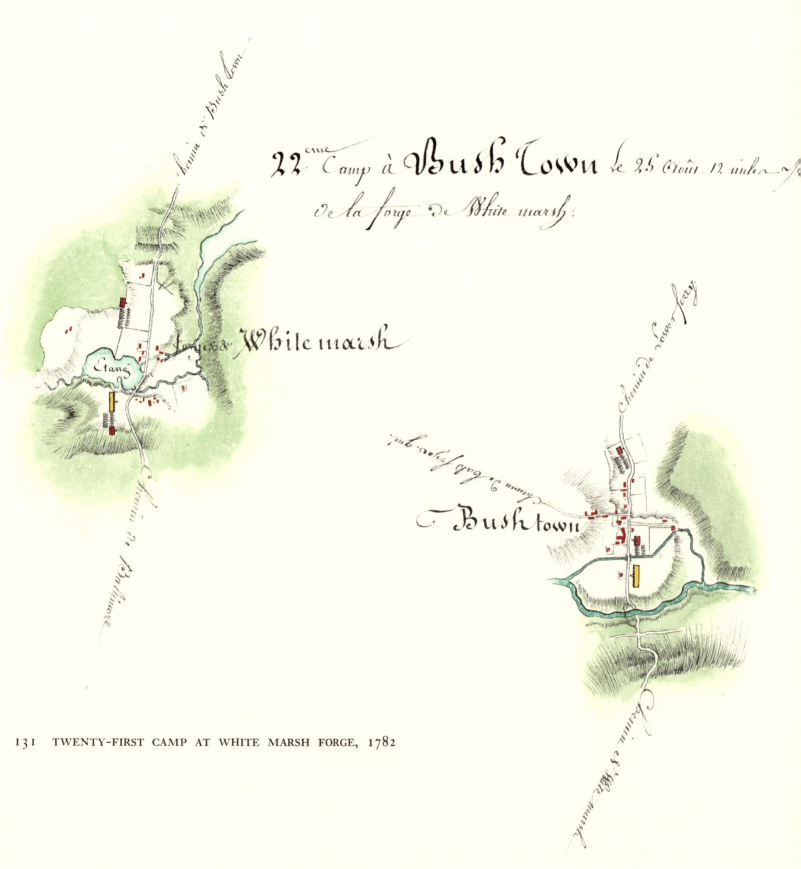

21 Camp à la forge de **Whitemarsh** le 24 Aoust.

12 Miles 1/2 de Baltimore.

22ᵉᵐᵉ Camp à **Bush Town** le 25 Aoust 12 miles 1/2 de la forge de White marsh.

Forge de **Whitemarsh**

Etang

Bushtown

131   TWENTY-FIRST CAMP AT WHITE MARSH FORGE, 1782

132   TWENTY-SECOND CAMP AT BUSH TOWN, 1782

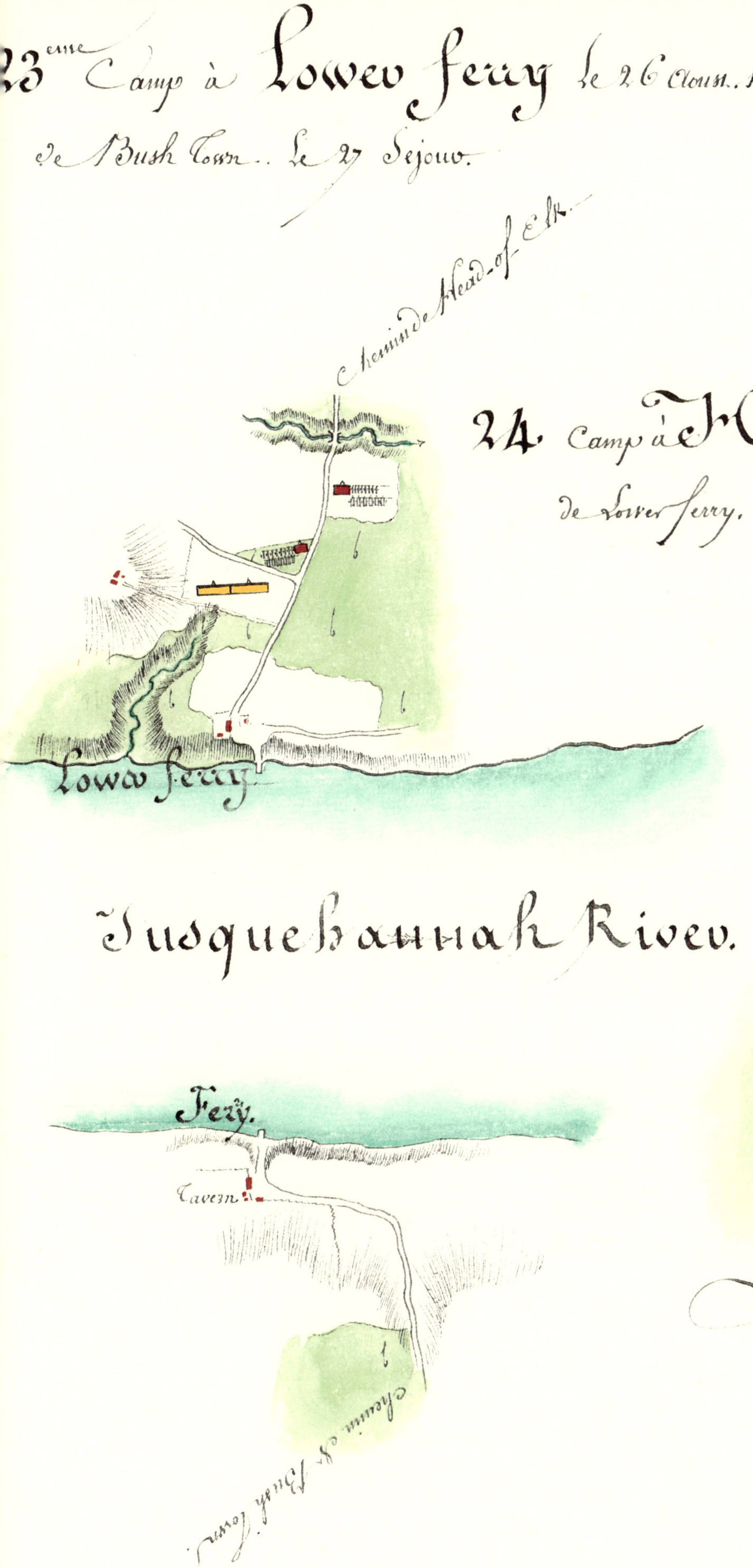

23ᵉᵐᵉ Camp à Lower ferry le 26 Aoust. 12. Miles
de Bush Town.. Le 27 Sejour.

Chemin de Head-of Elk.

24. Camp à Head-of. ELK le 28 Aoust 15 Miles
de Lower ferry.

Chemin de Newport.

Susquehannah River.

Ferry.

Tavern

Chemin de Bush Town.

Head-of Elk Bridge

Head-of ELK

Chemin de Lower ferry.

134   TWENTY-FOURTH CAMP AT HEAD OF ELK
[IN MARYLAND], 1782

133   TWENTY-THIRD CAMP AT LOWER FERRY, 1782

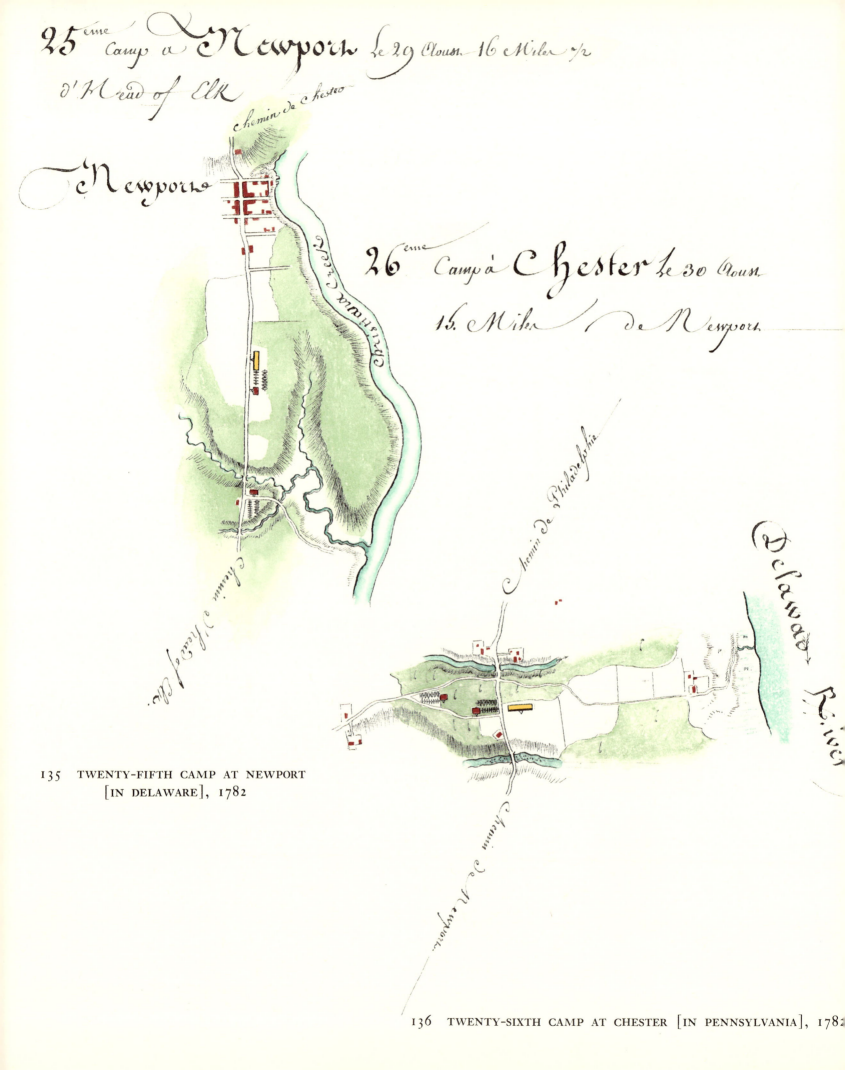

25ᵉᵐᵉ Camp à Newport le 29 Oust. 16 Miles ½
d'Head of Elk

chemin de chester

Newport

Christiana Creek

26ᵉᵐᵉ Camp à Chester le 30 Oust.
15. Miles   de Newport

chemin de Head of Elk

chemin de Philadelphia

Delaware River

chemin de Newport

135   TWENTY-FIFTH CAMP AT NEWPORT
      [IN DELAWARE], 1782

136   TWENTY-SIXTH CAMP AT CHESTER [IN PENNSYLVANIA], 1782

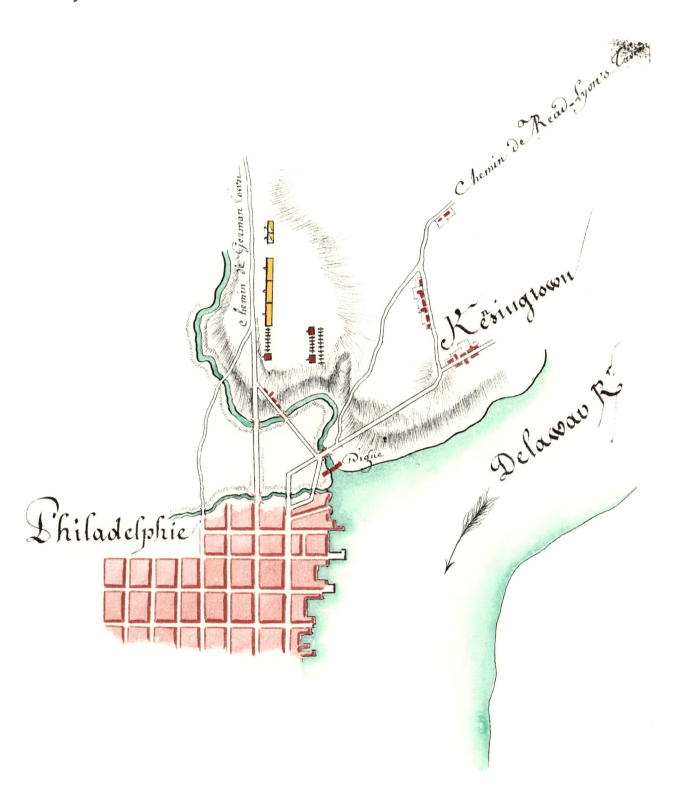

27eme Camp a Philadelphie le 31 Aoust

16 Miles de Chester. Le 1er Septembre Sejour.

Chemin de Read-Lyon's Caste

Chemin de German Coffe

Kesingtown

Delaware R.

Philadelphie

Digue

137 TWENTY-SEVENTH CAMP AT PHILADELPHIA, 1782

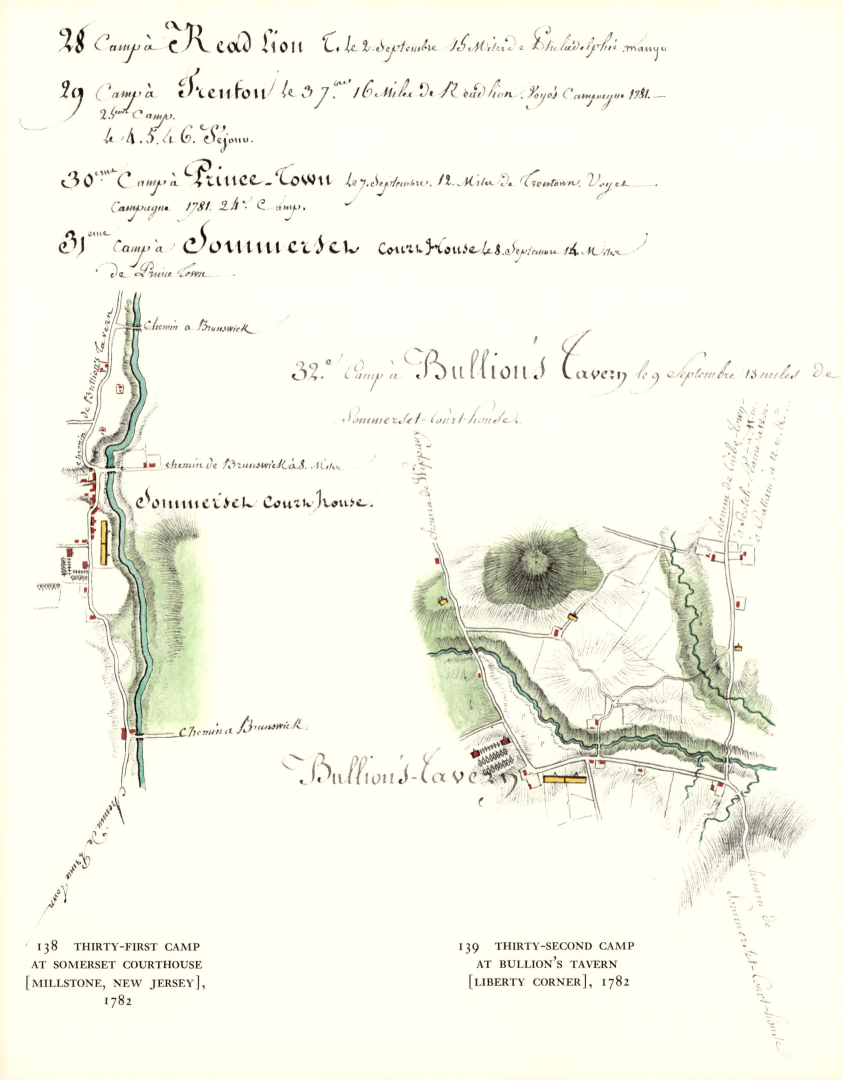

28 Camp à Read lion T. le 2 Septembre 15 Miles de Philadelphie manyu

29 Camp à Trenton le 3 7.re 16 Miles de Read lion. Voyes Campagne 1781. —
25eme Camp.
le 4. 5. & 6. Séjour.

30eme Camp à Prince-Town le 7 Septembre. 12. Miles de Trentown. Voyes
Campagne 1781. 24e Camp.

31eme Camp à Sommerset Court House le 8 Septembre 14 Miles
de Prince Town.

Chemin a Brunswick

chemin de Brullions Tavern

chemin de Brunswick à 8. Miles

Sommerset Court house.

Chemin a Brunswick

32.e Camp à Bullion's Tavern le 9 Septembre 13 miles de
Sommerset-Court-house.

chemin de Whippany

chemin de Cube Lown

a Prakam ce 12. M. &c

Bullion's-Tavern

138   THIRTY-FIRST CAMP
AT SOMERSET COURTHOUSE
[MILLSTONE, NEW JERSEY],
1782

139   THIRTY-SECOND CAMP
AT BULLION'S TAVERN
[LIBERTY CORNER], 1782

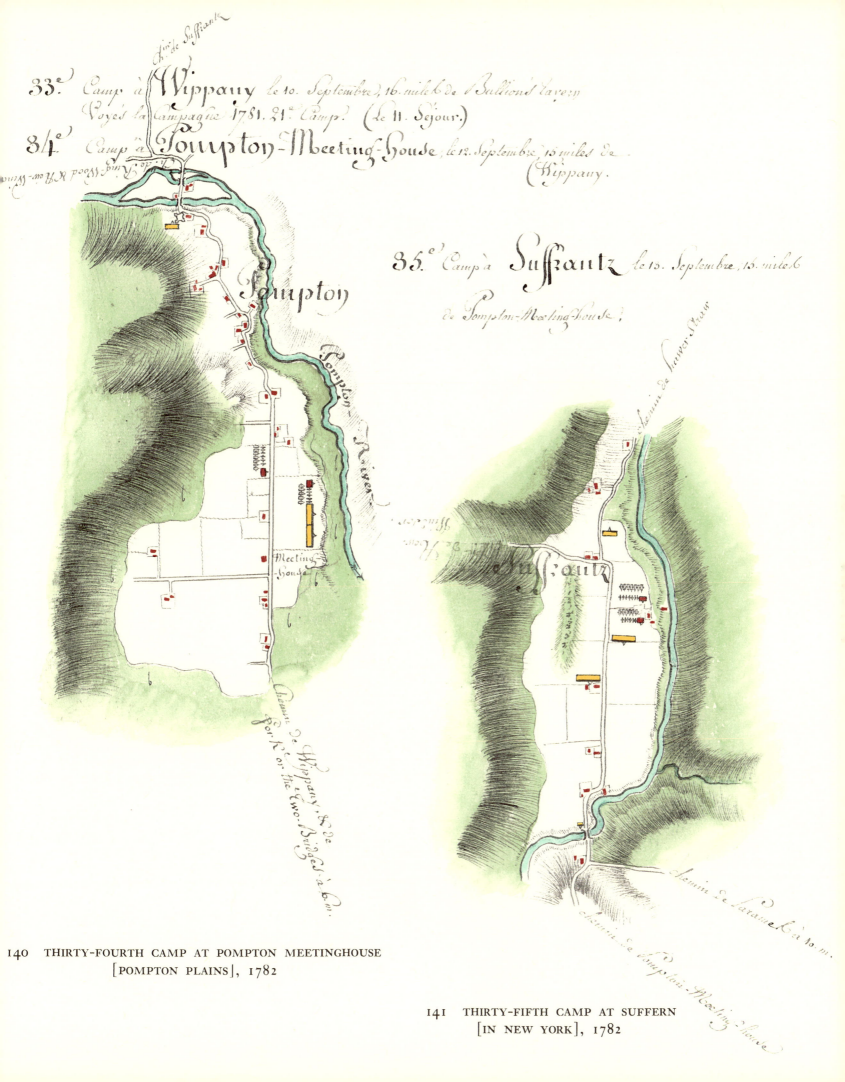

33.ᵉ *Camp à* Wippany *le 10. Septembre, 16. miles de l'Bullion's tavern*
(Voyes la Campagne 1781. 21.ᵉ Camp.) (*Le 11. Séjour.*)

34.ᵉ *Camp à* Pompton-Meeting-House *le 12. Septembre, 15. miles de Wippany.*

Pompton

Pompton-River

Meeting-House

35.ᵉ *Camp à* Suffrantz *le 13. Septembre, 15. miles de Pompton-Meeting-house;*

Suffrantz

140   THIRTY-FOURTH CAMP AT POMPTON MEETINGHOUSE
         [POMPTON PLAINS], 1782

141   THIRTY-FIFTH CAMP AT SUFFERN
         [IN NEW YORK], 1782

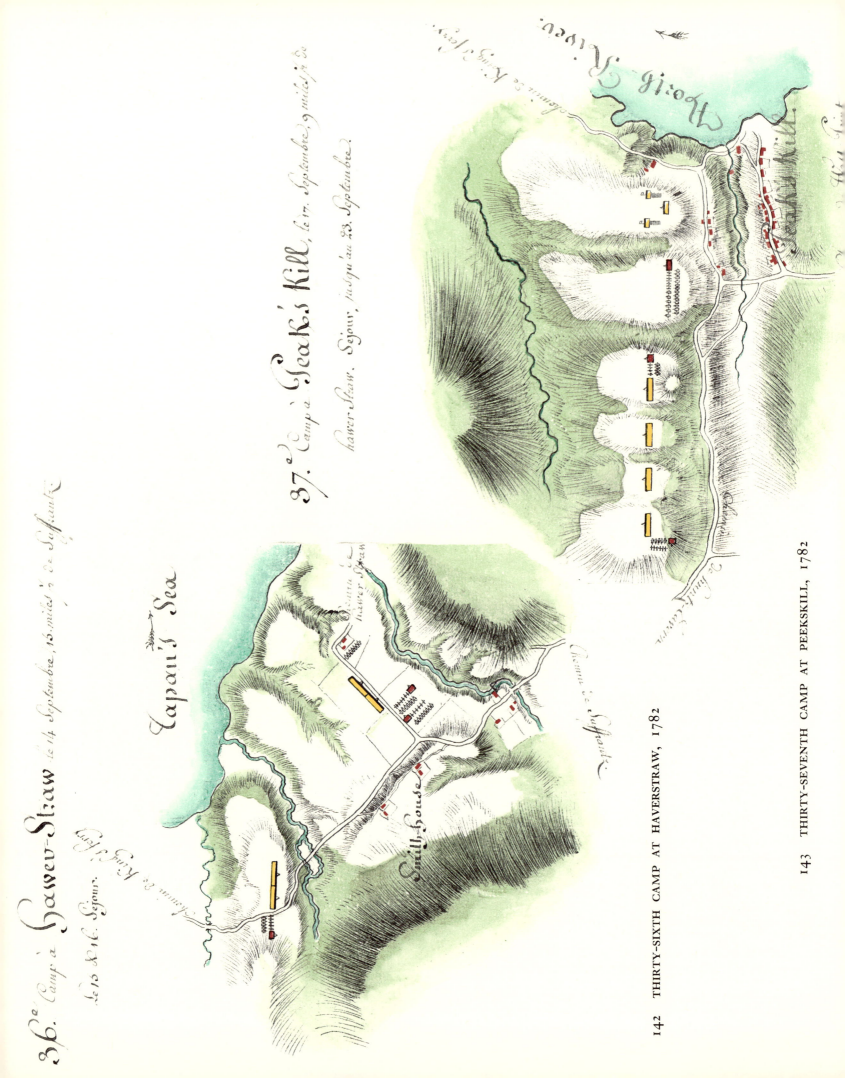

36.ᵉ Camp à Hauver-Straw le 14 Septembre, 15 miles ½ de Suffrein

Le 15 & 16. Séjour.

Tapaan's Sea

Smith-House

Chemin de King's-ferry

37.ᵈ Camp à Peaks Kill, le 17. Septembre, 9 miles ½ de

hauver-Straw. Séjour, jusqu'au 23. Septembre.

North River

142 THIRTY-SIXTH CAMP AT HAVERSTRAW, 1782

143 THIRTY-SEVENTH CAMP AT PEEKSKILL, 1782

144   ENCAMPMENT OF THE AMERICAN ARMY AT VERPLANCK'S POINT ON THE
NORTH RIVER IN 1782, AND THE RECEPTION OF THE FRENCH ARMY
ON ITS RETURN FROM VIRGINIA, BY JOHN TRUMBULL

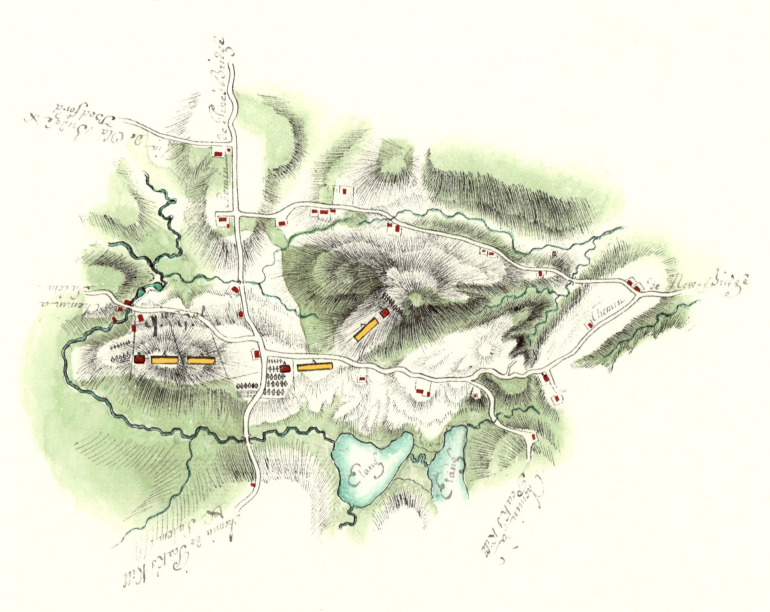

38ᵉ Camp à **Huntz Tavern** le 24 Septembre; 8 miles de Peaks Kill.

Séjour jusqu'au 21. Octobre.

145   THIRTY-EIGHTH CAMP AT HUNT'S TAVERN, 1782

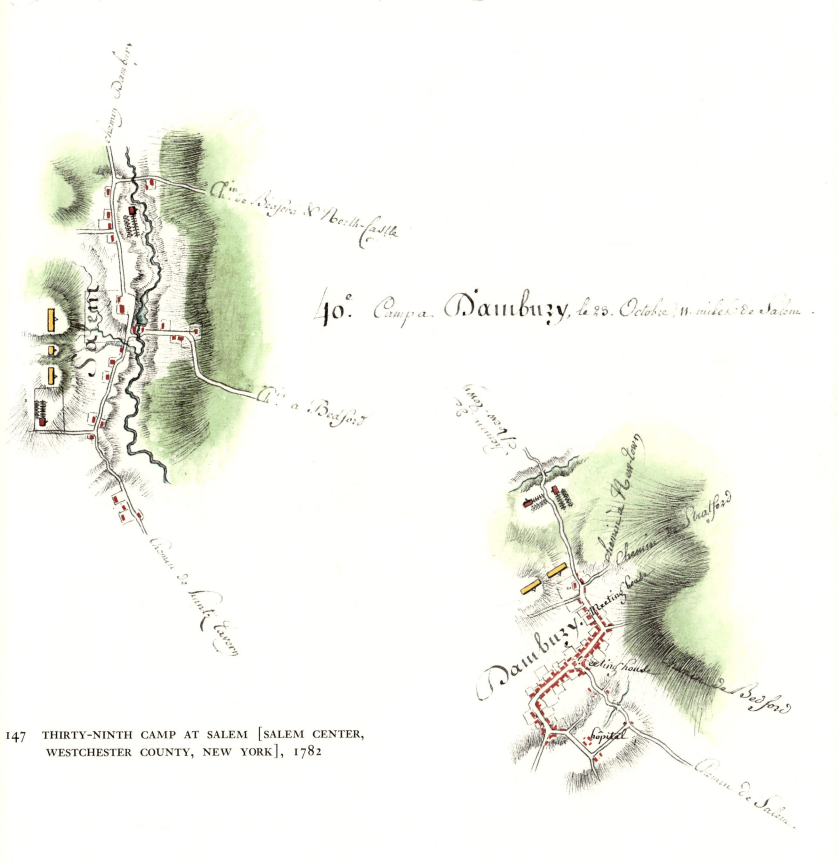

89.ᵉ *Camp a* Salem *le 22 Octobre, 13 miles ½ de hunt Tavern*

40.ᵉ *Camp a* Dambuzy, *le 23 Octobre, 11 miles de Salem.*

147 THIRTY-NINTH CAMP AT SALEM [SALEM CENTER,
WESTCHESTER COUNTY, NEW YORK], 1782

148 FORTIETH CAMP AT DANBURY [IN CONNECTICUT], 1782

41.ᵉ Camp à **New-Town** le 24 Octobre, 12 miles de *Danbury*, Voyez Campagne 1781, 10.ᵉ Camp. (le 25 Séjour.)

42.ᵉ Camp à **Break-Neck**, le 26 Octobre, 15 miles de *New-Town*, Voyez Campagne 1781, 9.ᵉ Camp.

43.ᵉ Camp à **Barn's Tavern** le 27 Octobre, 13 miles de *Break-Neck* Voyez Campagne 1781, 8.ᵉ Camp.

44.ᵉ Camp à **Farmington** le 28 Octobre, 13 miles de *Barn's Tavern*.

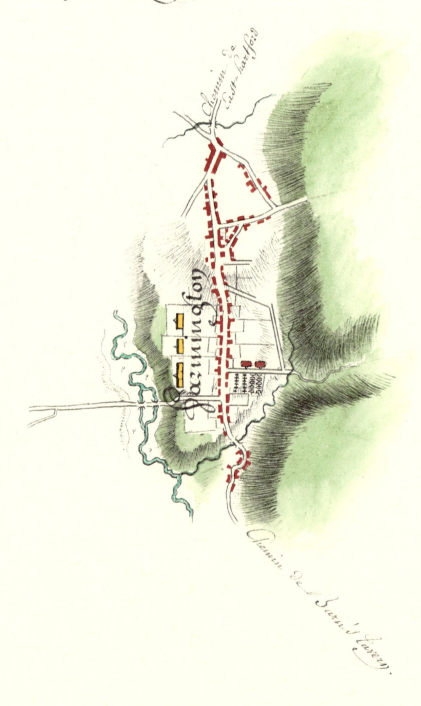

149   FORTY-FOURTH CAMP AT FARMINGTON, 1782

Tableau de La marche des Brigades de Bourbonnois et de Soissonnois Partant
du Camp de hunts taverne à un jour de distance l'une de l'autre pour se rendre a Eust-hart ford.

Octobre	Brigade de Bourbonnois	Milles	Brigade de Soissonnois	
Le 22	de hunts taverne a un demi mil endeça de Salem	13 ½		
Le 23	de Ce Camp a un demi mil audela de Dembury	11	de hunts taverne a un demi endeça de Salem	13 ½
Le 24	de Ce Camp a un mil et demi audela de New-ton	11	a un demi mil audela de Dembury	11
Le 25	Séjour		a un mil et demi audela de New-town	11
Le 26	de Ce Camp a Break-neck	13	Séjour	
Le 27	de Break-neck à Barons taverne	13	à Break-neck	13
Le 28	de Barons taverne a farmington	13	à Barons taverne	13
Le 29	de farmington a East hard-ford et passage du Conneticut	12 ½	à farmington	13
Le 20	Séjour		à East hard-ford et passage du Conneticut	12 ½
Le 31		Total — 87	Séjour	
				Total — 87

The sketch below was drawn on the verso of this slip of paper,
which contains marching orders for the army.

150 FIELD SKETCH FOR MAP OF THE CAMP AT FARMINGTON

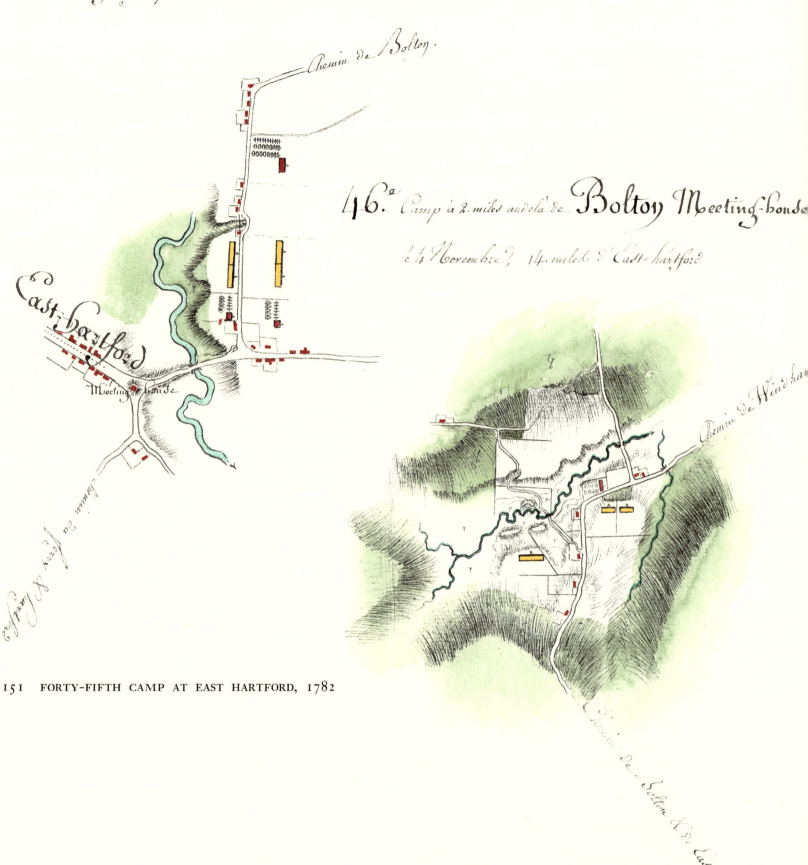

45.ᵉ Camp a East=Hartford, le 29 Octobre, 12. mile 687₂

Séjour jusqu'au 4. Novembre.

Chemin de Bolton.

East=hartford

Meeting=house

46.ᵉ Camp à 2. miles audelà de Bolton Meeting-house

le 4. Novembre, 14. miles d'East=hartford

Chemin de Winha...

151   FORTY-FIFTH CAMP AT EAST HARTFORD, 1782

152   FORTY-SIXTH CAMP, TWO MILES BEYOND
BOLTON MEETINGHOUSE, 1782

47.ᵉ Camp à Windham le 5. Novembre, 16 milet ½ de Bolton.
Le C. Séjour.

Chemin de Cantorbery.

Chemin de Bolton.

Windham

Chemin de Lebanon à 6.m.

Chemin de Mansfield 5.m.

Chemin de Bolton.

153   FORTY-SEVENTH CAMP AT WINDHAM, 1782

48.ᵉ Camp à Cantozbery le 7 Novembre, 10 miles de Windham.

Cantozbery

Chemin de Walen-Town

Meeting-house

Chemin de Windham

154   FORTY-EIGHTH CAMP AT CANTERBURY, 1782

49.ᵉ Camp à Walen-Town, le 8 Novembre, 10 miles de Cantozbery.

Chemin de Wilimansd Town

Walen-Town

Chemin de Cantozbery

155   FORTY-NINTH CAMP AT VOLUNTOWN
[STERLING HILL, CONNECTICUT], 1782

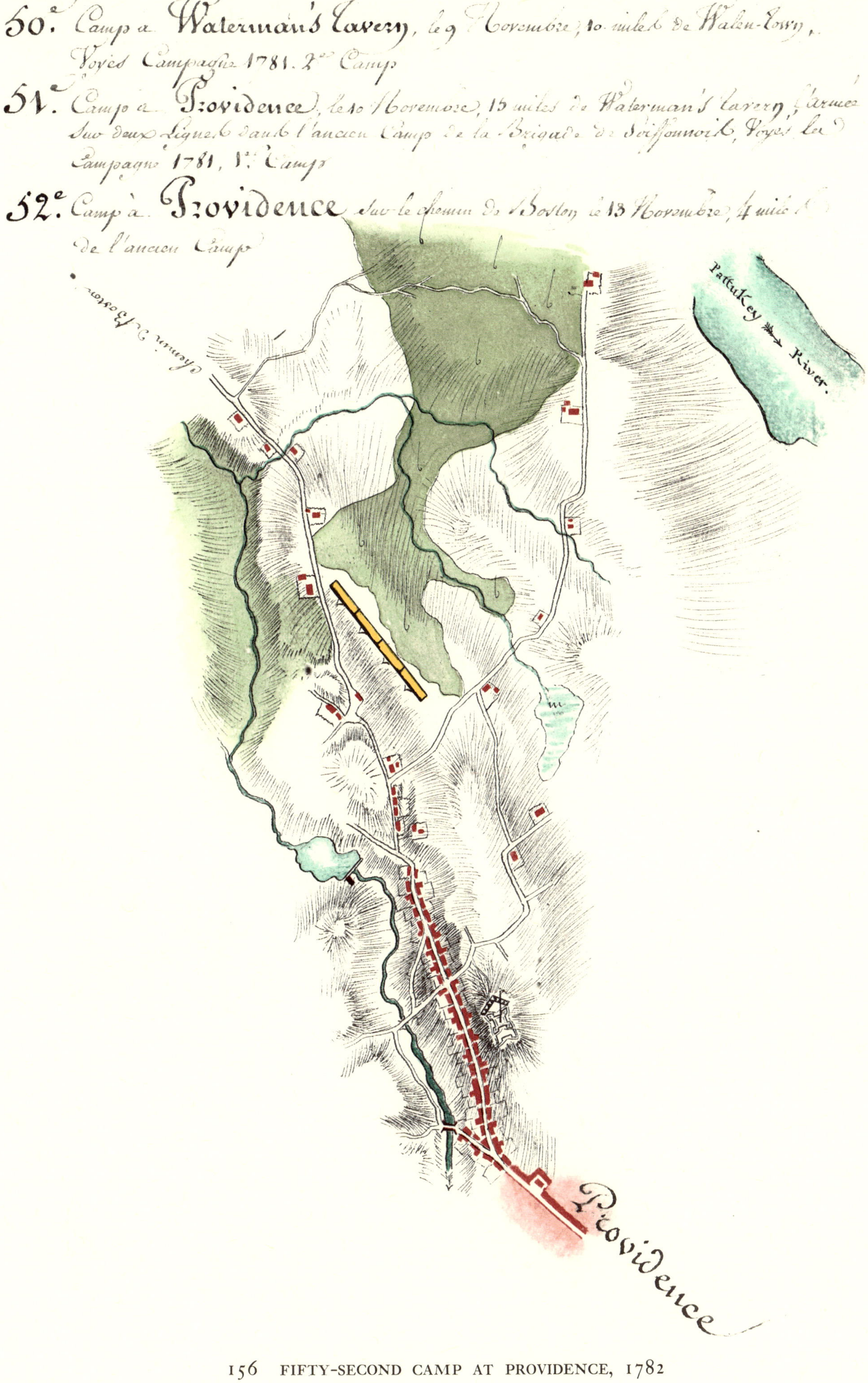

50. Camp à *Waterman's Tavern*, le 9 Novembre, 10 miles de Waten-Town, Voyés Campagne 1781. 2.° Camp

51. Camp à *Providence*, le 10 Novembre, 15 miles de Waterman's Tavern, l'armée sur deux Lignes dans l'ancien Camp de la Brigade de Soissonnois, Voyés la Campagne 1781, 1.° Camp

52.° Camp à *Providence* sur le chemin de Boston, le 13 Novembre, 4 miles de l'ancien Camp

Pattukey River.

chemin de Boston

Providence

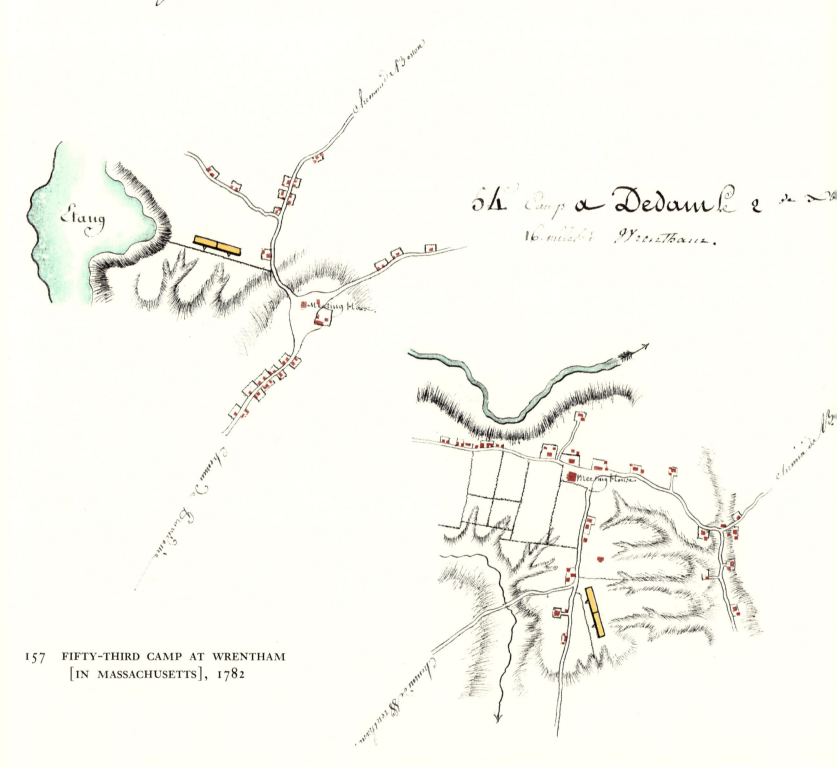

54ᵉ Camp à Dedam le 2 .ᵈ 8ᵇʳᵉ
16 milles de Wrentham.

Étang

157   FIFTY-THIRD CAMP AT WRENTHAM
       [IN MASSACHUSETTS], 1782

158   FIFTY-FOURTH CAMP AT DEDHAM, 1782

55ᵉ Camp à Boston le 3. ᵈ 8ᵇʳᵉ 11 Milles de Dedam.

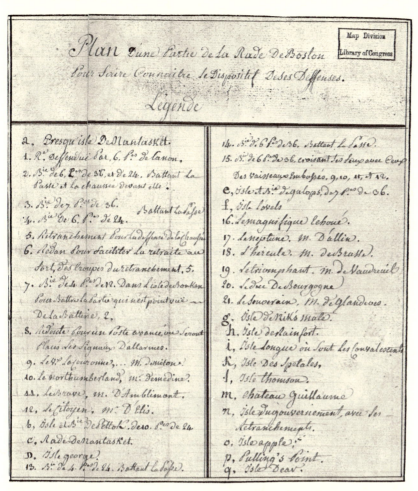

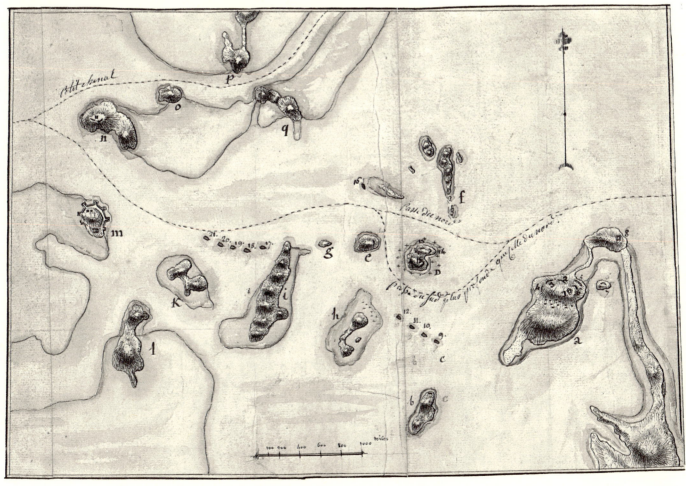

159   PLAN OF A PART OF THE ROADSTEAD OF BOSTON, SHOWING THE STATE OF ITS DEFENSES

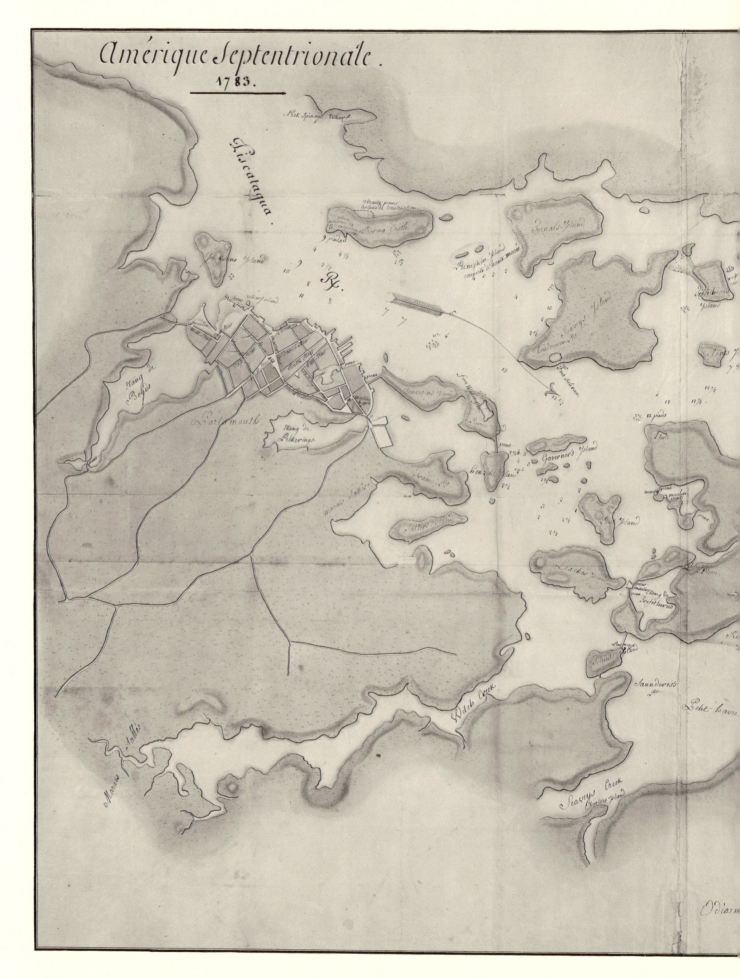

160   PLAN OF THE CITY AND HARBOR OF PORTSMOUTH IN NEW HAMPSHIRE, BY CRUBLIER D'OPTERRE

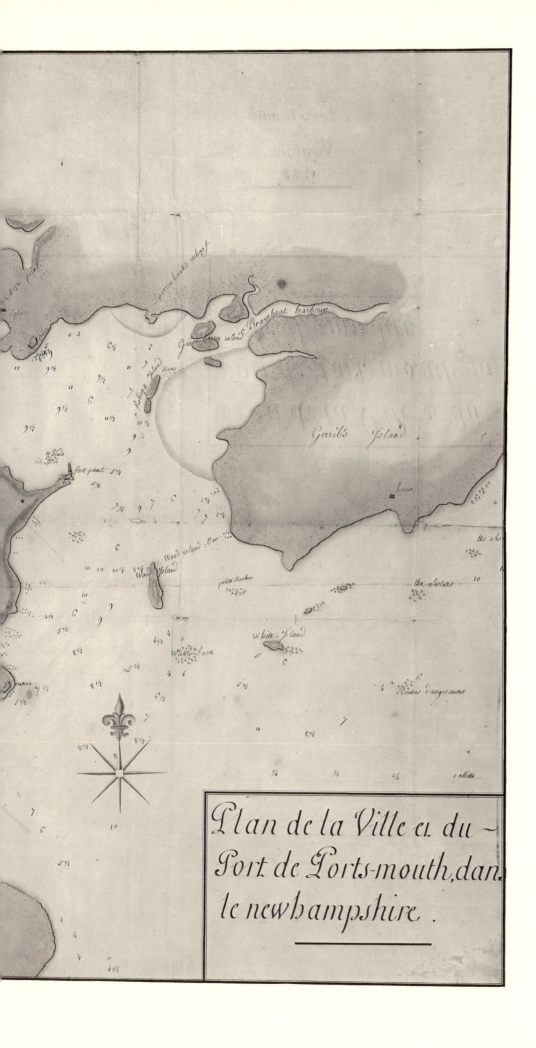

Sillery point

l'Eglise

parronbanks wharf

Braveboat harbour

Goos berry island

fishing Island Rocks

Gerrih's Island

Fort point

house

Wood island Bar

Wood Island

petite Roches

Isle Sh...

the Sisters

White Island

Whaleonback

Rôches dangereuses

¼   ½   ¾   1 Mille

*Plan de la Ville et du ~
Port de Ports-mouth, dan.
le new hampshire .*

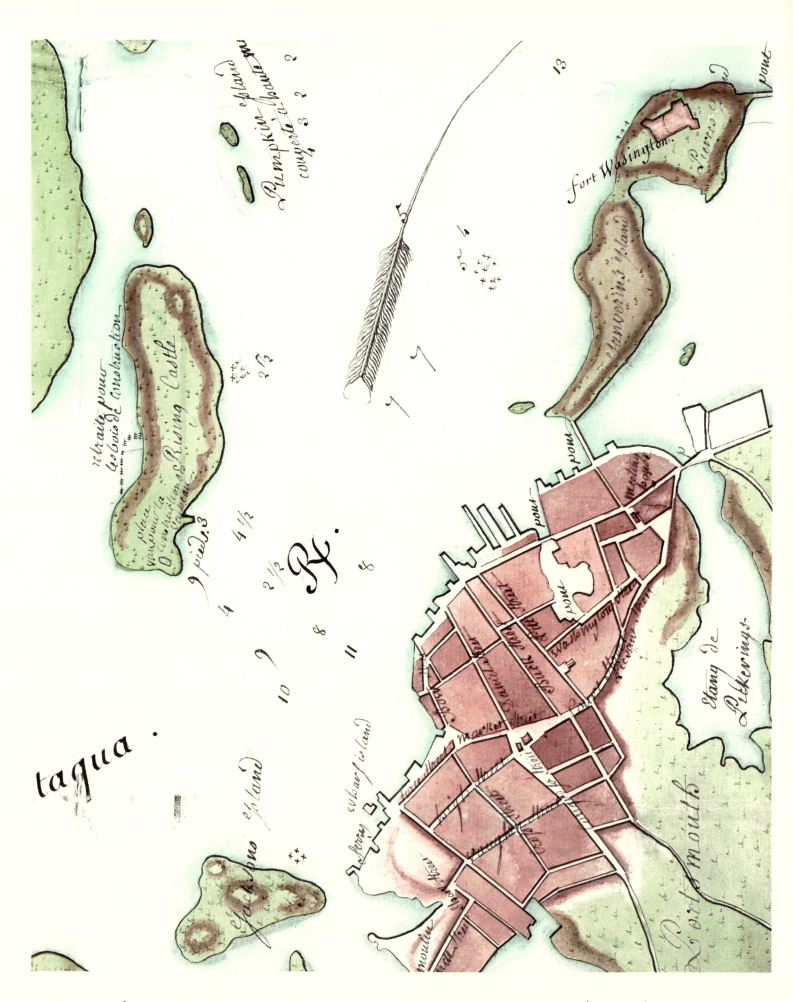

161 CITY OF PORTSMOUTH, NEW HAMPSHIRE. DETAIL FROM CRUBLIER D'OPTERRE'S MAP

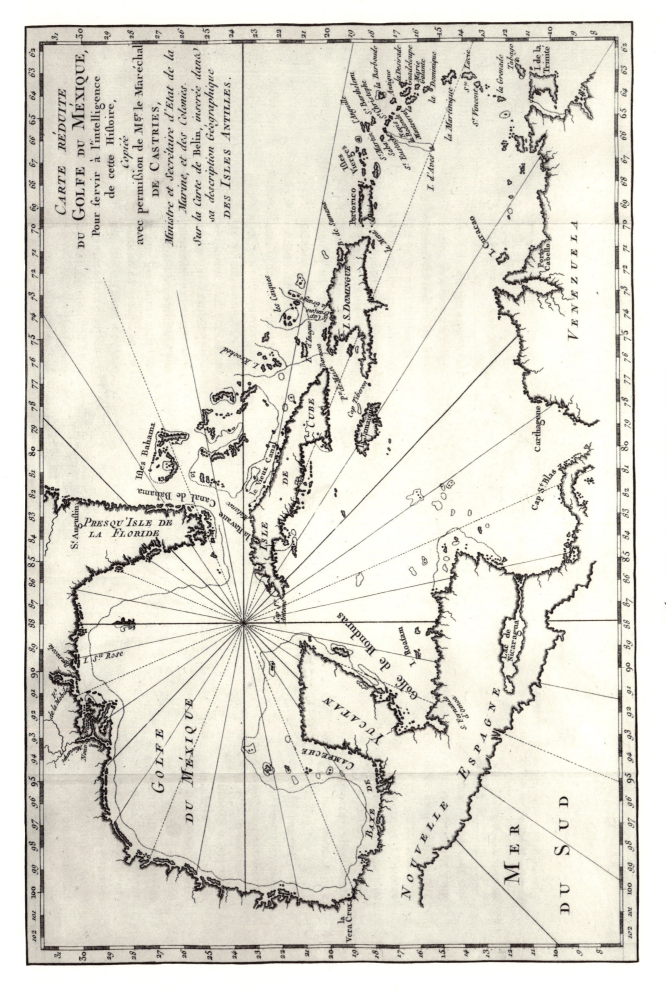

LE FORT ROYAL DANS L'ISLE DE LA MARTINIQUE
Vu du Mouillage.

N. Ozanne del.   Jⁿᵉ ᶠᶜⁱˢ Ozanne sculp.

164   FORT ROYAL, ISLAND OF MARTINIQUE

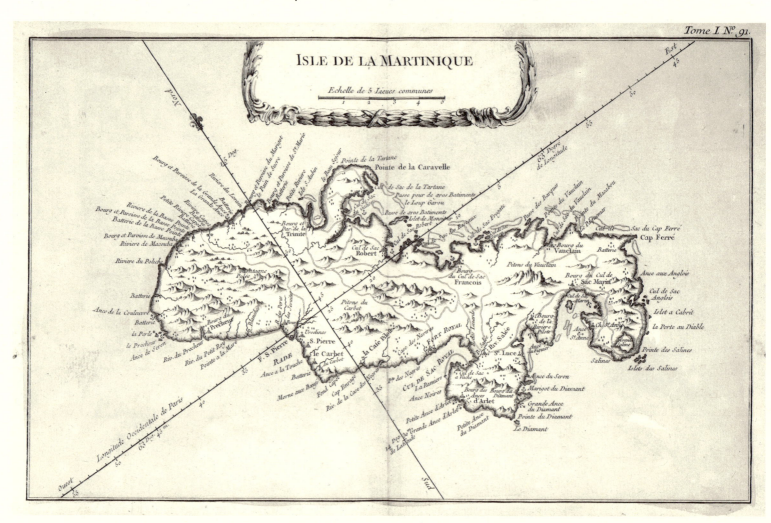

165   MAP OF THE ISLAND OF MARTINIQUE

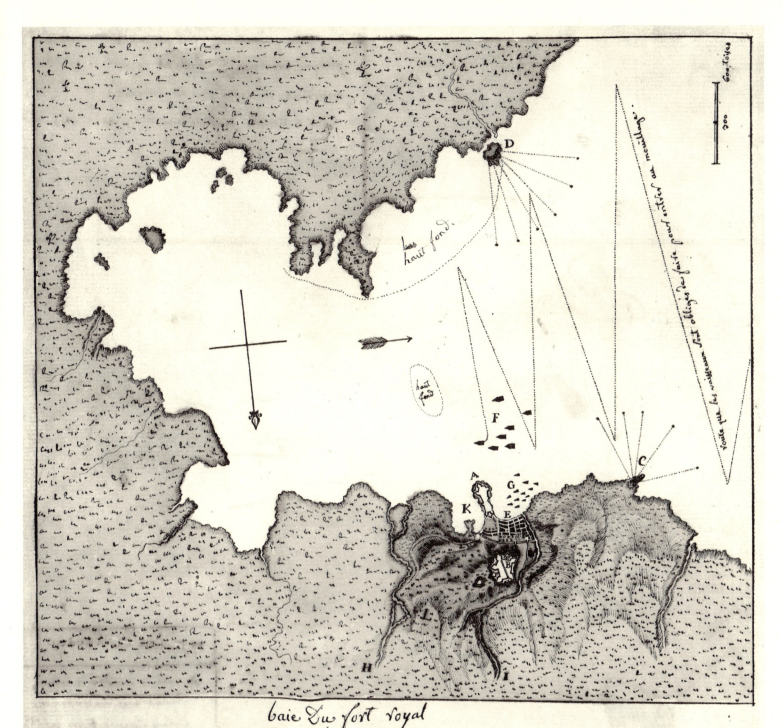

baie Du fort royal
De la martinique.

A, Le fort royal. B, le fort bourbon, c, redoute avancée du fort bourbon. C, pointe aux négres, dont les canons et mortiers

Défendent l'entrée de la baie, ainsi que ceux de Lilet a ramier D. E, La ville du fort royal, F, mouillage des gros

vaisseaux. G, mouillage des marchands. H rivière de monsieur, I rivière de l'hopital. K cul de Sac ou l'on

carenne les vaisseaux, et ou on peut en tenir cinq ou six pendant le temps des ouragans. L, point d'où l'on peut attaquer

en ouvrant une tranchée.

La ligne qui traverse le fort bourbon, exprime un corps de casernes casematté, chargé d'un parapet en terre derrière

lequel on pourroit capituler si le front attaqué étoit pris.

166   BAY OF FORT ROYAL [FORT-DE-FRANCE], MARTINIQUE, MAP BY DU PERRON, 1781

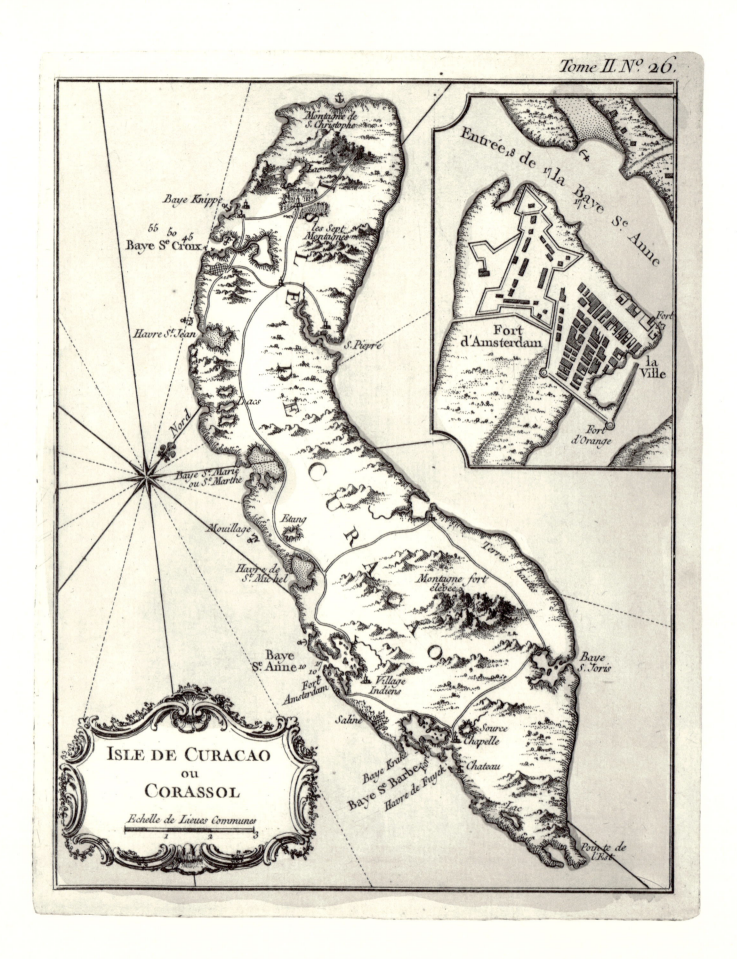

Entrée de la Baye Se Anne

Fort
d'Amsterdam

la Ville

Fort
d'Orange

Montagne de
S. Christophe

Lac

Baye Knippe

Baye Se Croix

les Sept
Montagnes

Havre St Jean

S. Pierre

Nord

Lacs

Baye Se Marie
ou Se Marthe

Mouillage

Etang

Havre de
St Michel

Montagne fort
élevée

Terres hautes

Baye
Se Anne

Fort
Amsterdam

Village
Indiens

Baye
S. Joris

Saline

Source

Chapelle

Chateau

Baye Krak

Baye Se Barbe

Havre de Fuyck

Lac

Pointe de
l'Est

ISLE DE CURAÇAO
ou
CORASSOL

Echelle de Lieues Communes

1   2   3

167   ISLAND OF CURAÇAO, WITH INSET OF FORT AMSTERDAM [WILLEMSTAD]

CARTE DES
CARACAS, CO...

Echelle de Cinquan...

Longitude de l'Isle de Fer

Longitude Occidentale du Merid.n de Paris

Latitude Septentrionale

Orchilla

Ifles d'Aves
la Grande Isle
la Petite Isle

I. Bonair
I. Roque

la Tortue Salée

Patillao ou la Roche Blanche
Cap Caudere
Cap Blanc ou Cap Cordillon
la Caneda
la Guayra
Mejo
Cap Blanc

Leon de Caracas
Saint Sebastien des Reos
St Gaspre

la Victoria
Turmero
Maracaye
R. Tacarigua
St Charles
Puebla novo ou Nouvelle Bourgade
Cejeda
Baraquicimeto
Trou de Baraquicimeto
Quibor
Tocuyo

Giutara
Valence
Lac de Valence
Porto Cabello ou Port des Cheveux

Golphe de ...
R. Neveri
R. Unare
La Puilla
Camanagotto
Santa Fe
Mesoma
Barcelona
Marcapana

C A R A C A S   C O

MA

Latitude Septentrionale

I. Curacao
L'Ascension
St Pierre
Petit Curacao
St Croix
St Marie
Ste Anne
St Barbe

I Bonaire
I Aruba

C. Coquibacoa
I. Monjos
VENEZUELA
ZAPARA
ABOS
Maracaibo
GOLPHE DE VENEZUELA

Cap St Roman

Pointe Rivelate
Tarutara
Chirobio R.
Pointe Seche
le Port Seche
Isles de Tuquaques
Porto Cabello ou Pt. des Cheveux
Pt. Estave
Porte Cabello ou Pt. des Cheveux

Coro
runas
Plaines de Carora
St Philippe de Carora

VENEZUELA

Nirva
Carache
Truxillo
Bocono
Negvipao
Domingo
Merida
Laguinillas
Rio. Chama
St Pierre

R. Motatan
Barbacones
Gibraltar
Tinoho

Pauraute

Lac de Maracayo ou Lac de Notre Dame
I Bonai
la Seiba
Rio. Hato de la Crux ou Habitation de la Crux

QUIRES

Macanabo

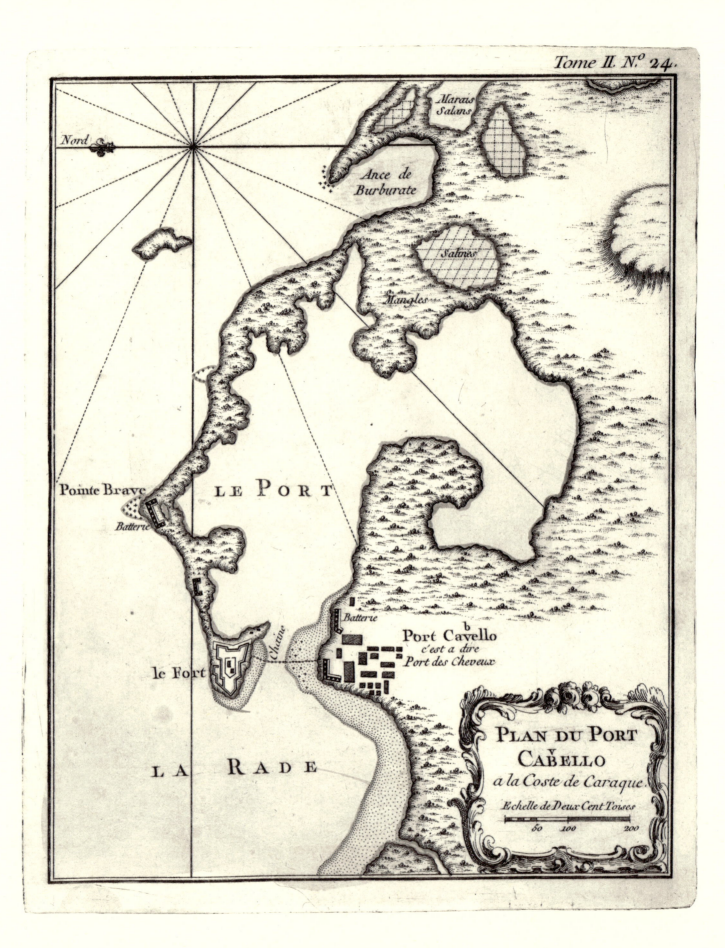

Nord

Marais Salans

Ance de Burburate

Salines

Mangles

Pointe Brave

LE PORT

Batterie

le Fort

Batterie

Chaine

Batterie

Port Cavello
c'est a dire
Port des Cheveux

LA RADE

PLAN DU PORT
CABELLO
a la Coste de Caraque.

Echelle de Deux Cent Toises

50   100   200

169   PLAN OF PUERTO CABELLO

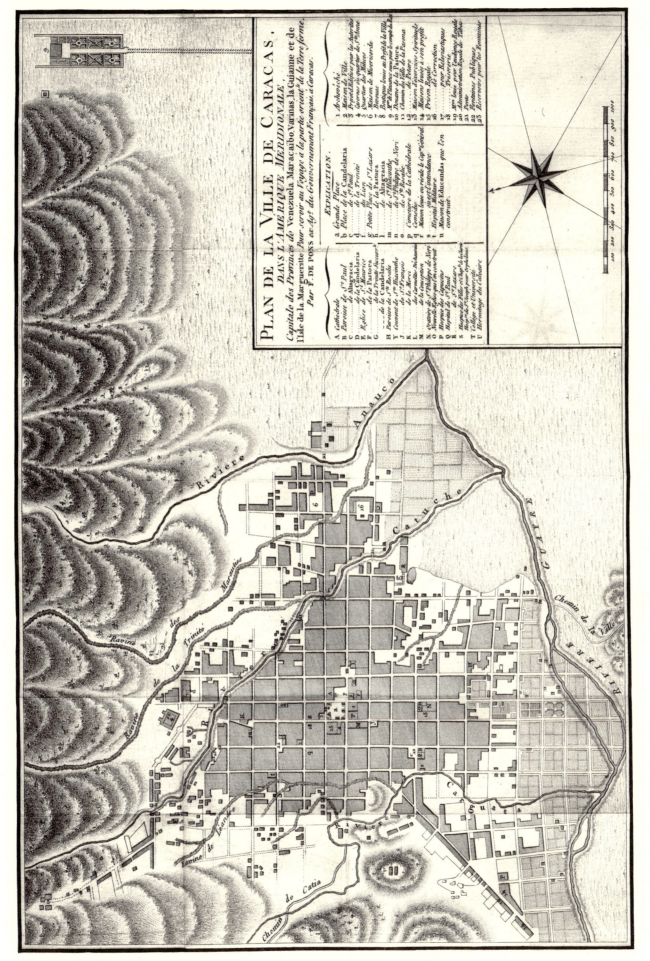

PLAN DE LA VILLE DE CARACAS,
DANS L'AMERIQUE MERIDIONALE,
Capitale des Provinces de Venezuela Maracaibo Varinas, la Guiane et de
l'Isle de la Marguerite. Pour servir au Voyage à la partie orient.ᵉ de la Terre ferme.
Par F. DE PONS ex-Ag.ᵗ du Gouvernement Français, à Caracas.

EXPLICATION.

A Cathédrale
B Paroisse de S.ᵗ Paul
C de Altagracia
D de la Candelaria
E Eglise de S.ᵗ Maurice
F de la Pastora
G de la Trinité
H Paroisse de S.ᵗ Rosalie
J Couvent de S.ᵗ François
K de la Merci
L des Carmelites Dechaussée
M de la Conception
N Oratoire de S.ᵗ Philippe de Neri
O Nouveau Couvent maintenant construit
P Hospice des Capucins
Q Hopital de S.ᵗ Paul
R de S.ᵗ Lazare
S Hospice des Filles ou chez les Sœurs
T Hospice S.ᵗ Joseph pour Orphelines
U Hermitage du Calvaire

a Grande Place
b Place de la Candelaria
c de S.ᵗ Paul
d de la Trinité
e du Lion
f Petite Place de l'Isleare
g d'Altagraca
h de la Pastora
l de S.ᵗ Hilacanthe
m de S.ᵗ Philippe de Neri
n de S.ᵗ Rosalie
o Comiche
p Cimetière de la Cathédrale
q Maison louée ou reste le Cap.ᵉ général
r Hôpital Militaire
s Hôtel de l'Intendance
t Maisons de Educandas que l'on
   construit.

1 Archeveché
2 Maison de Ville
3 Prison Militaire pour les Invalides
4 Caserne du quartier de S.ᵗ Anne
5 Quartier des Milices
6 Maison de Misericorde
7 Bureau
8 Boutique louée au Profit de la Ville
9 N.ᵗ de Finance ainsi par le comp.ᵗ du Roi
10 Douane de la Pastora
11 Chemin de la Valle de la Paroisse
12 de Petare
13 Maison d'exercice Spirituele
14 Maison louée à son profit
15 Prison Royale
16 de Correction
17 pour Educariseques
18 Trésorerie
19 Hₙᵗᵉ lieu pour l'audience Royale
20 Administration Royale du Tabac
21 Pente
22 Fontaines Publiques
23 Reservoir pour les Fontaines

ISLE DE
SAINT DOMINGUE
Echelle de 25 lieues communes

Latitude Septentrionale

Longitude Occidentale du Méridien de Paris.

PARTIE ESPAGNOLE

PARTIE FRANÇOISE

Cap S Nicolas
Isle de la Tortue
Port de Paix
Cap Samana
Baye de Samana
Ile de la Saone
S. Domingo
Port au Prince
Jacquemel
Cap Tiberon
La Vache
Cap de la Beate
Isle de la Beate
Baye du Neybe
La Gonave
Baye des Gonaves
S Marc
Baye S Marc
S Jago

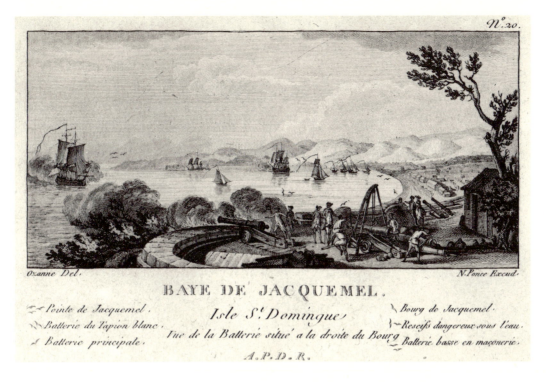

BAYE DE JACQUEMEL.

Isle S.t Domingue

Vue de la Batterie situé a la droite du Bourg

A.P.D.R.

Ozanne Del.

N. Ponce Excud.

↗ *Pointe de Jacquemel.*
↘ *Batterie du Tapion blanc.*
↙ *Batterie principale.*

Bourg de Jacquemel.
Reseifs dangereux sous l'eau.
Batterie basse en maçonerie.

172   JACMEL BAY, SAINT-DOMINGUE

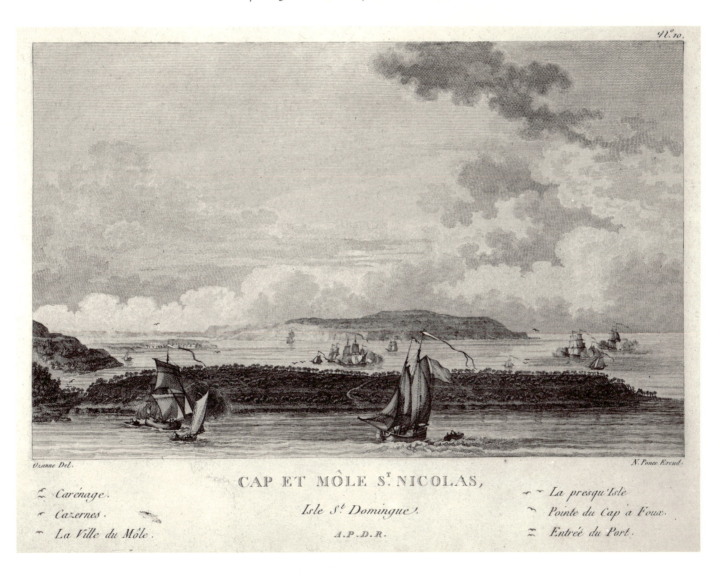

CAP ET MÔLE S.T NICOLAS,

Isle S.t Domingue.

A.P.D.R.

Ozanne Del.

N. Ponce Excud.

↗ *Carénage.*
↘ *Cazernes.*
↗ *La Ville du Môle.*

↗ *La presqu'Isle*
↘ *Pointe du Cap à Foux.*
↗ *Entrée du Port.*

173   CAPE AND MÔLE SAINT-NICOLAS, SAINT-DOMINGUE

LE CAP FRANÇOIS DANS   L'ISLE DE St. DOMINGUE,
Vu du   Mouillage.
Tiré d'un Recueil de différens Ports   des Isles Antilles dessinés en 1780.
Réunis à la Collection des Ports   de France, gravés par le Sr. Gouaz.
A Paris chez le Gouaz Graveur, rue St. Hyacinte, la 1re. Porte a gauche par la Place St. Michel.

5

174 THE FRENCH CAPE, SAINT-DOMINGUE

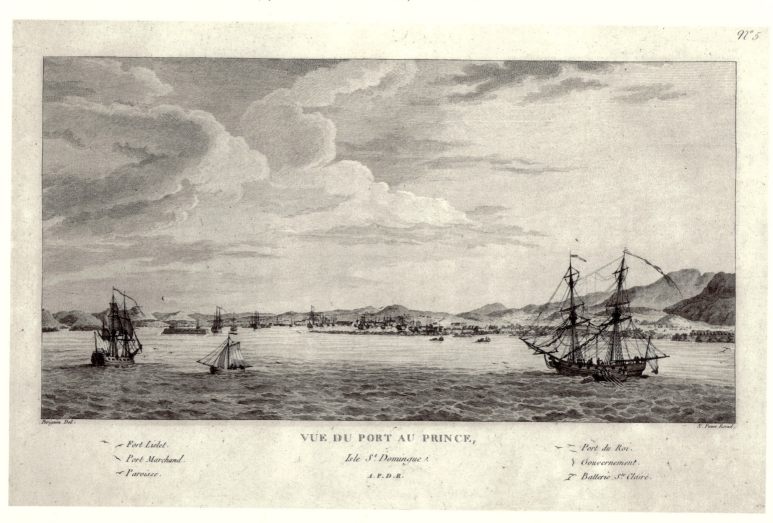

VUE DU PORT AU PRINCE,

Fort Lislet.   Port du Roi.
Port Marchand.   Isle St. Domingue.   Gouvernement.
Paroisse.   A.P.D.R.   Batterie Ste. Claire.

175 VIEW OF PORT-AU-PRINCE, SAINT-DOMINGUE

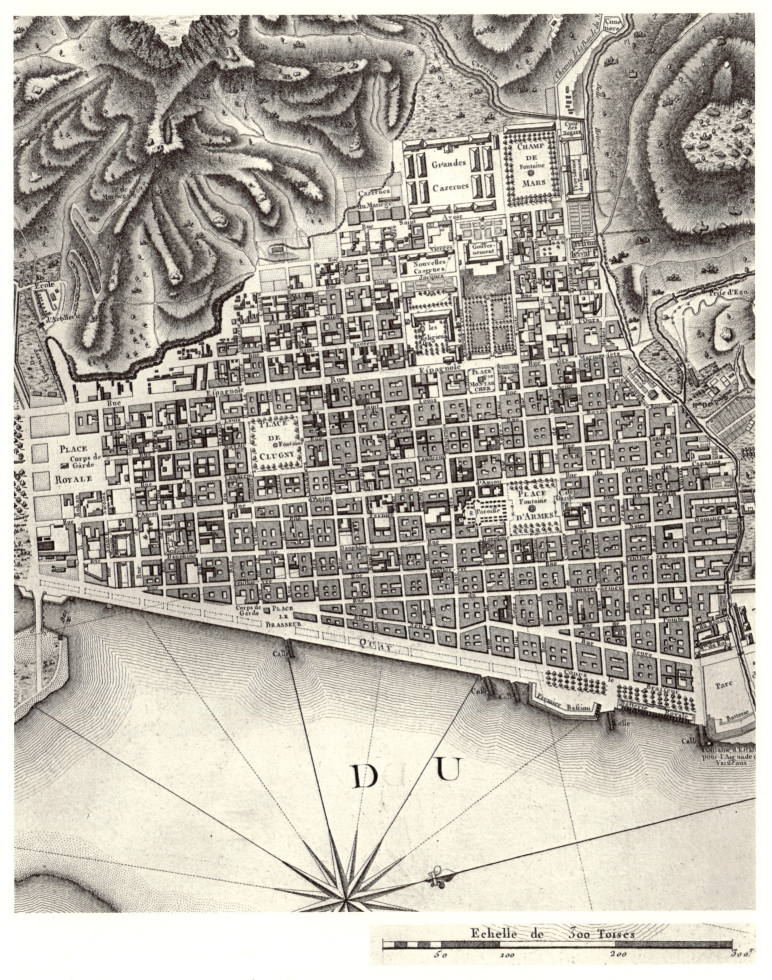

176 PLAN OF THE CITY OF THE FRENCH CAPE

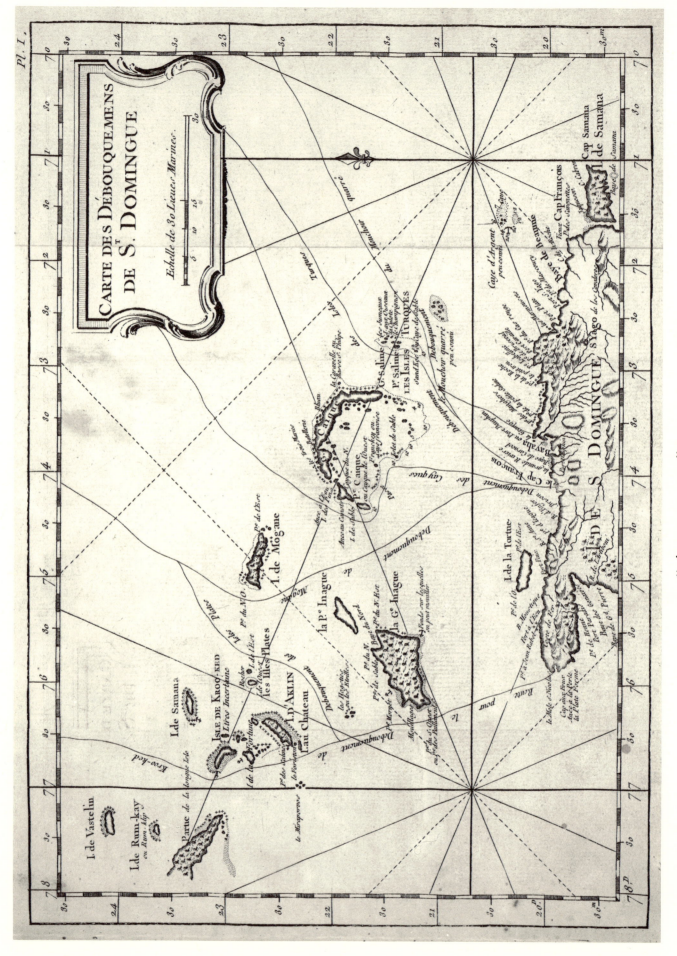

177   THE "DÉBOUQUEMENTS" OF SAINT-DOMINGUE

General Index

TO VOLUMES I AND II

G

I, xx–xxi, 309–10; view of in 1781, II, 128; Washington's visit (March 1781), I, 25, 241–42; winter quarters of Rochambeau's army (1780–81), I, 21ff, 124ff, 236ff. *See also* Rhode Island

New Rochelle, N. Y., French inhabitants of, I, 38n

Newtown, Conn.: camp at (1781), I, 30, 248, II, 13–14, 30–31, 130, 134; camp at (1782), I, 168, II, 189

New York defenses, reconnaissance of (July 1781), I, 36–38, 251–53; Adam painting, II, 139–41; maps, II, 136–39

Nicholson, James, Capt., I, 133n

Noailles, Louis, vicomte de, I, 52n, 60, 62, 134, 241, 266n; bounty for service at Yorktown (1782), I, 71

North Castle (Mount Kisco), N. Y.: bivouac at (Aug. 1781), II, 40–44, 146; camp at (1781), I, 32, 248, 254, II, 33, 130–31, 134–35; French hospital at, II, 135

North River (Hudson), origin and use of term, II, 9n

North Stratford (Monroe), Conn., II, 16

Nouvion, Ferdinand, I, 109

Nouvion, Jean-Baptiste-Théodore, Gen., I, 108–109

O

O'Connor, Antoine-François-Térance, I, 318

Octoraro Creek, camp of Lauzun Legion at (Sept. 1781), I, 53

O'Hara, Gen., I, 61; at surrender of Yorktown (1781), I, 148

Ollonne, Alexandre-Paul, comte d', I, 319, II, 173

Oneida Indians, *see* Indians

Onésime, Father, I, 89n

Opterre, *see* Crublier d'Opterre

Oxford, Conn., II, 16

Oyré, François-Ignace, chevalier d', engineer, II, 116n, 159

Ozanne, Jeanne-Françoise, II, 198

Ozanne, Nicolas, II, 202; view of Fort Royal, II, 198; view of Jacmel, II, 202; view of Môle Saint-Nicolas, II, 202

Ozanne, Pierre, "le cadet," view of The French Cape, II, 202; with d'Estaing's fleet (1778–79), II, 198

P

(The) Palisades, N. Y., I, 35–36, II, 49

Palys de Montrepos, engineer, II, 116n, 159

Paramus, N. J., Lauzun Legion at (1782), II, 184

Paris, Verger's description of (1783), I, 184–86

Parscau, *see* Duplessis-Parscau

Passaic Falls, N. J., description, I, 42

Pastour de Costebelle, *see* Costebelle

Peale, Charles Willson, I, 152n, II, 64n; portraits of Washington for Rochambeau and Chastellux, II, 166

Peale, James, painting of generals at Yorktown, II, 166–67

Pechot (pseudonym), *see* Tarragon

Peekskill, N. Y., II, 15, 36, 47–48; camp at (1781), I, 254–55; camp at (1782), I, 78, 165–66, II, 185–86; map, 37. *See also* Verplanck's Point

Pénandreff, M. de, I, 89n

Pennsylvania, I, 163

Pensacola, Battle of (May 1781), I, 38

Perdhomo, Emmanuel, *see* Prudhomme, don

Perrache de Franqueville, I, 199

Perryville, Md., *see* Lower Ferry

Peyton's Tavern, Va.: camp at (1782), I, 159, II, 177; wagon train camp at (1781), II, 93

Phalsbourg, France, I, 187

Philadelphia, Penna.: arrival of French army at (1781), I, 46, 134, II, 74–75, 145, 150; British occupation of (1777–78), II, 75–77; camp at (1782), I, 77–78, II, 183; celebration of birth of Dauphin, I, 77; descriptions of, I, 46–49, 162–63, II, 75; illuminations celebrating Yorktown surrender, I, 151n

Philipsburg, N. Y.: Berthier's rustic retreat at (July 1781), I, 250; camp at (1781), I, 32–36, 235n, 249, II, 33–34; maps, II, 131, 135–36, 139; foraging expedition from (1781), I, 38; Washington's camp at (July 1781), I, 248. *See also* White Plains

Phillips, Gen. William, I, 129

Pigott, Admiral, I, 86–87, 164n

Pines Bridge, N. Y., II, 16, 41–45; camp at (1781), I, 254; map, II, 38

Pinsun, I, 88n, 89

Plainfield, Conn., camp at (1781), I, 28, 247, II, 10–11, 22–23, 129, 133

Plancher, engineer, I, 89n, 116n, II, 159; bounty for service at Yorktown (1782), I, 71

plants: in the Atlantic Ocean, I, 119; in Connecticut, I, 28ff; in Martinique, I, 230; in Maryland, I, 75; in Rhode Island, I, 124–25; in Saint-Domingue, I, 280; in Venezuela, I, 93–94, 172, 267, 273, 275, 278; in Virginia, I, 67, 157–58. *See also* cotton plantations, indigo plantation, tobacco plantations

Plessis, Mauduit du, *see* Mauduit du Plessis

Plessis-Parscau, *see* Duplessis-Parscau

Pompton (Pompton Plains), N. J.: camp at (1781), I, 42, II, 55–56, 143, 148; camp at (1782), I, 164, II, 184–85

Ponce, Nicolas, engraver, II, 202–203

Pons, François R. J. de, I, 268n, 270n, 277n, II, 201

Pontdevaux, comte de, I, 67n

Pontoise, France, I, 184

Port-au-Prince, Saint-Domingue, I, 281; view of, II, 203

Portsmouth, N. H., I, 85, 256; French army and navy at, I, 170, II, 194–95; map by Crublier d'Opterre, II, 194–95

Portsmouth, Va.: destruction of British fortifications at (Nov. 1781), I, 65, II, 168; maps by Crublier d'Opterre, II, 167–68

Potomac River, ferry at Georgetown, II, 87–88; Posey's ferry, II, 90

Pottersville, R. I., *see* Waterman's Tavern

Pouzoullette, sieur de, I, 319

Pré-en-Pail, France, I, 183

Prescott, Gen. Richard, I, 43n, 124

Preudhomme de Borre, Philippe-Hubert, chevalier de, I, 343–44

Prez, Maj. de, I, 42, 130, 134

Princeton, N. J., I, 163–64; camp at (1781), II, 67, 70, 144, 149; camp at (1782), I, 163, II, 149, 184; orrery at the College of New Jersey, I, 44; rendezvous of Rochambeau

W

Y

Z